The Complete Book of Perfect Phrases for High-Performing Sales Professionals

But first, let's take a look at what is the most time-tested and traditional strategy: cold calling. Even though cold calling is the oldest strategy, it can also prove to be the most unrelenting, arduous, cruel, and grueling of all. In spite of that difficulty, there are times when it is the only option for some salespeople. More about that later.

Think about this situation logically and honestly. What are the chances of your encountering someone who has all five of the characteristics of a qualified prospective customer by cold calling, either by phone or by knocking on doors? You guessed it—extremely slim at best.

However, if there is no strong marketing effort, if brand awareness is low, if resources are limited, or if there is no other prospecting strategy available, this may be your only option. In that case or if cold calling is your strategy of choice, we will, of course, address what to say and when to say it. Nonetheless, at this point there might logically be some question in your mind about whether you should use this low-yield, yet deceptively inexpensive method of prospecting for any long term when so many other options, as explained in this book, could be available to you.

At the other end of the spectrum, inspired by today's technology, lots of salespeople have resorted to making unsolicited presentations through an array of digital tools—CDs, DVDs, e-mails, faxes, etc. And that may seem to be a really up-to-date strategy. But let's ask another very straightforward question. Have you ever received an unsolicited DVD, CD, or "spam" e-mail cleverly (sometimes not very cleverly) disguised as being important? Yes, probably a lot. However, here's the real question. How often have you personally looked at that DVD or listened to that CD? Have you ever opened an e-mail or read an unsolicited fax only to discover that you have been spammed with a clever but clearly manipulative headline? Although these tools of technology can be relatively inexpensive to use, they usually don't deliver the results you want—and they are deceptively expensive in terms of your reputation. So here's the moral of the story. Don't jump on the latest technological prospecting bandwagon. Or at least think about it before you do.

Selling's Number-One Secret

This most often overlooked and underappreciated secret is so important that it could make this book the most critical tool in your sales success library. After observing others sell for more than 30 years, managing salespeople for over 20, and personally selling for even longer than that, I have reached one simple but profound truth that will be repeated again and again in this book:

> **The secret to selling is to be in front of a qualified prospective customer when he or she is ready to buy, not when you need to make a sale.**

What does that mean? Simply this: timeliness is by far the single most important skill in prospecting—period.

This book is not so much about how to evaluate the myriad of strategies you could implement. Instead, it's really all about what to say when you are there, by phone, in person, or through another medium, regardless of how you get there.

However, you *do* need to have an appropriate strategy (or better yet, set of strategies) that clearly defines your prospecting effort. You must maintain the top-of-consciousness position in your prospective customers' minds in such a way that they think about you at the time they decide to pursue the purchase of a product or service that you sell.

Perfect Phrases for Lead Generation

This book will carefully recommend specific words and phrases linked to a wide array of strategies. There really is no other way to design it. What you say and how you say it are necessarily intertwined with what you do in order to get in front of a qualified prospective customer. Again, the primary purpose of this book is for you to know exactly what to say when you are in front of a qualified prospective customer at the right time. However, those words and phrases are contextualized by the strategy you use. There is no way around it.

But let me give you a warning. Don't allow these disarmingly simple tactics (words, phrases, terms, and approaches) to lead you to believe that you can do without an artfully defined prospecting strategy. Don't allow them to become the classic "tactics in search of a strategy." You must have a strategy. Choose which of the many prospecting approaches suggested in this book you may want to employ, *then* apply the right tactic at the right time with the right prospective customer, . . . and *then* use the right words!

Again, with whom should you use these phrases? You certainly will achieve better results if the person with whom you're using them is truly a qualified prospective customer. And, one more time, that single word, "qualified," is more critical than many salespeople believe it is. Long term, wasting too much time with too many of the wrong people is a sure way to guarantee sales failure.

Why are we revisiting this concept so soon after introducing it just a few pages back? Because it really is that important! And its fundamental value to prospecting can never, ever be overemphasized. And that is particularly true in a book like this—one that presents perfect phrases. Even the best phrases will misfire if used at the wrong time and in the wrong way. So, be warned!

A Word of Caution

Again, be careful not to use the words and phrases in this book with prospective customers who meet only the least important of the criteria—merely being willing to listen to you! Just because someone is willing to listen certainly doesn't mean that he or she is a qualified prospective customer. And that is a trap that has caught lots and lots of salespeople—and can be fatal to your sales career.

A final thought here: the only real inventory you have as a salesperson is your time. So don't waste it. Even if you are using the exact, right phrases, don't waste them on the wrong people.

The Three Biggest Myths in Lead Generation

Myth #1: "Prospecting Is a Numbers Game." That is simply not true. Prospecting is first and foremost a game of accuracy. It is all about delivering the right message to exactly the right people at precisely the right time and in the right way.

Of course, the more you do that, the more you will be able to prospect more effectively. Remember: it is important to be accurate, correct, and on target and not to waste a lot of time either with the wrong prospective customers or delivering the wrong message at the wrong time and in the wrong way.

Myth #2: "All Prospective Customers Are the Same." Based on where you are in your sales career, your years of experience, your prospecting resources, or your level of sales sophistication coupled with your product or service demands, this myth may or may not be meaningful to you. What does that mean? Early in their sales careers, lots of salespeople are told to "go out and see as many people as you can." They are told that sales is all about activity. However, once a salesperson has experienced enough sales success and/or failure and has worked with large numbers of prospective customers and customers/clients, he or she becomes aware of several realities:

- Some prospective customers will never buy, no matter what you say or do.
  Therefore, abandon them before they take up too much of your time.

- Some prospective customers will take up vast amounts of your time, regardless of how good or effective you are.
  Therefore, determine who they are and minimize your time with them.

- Some prospective customers are purely comparison and/or price shoppers.
  Therefore, determine who they are and never allow them to compare "apples to apples" or "drive you to your knees."

- Some prospective customers will never be profitable.
  Therefore, be sensitive to the future you face if you deal with too many price-shopping prospective customers.

- Some prospective customers are not strategically correct for you or your organization.
  Therefore, look at the bigger picture, not just the sale.

What does this all mean? This one, single thing: not all prospective customers are created equal.

Myth #3: "Positioning Is for Companies, Not for People." This assumption couldn't be more incorrect. To most prospective customers, you *are* your organization. And how you present yourself relative to minor concerns—such as timeliness, dress, style, image, grammar, etiquette, and demeanor—and to larger issues—such as how you establish yourself with regard to business acumen, implementing a strategy, possessing marketplace and technical knowledge, demonstrating expertise, and providing strong account management—positions you well or poorly. The choice is yours.

One more time: to every single prospective customer you see, you are your organization. As a consequence, you need to position yourself in the way that your prospective customers want to see you in order to help them solve their biggest issues. And they absolutely must be the same issues as your organization solves. Hopefully, your marketing department has figured that out and that there is close integration between your marketing message and your sales approach. If not, you have some work to do.

The Three Biggest Lead-Generation Mistakes and How to Avoid Them

Mistake #1: Dealing with the Wrong People at the Wrong Level. The principle here is that what you sell will determine the level of the person you should be contacting. It will also determine who, by title, you should not be seeing.

For example, an executive-level buyer may not be responsible for buying janitorial supplies. However, if you have positioned janitorial supplies as part of a broad-based cost-reduction solution, janitorial supplies might just be a part of your offering.

Here's the problem: far too many salespeople, for whatever reason, tend to enter accounts at too low a level and then never recover. Perhaps the person they call on doesn't really want them to move higher or perhaps the salesperson simply doesn't have the confidence to enter any higher in the account or move up.

This is a misplaced strategy and is a much bigger problem than most salespeople (or sales managers) realize.

Here's our first tactical secret. If you enter too low, tell your prospective customer that you are required by management to deal with higher-level decision makers and then report those findings to your manager. Further, say that you need that contact's help in getting to the higher level. Frankly, if your organization is a smart selling organization, that should be a requirement—either formally or informally. And it's the truth.

Mistake #2: Spending Too Much Time with Unqualified Prospective Customers. Remember the five characteristics of qualified buyers. Let's look at them again. All five are important.

1. They have an awareness of their need for whatever it is you sell.
2. They have both the authority and the ability to pay for it.
3. They have a legitimate sense of urgency relative to acquiring it.
4. They trust you and your organization.
5. They are willing to listen to you.

One more time: don't be fooled into believing that someone willing to listen to you is necessarily a qualified prospective customer. That is the fatal error in prospecting made by salespeople worldwide. Be sure you're not one of them, because it can become habit-forming—and very unprofitable. By the way, knowing this is such a universal flaw is perhaps the major key to prospecting. That's why we've mentioned it several times.

Mistake #3: Employing the Wrong Lead-Generation Strategy. Although this book is about the right words and phrases to use in generating leads, if your strategy is wrong, then even the best proven phrases will not succeed. This is also the second time we have made this point. Why? Like the decision to deal only with qualified prospective customers, the choice of strategy is critical to your long-term success. What's the bottom line to this? You must deploy a strategy that is consistent with how your customers buy your product or service rather than what you personally think is the best way to get in front of them. For example, don't try to forge partnerships with people who don't want to have partners or to develop relationships with prospective customers who want to buy in a transactional way.

What is the best strategy for you and your prospective customers? Only you can determine that. Perhaps these few observations might help:

- Who your present customers are . . . or are not
- Who your prospective customers are . . . and are not
- How your customers deal with salespeople like you
- What their policies are relative to purchases

However, your decision or strategy for prospecting could also be driven by the following factors:

- Where you are in your sales career
- Whether or not you have current or inherited business
- Your personal skill sets
- Tools you have at your disposal (digital, phone, etc.)
- The product or service you sell
- Who your best targeted prospective customers might be
- Budget considerations
- Marketing support
- Clerical support
- Purchasing patterns of prospective customers

Only you can review these issues. However, no words, no matter how well conceived or delivered, will offset a flawed strategy.

Now, let's start taking a look at the prospecting strategies you can deploy, defining them, outlining the components of each, discussing how to launch them, and considering the words to use to generate interest and responsiveness to you and your offer.

The Hardest Part of Prospecting

Acquiring new leads is the most difficult part of the sales profession. That is especially true if you're new to sales or in a new sales position. It's how you go from zero into ultimately building your book of business that will define your success. Then, the key to continuing that success is to avoid becoming complacent and, as a result, failing to find new business on a regular basis—and this is true no matter what you sell. There is, however, fundamental knowledge that you must acquire, based on what you sell and to whom you sell it. What does that mean? You need to engage prospective customers based on the way they buy— *not* based on the way you sell. In their expectations of the sales experience, your prospective customers generally will be *transactional* (they buy and move on), *relational* (they want a meaningful, ongoing interaction), or *strategic* (you jointly anticipate their future needs).

However, no matter what your strategy, eventually you will likely lose many of the accounts you win. There will come a time when you will be replaced for any of hundreds of reasons. It may not even be your fault. So let's face it, no matter what you sell or to whom you sell it, you do need to deal with this reality: learn to service your customers as well as you are able to do so and consistently go out and find others to replace them *before* they leave! And you need to do that every single day of your sales career—and that is true whether you have been in sales for 20 days or 20 years!

Here's the bottom line: providing excellent service to your accounts is, in the final analysis, the best form of prospecting, isn't it? However, sometimes even that isn't enough, no matter what you do.

Chapter 2
Your Direct Value Statement: What to Say

Your Direct Value Statement

What are your most common prospecting situations? They can likely be broken into at least the following categories:

- Face-to-face, formally or informally, on purpose or by chance
- By telephone
- At trade shows
- Through referrals from current customers
- Through referrals from people other than customers
- At networking events
- Response to mail, e-mail, or fax campaigns
- By selling current customers more

In each of these situations, you'll need to know the importance of your unique *Direct Value Statement* (DVS) and know how to use it. This is a straightforward, easy-to-say, and easy-to-understand statement that clearly and declaratively communicates the fundamental reason why your organization exists and why you're selling its products or services. It is likely the most important thing you'll learn in this book. Yet most salespeople never master the concept. In fact, surprisingly, some never even know it exists.

Sample Direct Value Statements

"We assist our clients in the banking industry to improve their profitability. We do this by reducing their fixed operational costs, improving employee performance, and geometrically expanding their marketing efforts."

The DVS is such an important concept that we'll be spending some time showing you how to design your own. Why is your personal DVS so important? Because it quickly, clearly, and precisely defines for a prospective customer exactly who you and your organization are, what you do, and how you do it. Better yet, it defines clearly what you do and how you do it in the way that it benefits your customers or clients. It also identifies your core customers.

Ultimately, your DVS will play a central role in virtually every prospecting situation in which you will ever find yourself. In fact, it will be referred to in practically every prospecting scenario explained in this book.

No matter your business, your DVS can always start with the same phrase:

"We assist clients (or customers) in the _____ industry (or business) to _____. We do this by _____."

However, in order to do that, you must really understand what end-result benefits you actually deliver to your customers.

You also need to know what end-result benefits your targeted prospective customers and current customers actually want to gain, enjoy, achieve, or have.[1]

Here are several examples:

- We assist our clients (or customers) in the industrial manufacturing industry (or business) *to design their products more efficiently.* We do this *by providing cost-effective design software.*
- We assist our clients (or customers) in the health-care industry (or business) *to provide first-rate care to their patients.* We do this *by providing practical, useful education behind our diagnostic products.*
- We assist our customers in the furniture industry (or business) *to earn greater add-on sales to their products.* We do this *by providing customer relationship tools and strategies.*

Using Direct Value Statements

Your DVS is extremely important in many venues. You can use it for gaining appointments, imbedding it into pre-approach communication tools, meeting people, and answering the inevitable question, "What do you do?"

Again, the structure is *always* the same: "We assist our _____ in the _____ industry (or business) to _____. We do this by _____."

No matter what your business, venture, service, or industry, this statement will work for you. Therefore, I'd urge you to give some very serious thought to answering these four questions when developing your own direct value statement.

- Do you work with individuals, organizations, enterprises, associations, or governments?

- Do you specialize in an industry? A specific segment? A unique market? A certain type of business?
- What do you assist your customers in doing? Reducing their costs? Improving their productivity? Reducing employee turnover? Maximizing financial returns? Gaining market share? Increasing stock value? Improving their profits?
- How do you do that? By improving processes? Improving manufacturing yield? Providing upgraded equipment? Offering education? Guaranteeing on-time delivery?[2]

If you cannot easily, quickly, and comfortably communicate the fundamental reason why people or organizations would choose to do business with you and precisely how you do what you do for your customers, you will surely have a very serious problem when prospecting for customers. In fact, this is so critical that if you can't verbalize those things, you may likely never even get your foot in the door.

In the final analysis, people will choose to do business with you in order to reduce or eliminate a problem, solve an issue, improve a situation, make easy purchases, or enhance their position. They are all vitally interested in solutions. That's really what it is all about.

Some more examples:

- We assist our clients (or customers) in the software industry (or business) *to reduce personnel costs.* We do this *by offering screening and assessment services, hiring systems, and retention programs.*
- We assist our clients in the long-term health industry (or business) *to provide better care to acutely ill patients.* We do this *by having the largest research facility in the world with*

the most scientists dedicated solely to critical, long-term care issues.

■ We assist design engineers in the metal fabrication industry (or business) *to provide real-time system feedback.* We do this *by having the most comprehensive troubleshooting software in the market.*

Your turn. Fill in the blanks of your Direct Value Statement.

We assist _____ [clients or customers] in _____ [industry or business] to _____ [what you help them to do]. We do this by _____ [what you do to help them].

Craft your DVS and use it over and over again. It will prove to be invaluable to you in gaining appointments with even the most difficult prospective customers.

Three Types of Contact

There are three primary situations in which you launch yourself from a "standing start"—you have no current customers, you have no one who can refer you, or you have absolutely no way to receive company-generated leads.

■ *Cold contact*—a phone or face-to-face interaction with a prospective customer who may never have seen or even heard of you or your organization.

■ *Warm contact*—a phone or face-to-face interaction that is preceded by a "pre-approach contact" by some direct means, to include referral. What makes this strategy "warm" instead of "hot" is simply the last sentence of any pre-approach communication (*purpose statement*) and the P.S. section of any communication. More about this later.

■ *Hot contact*—a phone or face-to-face interaction based on some form of pre-approach communication with a formal response mechanism that the prospective customer returns to you electronically, via response card/letter or other form (fax, e-mail, or phone, for example). More later here as well.

A few words of caution: if you are going to use broadcast faxing as a strategy, for example, be sure to comply with all current laws. Check them carefully. Although this book is not about laws, it is about prudent caution. So be careful. Along similar lines, if you are sending unsolicited e-mails, avoid spamming. Spamming is not a practice that well-positioned, professional salespeople do. However, if your organization wants to use the Internet to attract business and is willing to do what it takes to win the search engine and conversion wars with your site, that's a different story. It is also quite a different story if your organization's Web site is a destination site. However, seek advice on the proper, acceptable way to maximize the Web. It's not too difficult for any search engine to throw you out completely or at least place you at the bottom of your search category—fast. Don't do anything to cause that to happen.

Now, let's deal with some specific strategies you can employ—and employ them immediately!

Notes

1. *Perfect Phrases for the Sales Call* by William T. Brooks (McGraw-Hill, 2006), pp. 23–24.
2. *Perfect Phrases for the Sales Call* by William T. Brooks (McGraw-Hill, 2006), p. 25.

Chapter 3
Direct Methods
of Prospecting—
Cold, Warm, and Hot Calling:
What to Say

No matter what method you do choose, the secret to success is the same: it's the list. A lousy list will yield lousy results no matter what you send, say, or do. It all starts with having a good list; the tighter it is to your offering, solution, price point, etc., the better.

The second key is your offer. And that includes what you say. A later section will supply you with the precise words that will work with specific customer types (no matter what you sell); teaser copy you can use for envelopes, e-mail subject lines, or postcards; a sample document (word for word); exact words to use with each type of customer to describe your product or service, yourself, your organization, and your benefits; and words to avoid using at all costs. You'll also be supplied with ads to place either electronically or through conventional methods. You can also use these exact, precise phrases to engage in meaningful face-to-face or telephone conversations about your product or service, company, benefits, and relationships with your prospect.

In many of these situations, you will be using your Direct Value Statement. Prepare it carefully—and memorize it. Use it as indicated.

To see which methods work best for you, you may want to test your strategy. Try one form with 50 prospective customers and an alternative form with another 50. That's called a split test. Don't spend all your time or your entire budget on a bad list or a bad offer. Either way, you lose.

Cold Calling

Cold calling means that there is no previous contact at all between you and the prospective customer. Here, too, the list is essential. So be sure to work from a list that is tightly aligned with your targeted market. That is, at least, a start.

Now, a few words of caution. Cold calling is tough enough without hampering your effort with some of the manipulative methods currently being used in the sales world. Among those things to avoid at all costs are the following:

- Misrepresenting yourself on the phone. For example, having someone else call on your behalf and then tell the prospective customer to hold for you with reference to a "very important" issue you need to discuss or with reference to "file number X" that you must share with him or her.
- Calling under the guise of representing someone or some organization from which you know the prospective customer will take a call. For example, sounding as if you are someone whom your prospect considers a prospective customer.

■ Posing as a friend or acquaintance by using the person's first name and/or yours in order to have a gatekeeper put you through.

Now, let's take a look at some exact words or phrases you should use when cold calling a prospective customer directly. You'll notice that there are a lot more variables, options, and unknowns on cold calls than on warm or hot calls. That's because you simply can't control cold situations as you enter them. It's that simple. That's what makes cold calling so difficult.

A Receptionist or Gatekeeper Answers the Phone

You hear: "Good morning. Acme Corporation. How may I help you?"

You say: "Hello, my name is _____ with _____. I've got a problem and I need your help."

Remember: receptionists are trained to provide assistance to people who seek it.

You hear: "How can I help you?"

You say: "My name is _____. [Insert your Direct Value Statement.] I would like to talk with Ms. Johnson."

You hear: "I'm sorry, she's not available."

You say: "Do you know when she might be available?"

You hear: "I'm not sure."

You say: "I'd like to talk with her. Would you recommend that I leave a message with you or leave a voice-mail message for her?"

Work with the receptionist to achieve your one, single objective—an appointment. Always solicit that person's help for the best way to get your message to the prospective customer.

It is essential that you earn this person's support so that you can broaden your base of internal advocacy within your prospective customer's organization.[1]

1. *Perfect Phrases for the Sales Call* by William T. Brooks (McGraw-Hill, 2006), p. 46.

The Gatekeeper Is Positive and Receptive, but Your Prospective Customer Is Reluctant

Your prospective customer's gatekeeper answers the phone. His or her response is both positive and receptive. However, your prospective customer shows some resistance and reluctance.

You hear: "Hello, Ed Ryan's office. This is Barbara. How may I help you?"

You say: "Hello, Barbara. My name is _____ with _____. I'm wondering if Mr. Ryan is available."

You hear: "Yes, he is. May I ask you what this is in reference to?"

You say: "Certainly. As I said, my name is _____. I'm with _____. [Insert your Direct Value Statement.]"

You are connected.

You hear: "Hello. This is Ed Ryan."

You say: "Hello, Mr. Ryan. As I told Barbara, my name is _____ with _____. [Insert your Direct Value Statement.] I was wondering if it might be possible for us to get together so that I could show you exactly how we could possibly do the same for you."

Pause and wait for a response.

You hear: "That sounds good. However, I'm not interested in spending a lot of time looking at what you might have to offer right now."

You say: "I can understand that. My purpose, however, is not to sell you anything right now, anyway. I'd really like to have a chance to meet you personally, learn something about your situation, and, perhaps, give you some idea of what we do so that we might be a viable option for you at any time in the future when you might be interested in moving forward."

You hear: "I might be willing to listen. However, don't expect me to buy anything."

You say: "I certainly don't. In fact, I promise that we will only begin a dialogue around taking a look at what we have. Do you have your calendar available? Is there a time next week that's better than any other for us to get together?"

You hear: "How much time will this take?"

You say: "How much time could you spare? I promise I won't take any more time than you can give me."

Establish the time frame and confirm the day, time, and location. Be sure to reinforce that your meeting will take only as long as the prospective customer can set aside for it. Notice that you respond to a question ("How much time will this take?") with a question ("How much time can you spare?").

Don't ever assume that a prospective customer is or isn't interested in your product or service. Regardless of the prospect's interest, your goal is to deflect his or her belief that you will expect a purchase decision immediately—unless, of course, you are actually selling via a one-call close telephone strategy. (This strategy, however, is not what this book is about. It is about prospecting, not selling—and the two activities are very different.) Your goal is to emphasize your interest in determining whether you can help in any way and to introduce your product or service so your prospect will consider it or at least be aware of it. Never forget that. And never violate that promise. If, however, your prospective customer becomes very interested during your conversation, don't hesitate to move ahead as aggressively as necessary.[2]

2. *Perfect Phrases for the Sales Call* by Willilam T. Brooks (McGraw-Hill, 2006), p. 44–45.

The Gatekeeper Answers the Phone and Your Prospective Customer Is Positive and Receptive

You hear: "Margaret Smith's office. This is Barbara. How may I help you?"

You say: "Hello, Barbara. My name is _____ with _____. I'm wondering if Ms. Smith is available."

You hear: "Yes, she is. May I ask you what this is in reference to?"

You say: "Certainly. As I said, my name is _____. I'm with _____. [Insert your Direct Value Statement.]"

You are connected.

You hear: "Hello. This is Margaret Smith."

You say: "Hello, Ms. Smith. As I told Barbara, my name is _____ with _____. [Insert your Direct Value Statement.] I was wondering if it might be possible for us to schedule an appointment so that I could show you how we might possibly be able to do the same for you?"

Pause and wait for a response.

You hear: "That sounds interesting."

You say: "I can promise you this. If what we have, in your opinion, won't work for you, I'll certainly understand it and not take too much of your time. Does that make sense?"

You hear: "As long as you do that, I'll be happy to see you."

You say: "Good. Do you have your calendar handy? If so, let's go ahead and schedule an appointment. Is there a day next week that's particularly good for you?"

Agree on a time and date and schedule the appointment. This situation is not as rare as you may think. There are times when you will be able to get a good, positive first meeting. It is essential, however, that you remember that your singular, solitary goal is always to get an appointment—not to spend much time on the phone, make a presentation about your product or service, and try to make a sale. One more time: your single, primary goal is to gain an appointment.[3]

In many of these situations, you will note the overwhelming importance of your Direct Value Statement. You must prepare it carefully—and it is the only thing in this book that you must learn word for word. Use it at the most appropriate times and it will prove to be invaluable to you.

Should you receive questions with regard to your product or service, always defer them with the statement, "I can answer those questions when we get together. However, in order to answer them adequately, I'd like to ask you a few questions with reference to your concerns to see precisely how our solution can best be positioned to be of greatest value to you when we get together." Then, ask a few appropriate questions. Respond to each answer with something like "That's interesting. I think we can help with that. I'd like to prepare a few things for your review."

Never forget: all phone calls are always about one thing—getting an appointment. You are not making a sales presentation on the phone. Again, that's not the purpose of this section.

3. *Perfect Phrases for the Sales Call* by William T. Brooks (McGraw-Hill, 2006), pp. 46–47.

Your Prospective Customer Answers the Phone and Is Resistant

You hear: "Good morning, this is John Johnson."

You say: "Mr. Johnson, my name is _____ with _____. [Insert your Direct Value Statement.] Based on where you currently are in your planning, I'm wondering if you might want to invest some time with me. I'd simply like to ask you a few questions and see if we may be able to help you."

You hear: "I'm not interested in talking to anyone like you. I don't have the time, the interest, or the inclination."

You say: "I can understand that. However, I'd really like just to learn a little more about you and see if there may be some way we might be able to be of help to you, even if it's in the future. Does that sound like it might be acceptable to you?"

You hear: "No it's not."

You say: "I understand. If that's the case, I'd like to forward you some material. Do you prefer e-mail or regular mail?"

Make sure that you have the correct e-mail or mailing address. You can get this through an online service or additional research. Avoid having to ask the prospective customer for the address, especially if he or she is initially reluctant. The last thing you want to do is take more time, appear to be disorganized, and come across as just another cold caller.

You say: "I'll send you the material today. And if it's OK with you, I'll give you a call in a few days to make sure you have received it and see if you've had a chance to review it. If it looks like it might be of some mutual interest, we might be able to go from there. Does that sound OK?"

You hear: "Yes, that's fine."

Your strategy is designed solely to get materials into your prospective customer's hands because it is very clear at this point that trying to talk him or her into a meeting would likely prove to be counterproductive. This process will also give you a reason to make a warm call later as you follow up to determine if the prospective customer has received the materials and read them and to ask if he or she has any questions about them.[4] Again, your goal is to get a face-to-face appointment. Later on we'll discuss what we call nurturing or cultivating your prospective customer. You may even consider deploying that strategy at this point.

4. *Perfect Phrases for the Sales Call* by William T. Brooks (McGraw-Hill, 2006), pp. 48–49.

Your Prospective Customer Answers the Phone and Is Positive

You hear: "Good afternoon. Howard Smith."

You say: "Mr. Smith, my name is _____ with
_____. [Insert your Direct Value Statement.] The
purpose of my call is to discover if you might have an
interest in meeting with me to see if there is some way
that we could possibly be of service to you. Do you have
a few minutes so we might talk?"

You hear: "Well, tell me a little bit more about what it is that
you sell."

You say: "We have worked with lots of organizations such as
yours over the years and have found that once we are able
to establish a relationship we've been able to assist them
in unique and different ways. However, in order to see if
we might be able to be of some service to you, it's important that we have a face-to-face meeting. I'm wondering, is
there a time next week that might be best for you?"

Your sole strategy here is to gain an appointment, no
matter how positively responsive the prospective customer
may be. Never place yourself in the position of trying to
oversell. You'll note that you never attempt in this conversation to make a sales presentation. You simply state the benefits of your product or service and make an appointment.
The biggest mistake you can ever make here is to try to oversell a prospective customer who seems responsive.[5]

5. *Perfect Phrases for the Sales Call* by William T. Brooks (McGraw-Hill,
2006), pp. 49–50.

Your Prospective Customer Answers the Phone and Is Indifferent

You hear: "Good afternoon. Betty Johnson."

You say: "Ms. Johnson, my name is _____ with _____. [Insert your Direct Value Statement.] The purpose of my call is to see if there is some way that we may be able to establish a mutually convenient time to sit down and determine if we might be of some service or value to you and your organization."

You hear: "Well, I'm not that familiar with your organization and don't know anything about you. And, frankly, I'm not sure if we're in a position to make a decision at this point."

You say: "I can understand that. Very few of our customers are ever in the position to make a decision when we first contact them. However, I would like to send you some material that will give you a better understanding of who we are and what we offer. And then, if possible, I'd like to get back in touch with you in the next couple of days to determine if we might be able to pursue it further if the material looks interesting to you."

You hear: "Sure, that's OK. Go ahead and send the material."

It is important for you to make sure you have the proper address. Find it online or through some other source. Confirm with the prospective customer that you will call in a couple of days to set up an appointment for a meeting.[6]

However, always be aware that a request for information is, in most cases, a tactic to get you off the phone. This strategy, therefore, should only be used as a last resort to set up a follow-up call—and another opportunity to talk with your prospective customer in order to get a face-to-face appointment. You also may want to deploy the nurturing strategy at this point, but we'll discuss that later.

6. *Perfect Phrases for the Sales Call* by William T. Brooks (McGraw-Hill, 2006), pp. 50–51.

Leaving an Effective Cold Call Voice-Mail Message

This strategy should be used whenever you leave a cold calling voice-mail message, regardless of how you ended up in voice mail! However, in this example, you call and are able to make contact only through a voice-mail message.

You hear: "This is Mary Smith. I'm sorry that I'm not at my desk right now. Please leave a message and I'll get back with you at my earliest possible convenience."

You say: "My name is _____ with _____. [Insert your Direct Value Statement.] The purpose of my call is to see if there is some way that we might be able to be of some service or value to you. I certainly don't expect you to return my call. However, should you be so inclined, I would like to leave my number. [Give your number, twice, slowly.] If I don't hear from you in the next couple of days, I trust that you will be in a position to accept my phone call. So if I don't hear from you in a day or two, I'll give you a call to see if there is some way we might be able to get together."

Never expect your prospective customer to return a voice message! However, never oversell either. Leave a message that is benefit-rich, one that explains in detail the benefits the prospective customer will receive when doing business with you—in other words, your DVS.

Notice that you give your phone number twice. It is very important to do that because the person may not be able to make note of your number immediately. Be sure to give your number very slowly and clearly so that the prospective customer can understand it. Also notice that you are establishing a situation in which you will call that person again in a couple of days and he or she will be expecting your call.

You may even want to think about writing down your phone number as you give it. Why is that? Simply this: it makes you aware of the speed at which you're talking—your prospective customer can't write any faster than you can! Some people speak at a normal speed until they leave their phone number—and then they speed up! Those are the numbers I delete—forever. I'll bet you do, too. So will your prospective customer. Give your number very slowly and clearly.[7]

Also, remember the importance of tone. Your tone should convey "authoritative engagement"—you are clear, confident, exact, and in control but not heavy-handed or overconfident. How you speak may be as important as what you say.

7. *Perfect Phrases for the Sales Call* by William T. Brooks (McGraw-Hill, 2006), pp. 52–53.

Warm and Hot Calling: The Key Differences

You'll recall that what differentiates a warm or hot call from a cold contact is that in warm and hot contacts you have some sort of pre-approach communication. And this difference is critical.

The difference between a warm call and a hot call is that the warm pre-approach communication sets up some form of later communication from you while the hot contact allows the prospective customer to respond to you. He or she says, "Yes, I'm interested! Please contact me!"

What You Should Put into Your Pre-Approach Communication

The first thing you must know about any form of written prospecting communication is that there's a big difference between just seeing it and really reading it. It's the difference between sights and sounds.

What Prospective Customers See

Let's examine sights. That is everything you cause the prospective customer to see. Prospective customers can do one of three things with any material you fax, e-mail, or send to them. They can disregard it, they can simply look at it, or they can actually read it. And those are three separate and distinct activities.

Here's the first important thing to remember about those activities. Prospective customers "look before they read." They scan your materials before reading them.

Scanning might take only a microsecond, but it always happens because they can't avoid it. If they don't immediately toss your materials, they must first look at them before they can actually read them. That's a fact of life that no one can change.

While they're scanning, prospective customers are already starting to form what we will label as their primary perception. Therefore, even before they read the words in your materials, prospective customers are already leaning in one direction or another. They expect to either like or dislike what your words will say to them. And life is really all about expectations, isn't it? And so is sales.

Scanning is, of course, a purely visual experience. As soon as prospective customers start reading your words, their visual experience is joined by another experience, their audible experience, which is everything you cause them to hear. (Yes, hear!)

That happens because, with the rare exception of speed-readers, people actually read by saying words silently. Therefore, when they're reading, people really are both seeing and hearing. Surprising, isn't it?

What you can cause prospective customers to hear will be addressed later in great detail. But first, let's concentrate on what you can cause your prospective customers to see.

Ten Powerful Visual Presentation Principles

Whatever words you use, you have to make sure you create the right visual experience for the prospective customer. You must first pay attention to how your words look rather than what they say.

Let's look at some visual presentation principles. And please remember: these principles are just as effective for faxes, e-mails, cards, announcements, or letters. It really makes no difference.

PRINCIPLE 1: HAVE LOTS OF "AIR"
In the graphics design profession, "air" means "white space." You don't want your correspondence to look like a jumble of words from top to bottom.

At least half of the surface area of each page of the document should have no words on it. Again, this is true whether your pre-approach communication is a letter, a card, an e-mail, a fax, a digital newsletter, an invitation to an event, or anything else! And "at least" doesn't mean "roughly" or "approximately." It means "not less than"—nothing more!

PRINCIPLE 2: SET UP WIDE MARGINS

If the margins are wide, each line of text will be short. Research has discovered another crucially important fact: whether they're looking at a piece of paper or a computer screen, people have a viewing cone. A "viewing cone" is all a person looking at something sees without moving his or her eyes. Imagine the point of the cone touching a word on the correspondence where the prospective customers' eyes are focused. Peripheral vision allows them to see surrounding words at the same time, but to actually read those other words they must move their eyes. Try it with this page and you'll understand what this means.

The more prospective customers are forced to "change the viewing cone"—to move their eyes along a line of type—the more likely they are to stop reading. This is called "wear out": the eyes tire out if you make them work too much.

PRINCIPLE 3: WHEN IN DOUBT, USE RAGGED RIGHT

Obviously, most conventional communication is written with the left margin flush. For the right side, there are two approaches. Each gains and loses benefits for you.

It's possible to make the text flush right and flush left as shown in Example A on the next page. (I'm using xxxxxx instead of actual words because I want you to concentrate on the visual experience, not the audible experience. We'll get to the words later.)

Example A

xxxxxxxxxxxxxxxxxxxxxxxxxxxxxxxxxxxxxxxxxxxxxxxxxxxxxxxxxx
xxxxxxxxxxxxxxxxxxxxxxxxxxxxxxxxxxxxxxxxxxxxxxxxxxxxxxxxxx
xxxxxxxxxxxxxxxxxxxxxxxxxxxxxxxxxxxxxxxxxxxxxxxxxxxxxxxxxx
xxxxxxxxxxxxxxxxxxxxxxxxxxxxxxxxxxxxxxxxxxxxxxxxxxxxxxxxxx

The alternative is flush left and ragged right, as shown in Example B:

Example B

xxxxxxxxxxxxxxxxxxxxxxxxxxxxxxxxxxxxxxxxxxxxxxxxx
xxxxxxxxxxxxxxxxxxxxxxxxxxxxxxxxxxxxxxxxxxxxxxxxxxx
xxxxxxxxxxxxxxxxxxxxxxxxxxxxxxxxxxxxxxxxxxxxxxxxx
xxxxxxxxxxxxxxxxxxxxxxxxxxxxxxxxxxxxxxxxxxxxxxxxxxx.

- Example A creates the perception that the contents of your printed or digital document are very knowledgeable and authoritative.
- Example B will be perceived as more reader-friendly and easier to read than Example A.

It's usually best to follow Example B because your pre-approach materials should be perceived as informal communication, not as formal documents. And that's particularly true in lead generation. Most salespeople make the mistake of being too formal in their communication to prospects. While the tone and style should certainly be professional, it should also be both informal and conversational.

PRINCIPLE 4: KEEP THE PARAGRAPHS SHORT

The shorter the paragraph, the more likely prospective customers will read it. The "words" (xxxx) in a single paragraph in Example C are made to appear more reader-friendly by separating them into three paragraphs, as shown in Example D.

Example C

XXXXXXXXXXXX XXXXXXXXXXXXXXX XXXXXXXXXXXXXXXXXXXXXXXXX
XXXXXXXXXXXXXX XXXXXXXXX XXXXXXXXXXXXXXXXXXXXX.
XXXXXXXXXXXXXXXXXXXXX XXXXXXXXXXXXXXXX XXXXXXXX
XXXXXXXXX XXXXXXXXXXXXX XXXXXXXXXXX XXXXXXXXXXXXXXXXX
XXXXXXXXXXXX XXXXXXXXXXXXX XXXXXXXXXXXXXXXX XXXXXX
XXXXXXXXXXX XXXXXXXXXXXXX XXXXXXXXX XXXXXXXXXXX
XXXXXXXXXXXXXXXXXX XXXXXXXXXX XXXXXXXXXXXX.

Example D

XXXXXXXXXXX XXXXXXXXXXXXXXX XXXXXXXXXXXXXXX
XXXXXXXXXXXXXXXXXXXXXXXXXXXXXXX XXXXXXX XXXXXX
XXXXXXXXXXXX XXXXXXXXXX XXXXXXXXXXXXXXXXXXXXXXXXXXX.

XXXXXXXXXXXXXXXXXXXXXXXXXXXX XXXXXXXXXXXXXXXXXXX.
XXXXXXXXXXXXXXXXXXXXXXXXXXXXXXXXXXXXX
XXXXXXXXXXXX XXXXXXXXXXXX XXXXXXXXXX XXXXXX.

XXXXXXXXXXXXXXXXXXXXXXXXXX XXXXXXXXX XXXXXXXXXXXXXXXX.
XXXXXXXXXXXXXXXXXXX XXXXXXXXXX XXXXXXXXXX
XXXXXXXXXXX XXXXXXX XXXXXXXXXXXXX XXXXXXXXXX.

PRINCIPLE 5: KEEP THE SENTENCES SHORT

Take the same approach as with long paragraphs—break them up. Turn a long sentence into two or three shorter sentences or break it with a dash (—).

Techniques of that sort keep the prospective customer reading because they "move the eye along." A dash inspires "visual curiosity" because most readers want to know what follows the dash. Look at Example D again. Now notice how the text is modified in Example E.

Example E

XXXXXXXXXXXXX XXXXXXXXXXXXXXXX XXXXXXXXXXXXXXXXXX
XXXXXXXXXX XXXXXXXXXXXXX XXXXXXXXXXX XXXXXXX XXXXXX
XXXXXXXXXXXX XXXXXXXXXXX XXXXXXXXXXX XXXXXXXXXXXXXXXXXXX.

XXXXXXXXXX XXXXXXXXXXXXXXXX XXXXXXXXXXXXXXXXXXX.
XXXXXXXXXXXXXXXXXXXXXX—XXXXXXXXXXXXXXXXXXXX
XXXXXXXXXXXXX XXXXXXXXXXXXX XXXXXXXXXX XXXXXX.

XXXXXXXXXXXXXXXXXXXXXXXXXX—XXXXXXXX XXXXXXXXXXXXXXXXX.
XXXXXXXXXXXXX XXXXXXXXXXX XXXXXXXXXXXXXX
XXXXXXXXXXXXXX XXXXXXXXXXXXXXXXX XXXXXXXXXX.

A dash instead of a period might be preferable. Periods are "stoppers" because they usually cause the eye to temporarily stop reading. Any time that happens, you risk losing the prospective customer completely.

PRINCIPLE 6: CREATE A LOT OF VISUAL VARIETY

Quotation marks, italics, boldface, underlining, and so on create the perception of visual variety. They make your letters more appealing during the scanning process.

PRINCIPLE 7: DON'T ITALICIZE OR UNDERLINE MORE THAN ABOUT THREE WORDS IN A ROW

Compare Examples F and G. Notice how Example G gives the eye too much to handle:

> **Example F**
> Don't italicize or underline more than *about three words* in a row. Here too, the issue is wear out.
>
> **Example G**
> *Don't italicize or underline more than about three words in a row. Here too, the issue is wear out.*

PRINCIPLE 8: DON'T MAKE UNDERLINES SOLID

Example G is bad enough with extensive italics, but it can be made even worse if the words are underlined continuously. Notice how the words appear when this principle is violated, how they seem to run together.

> **Example G** (redone)
> <u>Don't italicize or underline more than about three words in a row. Here too, the issue is wear out.</u>

PRINCIPLE 9: AVOID THE USE OF ALL CAPS

Compare Examples H and I and see for yourself. (In heads, as used in this book, all caps can be OK, as long as they are not excessive.)

Example H

ALL CAPS are very difficult for the eye to read and accelerate wear out.

Example I

ALL CAPS ARE VERY DIFFICULT FOR THE EYE TO READ AND ACCELERATE WEAR OUT.

PRINCIPLE 10: USE "PRIME TIME WINDOWS" (PTWs) TO THEIR FULL POTENTIAL

PTWs are communication opportunities that prospective customers give you—moments in time when they're paying attention. Every communication has three of these "PTWs." Almost every prospective customer will read a headline, the first sentence, and P.S. message of any correspondence. And yes, you can put headlines into e-mails (subject line), fax correspondence, invitations, ads, and even letters:

HEADLINE (PTW)
Dear Xxxxxxx:

Xxxxxxxxxxxxxxxx xxxxxxx xxxxxxxxxxxxxxxxxxxxxxxx.
(PTW)
Xxxxxxxx xxxxxxxxxxxxxxxxxxxxxx xxxxxxxxxxxxxxxxxxxxxxxx
xxxxxxxxxxxxx—xxxxxxxxxxxxxxxxxxxx xxxxxxxxxx.
Xxxxxxxxxxxxx

xxxxxxxxxxxxxxxxxxxxxxxx xxxxxxxxxxxxxxxxxxxxxx.
Xxxxxxxxxxxxxxxxxx xxxxxxxxxxxxx … xxxxxxxxxxxxxxxxxxxx
xxxxxxxxxxxxxxxxxxxxxxxx.

Xxxxxxxxxxxxxxxxxxxxx xxxxxxxxxxxxxx.
Xxxxxxxxxxxxxxxxxxxxxxxx xxxxxxxxxxxxxxxx … xxxxxxxxxxx
xxxxxxxxxxxxxxxxxx. xxxxxxxxxxx xxxxxxxxxxxxxx.
(Your name and title)
P. S. xxxxxx xxxxxxxxx (PTW)

Again, almost every prospective customer will read the P.S. at the end of your correspondence. This P.S. should be a rephrasing of the original headline coupled with a recap of your Purpose Statement. Shortly, you'll see a sample of this.

Remember that your purpose will be different depending on whether the contact is warm or hot; as a rule, you will be reminding a warm prospective customer that you'll contact him or her, while you will be asking a hot prospective customer, a second time, to respond to you by registering interest in having you contact him or her.

What Prospective Customers Hear

The other half of the equation for the pre-approach communication is the audible experience—everything you cause your prospective customers to hear.

The Prime Time Window in your pre-approach prospecting communications should always be dedicated to your Primary Bonding Statement (which we'll consider later) and nothing but that Primary Bonding Statement.

Here are the components, with the Prime Time Windows (PTW) and White Space noted:

Headline (PTW)

Dear _____:

(PTW) Primary Bonding Statement

White Space

Product or Service Statement

White Space

Provider Statement

White Space

Benefit Statement

Direct Value Statement

Purpose Statement

(Closing),

(Your Name and Title)

(PTW) P.S. A Modified Bonding Statement

Five points here are most important:

1. The *Primary Bonding Statement* should be your first and/or second paragraphs. This is a statement of the type of relationship you would propose having with the prospective

buyer. Each one is uniquely branded to match the precise buying relationship that each specific prospective customer wants to have with any supplier or vendor from whom he or she purchases anything, including your product or service. This is important!

2. Make no mention of price in your communication (unless your strategy is to be the low price provider) because it's much too early in your sales process for that.

3. There's no established sequence for the Product or Service Statements, the Provider Statement, and the Benefit Statement.

4. The *Purpose Statement* is your reason for the communication; that is, you want to arrange a meeting, talk with the prospective customer on the phone, or whatever.
Ironically, research reveals that your purpose for writing is the least important component of the document—unless you are asking the prospective customer to take the physical action of responding to you in some directed and tangible way. That, then, becomes a hot communication.

   If the Primary Bonding Statement works, it's not difficult to have a prospective customer agree to the next step, which is almost always the subject of the Purpose Statement. If it doesn't work, your purpose won't matter, it won't happen, and it may go nowhere at all—except the trash can or the delete button.

5. Again, please note that these statements are the identical verbiage you can use in any type of communication with the prospective customer. Don't worry about being repetitious. Prospective customers don't remember the words you say or write, anyway. They remember only the good

feelings created by those words. This book is not about what you do when you are in front of a qualified prospective customer, but rather about how to get there. And, in many cases, you get there with feelings—the feelings you create.

A Sample Pre-Approach Communication Document

Here is a sample letter to a very, very specific type of prospective customer designed to establish a warm relationship. Chapter 4 will cover pre-approach campaigns for this prospective customer and 24 others.

Being Your Own Person (PTW) [Headline]

White Space

Dear [Name]:

White Space

There's nothing like calling your own shots. **(PTW) (Primary Bonding Statement)**

White Space

When you're free to do that, the business will usually move along the way you want it to, and you will wind up being able to do what you want with it. **(Primary Bonding Statement)**

White Space

When you have everything running like clockwork and you don't have people knocking on your door and turning your world upside down, you'll be able to keep things on

---

track and maintain control over what's really important. **(Primary Bonding Statement)**

White Space

Of course, benefits like that only come from the best products or services—the ones that are safe because they're easy to understand. So you don't need to move mountains to know what they're all about. **(Product or Service Statement)**

White Space

You might find that our product/service is just that kind of product/service.

White Space

But I'm talking about a lot more than a product/service or a bunch of benefits. **(Benefit Statement)**

White Space

I'm also talking about a relationship with the people around you. They absolutely must be experts in the areas where you simply don't have the time.

And you should be able to count on them to be honest and straightforward.

I like to think that describes [your organization]. **(Provider Statement)**

White Space

[Your organization] works with [organizations like the prospective customer's] to [collect overdue accounts inexpensively (for example)]. We do this by [offering our outsourced services]. **(Direct Value Statement)**

White Space

However, instead of going on about [your product/service] and [your organization], let me simply say that you might find it worthwhile to have a brief chat with me to evaluate for yourself what I've been talking about. Therefore, I'll call you in the next couple of days to pursue your interest further. (**Purpose Statement:** to establish the expectations of a warm prospective customer)

White Space

Sincerely,

[Your Name and Title]

White Space

P.S. Calling your own shots is what it's all about. Knowing that, that's how we work with clients like you. I look forward to our phone conversation! (**PTW**)

Remember: to elevate this prospective customer to hot status, simply modify your Purpose Statement and P.S. For example, your Purpose Statement might be "So that we might better discuss your specific situation, simply fill out and return the enclosed, postage-paid card and I will personally call you immediately." Your P.S. might be "Calling your own shots is what it's all about. Knowing that, that's why we work with clients like you. Again, if you'd like to learn more about how we can help you do that, please return the enclosed postage-paid card!"

Notice that the *Primary Bonding Statement* is divided into three paragraphs because you want to make your first paragraph as short as possible:

There's nothing like calling your own shots.

Then you build on that opening:

> When you're free to do that, the business will usually move along the way you want it to, and you wind up being able to do anything you want with it.

> When you have everything running like clockwork and you don't have people knocking on your door and turning your world upside down, you'll be able to keep things on track and maintain control over what's really important.

Let's look at the Purpose Statement one more time. Again, remember that this statement merely establishes what you want the prospective customer to do in response to your communication. A warm communication will require that you make a lot of calls because you are telling them that you'll do that work—you'll contact them. Again, here's our example of a warm Purpose Statement:

> Instead of going on about [your product/service] and [your organization], let me simply say that you might find it worthwhile to have a brief chat with me to evaluate for yourself what I've been talking about. Therefore, I'll call you in the next couple of days.

Now, again, let's see how a hot communication might work:

> Instead of going on about [your product/service] and [your organization] in this communication, perhaps you'd like to learn more. Simply return the enclosed, postage-paid card (form, fax-back form, etc.) and I'll be in touch with you personally so we can pursue things further.

Clearly, this will create less work for you, as a smaller percentage of prospective customers will respond to you. However, they are much better prospective customers because they are actually expressing interest. In order to react to their interest, however, you must have a good list, of course, and you must be willing to send at least three documents to them on a regular, tight schedule. Send one document and you'll get virtually no response, no matter what words you use! Two will be better— and three will be great.

In addition to the White Space and the Statements are these low-key ways to refer to your organization and your product or service:

"I like to think that describes [your organization]."

"You might find that our product/service is just that kind of product/service."

The Direct Value Statement clarifies what you do. Again, you see how critical learning and committing your DVS to your memory can be!

As suggested, effective communication of any type whatsoever should be sent in a series of at least three. You communicate with the same prospective customer at regular intervals, because the more often pre-approach documents are able to put you and your message in front of a prospective customer, the greater your chance of making your Purpose Statement— what you want them to do, whether accept your call or send something back to you—become reality.

As mentioned earlier, three is the ideal number unless you are establishing a sophisticated nurture process. (But more about that later.)

So keep sending those "uninterrupted commercials." In fact, in our organization, a warm or hot prospective customer can receive as many as 27 different nurturing communications from us over a one-year period! That's a lot more than three . . . and in each one of the initial three contacts we give them a chance to request (yes, request) the next 24. You'll see how we do this later. And they have the option to opt out at any time. It's called nurture or cultivation prospecting—and it really works!

Chapter 4
Pre-Approach Campaigns
What to Say or Write to
25 Types of Prospective Customers

The Process of a Pre-Approach Campaign

This chapter presents perfect phrases to use in a pre-approach campaign for each of 25 types of potential customers. These phrases work with your Direct Value Statement, your Purpose Statement, and your response mechanism of choice within any basic campaign strategy.

The process is the same for every single prospective customer. You simply plug in the different, targeted words and phrases for each type of prospective customer. (For each type of prospective customer, there is also a list of words that have tested as being really negative, distasteful, or, at best, neutral. Don't use them unless you are describing your competitors!)

Here's what to do:

■ Find a source that can teach you the fundamentals of direct response methods. Learn as much as you can about it before you do it.

- Get a strong list and test several samples with a small percentage of the list. Don't waste your resources on 1,000 people when a test of several hundred on the list will work.
- Ensure that your documents contain the following:
    - Envelope or Subject Teaser Copy for E-mails or Faxes (specific to the type of prospective customer)
    - Headline (specific to the type of prospective customer)
    - Entire Pre-Approach Communication (specific to the type of prospective customer)
    - Purpose Statement (what you want the prospective customer to do: if warm, expect a call; if hot, return some form of response tool specific to the type of prospective customer)
    - Direct Value Statement
    - Response Mechanism (described later)
    - P.S. (warm or hot)

The reason the pre-approach words and phrases you'll find in this chapter are so effective is because they focus on what prospective customers want. And wants are not specific to a product or service.

Why is that? Product or service references deal with needs, while buying motives spring from wants—and wants are universal. Selling is about how the prospective customers perceive things. It's not just about the needs they have to solve a problem, resolve an issue, or deal with a situation. Instead, this chapter will deal with the precise words and phrases that target what your prospective customers want emotionally from any product or service—including yours, regardless of what you sell.

Each of the following 25 prospective customer types will be presented in the same format. We'll begin with an entrepreneur with a general business background—the same prospective customer as in the example at the end of Chapter 3. So here we go!

Type 1. Entrepreneur with a General Business Background

SAMPLE HEADLINE

- Staying in Control … Your Way

WORDS TO USE IN YOUR PRIMARY BONDING STATEMENT

- Being in charge
- Calling your own shots
- Personal independence
- Being your own person
- Making the business run your way
- Having complete control over the business

WORDS TO USE TO DESCRIBE YOUR PRODUCT OR SERVICE

- Designed specifically for your unique situation
- Practical
- Street-smart
- Nothing theoretical or abstract
- Won't put any demands on your time
- Won't strain your resources

WORDS TO USE TO DESCRIBE YOUR ORGANIZATION

- Flexible
- Responsive
- Accommodating/Willing to make accommodations
- Never try to put a square peg in a round hole
- Recognizes your uniqueness
- Thorough

- Follows through on everything
- Covers all the bases for you
- Willing to do whatever it takes
- Makes sure every detail is covered

WORDS TO USE TO DESCRIBE THE BENEFITS OF YOUR PRODUCT OR SERVICE

- Order (in their business)
- Control
- Be in control automatically
- Order that reflects your personal wishes
- No more chaos
- Never tolerate disorder again

WORDS TO AVOID WITH AN ENTREPRENEUR WITH A GENERAL BUSINESS BACKGROUND

These words may appear not to be negative. However, they are emotionally charged with negativity to this specific prospective customer. So … be careful! Don't use them in any communication with this type of prospective customer!

- Organization
- Sophisticated
- Employee
- Theoretical
- Standardized
- Uniform
- The same for everyone
- Structured
- Procedures
- Growth
- Profitability

ENVELOPE TEASER COPY OR DIGITAL SUBJECT LINE COPY

- Inside—"How to Be Your Own Person and Run Your Business Your Way!"

SAMPLE PRE-APPROACH COMMUNICATION: ENTREPRENEUR WITH A GENERAL BUSINESS BACKGROUND

Staying in Control … Your Way **(PTW)**

White Space

Dear (Name),

(Primary Bonding Statement) There's nothing like being your own person …, doing whatever you want to do, whenever you want to do it. **(PTW)**

(Describing Your Product or Service) To help you get there, any product or service must be specific to your unique situation. It also needs to be practical and street-smart.

White Space

(Describing Your Organization) But even the best product or service won't do you much good unless it comes from an organization made up of people who are willing to do whatever it takes to make sure every detail is covered.

White Space

(Describing Your Benefits) Then, you'll have control over a business that reflects your personal wishes and keeps you in control.

White Space

I believe you'll see that [your product/service] and [your

organization] can be all that for you. But you should be free to make that decision for yourself.

White Space

[Insert your Direct Value Statement and Purpose Statement.]

[Add appropriate warm or hot P.S.]

FOR A FAX, AN E-MAIL, OR A PRINT AD

Being Your Own Person **(PTW)**

There's nothing like being your own person—doing whatever you want to do, whenever you want to do it. **(PTW)**

White Space

To help you get there, a product or service has to be specific to your unique situation. It also should be practical and very street-smart.

White Space

But even the best product or service won't do you much good unless it comes from people who are willing to do whatever it takes to make sure every detail is covered.

White Space

Then, you'll have control over a business that reflects your personal wishes.

We like to think that [your product or service] and [your organization] can be all that for you. But you should be free to make that decision for yourself.

[Insert your Direct Value Statement and Purpose Statement.]

[Add appropriate warm or hot P.S.]

A warm P.S. for this prospective customer might be:

P.S. If staying in control is important to you, then we do need to talk. I'll give you a call in the next few days so we can pursue things further!

A hot P.S. for this prospective customer would be:

P.S. If staying in control is important to you, please return the enclosed self-addressed card, and we will be in touch with you!

Why These Phrases Work

Remember earlier that we indicated the differences between needs and wants. All of these pre-approach communication devices are based on that concept—people always buy what they want. For example, a person may need a car, but will always buy the one he or she wants—the sports car with the full package or the SUV with the right color combinations.

How did we do the research on this? It's important for you to know so that you can have faith and confidence in the words we'll suggest that you use.

After decades of research with thousands of prospective customers, there are some pure scientific facts that we have collected through a very straightforward process. Here's that process:

1. We'd select a type of prospective customer to contact (for example, the CEOs of high-technology manufacturing firms, the owners of companies with fewer than 50 employees, and so on).

2. We wanted sample groups of between 30 and 100, depending on the type of prospective customer. It rarely took long to get sample groups together

because we found that most people like to participate in research.

3. After getting a good list in each category, we'd call the prospective customers and ask if they'd like to participate in a research project.

4. In exchange for their participation, we offered what's known in the research industry as a "premium." In other words, we gave something away to get them to take part. It could be free consulting, free research data, or anything of that nature.

5. To earn their premium, they had to answer some research questions, then let us observe meetings they'd have with salespeople who were trying to sell something to them, and finally answer some more questions after the meeting.

6. We promised strict confidentiality—no names, no sharing information with competitors or with the people who were trying to sell to them, and no publishing information that could be traced back to them personally.

7. Our questions covered a host of issues: what they liked and didn't like about the approaches used by salespeople, what they could remember about what the salespeople said, whether or not they believed what they heard, and so on. We also asked them to review product brochures and other forms of marketing literature and give us feedback.

With some types of prospective customers, the selling medium was always cold or warm phone calls rather than establishing in-person meetings. For example, a lot of purchasing professionals are bombarded daily with calls. So we'd listen in on those inbound calls.

Here's the twist. All of this was done under the premise of evaluating the sales approaches being used by the salespeople contacting them. However, the prospective customers themselves were actually the subjects of the research! Since they were unaware of that focus, their reactions were far more spontaneous. They opened up in a way they never would have done if they had known what we were really studying.

But that's not trickery. Rather, it's an example of an accepted research technique known as "unconscious indirect testing." The fundamental principle of unconscious indirect testing is to never let the "respondent" (the person you're studying) know either what you're really trying to find out or that you're doing research at all.

Not letting the respondents know that we were doing research helped when we worked with prospective customers who weren't inclined to take part in sales research, such as physicians, attorneys, and so on. In those cases, we took the opposite approach. Instead of trying to contact those prospective customers directly, we approached companies that were selling to them and offered them the same "premium" if they'd let us accompany their salespeople or listen in on their phone calls to the prospective customers we wanted to study.

A lot of research was also collected through telephone surveys and "intercepts," such as stopping people in shopping malls and industrial parks. Here, too, we used unconscious indirect testing.

The questions we used across the board were open-ended and designed to deflect the respondents' attention away from our true purpose. In some cases, we'd ask a prospective customer who had just dealt with a salesperson, "If you were that person's sales manager, what would you tell him/her to do in order to present the product/service better?" While that seems like a perfectly obvious question, our purpose in asking it was not.

The specific recommendation that the prospective customer would make in the capacity of a sales manager wasn't the issue. We wanted instead to find out which part of the presentation the prospective customer focused on. That would tell us precisely when and where his or her decisive perceptions were being formed.

What Do You Want Your Prospective Customer to Do?

Whether it is an e-mail, a fax, a letter, a direct mail piece, or an ad, you want your prospective customer to take some mental or physical action. What does that mean? To anticipate and expect a phone call (warm) or to expend the effort to fill out a form, send back a response card, return a fax-back form, go to a Web site, make a phone call, request more information, etc. (hot). You may want to determine if the prospective customer wants to hear from you repetitively. Again, that is called nurture or cultivation prospecting. More about that later: that's a promise.

This is important! Don't forget why you're making contact.

Let's take a look at just one sample of a response form that can convert any prospective customer into a hot prospective customer merely by having him or her fill it out and forward it to you. In this example, we ask the prospective customer to fill out a simple form that we can ask them to return via a postage-paid envelope or card or we can use as a simple fax-back form. We could even use it as a form on a Web site. Remember: once your prospective customer has responded to you, that single action has communicated to you that he or she wants to hear from you. The prospective customer has requested more information—and has thus become "hot." Other than a referral, this is the best lead. Here's a sample that you can use, adapt, or modify.

Yes, I'd like to learn how (your product or service) can help me to continue to stay in better control of my business! **(PTW)***

My Name _____

My Job Title _____

My Organization _____

My Address _____

_____

My Office Phone _____

My Home Phone (optional) _____

My Cell Phone (optional) _____

My Fax _____

My E-Mail _____

What method of communication do you prefer? (Please
   check all those that apply.)

❏ Office Phone   ❏ Fax

❏ Home Phone   ❏ E-Mail

❏ Cell Phone

Is there a preferred time of the day to contact you?

❏ Yes   ❏ No   If so, when? _____

Thank you.

*Remember: you must modify the PTW to reflect the Primary Want of the specific type of prospective customer. (We sometimes call this their "Emotional Agenda.")

Now that you understand the process for developing pre-approach documents, let's look at how you can develop exact, precise pre-approach documents for 24 more types of prospective customers.

Type 2. Entrepreneur with a Financial Background

SAMPLE HEADLINE

- Be Your Own Person ... in a Financially Stable Business

WORDS TO USE IN YOUR PRIMARY BONDING STATEMENT

- Being in charge
- Calling your own shots
- Personal independence
- Being your own person
- Making the business run your way
- Doing whatever you want to do, whenever you want to do it
- Having complete control over your business
- Making the business run by the numbers
- Having a financially stable business
- Being financially solid
- Having a guaranteed future

WORDS TO USE TO DESCRIBE YOUR PRODUCT OR SERVICE

- Balanced
- Takes the key priorities into account
- Risk-free
- Scientifically designed and developed
- Designed with finances and operations in mind
- Based on what a business is all about
- Doesn't make you dependent on guesswork
- You can know, rather than guess

WORDS TO USE TO DESCRIBE YOUR ORGANIZATION

- Sensible
- No-nonsense
- No extravagant claims
- Financially stable
- Has a financial impact that's proportionate to the price
- Gives you a reasonable return on investment

WORDS TO USE TO DESCRIBE THE BENEFITS OF YOUR PRODUCT OR SERVICE

- Order (in their business)
- Control
- Be in control automatically
- Order that reflects your personal wishes
- No more chaos
- Never tolerate disorder again
- Have the business run by the numbers
- Run quantifiably
- Keep your internal systems and procedures running smoothly

WORDS TO AVOID WITH AN ENTREPRENEUR WITH A FINANCIAL BACKGROUND

These words may appear not to be negative. However, they are emotionally charged with negativity to this specific prospective customer. So . . . be careful! Don't use them in any communication with this type of prospective customer!

- A huge return on investment
- Intuition
- Feelings

- Perception
- Employee
- Flexible pricing
- Innovative
- Experimental
- Bold
- Daring
- Take everyone's wishes into account

ENVELOPE TEASER COPY OR DIGITAL SUBJECT LINE COPY

- Inside—"Being Your Own Person … in a Financially Stable Business"

SAMPLE PRE-APPROACH COMMUNICATION: ENTREPRENEUR WITH A FINANCIAL BACKGROUND

Be Your Own Person … in a Financially Stable Business **(PTW)**

Dear (Name),

(Primary Bonding Statement) There's nothing like being your own person … doing whatever you want to do, whenever you want to do it—and doing it in a financially solid business. **(PTW)**

(Describing Your Product or Service) To help you get there, any product or service has to be risk-free and designed with finances and operations in mind.

(Describing Your Organization) But even the best product or service won't do you much good unless it comes from a financially stable organization that's governed by sensible, no-nonsense thinking.

(Describing Your Benefits) Then, you have a business that runs by the numbers — with YOUR systems and procedures running smoothly.

I believe you'll see [your product/service] and [your organization] can be all that for you. But you should be free to make that decision for yourself.

[Insert your Direct Value Statement and Purpose Statement.]

[Add appropriate warm or hot P.S.]

Now, let's look at two specifically different pre-approach tools for this same type of prospect. One will be "warm" and the other "hot," but both, again, for this same prospect, an entrepreneur with a financial background. All others will follow this model.

Approach 1

Be Your Own Person ... In a Financially Stable Business **(PTW)**

Dear (Name),

(Primary Bonding Statement) There's nothing like being your own person ... doing whatever you want to do, whenever you want to do it—and doing it in a financially solid business. **(PTW)**

(Describing Your Product or Service) To help you get there, any product or service has to be risk-free and designed with finances and operations in mind.

(Describing Your Organization) But even the best product or service won't do you much good unless it comes from a financially stable organization that's governed by sensible, no-nonsense thinking.

(Describing Your Benefits) Then, you have a business that runs by the numbers—with YOUR systems and procedures running smoothly.

I believe you'll see [your product/service] and [your organization] can be all that for you. But you should be free to make that decision for yourself.

(Sample Direct Value Statement) We assist sales-driven organizations in the air-conditioning and repair business to improve their sales team's performance. We do this by providing state-of-the-art training and development systems.

(Sample "Warm" Purpose Statement) I look forward to the opportunity to talk with you about how we can do the same for you. I will contact you in the next few days to set up an appointment.

(Sample "Warm" P.S.) P.S. If you're interested in ensuring that you stay in control of your business in a predictable way, we need to talk!

Approach 2

Be Your Own Person … in a Financially Stable Business **(PTW)**

Dear (Name),

(Primary Bonding Statement) There's nothing like being your own person … doing whatever you want to do, whenever you want to do it. And doing it in a financially solid business. **(PTW)**

(Describing Your Product or Service) To help you get there, any product or service has to be risk-free and designed with finances and operations in mind.

(Describing Your Organization) But even the best product or service won't do you much good unless it comes from a financially stable organization that's governed by sensible, no-nonsense thinking.

(Describing Your Benefits) Then, you have a business that runs by the numbers—with YOUR systems and procedures running smoothly.

I believe you'll see [your product/service] and [your organization] can be all that for you. But you should be free to make that decision for yourself.

(Sample Direct Value Statement) We assist sales-driven organizations in the air-conditioning and repair business to improve their sales team's performance. We do this by providing state-of-the-art training and development systems.

(Sample "Hot" Purpose Statement) To ensure that you can continue to be in control of a predictable business, please return the enclosed fax-back form. Once I receive it, I will send you some additional material for your review. We can then, of course, set up a mutually acceptable time for a meeting.

(Sample "Hot" P.S.) P.S. Please return the enclosed form so that being in control of your business predictably can be a way of life!

FOR A FAX, AN E-MAIL, OR A PRINT AD

Being Your Own Person …
in a Financially Stable Business **(PTW)**

There's nothing like being your own person … doing whatever you want to do, whenever you want to do it in a financially solid business. **(PTW)**

To help you get there, any product or service has to be risk-free and designed with finances and operations in mind.

But even the best product or service won't do you much good unless it comes from a financially stable organization that's governed by sensible, no-nonsense thinking.

Then you have a business that runs by the numbers—with YOUR systems and procedures running smoothly. And whatever you buy should be priced according to a proven textbook formula.

We like to think [your product or service] and [your organization] can be all that for you. But you should be free to make that decision for yourself.

[Insert your Direct Value Statement and Purpose Statement.]

[Add appropriate warm or hot P.S.]

Type 3. Accountant (Principal)

SAMPLE HEADLINE

- Know How to Protect Yourself

WORDS TO USE IN YOUR PRIMARY BONDING STATEMENT

- Predictability
- Knowing how things are going to turn out
- Knowing what's coming
- Protecting yourself

WORDS TO USE TO DESCRIBE YOUR PRODUCT OR SERVICE

- Allows for a manageable practice
- Makes business a pleasurable experience
- Helps create a rewarding practice
- Compensates for what you haven't learned yet

WORDS TO USE TO DESCRIBE YOUR ORGANIZATION

- Financially stable
- No extravagant claims
- Support/Supportive
- Goes the extra mile
- Takes the extra time
- A reasonable return on investment

WORDS TO USE TO DESCRIBE THE BENEFITS OF YOUR PRODUCT OR SERVICE

- Balance
- Proportion

- Bring some balance back into your life
- Put everything in proportion

WORDS TO AVOID WITH AN ACCOUNTANT (PRINCIPAL)

These words may appear not to be negative. However, they are emotionally charged with negativity to this specific prospective customer. So ... be careful! Don't use them in any communication with this type of prospective customer!

- Have a pretty good idea about what's coming
- Take a chance
- Art
- Art form
- Fairly well balanced
- Intuition
- Intuitive
- A huge return on investment
- Stay on the job
- Profit margins that feel right

ENVELOPE TEASER COPY OR DIGITAL SUBJECT LINE COPY

Inside—"Know How to Protect Yourself"

SAMPLE PRE-APPROACH COMMUNICATION: ACCOUNTANT (PRINCIPAL)

Know How to Protect Yourself **(PTW)**

Dear (Name),

(Primary Bonding Statement) There's no substitute for predictability, for knowing how things are going to turn out so that you can protect yourself. **(PTW)**

(Describing Your Product or Service) That's what makes a manageable practice possible and makes doing business a pleasurable experience.

(Describing Your Organization) Financially stable companies are the ones that deliver products and services like that—companies that are dedicated to support and giving you a reasonable return on investment.

(Describing Your Benefits) They're the ones that can bring some balance back into your life and help you put everything in proportion.

I believe you'll see [your product/service] and [your organization] can be all that for you. But you should be free to make that decision for yourself.

[Insert your Direct Value Statement and Purpose Statement.]

[Add appropriate warm or hot P.S.]

FOR A FAX, AN E-MAIL, OR A PRINT AD

Know How to Protect Yourself **(PTW)**

There's no substitute for predictability, for knowing how things are going to turn out so that you can protect yourself. That's what makes a manageable practice possible and makes doing business a pleasurable experience. **(PTW)**

Financially stable companies are the ones that deliver products and services like that—companies that are dedicated to support and giving you a reasonable return on investment.

They're the ones that can bring some balance back into your life and help you put everything in proportion.

Whatever you buy should be priced according to a textbook formula.

We like to think [your product/service] and [your organization] can be all that for you. But you should be free to make that decision for yourself.

[Insert your Direct Value Statement and Purpose Statement.]

[Add appropriate warm or hot P.S.]

Type 4. Architect (Principal)

SAMPLE HEADLINE

- Your Creativity … the Key

WORDS TO USE IN YOUR PRIMARY BONDING STATEMENT

- Knowing your creativity is the key to a successful project
- Being validated
- Using your value
- The valuable work you do for them
- Acceptance of your work and clients' appreciation for it
- Having everything you need to keep doing it
- Having work that's not compromised
- Utilizing your own ideas
- Make your own statement

WORDS TO USE TO DESCRIBE YOUR PRODUCT OR SERVICE

- Unique
- Novel
- Makes real creativity possible
- Value that's obvious to everyone
- It stands behind you
- Convincing
- Not a technical nightmare/not overly technical
- Not be limited by a lack of imagination or vision
- Prestigious
- Practicality that isn't excessive

WORDS TO USE TO DESCRIBE YOUR ORGANIZATION

- Sensitive to design priorities
- Doesn't sit in judgment
- Nonjudgmental
- Able to see past personal profit and loss statement
- Responsive
- Empathetic/Empathy

WORDS TO USE TO DESCRIBE THE BENEFITS OF YOUR PRODUCT OR SERVICE

- Enhance the environment
- Make a permanent statement

WORDS TO AVOID WITH AN ARCHITECT (PRINCIPAL)

These words may appear not to be negative. However, they are emotionally charged with negativity to this specific prospective customer. So . . . be careful! Don't use them in any communication with this type of prospective customer!

- Profitable
- Bottom line
- Temporary
- Transitory
- Dollars and cents
- Industry standard
- Practical to the "Nth" degree
- Needs to be defended
- Someone else's idea(s)
- Share the spotlight
- Make judgments
- Highly technical

- Technological
- Value that isn't immediately obvious

ENVELOPE TEASER COPY OR DIGITAL SUBJECT LINE COPY

- Inside—"Your Creativity … the Key"

SAMPLE PRE-APPROACH COMMUNICATION: ARCHITECT (PRINCIPAL)

Your Creativity … the Key **(PTW)**

Dear (Name),

(Primary Bonding Statement) Your creativity is the key to a successful project, especially when it's not compromised. So you should have everything you need to keep doing it.

(Describing Your Product or Service) One of those things is a unique product or service that makes real creativity possible—a product or service that isn't limited by a lack of imagination or vision.

(Describing Your Organization) Besides the product or service, it's also vital to have a relationship with people who are sensitive to design priorities. They should also not sit in judgment of everyone and must be able to see past their own profit and loss statement.

(Describing Your Benefits) Put all those things together and you can enhance the environment and make a permanent statement at the same time.

I believe you'll see [your product/service] and [your organization] can be all that for you. But you should be free to make that decision for yourself.

[Insert your Direct Value Statement and Purpose Statement.]

[Add appropriate warm or hot P.S.]

FOR A FAX, AN E-MAIL, OR A PRINT AD

Your Creativity … the Key **(PTW)**

Your creativity is the key to a successful project, especially when it's not compromised. So you should have everything you need to keep doing it. **(PTW)**

One of those things is a unique product or service that makes real creativity possible—a product or service that isn't limited by a lack of imagination or vision.

Besides the product or service, it's also vital to have a relationship with people who are sensitive to design priorities. They should also not sit in judgment of everyone and must be able to see past their own profit and loss statement.

Put all those things together, and you can enhance the environment and make a permanent statement at the same time.

To get that, you shouldn't have to pay a price that isn't fair, even to the most demanding observer.

We like to think [your product/service] and [your organization] can be all that for you. But you should be free to make that decision for yourself.

[Insert your Direct Value Statement and Purpose Statement.]

[Add appropriate warm or hot P.S.]

Type 5. Attorney (Litigating)

SAMPLE HEADLINE

- Control Through Leverage

WORDS TO USE IN YOUR PRIMARY BONDING STATEMENT

- Maintain control
- Not getting emotionally bogged down
- Continuing to win
- Dominating
- Controlling the outcome
- Keeping leverage
- Doing it without paying an emotional price

WORDS TO USE TO DESCRIBE YOUR PRODUCT OR SERVICE

- Sophisticated
- Capable of quick implementation
- Well thought out
- Gives you a substantial competitive advantage
- Credible

WORDS TO USE TO DESCRIBE YOUR ORGANIZATION

- Has an exceptional capacity for preparation
- Sound internal procedures
- Able to perform under difficult circumstances
- Tough-minded
- Workers/people who have their act together

WORDS TO USE TO DESCRIBE THE BENEFITS OF YOUR PRODUCT OR SERVICE

- Sparks bulletproof performance
- Have greater persuasiveness
- Adaptability
- Create magnetic attraction
- Shape influence
- Have significant impact on others

WORDS TO AVOID WITH A LITIGATING ATTORNEY

These words may appear not to be negative. However, they are emotionally charged with negativity to this specific prospective customer. So ... be careful! Don't use them in any communication with this type of prospective customer!

- Profitable
- Bottom line
- Temporary
- Transitory
- Dollars and cents
- Industry standard
- Practical to the "Nth" degree
- Needs to be defended
- Someone else's idea(s)
- Share the spotlight
- Make judgments
- Highly technical
- Technological
- Value that isn't immediately obvious

ENVELOPE TEASER COPY OR DIGITAL SUBJECT LINE COPY

■ Inside—"Control Through Leverage"

SAMPLE PRE-APPROACH COMMUNICATION: LITIGATING ATTORNEY

Control Through Leverage **(PTW)**

Dear (Name),

(Primary Bonding Statement) It's great to have the leverage that puts you in control of things . . . especially if you can do it without paying a heavy personal price. **(PTW)**

(Describing Your Product or Service) That is possible when you have a sophisticated product or service that is so well thought out and so credible that it gives you a substantial competitive advantage.

(Describing Your Organization) Products and services like that are backed by people who have their act together and can perform for you under difficult circumstances.

(Describing Your Benefits) With help like that, you can be sure of bulletproof performance that has a significant impact.

I believe you'll see [your product/service] and [your organization] can be all that for you. But you should be free to make that decision for yourself.

[Insert your Direct Value Statement and Purpose Statement.]

[Add appropriate warm or hot P.S.]

FOR A FAX, AN E-MAIL, OR A PRINT AD

Control Through Leverage **(PTW)**

It's great to have the leverage that puts you in control of things ... especially if you can do it without paying a heavy personal price. **(PTW)**

That is possible when you have a sophisticated product or service that is so well thought out and so credible that it gives you a substantial competitive advantage.

Products and services like that are backed by people who have their act together and can perform for you under difficult circumstances.

With help like that, you can be sure of bulletproof performance that has a significant impact.

Plus, all of that should come to you at a price that takes professional priorities into account.

We like to think [your product/service] and [your organization] can be all that for you. But you should be free to make that decision for yourself.

[Insert your Direct Value Statement and Purpose Statement.]

[Add appropriate warm or hot P.S.]

Type 6. Attorney (Non-Litigating)

SAMPLE HEADLINE

- Anticipating the Future

WORDS TO USE IN YOUR PRIMARY BONDING STATEMENT

- Minimizing your exposure
- Anticipating future events
- Inoculating yourself from risk
- Avoiding major mistakes
- Keeping from getting down and dirty
- Making sure things stay out of court

WORDS TO USE TO DESCRIBE YOUR PRODUCT OR SERVICE

- Completely predictable
- Predictable performance
- Precision/Precise
- Keeps human frailty to a minimum
- Makes things happen for you as automatically as possible
- Automatic

WORDS TO USE TO DESCRIBE YOUR ORGANIZATION

- Runs like a clock
- Like clockwork
- Spells everything out
- Leaves nothing to chance

WORDS TO USE TO DESCRIBE THE BENEFITS OF YOUR PRODUCT OR SERVICE

- Zero failure rate
- Reduce your dependence on other people
- Free of people-dependence
- No hidden hand grenades
- Make sure no one throws a wrench into your future

WORDS TO AVOID WITH A NON-LITIGATING ATTORNEY

These words may appear not to be negative. However, they are emotionally charged with negativity to this specific prospective customer. So … be careful! Don't use them in any communication with this type of prospective customer!

- Take a chance
- Always be ready to go to court
- Take a bold position
- Litigate
- Fairly predictable
- Let people do their thing
- Let people exercise their discretion
- Depend on people
- Minimal failure rate
- Flexible interpretation
- Close to the mark
- Nearly right on target

ENVELOPE TEASER COPY OR DIGITAL SUBJECT LINE COPY

▪ Inside—"Anticipating the Future"

SAMPLE PRE-APPROACH COMMUNICATION: NON-LITIGATING ATTORNEY

Anticipating the Future **(PTW)**

Dear (Name),

(Primary Bonding Statement) You have to be able to anticipate future events so that you can avoid major mistakes and make sure things stay out of court. **(PTW)**

(Describing Your Product or Service) A completely predictable and highly precise product or service can help you achieve that by making things happen for you as automatically as possible.

(Describing Your Organization) But products and services like that—the ones that run like clockwork—only come from suppliers who spell everything out and leave nothing to chance.

(Describing Your Benefits) That combination will help you achieve a zero failure rate and make sure no one throws a wrench into your future.

I believe you'll see [your product/service] and [your organization] can be all that for you. But you should be free to make that decision for yourself.

[Insert your Direct Value Statement and Purpose Statement.]

[Add appropriate warm or hot P.S.]

FOR A FAX, AN E-MAIL, OR A PRINT AD

Anticipating the Future **(PTW)**

You have to be able to anticipate future events so that you can avoid major mistakes and make sure things stay out of court. **(PTW)**

A completely predictable and highly precise product or service can help you achieve that by making things happen for you as automatically as possible.

But products and services like that—the ones that run like clockwork—only come from suppliers who spell everything out and leave nothing to chance.

That combination will help you achieve a zero failure rate and make sure no one throws a wrench into your future.

Plus, all that should come to you at a price that takes professional priorities into account.

We like to think [your product/service] and [your organization] can be all that for you. But you should be free to make that decision for yourself.

[Insert your Direct Value Statement and Purpose Statement.]

[Add appropriate warm or hot P.S.]

Type 7. CEO with an Engineering Background

SAMPLE HEADLINE

- Protect What You've Built with Fail-Safe Predictability

WORDS TO USE IN YOUR PRIMARY BONDING STATEMENT

- Minimizing your risks
- Going one step at a time
- Career
- Spreading the risk
- Protecting what you've built
- Major career investment
- Going straight down the middle
- Making the business run predictably
- Establishing fail-safe predictability
- Being able to quantify everything
- Making sure that important decisions are quantified
- Quantification
- Self-evident/Obvious
- Beyond question
- Predictability

WORDS TO USE TO DESCRIBE YOUR PRODUCT OR SERVICE

- Minimizes/Eliminates the "human factor"
- Protects you from the "human factor"
- Reliable
- Industry standard
- Proven
- Tested

- Proven reliability
- Tested reliability

WORDS TO USE TO DESCRIBE YOUR ORGANIZATION

- Proven designs are collected
- Proven designs are used
- Quantified designs
- Designs from real-world applications
- Large install base
- Applications like/similar to/identical to yours
- Not dependent on the "human factor"

WORDS TO USE TO DESCRIBE THE BENEFITS OF YOUR PRODUCT OR SERVICE

- Stabilize the work environment
- No surprises
- No guesswork
- Controllable progress

WORDS TO AVOID WITH A CEO WITH AN ENGINEERING BACKGROUND

These words may appear not to be negative. However, they are emotionally charged with negativity to this specific prospective customer. So . . . be careful! Don't use them in any communication with this type of prospective customer!

- Educated guess
- Intuition
- State of the art
- Feelings
- Perception
- Cutting edge

- Pushing the edge of the envelope
- Innovative
- Experimental
- New
- Daring
- People
- Human ingenuity
- Pioneering
- Revolutionary
- Accountability
- Stand up and be counted
- Substantial change

ENVELOPE TEASER COPY OR DIGITAL SUBJECT LINE COPY

- Inside—"Protect What You've Built with Fail-Safe Predictability"

SAMPLE PRE-APPROACH COMMUNICATION: CEO WITH AN ENGINEERING BACKGROUND

Protect What You've Built with Fail-Safe Predictability **(PTW)**

Dear (Name),

(Primary Bonding Statement) You made a major investment in your career. And to protect what you've built, you need to establish fail-safe predictability to make sure that important decisions are quantified and beyond question. **(PTW)**

(Describing Your Product or Service) With all that you've accomplished, this isn't the time for conflicts and controversy. You want proven, industry-standard products and services with proven reliability.

(Describing Your Organization) That happens when proven designs are collected from real-world applications within a large install base.

(Describing Your Benefits) So you'll wind up with a stabilized work environment where there are no surprises and controllable progress.

I believe you'll see [your product/service] and [organization] can be all that for you. But you should be free to make that decision for yourself.

[Insert your Direct Value Statement and Purpose Statement.]

[Add appropriate warm or hot P.S.]

FOR A FAX, AN E-MAIL, OR A PRINT AD

Protect What You've Built
with Fail-Safe Predictability **(PTW)**

You made a major investment in your career. And to protect what you've built, you need to establish fail-safe predictability to make sure that important decisions are quantified and beyond question. **(PTW)**

With all that you've accomplished, this isn't the time for conflicts and controversy. You want proven, industry-standard products and services with proven reliability.

That happens when proven designs are collected from real-world applications within a large install base.

So you'll wind up with a stabilized work environment where there are no surprises and controllable progress.

And whatever you buy should have a stable price that isn't subject to wide swings.

We like to think [your product/service] and [your organization] can be all that for you. But you should be free to make that decision for yourself.

[Insert your Direct Value Statement and Purpose Statement.]

[Add appropriate warm or hot P.S.]

Type 8. CEO with a Financial Background

SAMPLE HEADLINE

- Protect What You've Built ... by the Numbers

WORDS TO USE IN YOUR PRIMARY BONDING STATEMENT

- Minimizing risks
- Going one step at a time
- Career
- Spreading the risk
- Protecting what's been built
- Major career investment
- Going straight down the middle
- Maintaining operation by the numbers
- Doing exactly what has to be done
- Insulating yourself
- Having the security of knowing
- Keeping a firm grasp of reality
- Moving risk as far from yourself as possible
- Keeping a big margin between yourself and dangerous risks
- Knowing is always better than guessing

WORDS TO USE TO DESCRIBE YOUR PRODUCT OR SERVICE

- No conflicts
- Free of controversy
- Integration without disrupting anything
- No interruptions

- Nothing offensive about it
- People won't find anything to argue with
- Won't produce any arguments
- Keeps everything controllable
- Stays on an even keel
- Balanced
- Takes the key standards into account
- Risk-free
- Scientifically designed and developed
- Designed with finances and operations in mind
- Based on what business is all about
- Doesn't make you dependent on guesswork
- Keeps people off your back/out of your hair

WORDS TO USE TO DESCRIBE YOUR ORGANIZATION

- Stable
- Doesn't believe in radical change
- Widely accepted
- Undemanding
- Known for not rocking the boat
- Knows how things are supposed to be done
- Moderate
- Restrained
- Nonconfrontational
- Intelligent risk taker
- Sensible
- No-nonsense
- No extravagant claims
- Financially stable
- Gives you a reasonable return on investment

- People who don't get carried away
- Don't destroy their credibility and yours too

WORDS TO USE TO DESCRIBE THE BENEFITS OF YOUR PRODUCT OR SERVICE

- Put the right standards in place
- Make sure the organization doesn't lose its moorings
- Create a solid foundation
- Achieve a consensus

WORDS TO AVOID WITH A CEO WITH A FINANCIAL BACKGROUND

These words may appear not to be negative. However, they are emotionally charged with negativity to this specific prospective customer. So . . . be careful! Don't use them in any communication with this type of prospective customer!

- Educated guess
- Confront
- Bold people
- Revolutionary
- Flexible standards
- Play to win
- Spend a lot of time with other people
- Ambition
- Stand out from the crowd
- Terrific return on investment
- Dramatic
- Accountability
- Stand up and be counted
- Pioneering
- Substantial change

ENVELOPE TEASER COPY OR DIGITAL SUBJECT LINE COPY

■ Inside—"Protect What You've Built ... by the Numbers"

SAMPLE PRE-APPROACH COMMUNICATION: CEO WITH A FINANCIAL BACKGROUND

Protect What You've Built ... by the Numbers **(PTW)**

Dear (Name),

(Primary Bonding Statement) You made a major investment in your career. And to protect what you've built, you need the security of knowing that everything is operating by the numbers . . . because knowing is better than guessing. **(PTW)**

(Describing Your Product or Service) With all that you've accomplished, this isn't the time for conflicts and controversy. You want risk-free products and services that take the key standards into account and don't make you dependent on guesswork.

(Describing Your Organization) And if they don't get carried away with themselves, suppliers will be able to give you a reasonable return on investment.

(Describing Your Benefits) The bottom line is that the organization won't lose its moorings because you'll have a solid foundation in place.

I believe you'll see that [your product/service] and [your organization] can be all that for you. But, you should be free to make the decision for yourself.

[Insert your Direct Value Statement and Purpose Statement.]

[Add appropriate warm or hot P.S.]

FOR A FAX, AN E-MAIL, OR A PRINT AD

Protect What You've Built ... by the Numbers **(PTW)**

You made a major investment in your career. And to protect what you've built, you need the security of knowing that everything is operating by the numbers ... because knowing is better than guessing. **(PTW)**

With all that you've accomplished, this isn't the time for conflicts and controversy. You want risk-free products and services that take the key standards into account and don't make you dependent on guesswork.

And if they don't get carried away with themselves, suppliers will be able to give you a reasonable return on investment.

The bottom line is that the organization won't lose its moorings because you'll have a solid foundation in place.

And the only price you should have to pay is prudent and thorough thought.

We like to think [your product/service] and [your organization] can be all that for you. But you should be free to make that decision for yourself.

[Insert your Direct Value Statement and Purpose Statement.]

[Add appropriate warm or hot P.S.]

Type 9. CEO with a General Non-Entrepreneurial Background

SAMPLE HEADLINE

- Protect What You've Built

WORDS TO USE IN YOUR PRIMARY BONDING STATEMENT

- Minimizing risks
- Going one step at a time
- Career
- Spreading the risk
- Protecting what's been built
- Major career investment
- Going straight down the middle

WORDS TO USE TO DESCRIBE YOUR PRODUCT OR SERVICE

- No conflicts
- Free of controversy
- Integration without disrupting anything
- No interruptions
- Nothing offensive about it
- People won't find anything to argue with
- Won't produce any arguments
- Keeps everything controllable
- Stays on an even keel

WORDS TO USE TO DESCRIBE YOUR ORGANIZATION

- Stable
- Doesn't believe in radical change

- Widely accepted
- Doesn't make demands on you
- Known for not rocking the boat
- Knows how things are supposed to be done
- Moderate
- Restrained
- Nonconfrontational
- Respectable
- Not daring

WORDS TO USE TO DESCRIBE THE BENEFITS OF YOUR PRODUCT OR SERVICE

- Get everyone on board
- Get everyone's agreement
- Look good
- Create the right image, inside and outside the organization
- Put all the possible objections to rest
- Resolve everyone's concerns
- Achieve a consensus

WORDS TO AVOID WITH A CEO WITH A GENERAL NON-ENTREPRENEURIAL BACKGROUND

These words may appear not to be negative. However, they are emotionally charged with negativity to this specific prospective customer. So . . . be careful! Don't use them in any communication with this type of prospective customer!

- Daring
- Confront
- Take someone on

- Revolutionary
- New
- Play to win
- Do an end run
- Ambition
- Stand out from the crowd
- Goal-orientation
- Competitiveness
- Accountability
- Stand up and be counted
- Override objections
- Substantial change

ENVELOPE TEASER COPY OR DIGITAL SUBJECT LINE COPY

- Inside—"Protect What You've Built"

SAMPLE PRE-APPROACH COMMUNICATION: CEO WITH A GENERAL NON-ENTREPRENEURIAL BACKGROUND

Protect What You've Built **(PTW)**

Dear (Name),

(Primary Bonding Statement) You made a major investment in your career. And to protect what you've built, you have to minimize your risks and go straight down the middle. **(PTW)**

(Describing Your Product or Service) With all that you've accomplished, this isn't the time for conflicts and controversy. You want products and services that won't produce any arguments and will help you keep everything on an even keel.

(Describing Your Organization) And if they know how things are supposed to be done, a supplier will be restrained enough to not rock the boat and will give you that kind of product or service.

(Describing Your Benefits) Then, you can get everyone on board by putting all the possible objections to rest and resolving everyone's concerns.

I believe you'll see [your product/service] and [your organization] can be all that for you. But you should be free to make that decision for yourself.

[Insert your Direct Value Statement and Purpose Statement.]

[Add appropriate warm or hot P.S.]

FOR A FAX, AN E-MAIL, OR A PRINT AD

Protect What You've Built **(PTW)**

You made a major investment in your career. And to protect what you've built, you have to minimize your risks and go straight down the middle. **(PTW)**

With all that you've accomplished, this isn't the time for conflicts and controversy. You want products and services that won't produce any arguments and will help you keep everything on an even keel.

And if they know how things are supposed to be done, a supplier will be restrained enough to not rock the boat and will give you that kind of product or service.

Then, you can get everyone on board by putting all the possible objections to rest and resolving everyone's concerns.

And the only price you should have to pay is prudent and thorough thought.

We like to think [your product/service] and [your organization] itself can be all that for you. But, you should be free to make that decision for yourself.

[Insert your Direct Value Statement and Purpose Statement.]

[Add appropriate warm or hot P.S.]

Type 10. Chief Financial Officer

SAMPLE HEADLINE

- Reality, Not Guesswork

WORDS TO USE IN YOUR PRIMARY BONDING STATEMENT

- Maintaining operation by the numbers
- Doing exactly what has to be done
- Insulating yourself
- Having the security of knowing
- Having a firm grasp of reality
- Moving risk as far from yourself as possible
- Keeping a big margin between yourself and dangerous risks
- Knowing is always better than guessing

WORDS TO USE TO DESCRIBE YOUR PRODUCT OR SERVICE

- Balanced
- Takes the key standards into account
- Risk-free
- Scientifically designed and developed
- Designed with finances and operations in mind
- Based on what a business is all about
- Doesn't make you dependent on guesswork
- Keeps people off your back/out of your hair

WORDS TO USE TO DESCRIBE YOUR ORGANIZATION

- Sensible
- No-nonsense
- No extravagant claims

- Financially stable
- Has a financial impact that is proportionate to the price
- Gives you a reasonable return on investment
- People who do not get carried away
- People who will not destroy their credibility and yours too

WORDS TO USE TO DESCRIBE THE BENEFITS OF YOUR PRODUCT OR SERVICE

- Have everything running like clockwork
- Do not have people knocking on your door
- Keep everything from being turned upside-down
- Be able to keep things on track
- Maintain control over what is really important

WORDS TO AVOID WITH A CHIEF FINANCIAL OFFICER

These words may appear not to be negative. However, they are emotionally charged with negativity to this specific prospective customer. So . . . be careful! Don't use them in any communication with this type of prospective customer!

- Educated guess
- Risk-taker
- Intuition
- Aesthetic
- Keep your door open for people
- Interaction
- Interactive
- Relationship-oriented
- Intimate
- Let people do their thing
- Operating flexibility
- Top-to-bottom revision

- Creative outlook
- Take a chance
- Gut instinct
- Instinctive

ENVELOPE TEASER COPY OR DIGITAL SUBJECT LINE COPY

- Inside—"Reality, Not Guesswork"

SAMPLE PRE-APPROACH COMMUNICATION: CHIEF FINANCIAL OFFICER

Reality, Not Guesswork **(PTW)**

Dear (Name),

(Primary Bonding Statement) The kind of performance you can count on is based on reality … not guesswork. It comes from operating by the numbers with everyone doing exactly what has to be done so that you can move risk as far from yourself as possible. **(PTW)**

(Describing Your Product or Service) That can be virtually ensured when you have products and services that are balanced because they take the key standards into account. In addition, they are designed with both finances and operations in mind.

(Describing Your Organization) And if they do not get carried away with themselves, a supplier will be able to give you a reasonable return on investment.

(Describing Your Benefits) The bottom line is that you will not have people knocking on your door and turning everything upside-down.

I believe you'll see [your product/service] and [your organization] can be all that for you. But you should be free to make that decision for yourself.

[Insert your Direct Value Statement and Purpose Statement.]

[Add appropriate warm or hot P.S.]

FOR A FAX, AN E-MAIL, OR A PRINT AD

Reality, Not Guesswork **(PTW)**

The kind of performance you can count on is based on reality … not guesswork. It comes from operating by the numbers with everyone doing exactly what has to be done so that you can move risk as far from yourself as possible. **(PTW)**

That can be virtually ensured when you have products and services that are balanced because they take the key standards into account. In addition, they are designed with both finances and operations in mind.

And if they do not get carried away with themselves, a supplier will be able to give you a reasonable return on investment.

The bottom line is that you will not have people knocking on your door and turning everything upside-down.

And the only cost you should pay must be an exercise in textbook pricing.

We like to think [your product/service] and [your organization] can be all that for you. But you should be free to make that decision for yourself.

[Insert your Direct Value Statement and Purpose Statement.]

[Add appropriate warm or hot P.S.]

Type 11. Corporate Executive

SAMPLE HEADLINE

- Staying in the Mainstream

WORDS TO USE IN YOUR PRIMARY BONDING STATEMENT

- Teamwork
- Not sticking your neck out
- Staying in the mainstream
- Sensible responsibilities
- Being involved in all the important decisions
- Keeping steadily advancing
- Protecting yourself from unwarranted intrusions
- Keeping everything on a safe course
- Insulating yourself

WORDS TO USE TO DESCRIBE YOUR PRODUCT OR SERVICE

- Supports what you have already accomplished
- Is not a departure from what you are doing
- Right in line with the direction you are taking

WORDS TO USE TO DESCRIBE YOUR ORGANIZATION

- Good team players
- Widely accepted
- Blend in well with everyone
- Committed to a team approach

WORDS TO USE TO DESCRIBE THE BENEFITS OF YOUR PRODUCT OR SERVICE

- Nothing you have to defend or explain
- Nothing you have to apologize for
- Results everyone accepts
- The outcome everyone approves

WORDS TO AVOID WITH A CORPORATE EXECUTIVE

These words may appear not to be negative. However, they are emotionally charged with negativity to this specific prospective customer. So … be careful! Don't use them in any communication with this type of prospective customer!

- Accountability
- Plot an unusual course
- Considerable responsibilities
- Keep your door open to everyone
- Be out in front
- Lead the pack
- A departure
- Shift direction
- Change from the ground up
- Substantial change
- Defend
- Explain
- Surprising results
- Unexpected

ENVELOPE TEASER COPY OR DIGITAL SUBJECT LINE COPY

- Inside—"Staying in the Mainstream"

SAMPLE PRE-APPROACH COMMUNICATION: CORPORATE EXECUTIVE

Staying in the Mainstream **(PTW)**

Dear (Name),

(Primary Bonding Statement) You should be able to stay in the mainstream—with sensible responsibilities—while being involved in all the important decisions as you keep everything on a safe course. **(PTW)**

(Describing Your Product or Service) That requires products and services to support what you've already accomplished because they are right in line with the direction you are taking.

(Describing Your Organization) It also requires good team players who are widely accepted for blending in well with everyone.

(Describing Your Benefits) When you get that, there's nothing you have to defend or apologize for because the results are what everyone expects.

I believe you'll see [your product/service] and [your organization] can be all that for you. But you should be free to make that decision for yourself.

[Insert your Direct Value Statement and Purpose Statement.]

[Add appropriate warm or hot P.S.]

FOR A FAX, AN E-MAIL, OR A PRINT AD

Staying in the Mainstream **(PTW)**

You should be able to stay in the mainstream—with sensible responsibilities—while being involved in all the important decisions as you keep everything on a safe course. **(PTW)**

That requires products and services to support what you have already accomplished because they are right in line with the direction you are taking.

It also requires good team players who are widely accepted for blending in well with everyone.

When you get that, there is nothing you have to defend or apologize for because the results are what everyone expects.

On top of that, they expect a price that is in line with the industry.

We like to think [your product/service] and [your organization] itself can be all that for you. But you should be free to make that decision for yourself.

[Insert your Direct Value Statement and Purpose Statement.]

[Add appropriate warm or hot P.S.]

Type 12. Dentist/Orthodontist

SAMPLE HEADLINE

- The Way You Plan It

WORDS TO USE IN YOUR PRIMARY BONDING STATEMENT

- Solidly prestigious
- Orderly
- Everything happening the way you plan it
- Avoiding gambling
- Keeping clear of unpleasant surprises

WORDS TO USE TO DESCRIBE YOUR PRODUCT OR SERVICE

- Uncomplicated
- Practical
- Doesn't require much/any attention
- Won't distract you from practicing your art
- Not be bothered by people

WORDS TO USE TO DESCRIBE YOUR ORGANIZATION

- Plain talk
- Expertise
- We have simple, straightforward answers
- There's no substitute for honesty
- Nothing hidden

WORDS TO USE TO DESCRIBE THE BENEFITS OF YOUR PRODUCT OR SERVICE

- Protect yourself from situations you don't want

- Keep certain people at a distance
- Protect your professional privacy

WORDS TO AVOID WITH A DENTIST/ORTHODONTIST

These words may appear not to be negative. However, they are emotionally charged with negativity to this specific prospective customer. So ... be careful! Don't use them in any communication with this type of prospective customer!

- Surprise
- Vary from the plan
- Interaction
- Interactive
- Consultant
- Business
- Businesslike
- Business priorities
- System
- Marketing
- New horizons
- Marketing
- Salesmanship

ENVELOPE TEASER COPY OR DIGITAL SUBJECT LINE COPY

- Inside—"The Way You Plan It"

SAMPLE PRE-APPROACH COMMUNICATION: DENTIST/ORTHODONTIST

The Way You Plan It **(PTW)**

Dear (Name),

(Primary Bonding Statement) Everything should happen the way you plan it, without any unpleasant surprises. **(PTW)**

(Describing Your Product or Service) And you'll never be surprised by an uncomplicated, practical product or service that won't distract you from the practice of your art.

(Describing Your Organization) To go along with that product or service, you should have suppliers who give you simple, straightforward answers along with plain talk and the benefit of their expertise.

(Describing Your Benefits) There's no better way to protect your professional privacy.

I believe you'll see [your product/service] and [your organization] can be all that for you. But you should be free to make that decision for yourself.

[Insert your Direct Value Statement and Purpose Statement.]

[Add appropriate warm or hot P.S.]

FOR A FAX, AN E-MAIL, OR A PRINT AD

The Way You Plan It **(PTW)**

Everything should happen the way you plan it, without any unpleasant surprises. **(PTW)**

And you'll never be surprised by an uncomplicated, practical product or service that won't distract you from the practice of your art.

To go along with that product or service, you should have suppliers who use plain talk to give you simple, straightforward answers and the benefit of their expertise.

There's no better way to protect your professional privacy.

And there's no better price than the one that's directly related to value.

We like to think [your product/service] and [your organization] can be all that for you. But you should be free to make that decision for yourself.

[Insert your Direct Value Statement and Purpose Statement.]

[Add appropriate warm or hot P.S.]

Type 13. Entrepreneur with an Engineering Background

SAMPLE HEADLINE

- Be Your Own Person ... in a Fail-Safe Business

WORDS TO USE IN YOUR PRIMARY BONDING STATEMENT

- Being in charge
- Calling your own shots
- Personal independence
- Being your own person
- Make the business run your way
- Doing whatever you want to do, whenever you want to do it
- Having complete control over your business
- Making the business run predictably
- Establishing fail-safe predictability
- Being able to quantify everything
- Making sure that important decisions are quantified
- Quantification
- Self-evident/Obvious
- Beyond question

WORDS TO USE TO DESCRIBE YOUR PRODUCT OR SERVICE

- Minimizes/Eliminates the "human factor"
- Protects you from the "human factor"
- Reliable
- Industry standard

- Proven
- Tested
- Proven reliability
- Tested reliability

WORDS TO USE TO DESCRIBE YOUR ORGANIZATION

- Proven designs are collected
- Proven designs are used
- Quantified designs
- Designs from real-world applications
- Large install base
- Applications like/similar to/identical to yours
- Not dependent on the "human factor"

WORDS TO USE TO DESCRIBE THE BENEFITS OF YOUR PRODUCT OR SERVICE

- Order (in their business)
- Control
- Be in control automatically
- Order that reflects your personal wishes
- No more chaos
- Never tolerate disorder again

WORDS TO AVOID WITH AN ENTREPRENEUR WITH AN ENGINEERING BACKGROUND

These words may appear not to be negative. However, they are emotionally charged with negativity to this specific prospective customer. So … be careful! Don't use them in any communication with this type of prospective customer!

- State of the art
- Intuition

- Feelings
- Perception
- Cutting edge
- Pushing the edge of the envelope
- Innovative
- Experimental
- Bold
- Daring
- People
- Human ingenuity

ENVELOPE TEASER COPY OR DIGITAL SUBJECT LINE COPY

- Inside—"Being Your Own Person ... in a Fail-Safe Business"

SAMPLE PRE-APPROACH COMMUNICATION: ENTREPRENEUR WITH AN ENGINEERING BACKGROUND

Be Your Own Person ... in a Fail-Safe Business **(PTW)**

Dear (Name),

(Primary Bonding Statement) There's nothing like being your own person ... doing whatever you want to do, whenever you want to do it in a business that gives you fail-safe predictability. **(PTW)**

(Describing Your Product or Service) And you can only get there with an industry-standard product or service that's both reliable and proven.

(Describing Your Organization) But even the best product or service won't do you much good unless it has a proven design that's been quantified in a real-world application.

(Describing Your Benefits) Then, you'll have order that reflects your personal wishes.

I believe you'll see [your product/service] and [your organization] can be all that for you. But you should be free to make that decision for yourself.

[Insert your Direct Value Statement and Purpose Statement.]

[Add appropriate warm or hot P.S.]

FOR A FAX, AN E-MAIL, OR A PRINT AD

Being Your Own Person … in a Fail-Safe Business **(PTW)**

There's nothing like being your own person … doing whatever you want to do, whenever you want to do it in a business that gives you fail-safe predictability.

You can get there with an industry-standard product or service that's both reliable and proven.

But even the best product or service won't do you much good unless it has a proven design that's been quantified in a real-world application. Then, you'll have order that reflects your personal wishes.

And whatever you buy should have a stable price that isn't subject to wide swings.

We like to think that [your product/service] and [your organization] can be all that for you. But you should be free to make that decision for yourself.

[Insert your Direct Value Statement and Purpose Statement.]

[Add appropriate warm or hot P.S.]

Type 14. Entrepreneur with an Operations Background

SAMPLE HEADLINE

■ Be Your Own Person … in a Business That Hums Along

WORDS TO USE IN YOUR PRIMARY BONDING STATEMENT

■ Being in charge
■ Calling your own shots
■ Personal independence
■ Being your own person
■ Making the business run your way
■ Doing whatever you want to do, whenever you want to do it
■ Having complete control over your business
■ Concrete
■ A clear-cut environment
■ Keeping the business humming along
■ Tangible
■ Real/Real-world
■ Having everything in its place
■ Getting things organized
■ Order/Orderly
■ Keeping everything buttoned down

WORDS TO USE TO DESCRIBE YOUR PRODUCT OR SERVICE

■ Designed specifically for your unique situation (e.g., "for small businesses" or "for industrial distribution")

- Practical
- Street-smart
- Nothing theoretical or abstract about it
- Won't put any demands on your time
- Won't strain your resources

WORDS TO USE TO DESCRIBE YOUR ORGANIZATION

- Regular people
- Down-to-earth
- Just like you
- Think the way you do
- Your ideas and opinions matter
- Straightforward
- Nothing slick

WORDS TO USE TO DESCRIBE THE BENEFITS OF YOUR PRODUCT OR SERVICE

- Keep it running
- Maintain the performance you want
- Keep getting the results you want
- Get your hands around what you want and hold onto it
- Consistent results
- Consistency

WORDS TO AVOID WITH AN ENTREPRENEUR WITH AN OPERATIONS BACKGROUND

These words may appear not to be negative. However, they are emotionally charged with negativity to this specific prospective customer. So ... be careful! Don't use them in any communication with this type of prospective customer!

- Sophisticated
- Theoretical
- Abstract
- Standardized
- Uniform
- The same for everyone
- Structured
- Growth
- Profitability
- Keep things flexible
- Experimental
- Elite
- Complex
- Clever
- Stop and reorganize

ENVELOPE TEASER COPY OR DIGITAL SUBJECT LINE COPY

- Inside—"Being Your Own Person … in a Business That Hums Along"

SAMPLE PRE-APPROACH COMMUNICATION: ENTREPRENEUR WITH AN OPERATIONS BACKGROUND

Be Your Own Person ... in a Business That Hums Along **(PTW)**

Dear (Name),

(Primary Bonding Statement) There's nothing like being your own person . . . doing whatever you want to do, whenever you want to do it in a business that hums along with everything in place. **(PTW)**

(Describing Your Product or Service) To help you get there, a product or service has to be specific to your unique situation. It also should be practical and very street-smart.

(Describing Your Organization) But even the best product or service won't do you much good unless it comes from down-to-earth, straightforward people who think the way you do.

(Describing Your Benefits) Then, you'll be able to get your hands around what you want and hold onto it.

I believe you'll see [your product/service] and [your organization] can be all that for you. But you should be free to make that decision for yourself.

[Insert your Direct Value Statement and Purpose Statement.]

[Add appropriate warm or hot P.S.]

FOR A FAX, AN E-MAIL, OR A PRINT AD

Being Your Own Person ... in a Business
That Hums Along **(PTW)**

There's nothing like being your own person ... doing whatever you want to do, whenever you want to do it in a business that hums along with everything in place. **(PTW)**

To help you get there, a product or service has to be specific to your unique situation. It also should be practical and very street-smart.

But even the best product or service won't do you much good unless it has a proven design that's been quantified in a real-world application. Then, you'll be able to get your hands around what you want and hold onto it.

And whatever you buy should have a stable price that isn't subject to wide swings.

We like to think that [your product/service] and [your organization] can be all that for you. But you should be free to make that decision for yourself.

[Insert your Direct Value Statement and Purpose Statement.]

[Add appropriate warm or hot P.S.]

Type 15. Facilities Manager

SAMPLE HEADLINE

- Hands-on Performance

WORDS TO USE IN YOUR PRIMARY BONDING STATEMENT

- Concrete results
- Clear-cut tasks
- Tangible
- Real
- Real-world
- Hands-on
- Perform/Performance

WORDS TO USE TO DESCRIBE YOUR PRODUCT OR SERVICE

- Built-in simplicity
- Simple to figure out
- Not rocket science
- Easy for people to use

WORDS TO USE TO DESCRIBE YOUR ORGANIZATION

- Regular people
- Down-to-earth
- Just like you
- Think the way you do
- Your ideas and opinions matter
- Straightforward
- Nothing slick

WORDS TO USE TO DESCRIBE THE BENEFITS OF YOUR PRODUCT OR SERVICE

- Keep it running
- Maintain the performance you want
- Keep getting the results you want
- Get your hands around what you want and hold onto it
- Consistent results

WORDS TO AVOID WITH A FACILITIES MANAGER

These words may appear not to be negative. However, they are emotionally charged with negativity to this specific prospective customer. So ... be careful! Don't use them in any communication with this type of prospective customer!

- Sophisticated
- Elite
- Complex
- Theoretical
- Theorize
- Abstract
- Hypothetical
- Imagine
- Speculate
- Speculation
- Formal
- Technological

ENVELOPE TEASER COPY OR DIGITAL SUBJECT LINE COPY

- Inside—"Hands-on Performance"

SAMPLE PRE-APPROACH COMMUNICATION: FACILITIES MANAGER

Hands-on Performance **(PTW)**

Dear (Name),

(Primary Bonding Statement) The real world demands clear-cut, tangible results that can only come from hands-on performance. **(PTW)**

(Describing Your Product or Service) That's only possible when you have products and services with built-in simplicity—the ones that are easy to figure out and easy for people to use.

(Describing Your Organization) Along with that, you should be able to work with regular, down-to-earth people who think the way you do—you need a straightforward supplier.

(Describing Your Benefits) They'll help you maintain the performance you want and the consistent results you can get your hands around.

I believe you'll see [your product/service] and [your organization] can be all that for you. But you should be free to make that decision for yourself.

[Insert your Direct Value Statement and Purpose Statement.]

[Add appropriate warm or hot P.S.]

FOR A FAX, AN E-MAIL, OR A PRINT AD

Hands-on Performance **(PTW)**

The real world demands clear-cut, tangible results that can only come from hands-on performance. **(PTW)**

That's only possible when you have products and services

with built-in simplicity—the ones that are easy to figure out and easy for people to use.

Along with that, you should be able to work with regular, down-to-earth people who think the way you do—you need a straightforward supplier.

They'll help you maintain the performance you want and the consistent results you can get your hands around.

And they'll give you a stable price as well.

We like to think [your product/service] and [your organization] can be all that for you. But you should be free to make that decision for yourself.

[Insert your Direct Value Statement and Purpose Statement.]

[Add appropriate warm or hot P.S.]

Type 16. Franchisee

SAMPLE HEADLINE

- Be in Charge

WORDS TO USE IN YOUR PRIMARY BONDING STATEMENT

- Turnkey
- Owning your own turnkey business
- Being in charge
- Personal independence
- Being your own person

WORDS TO USE TO DESCRIBE YOUR PRODUCT OR SERVICE

- Proven
- Debugged
- Accepted/Popular
- Respected
- Runs/Operates the same way every day
- Safe
- Dependable

WORDS TO USE TO DESCRIBE YOUR ORGANIZATION

- Steady
- Reliable
- Excellent marketing capability
- Always available to you

WORDS TO USE TO DESCRIBE THE BENEFITS OF YOUR PRODUCT OR SERVICE

- Decisions that are obvious
- Take the risk out of decision making

WORDS TO AVOID WITH A FRANCHISEE

These words may appear not to be negative. However, they are emotionally charged with negativity to this specific prospective customer. So … be careful! Don't use them in any communication with this type of prospective customer!

- Experimental
- Currently being tested
- Make far-reaching decisions
- Flexible values and priorities
- Implement your own ideas
- Challenge
- Substantially debugged
- Changing routines and procedures
- Stretch your capabilities
- Risk-taker
- Use your marketing capability
- Don't depend on anyone but yourself
- Rewards that are worth the risk

ENVELOPE TEASER COPY OR DIGITAL SUBJECT LINE COPY

- Inside—"Be in Charge"

SAMPLE PRE-APPROACH COMMUNICATION: FRANCHISEE

Be in Charge **(PTW)**

Dear (Name),

(Primary Bonding Statement) Personal independence comes from owning a turnkey business that lets you be in charge and be your own person. **(PTW)**

(Describing Your Product or Service) A business like that uses proven, debugged products and services that are respected because they run the same way every day. They're safe and dependable.

(Describing Your Organization) You can get dependable products and services from steady companies with excellent marketing capability, companies that are always available to you.

(Describing Your Benefits) There's no better way to take the risk out of decision making.

I believe you'll see [your product/service] and [your organization] can be all that for you. But you should be free to make that decision for yourself.

[Insert your Direct Value Statement and Purpose Statement.]

[Add appropriate warm or hot P.S.]

FOR A FAX, AN E-MAIL, OR A PRINT AD

Be in Charge **(PTW)**

Personal independence comes from owning a turnkey business that lets you be in charge and be your own person. **(PTW)**

A business like that uses proven, debugged products and services that are respected because they run the same way every day. They're safe and dependable.

You can get dependable products and services from steady companies with excellent marketing capability, companies that are always available to you.

There's no better way to take the risk out of decision making.

And there's no better price than the one that's prudent and sensible.

We like to think [your product/service] and [your organization] itself can be all that for you. But you should be free to make that decision for yourself.

[Insert your Direct Value Statement and Purpose Statement.]

[Add appropriate warm or hot P.S.]

Type 17. Hospital Administrator

SAMPLE HEADLINE

- Getting Impressive Results

WORDS TO USE IN YOUR PRIMARY BONDING STATEMENT

- Hospitals that run the best are the ones where the administrator is in control
- Stay in control
- Getting results that impress the people who are watching
- The world pays attention to people who get results
- Taking control and staying in control
- Putting control and authority where they belong
- Moving in the direction you want to go
- Climbing the next step up the ladder

WORDS TO USE TO DESCRIBE YOUR PRODUCT OR SERVICE

- A reasonable life cost
- Flexible
- Adaptable to all kinds of challenges
- Responsive to change

WORDS TO USE TO DESCRIBE YOUR ORGANIZATION

- Marketing-oriented
- Sensitive to business requirements
- Understands what the priorities are

WORDS TO USE TO DESCRIBE THE BENEFITS OF YOUR PRODUCT OR SERVICE

- Success on a large scale
- Significant success
- Impress the right people
- Being in the forefront with the people who matter

WORDS TO AVOID WITH A HOSPITAL ADMINISTRATOR

These words may appear not to be negative. However, they are emotionally charged with negativity to this specific prospective customer. So … be careful! Don't use them in any communication with this type of prospective customer!

- Small
- On a small scale
- Physician-oriented
- Medicine
- A reasonable return on investment
- Work well with everyone
- Share decision making
- Doesn't need proof
- Quiet success
- Accommodating
- Compromise
- Flexible priorities

ENVELOPE TEASER COPY OR DIGITAL SUBJECT LINE COPY

- Inside—"Getting Impressive Results"

SAMPLE PRE-APPROACH COMMUNICATION: HOSPITAL ADMINISTRATOR

Getting Impressive Results **(PTW)**

Dear (Name),

(Primary Bonding Statement) The hospitals that run the best are the ones where the administrator is in control and stays in control. They get results that impress the people who are watching. **(PTW)**

(Describing Your Product or Service) From your standpoint, therefore, no product or service serves you and the hospital better than the ones that are flexible and adaptable to all kinds of challenges.

(Describing Your Organization) The suppliers who serve you best are marketing-oriented because they understand what the priorities are.

(Describing Your Benefits) They'll help you achieve success on a large scale.

I believe you'll see [your product/service] and [your organization] can be all that for you. But you should be free to make that decision for yourself.

[Insert your Direct Value Statement and Purpose Statement.]

[Add appropriate warm or hot P.S.]

FOR A FAX, AN E-MAIL, OR A PRINT AD

Getting Impressive Results **(PTW)**

The hospitals that run the best are the ones where the administrator is in control and stays in control. They get results that impress the people who are watching. **(PTW)**

From your standpoint, therefore, no product or service serves you and the hospital better than the ones that are flexible and adaptable to all kinds of challenges.

The suppliers who serve you best are marketing-oriented because they understand what the priorities are.

They'll help you achieve success on a large scale and their price will make a high return on investment possible.

We like to think [your product/service] and [your organization] can be all that for you. But you should be free to make that decision for yourself.

[Insert your Direct Value Statement and Purpose Statement.]

[Add appropriate warm or hot P.S.]

Type 18. Human Resources/Training Executive

SAMPLE HEADLINE

- The Respect and Recognition You Deserve

WORDS TO USE IN YOUR PRIMARY BONDING STATEMENT

- Getting recognition
- Being respected for what you do
- Getting credit (you probably do a lot more than you get credit for)
- Gaining respect
- Continuing to do important work
- Making a big contribution
- Remaining essential to your organization's success

WORDS TO USE TO DESCRIBE YOUR PRODUCT OR SERVICE

- Fits right in with what you're doing
- Builds on what you've already accomplished
- Adds to what you already have
- Doesn't negate anything you've done
- New
- Unique
- Designed to be easily controlled
- Gives you control over the outcome
- Easy to adapt to your purposes

WORDS TO USE TO DESCRIBE YOUR ORGANIZATION

- People
- Dependable

- Relationship-oriented
- Loyal
- Your external support staff
- Interactive

WORDS TO USE TO DESCRIBE THE BENEFITS OF YOUR PRODUCT OR SERVICE

- Gain more influence
- Get your point across more persuasively
- Be taken at your word
- Get people to start listening
- Be accepted for who you are and what you do

WORDS TO AVOID WITH A HUMAN RESOURCES/TRAINING EXECUTIVE

These words may appear not to be negative. However, they are emotionally charged with negativity to this specific prospective customer. So ... be careful! Don't use them in any communication with this type of prospective customer!

- Technological
- Staff person
- Rebuild from the ground up
- Ready to clean things up
- Been around for a long time
- Organization
- Hierarchy
- Structure
- Traditional
- Leave you alone
- Surprise

- An independent supplier
- Replace
- Substitute

ENVELOPE TEASER COPY OR DIGITAL SUBJECT LINE COPY

- Inside—"The Respect and Recognition You Deserve"

SAMPLE PRE-APPROACH COMMUNICATION: HUMAN RESOURCES/TRAINING EXECUTIVE

The Respect and Recognition You Deserve **(PTW)**

Dear (Name),

(Primary Bonding Statement) It's not easy getting the respect and recognition you deserve—even though you're doing very important work and making a big contribution. **(PTW)**

(Describing Your Product or Service) So you need to build on what you've already accomplished with unique products and services that fit right in with what you're doing and let you adapt them to your purposes.

(Describing Your Organization) Only relationship-oriented people can appreciate the importance of that and, as a result, they're willing to be your external support staff—dependable and loyal.

(Describing Your Benefits) That's when you'll have your best chance to gain more influence and get your point across more persuasively. People will start listening and you'll be accepted for who you are and what you do.

I believe you'll see [your product/service] and [your organization] can be all that for you. But you should be free to make that decision for yourself.

[Insert your Direct Value Statement and Purpose Statement.]

[Add appropriate warm or hot P.S.]

FOR A FAX, AN E-MAIL, OR A PRINT AD

The Respect and Recognition You Deserve **(PTW)**

It's not easy getting the respect and recognition you deserve—even though you're doing very important work and making a big contribution. **(PTW)**

So, you need to build on what you've already accomplished with unique products and services that fit right in with what you're doing and let you adapt them to your purposes.

Only relationship-oriented people can appreciate the importance of that and, as a result, they're willing to be your external support staff—dependable and loyal.

That's when you'll have your best chance to gain more influence and get your point across more persuasively. People will start listening and you'll be accepted for who you are and what you do.

Obviously, the price for all that can be easily justified by the benefits.

We like to think [your product/service] and [your organization] can be all that for you. But you should be free to make that decision for yourself.

[Insert your Direct Value Statement and Purpose Statement.]

[Add appropriate warm or hot P.S.]

Type 19. Medical/Dental Office Manager

SAMPLE HEADLINE

■ They All Depend on You

WORDS TO USE IN YOUR PRIMARY BONDING STATEMENT

■ Staying on top of everything in the practice
■ Keeping everything on track, no matter what comes at you
■ Everyone depending on you
■ Making sure everyone gets what they need
■ Remaining a valuable member
■ Everything revolving around you

WORDS TO USE TO DESCRIBE YOUR PRODUCT OR SERVICE

■ For the person who's in the middle of everything
■ Won't have to spend hours studying it before you can understand how to use it
■ Based on common sense

WORDS TO USE TO DESCRIBE YOUR ORGANIZATION

■ Never puts you under the gun
■ Understands what you're going through
■ Pays attention to what you have to say

WORDS TO USE TO DESCRIBE THE BENEFITS OF YOUR PRODUCT OR SERVICE

■ You've earned the right
■ Have people pay attention to you

- Listen to what you have to say
- You've paid your dues

WORDS TO AVOID WITH A MEDICAL/DENTAL OFFICE MANAGER

These words may appear not to be negative. However, they are emotionally charged with negativity to this specific prospective customer. So … be careful! Don't use them in any communication with this type of prospective customer!

- Stand-alone
- Stand by yourself
- Independent
- Independent action
- Go your own way
- Requires study
- Highly technical
- Data-dependent
- Rational evaluation
- Analysis
- Scheme
- Investment
- Investment opportunity

ENVELOPE TEASER COPY OR DIGITAL SUBJECT LINE COPY

- Inside—"They All Depend on You"

SAMPLE PRE-APPROACH COMMUNICATION: MEDICAL/DENTAL OFFICE MANAGER

They All Depend on You **(PTW)**

Dear (Name),

(Primary Bonding Statement) You stay on top of everything in the practice—keeping everything on track no matter what comes at you and making sure everyone gets what they need. That's why they all depend on you. **(PTW)**

(Describing Your Product or Service) So you should have products and services that are designed for the person who's in the middle of everything—the products that are based on common sense.

(Describing Your Organization) Those products and services come from people who never put you under the gun because they understand what you go through and pay attention to what you have to say.

(Describing Your Benefits) And you've earned the right to have that—you've paid your dues.

I believe you'll see [your product/service] and [your organization] can be all that for you. But you should be free to make that decision for yourself.

[Insert your Direct Value Statement and Purpose Statement.]

[Add appropriate warm or hot P.S.]

FOR A FAX, AN E-MAIL, OR A PRINT AD

They All Depend on You **(PTW)**

You stay on top of everything in the practice—keeping everything on track no matter what comes at you and making sure everyone gets what they need. That's why they all depend on you.

You should have products and services that are designed for the person who's in the middle of everything—the products that are based on common sense.

Those products and services come from people who never put you under the gun because they understand what you go through and pay attention to what you have to say.

And you've earned the right to have that—you've paid your dues.

Plus, it should be easy to get the approval to buy them.

We like to think [your product/service] and [your organization] can be all that for you. But you should be free to make that decision for yourself.

[Insert your Direct Value Statement and Purpose Statement.]

[Add appropriate warm or hot P.S.]

Type 20. Oncologist

SAMPLE HEADLINE

■ Out in Front

WORDS TO USE IN YOUR PRIMARY BONDING STATEMENT

■ Discovering the extraordinary
■ Constantly breaking new ground
■ Being right
■ Not idly exploring
■ Looking for answers
■ Having major impact
■ Being out in front
■ Breaking through traditional patterns
■ Never hanging back in the rear
■ Being a leader, not a follower
■ Remaining a part of the greatest battle the human race has ever fought

WORDS TO USE TO DESCRIBE YOUR PRODUCT OR SERVICE

■ Beyond question or doubt
■ Current, up-to-date
■ Not over the edge
■ Unimpeachable data
■ Not state of the art
■ Accepted protocols

WORDS TO USE TO DESCRIBE YOUR ORGANIZATION

- Stand behind product/service
- Constantly acquires more and more information
- Share information with customers
- Understand how you want the relationship to work
- Intellectually curious
- Doesn't challenge its customers

WORDS TO USE TO DESCRIBE THE BENEFITS OF YOUR PRODUCT OR SERVICE

- Stay on the cutting edge
- Out in front
- In the lead

WORDS TO AVOID WITH AN ONCOLOGIST

These words may appear not to be negative. However, they are emotionally charged with negativity to this specific prospective customer. So ... be careful! Don't use them in any communication with this type of prospective customer!

- Play it safe
- Low-risk
- Low-pressure
- Take the pressure off
- State of the art
- Be a team member
- Teamwork
- Cut people some slack
- Conjecture
- Theory
- Hypothesis
- Flexible standards

ENVELOPE TEASER COPY OR DIGITAL SUBJECT LINE COPY

- Inside—"Out in Front"

SAMPLE PRE-APPROACH COMMUNICATION: ONCOLOGIST

Out in Front **(PTW)**

Dear (Name),

(Primary Bonding Statement) You have to be right because you're constantly breaking new ground—you're out in front rather than back in the rear. **(PTW)**

(Describing Your Product or Service) That's why it's so important for you to have an up-to-date product or service based on accepted protocols and with validity that is beyond question or doubt.

(Describing Your Organization) Behind that product or service should be standing a well-informed supplier who understands how you want the relationship to work.

(Describing Your Benefits) After all, you have to stay out in front, on the cutting edge.

I believe you'll see [your product/service] and [your organization] can be all that for you. But you should be free to make that decision for yourself.

[Insert your Direct Value Statement and Purpose Statement.]

[Add appropriate warm or hot P.S.]

FOR A FAX, AN E-MAIL, OR A PRINT AD

Out in Front **(PTW)**

You have to be right because you're constantly breaking new ground—you're out in front rather than back in the rear. **(PTW)**

That's why it's so important for you to have an up-to-date product or service based on accepted protocols and with validity that is beyond question or doubt.

Behind that product or service should be standing a well-informed supplier who understands how you want the relationship to work.

After all, you have to stay out in front, on the cutting edge.

And the price for a product or service that helps you stay at the cutting edge should be one that's easily justified.

We like to think [your product/service] and [your organization] can be all that for you. But you should be free to make that decision for yourself.

[Insert your Direct Value Statement and Purpose Statement.]

[Add appropriate warm or hot P.S.]

Type 21. Pathologist

SAMPLE HEADLINE

- As Important as Anyone

WORDS TO USE IN YOUR PRIMARY BONDING STATEMENT

- Being recognized as being just as important in the hospital as everyone else
- Supplying services the hospital couldn't get along without
- Not taking a back seat to anyone
- Professionals depending on you
- Being accepted

WORDS TO USE TO DESCRIBE YOUR PRODUCT OR SERVICE

- Fast
- Avoids costly mistakes
- Precise/Precision
- Easy to use
- Helps take the pressure off

WORDS TO USE TO DESCRIBE YOUR ORGANIZATION

- Careful about everything it does
- Never rushes
- Meticulous
- Patience/Patient

WORDS TO USE TO DESCRIBE THE BENEFITS OF YOUR PRODUCT OR SERVICE

- Predictable
- Free from interference

- Reproducible results
- Stress-free
- Keep you protected from people you don't want to deal with

WORDS TO AVOID WITH A PATHOLOGIST

These words may appear not to be negative. However, they are emotionally charged with negativity to this specific prospective customer. So … be careful! Don't use them in any communication with this type of prospective customer!

- Pecking order
- In a hurry
- Rank/Ranking
- Eager to get on with it
- Variance
- Defend
- Communicate
- Interact
- Interactive
- Persuasive
- Persuade
- Exert influence over others

ENVELOPE TEASER COPY OR DIGITAL SUBJECT LINE COPY

- Inside—"As Important as Anyone"

SAMPLE PRE-APPROACH COMMUNICATION: PATHOLOGIST

As Important as Anyone **(PTW)**

Dear (Name),

(Primary Bonding Statement) You're as important in the hospital as everyone else. In fact, the hospital couldn't get along without your services. So you don't have to take a back seat to anyone. **(PTW)**

(Describing Your Product or Service) That means you deserve precise products and services that are easy to use and help take the pressure off.

(Describing Your Organization) You also deserve suppliers who are careful about everything they do—who are patient and meticulous in their work.

(Describing Your Benefits) Then, you'll have reproducible results in a stress-free environment that keeps you protected from people you don't want to deal with.

I believe you'll see [your product/service] and [your organization] can be all that for you. But you should be free to make that decision for yourself.

[Insert your Direct Value Statement and Purpose Statement.]

[Add appropriate warm or hot P.S.]

FOR A FAX, AN E-MAIL, OR A PRINT AD

As Important as Anyone **(PTW)**

You're as important in the hospital as everyone else. In fact, the hospital couldn't get along without your services. So you don't have to take a back seat to anyone. **(PTW)**

That means you deserve precise products and services that are easy to use and help take the pressure off.

You also deserve suppliers who are careful about everything they do—who are patient and meticulous in their work.

Then, you'll have reproducible results in a stress-free environment that keeps you protected from people you don't want to deal with.

Plus, you'll have the benefit of a price that justifies itself.

We like to think [your product/service] and [your organization] can be all that for you. But you should be free to make that decision for yourself.

[Insert your Direct Value Statement and Purpose Statement.]

[Add appropriate warm or hot P.S.]

Type 22. Primary Care Physician

SAMPLE HEADLINE

- To Practice Your Art

WORDS TO USE IN YOUR PRIMARY BONDING STATEMENT

- Maintaining independence
- Using professional discretion
- Being free from bureaucratic regulation
- Practicing medicine instead of pushing paper
- Never being treated like a vendor again
- Practicing your art without outside interference
- Fulfilling the reason you went to medical school
- You didn't go to medical school to become an office manager

WORDS TO USE TO DESCRIBE YOUR PRODUCT OR SERVICE

- Easy to use
- Doesn't require extraordinary (or any) attention
- Won't take you away from the practice of medicine
- Doesn't get in your way

WORDS TO USE TO DESCRIBE YOUR ORGANIZATION

- Plain talk
- Expertise
- Simple, straightforward answers
- There's no substitute for honesty
- Nothing hidden

WORDS TO USE TO DESCRIBE THE BENEFITS OF YOUR PRODUCT OR SERVICE

- Less outside interference
- More empathy for your situation
- Not bothered or distracted
- Able to practice medicine the way you want to

WORDS TO AVOID WITH A PRIMARY CARE PHYSICIAN

These words may appear not to be negative. However, they are emotionally charged with negativity to this specific prospective customer. So … be careful! Don't use them in any communication with this type of prospective customer!

- Organization
- Business
- Businesslike
- Business priorities
- Structure
- Insurance
- Invest/Investment
- Law
- Consultant
- System
- Complex
- Technical
- Marketing
- New horizons

ENVELOPE TEASER COPY OR DIGITAL SUBJECT LINE COPY

- Inside—"To Practice Your Art"

SAMPLE PRE-APPROACH COMMUNICATION: PRIMARY CARE PHYSICIAN

To Practice Your Art **(PTW)**

Dear (Name),

(Primary Bonding Statement) You didn't go to medical school to become an office manager. You wanted to practice your art without outside interference or a lot of paper pushing. **(PTW)**

(Describing Your Product or Service) For that reason, you certainly don't want any products or services that require extraordinary attention or take you away from the practice of medicine.

They simply shouldn't get in your way.

(Describing Your Organization) Your suppliers shouldn't get in your way either. They should use plain talk to give you simple, straightforward answers and the benefit of their expertise.

(Describing Your Benefits) Then, you'll be able to practice medicine the way you want to.

I believe you'll see [your product/service] and [your organization] can be all that for you. But you should be free to make that decision for yourself.

[Insert your Direct Value Statement and Purpose Statement.]

[Add appropriate warm or hot P.S.]

FOR A FAX, AN E-MAIL, OR A PRINT AD

To Practice Your Art **(PTW)**

You didn't go to medical school to become an office manager.

You wanted to practice your art without outside interference or a lot of paper pushing. **(PTW)**

For that reason, you certainly don't want any products or services that require extraordinary attention or take you away from the practice of medicine. They simply shouldn't get in your way.

Your suppliers shouldn't get in your way either. They should use plain talk to give you simple, straightforward answers and the benefit of their expertise.

Then, you'll be able to practice medicine the way you want to—and when you have that, it's easy to translate the cost of a product or service into its value.

We like to think [your product/service] and [your organization] can be all that for you. But you should be free to make that decision for yourself.

[Insert your Direct Value Statement and Purpose Statement.]

[Add appropriate warm or hot P.S.]

Type 23. Purchasing Agent/Manager

SAMPLE HEADLINE

- You're Doing Important Work

WORDS TO USE IN YOUR PRIMARY BONDING STATEMENT

- Getting recognition
- Being respected for what you do
- Getting credit (you probably do a lot more than you get credit for)
- Gaining respect
- Continuing to do important work
- Making a big contribution
- Remaining essential to your organization's success

WORDS TO USE TO DESCRIBE YOUR PRODUCT OR SERVICE

- Easy to understand
- A safe purchase
- Doesn't require a lot of technical education
- Not technically challenging

WORDS TO USE TO DESCRIBE YOUR ORGANIZATION

- Sincere
- Nonjudgmental
- Patient
- Not technically obsessed with its product or service
- More interested in its customers than in what it's selling
- Doesn't attach any strings to a relationship with customers
- People

WORDS TO USE TO DESCRIBE THE BENEFITS OF YOUR PRODUCT OR SERVICE

- Things should run smoothly for you
- Quietly
- No crises
- Decisions that are certain and sure

WORDS TO AVOID WITH A PURCHASING AGENT/MANAGER

These words may appear not to be negative. However, they are emotionally charged with negativity to this specific prospective customer. So ... be careful! Don't use them in any communication with this type of prospective customer!

- Challenging
- Highly technical
- Technology
- Technological
- Complex
- Make a judgment
- Education
- No-brainer
- Conditional
- Systematology
- Noninteractive
- Independent
- Requires study

ENVELOPE TEASER COPY OR DIGITAL SUBJECT LINE COPY

- Inside—"You're Doing Important Work"

SAMPLE PRE-APPROACH COMMUNICATION: PURCHASING AGENT/MANAGER

You're Doing Important Work **(PTW)**

Dear (Name),

(Primary Bonding Statement) You should get respect for what you do, and you probably do a lot more than you get credit for—the important work that makes a big contribution to your organization's success. **(PTW)**

(Describing Your Product or Service) You can improve that situation with products and services that are safe purchases because they're easy to understand and don't require a lot of technical education.

(Describing Your Organization) It takes special people to come out with a product or service like that—people who are more interested in the customer than in what they're selling.

(Describing Your Benefits) With teammates like that, things will run smoothly for you—quietly, without crises.

I believe you'll see [your product/service] and [your organization] can be all that for you. But you should be free to make that decision for yourself.

[Insert your Direct Value Statement and Purpose Statement.]

[Add appropriate warm or hot P.S.]

FOR A FAX, AN E-MAIL, OR A PRINT AD

You're Doing Important Work **(PTW)**

You should get respect for what you do, and you probably do a lot more than you get credit for—the important work that makes a big contribution to your organization's success. **(PTW)**

You can improve that situation with products and services that are safe purchases because they're easy to understand and don't require a lot of technical education.

It takes special people to come out with a product or service like that—people who are more interested in the customer than in what they're selling.

With teammates like that, things will run smoothly for you—quietly, without crises.

Then, the price can be easily translated into the benefits you get.

We like to think [your product/service] and [your organization] can be all that for you. But you should be free to make that decision for yourself.

[Insert your Direct Value Statement and Purpose Statement.]

[Add appropriate warm or hot P.S.]

Type 24. Radiologist

SAMPLE HEADLINE

- The Most Important Specialty

WORDS TO USE IN YOUR PRIMARY BONDING STATEMENT

- Having the most important specialty
- Having the most riding on it
- Being right at the center of everything
- Running hospitals the way they used to
- Keeping your art more important than mere numbers
- Using your art to prevent the hospital from coming to a grinding halt

WORDS TO USE TO DESCRIBE YOUR PRODUCT OR SERVICE

- Ahead of the development curve
- State of the art
- Won't turn you into a manual laborer
- Easy to manage
- Performs for you to its full potential
- Doesn't force you to do the things you don't want to do

WORDS TO USE TO DESCRIBE YOUR ORGANIZATION

- First-class reputation
- Strong innovators
- The very best support available

WORDS TO USE TO DESCRIBE THE BENEFITS OF YOUR PRODUCT OR SERVICE

- Be the best qualified to be in charge
- Take the lead and hold it
- Control the important decisions

WORDS TO AVOID WITH A RADIOLOGIST

These words may appear not to be negative. However, they are emotionally charged with negativity to this specific prospective customer. So … be careful! Don't use them in any communication with this type of prospective customer!

- Budget
- Committee
- Bottom line
- Marketing
- Cost-effectiveness
- Equal
- Equality
- Interaction
- Interactive
- Work in tandem
- Consider the other person's point of view
- Teamwork

ENVELOPE TEASER COPY OR DIGITAL SUBJECT LINE COPY

- Inside—"The Most Important Specialty"

SAMPLE PRE-APPROACH COMMUNICATION: RADIOLOGIST

The Most Important Specialty **(PTW)**

Dear (Name),

(Primary Bonding Statement) Your specialty is the most important because it has the most riding on it. Without you and your art, the hospital would come to a grinding halt. **(PTW)**

(Describing Your Product or Service) So you must have products and services that are ahead of the development curve and, at the same time, will perform for you to their full potential.

(Describing Your Organization) That means you need to make contact with suppliers with first-class reputations. Plus, they have to be strong innovators who give you the very best support available.

(Describing Your Benefits) If they're the right kind of people, they can help you take the lead and hold it while you control the important decisions.

I believe you'll see [your product/service] and [your organization] can be all that for you. But you should be free to make that decision for yourself.

[Insert your Direct Value Statement and Purpose Statement.]
[Add appropriate warm or hot P.S.]

FOR A FAX, AN E-MAIL, OR A PRINT AD

The Most Important Specialty **(PTW)**

Your specialty is the most important because it has the most riding on it. Without you and your art, the hospital would come to a grinding halt. **(PTW)**

So you must have products and services that are ahead of the development curve and, at the same time, will perform for you to their full potential.

That means you need to make contact with suppliers with first-class reputations. Plus, they have to be strong innovators who give you the very best support available.

If they're the right kind of people, they can help you take the lead and hold it while you control the important decisions.

And their price should be easily justified.

We like to think [your product/service] and [your organization] can be all that for you. But you should be free to make that decision for yourself.

[Insert your Direct Value Statement and Purpose Statement.]

[Add appropriate warm or hot P.S.]

Type 25. Surgeon

SAMPLE HEADLINE

- Being the Leader

WORDS TO USE IN YOUR PRIMARY BONDING STATEMENT

- Being the leader
- Taking a leadership position
- Holding the patient's welfare in your hands
- Being out in front
- Showing the way for others to follow
- Fulfilling the most important role
- Ranking the highest of all
- Being right in the front lines

WORDS TO USE TO DESCRIBE YOUR PRODUCT OR SERVICE

- Easy to use
- Prestigious
- Elite
- Very highly regarded
- Contributes to quick action
- Pragmatic

WORDS TO USE TO DESCRIBE YOUR ORGANIZATION

- Supportive
- Quick-acting
- Can perform well under difficult conditions
- Turn around and respond at a moment's notice

WORDS TO USE TO DESCRIBE THE BENEFITS OF YOUR PRODUCT OR SERVICE

- Faster action
- More reliable procedures
- No complications

WORDS TO AVOID WITH A SURGEON

These words may appear not to be negative. However, they are emotionally charged with negativity to this specific prospective customer. So … be careful! Don't use them in any communication with this type of prospective customer!

- Deliberate action
- Move one step at a time
- Never let themselves be rushed
- Committee
- Budget
- Marketing
- Equal
- Equality
- Share the spotlight
- Complexities
- Economics
- Technological
- Quiet working conditions

ENVELOPE TEASER COPY OR DIGITAL SUBJECT LINE COPY

- Inside—"Being the Leader"

SAMPLE PRE-APPROACH COMMUNICATION: SURGEON

Being the Leader **(PTW)**

Dear (Name),

(Primary Bonding Statement) Being the leader—being out in front—means you have to show the way for others to follow. That puts you right in the front lines, holding the patient's welfare in your hands. **(PTW)**

(Describing Your Product or Service) That's why you can't waste your time with products and services that aren't pragmatic and easy to use. You need the ones that are the most highly regarded—the elite.

(Describing Your Organization) And if that isn't enough, you also need suppliers who act quickly, who can perform well under difficult conditions, and who can turn around and respond at a moment's notice.

(Describing Your Benefits) Then, you'll get faster action with no complications.

I believe you'll see [your product/service] and [your organization] can be all that for you. But you should be free to make that decision for yourself.

[Insert your Direct Value Statement and Purpose Statement.]

[Add appropriate warm or hot P.S.]

FOR A FAX, AN E-MAIL, OR A PRINT AD

Being the Leader **(PTW)**

Being the leader—being out in front—means you have to show the way for others to follow. That puts you right in the front lines, holding the patient's welfare in your hands. **(PTW)**

That's why you can't waste your time with products and services that aren't pragmatic and easy to use. You need the ones that are the most highly regarded—the elite.

And if that isn't enough, you also need suppliers who act quickly, who can perform well under difficult conditions, and who can turn around and respond at a moment's notice.

Then, you'll get faster action with no complications.

One more thing: you should never pay a price that can't be easily justified.

We like to think [your product/service] and [your organization] can be all that for you. But you should be free to make that decision for yourself.

[Insert your Direct Value Statement and Purpose Statement.]

[Add appropriate warm or hot P.S.]

Chapter 5
Contacting Warm and Hot Prospective Customers: What to Say

Warm Call Phrases and Situations

Let's face it, even with the greatest pre-approach letter ever conceived, a lot of warm prospective customers will claim they never received your letter, won't communicate to the gatekeeper they did, may admit to receiving it but claim they never read it, actually have not read it, or have read it and are still not interested in accepting your call. However, look at it this way. Sending a pre-approach letter will give you a reason for making the call or at least make you feel more comfortable about making the contact!

So, let's start with the more difficult situations.

The Gatekeeper Is Resistant

You hear: "Good afternoon. Ms. Smithson's office. This is Barbara speaking."

You say: "Good afternoon, Barbara. My name is _____ with _____. [Insert your Direct Value Statement.] I'm following up on some material I sent to Ms. Smithson last week. I'm wondering if Ms. Smithson is available?"

You hear: "She doesn't take calls from people trying to sell her something."

You say: "I can understand that. However, I'm following up on some information I sent her."

You hear: "I know she won't take your call. She never takes calls."

You say: "I do understand. But maybe you could help me. Does she ever personally talk with people who have sent her materials?"

You hear one of two responses: (A) "Well, yes, she does occasionally" or (B) "No, she doesn't."

If (A), you say: "Great. Would it be acceptable if I left her a voice mail or would you suggest that I leave my number with you so you can pass it on to her?"

If (B), you say: "I would like to talk to her now. But if not, perhaps I could follow up tomorrow with a phone call to see if she has had a chance to review the material."

This situation, unfortunately, is not unusual or uncommon. Many gatekeepers are given the primary duty of keeping out callers no matter what: they are the buffers. Never forget: your goal is simple, straightforward, and clear—to get an appointment with the prospective customer. That's it. And here's the point: never, ever alienate the gatekeeper. In fact, you should work diligently to get that person on your side. However, if you must, you may need to circumvent that person's role by going directly to voice mail and leaving a powerful, benefit-rich message hoping to have the prospective customer either eagerly expect your next call or tell the gatekeeper to anticipate your call.

The Gatekeeper Is Positive, Prospective Customer Is Resistant

The gatekeeper answers the phone. Her response is positive and receptive. However, when you get to talk with your prospective customer, there is some degree of resistance and reluctance.

You hear: "Hello. Margaret Smith's office. This is Barbara. How may I help you?"

You say: "Hello, Barbara. My name is _____. [Insert your Direct Value Statement.] I'm wondering if Ms. Smith is available."

You hear: "Yes, she is. May I ask you what this is in reference to?"

You say: "Certainly. As I said, my name is _____. I'm with _____ and I had indicated to her that I would follow up on the material I recently sent to her."

You are connected.

You hear: "Hello. This is Margaret Smith."

You say: "Hello, Ms. Smith. As I told Barbara, my name is _____ with _____. I sent you a letter recently and I am just following up. [Insert your Direct Value Statement.] I was wondering if it might be possible for us to get together so that I could show you exactly how we could possibly do the same for you."

You hear: "That sounds good. However, I'm not interested in spending a lot of time looking at what you have to offer right now."

You say: "I can understand that. My purpose, however, is not to sell you anything. I'd really like to have a chance to meet you personally, learn something about your situation, and perhaps give you some idea of what we do so that we might be a viable option for you at a time when you might be interested in moving forward in the future."

You hear: "I might be willing to listen. However, don't expect me to buy anything."

You say: "I certainly don't. In fact, I promise that we will only begin a dialogue around taking a look at what we have. I'm wondering, do you have your calendar available? Is there a time next week that's better than any other for us to get together?"

You hear: "How much time will this take?"

You say: "How much time could you spare? I promise I won't take any more time than you can give me."

Note: Suggest a specific time frame and then set a day, a time, and a location. Be sure to emphasize that your meeting will take only as much time as the prospective customer can spare. Notice, again, that you respond to a question with a question ("How much time will this take?" "How much time can you spare?").

At this stage, don't assume that the prospective customer is or is not interested in your product or service. Your primary purpose is to assure him or her that you will not be expecting a purchase decision immediately. Your goal is to emphasize your interest in determining whether you can be of help in any way and to introduce your product or service to your prospective customer. Never forget that—and never violate that promise. If, however, your prospective customer develops interest during your visit, don't hesitate to move ahead as aggressively as necessary.

The Gatekeeper Is Officious

You hear: "Good morning. Ms. Johnson's office. This is Linda speaking. How may I help you?"

You say: "Hello, Linda. My name is _____ with _____. I've got a problem and I need your help."

Note: People in positions such as hers are trained to provide assistance to people who seek it.

You hear: "How can I help you?"

You say: "Linda, my name is _____ and I'm calling to determine if Ms. Johnson received my recent correspondence. [Insert your Direct Value Statement.] I would like to talk with Ms. Johnson, leave a message with you, leave a voice-mail message, or send Ms. Johnson some additional information. Which would you suggest that I do?"

Work with the gatekeeper to achieve your one, single objective—an appointment. Always solicit that person's help in suggesting the best way to get your message to your prospective customer.

It is essential that you earn this person's endorsement and support so that you can broaden your base of internal advocacy within your prospective customer's organization.

The Gatekeeper Is Receptive, Prospective Customer Is Positive

You hear: "Hello. Margaret Smith's office. This is Barbara. How may I help you?"

You say: "Hello, Barbara. My name is _____ with _____. I'm wondering if Ms. Smith is available."

You hear: "Yes, she is. May I ask you what this is in reference to?"

You say: "Certainly. As I said, my name is _____. I'm with _____. [Insert your Direct Value Statement.]"

You are connected.

You hear: "Hello. This is Margaret Smith."

You say: "Hello, Ms. Smith. As I told Barbara, my name is _____ with _____. [Insert your Direct Value Statement.] I'm calling to check and see if you received the recent correspondence (letter, e-mail, fax, card, announcement, etc.) I sent you. [Wait for a response.] I was wondering if it might be possible for us to schedule an appointment so that I could show you how we might be able to help you with _____."

You hear: "Your correspondence did look interesting."

You say: "Good. But I can promise you this: if what we have, in your opinion, won't work for you, I'll certainly understand and not take too much of your time. Does that make sense?"

> ***You hear:*** "As long as you do that, I'll be happy to see you."
>
> ***You say:*** "Good. Do you have your calendar handy? If so, let's go ahead and schedule an appointment. Is there a day next week that's particularly good for you?"

This situation is not as rare as you may think. There are times when you will be able to get a good, positive first contact. It is essential, however, that you remember that your single, solitary goal is always the same in every case—to get an appointment. Your goal is not to spend a lot of time on the phone, to make a sale, or give a presentation about your product or service. One more time: your single, primary goal is to gain an appointment—not to sell!

This situation shows the overwhelming importance of your Direct Value Statement. You must have it carefully prepared and it is the only thing in this book that you need to learn word for word. Use it at the most appropriate times and it will prove to be invaluable to you.

Should you receive questions with regard to your product or service, always defer them with the statement, "I can answer those questions when we get together. However, in order to answer them adequately, I'd like to ask you a few questions to see precisely how our solution can best be positioned to be of greatest value to you when we get together."

Never forget: all phone calls are always about one thing: getting an appointment—not making a sales presentation on the phone.

Your Prospective Customer Answers the Phone and Is Negative

You hear: "Good morning. This is John Johnson."

You say: "Mr. Johnson, how are you today? My name is _____ with _____. [Insert your Direct Value Statement.] You may recall receiving my recent correspondence. Have you had a chance to review it? [Pause.] The purpose of my call is to see if there is some way that we may be able to get together and discuss some things that might be of mutual interest."

You hear: "I'm not interested in talking to anyone like you. I don't have the time, the interest, or the inclination."

You say: "I can understand that. I'm wondering though if I might be able to send some additional targeted material that you can react to and then I'll call to follow up and see if there is some way that we might be able to establish a meeting. Does that sound like it might be acceptable to you?"

You hear: "Yes, that's OK. Just go ahead and send the material."

Note: Make sure that you have the correct address. You can get it through an online service or additional research. Avoid needing to ask your prospective customer, especially if he or she is initially reluctant. The last thing you want to do is take more time, appear to be disorganized, or to come across as "just another cold caller," even though you are a "warm" caller.

> **You say:** "I'll send you the material today. And if it's OK with you, I'll give you a call in a few days to make sure you have received it and to see if you've had a chance to review it. If it looks like it might be of some mutual interest, we might be able to go from there. Does that sound OK?"
>
> **You hear:** "Yes, that's fine."

Your strategy is designed solely to get materials into your prospective customer's hands because it is very clear at this point that trying to talk him or her into a meeting would likely prove to be counterproductive. This process will also give you a reason to make another warm call at a later point as you follow up to ensure he or she has received it and read it or to check whether there are any questions about it. However, be cautious here, because the prospective customer's agreement to have you forward some additional material may be a stall—their veiled attempt to defer telling you no. Be careful!

Your Prospective Customer Answers the Phone and Is Positive

You hear: "Good afternoon. Howard Smith."

You say: "Mr. Smith, my name is _____ with _____. [Insert your Direct Value Statement.] The purpose of my call is to discover if you might have an interest in meeting with me to see if there is some way that we might be of service to you. You may recall receiving my recent correspondence. Have you had a chance to review it?"

You hear: "Yes, but tell me a little bit more about what it is that you sell."

You say: "As I explained in my (letter, e-mail, fax, card, etc.), we _____."

Maybe the prospective customer has not read your communication.

You hear: "No."

You say: "OK, I understand. As I explained in my (letter, e-mail, fax, card, etc.), we _____. We have worked with lots of organizations such as yours over the years and have found that once we are able to establish a relationship we've been able to assist them in unique and different ways. Again, [insert your Direct Value Statement]. However, in order to see if we might be able to be of some service specifically to you, it's important that we have a face-to-face meeting. I'm wondering, is there a time next week that might be best for you?"

One more time: your sole strategy is to gain an appointment, no matter how positively responsive the prospective customer may be. Never place yourself in the position of trying to oversell on the phone. You'll note that there is never an attempt in any of the conversations in this book to make a sales presentation. The entire conversation is solely about telling the benefits of your particular product or service and establishing an appointment. The biggest mistake you can ever make here is to try to oversell an apparently responsive prospective customer. Remember: you are selling an appointment, not your product or service. And there is a big, big difference between the two.

Your Prospective Customer Answers the Phone and Is Neutral

You hear: "Good afternoon. Betty Johnson."

You say: "Ms. Johnson, my name is _____ with _____. [Insert your Direct Value Statement.] The purpose of my call is to see if you have had a chance to read my recent correspondence. Have you had a chance to review it?"

You hear: "Well, I did review your material but I'm just not that familiar with your organization and don't know much about it. And, frankly, I'm not sure if we're in a position to make a decision at this point."

You say: "I can understand that. Very few of our customers are ever in the position to make a decision when we first contact them. However, I would like to send you some additional material that will give you a better understanding of who we are and what we offer. And then, if possible, I'd like to get back in touch with you in the next couple of days to determine if we might be able to pursue it further if the material looks interesting to you."

You hear: "Sure, that's OK. Go ahead and send the material."

Note: Again, it is essential for you to have the exact and proper address (physical or e-mail). Secure it online or through some other source. Confirm that you will call in a few days to set up an appointment for a meeting. Don't be concerned that this may be a stall. If so, his or her situation could change, problems could arise, or a specific application for your product or service could surface at any time. Your goal? To stay in front of your prospective customer!

You Get Voice Mail

You should use this strategy whenever you leave a voice-mail message, regardless of how you get to voice mail! As you'll recall, we presented this strategy in Chapter 3. However, it bears repeating—particularly in this context.

You hear: "This is Mary Smith. I'm not at my desk right now. Please leave a message and I'll get back with you at my earliest possible convenience."

You say: "My name is _____ with _____. [Insert your Direct Value Statement.] Perhaps you may recall receiving my recent correspondence. However, the real purpose of my call is to see if there is some way that we might be able to be of some service or value to you. I certainly don't expect you to return my call. However, should you be so inclined, I would like to leave my number. [Leave your number, twice, slowly.] If I do not hear from you in the next couple of days, I will give you a call to see if there is some way we might be able to get together. I trust that you will be in a position to accept my call."

Never expect your prospective customer to return a voice message! However, you never want to oversell. You want to leave a message that is benefit-rich, that explains in great detail the benefits the prospective customer will receive when doing business with you—your DVS.

Leave your phone number twice. It is very important to do that because the prospective customer may need a moment to be able to jot it down. Be sure to leave your number very slowly and precisely so that it can be understood. Do your best to prepare the prospective customer to be expecting another call from you within a few days.

You'll recall that we have also suggested that you think about writing your phone number down as you leave it, to ensure that you give it slowly enough. You want to make it as easy as possible for your prospective customer to make note of it.

Hot Call Phrases and Situations: The Gatekeeper Answers the Phone

You hear: "Good afternoon. Mr. Price's office. This is Janet speaking. How may I help you?"

You say: "Hello, Janet. My name is _____ with _____. [Insert your Direct Value Statement.] I recently provided some materials to Mr. Price and he personally responded by requesting additional information about our organization. Do you know if he has received them?"

You hear: (A) "I don't know" or (B) "Yes, he has" or (C) "No, he hasn't."

If (A), you say: "I sent it last week. I'm wondering if I could talk with Mr. Price to see if he has received it and had a chance to review what he was most interested in. Could you please connect us?"

If (B), you say: "I'd like to talk with him to see what he thought of the information he requested. Could you please connect us?"

If (C), you say: "I understand he's extremely busy, but I received his request at the end of last week. Would you suggest that I resend the material he personally requested . . . or do you think that he might have received it without your knowledge? I wonder if you might connect us so that I can track this down."

Remember: your sole goal is to speak directly with your prospective customer in order to gain an appointment. You want to be sure to use the powerful phrase "personally requested." The material you send to a warm prospective customer is merely intended to give you a reason to have a discussion in order to gain an appointment. The hot prospective customer, again, is someone who has indicated an interest in being contacted. Which one is a stronger lead, warm or hot?

Your secondary goal, as in all of these scenarios, is to develop an internal advocate as early as possible. Quite often, that person is the gatekeeper. Here's another great phrase.

You say: "Janet, I know that Mr. Price counts a great deal on you to keep things straight. I'm wondering if you might be able to help me."

The reason for saying this is that often people in this position thrive on "reflected valuation." What does that mean? That a great deal of their personal value emanates from the worth or value that is placed upon them by their superiors. In this case, that's your prospective customer.

Never forget: you need to maximize the opportunity for leverage. Leverage the materials you've sent and your opportunity to have a discussion with the gatekeeper or buffer, to determine your prospective customer's receptivity, and to gain access to the prospective customer in order to engage in further dialogue.

Hot Call Phrases and Situations: Your Prospective Customer Answers the Phone

You hear: "Hello. This is Doris Maloney."

You say: "Hello, Ms. Maloney. My name is
_____. [Insert your Direct Value
Statement.] I'm calling you in response to your communication with us. As you may recall, you [called, left a message, sent in a response form, etc.] with reference to our
[product/service]."

You hear: "Yes, I recall doing that."

You say: "Good. Is there something in particular that I might
be able to help you with?"

Your goal here is to use the response as a springboard to
determine why he or she responded and as a way to lead you
to additional issues that he or she may want to have solved.
You want to establish a face-to-face appointment if relevant,
to make a telephone sales presentation if appropriate, or to
deduce that the prospective customer is not qualified.

You'll notice that there are only two scenarios here relative to dealing with hot prospective customers. There are
eight for dealing with warm prospective customers and (in
Chapter 3) seven for dealing with cold prospective customers. Why is that?

In going from cold to warm and then to hot, you reduce
the variables with which you'll have to deal. There is more
work up front. However, as with many things in life, the
preparation makes the rest of the process easier and more
predictable.

Chapter 6
Always Confirm Every Appointment:
What to Say or Write

Confirming Appointments

Never, never, never go on any appointment unless you have first contacted your prospective customer to confirm the time, date, location, and time frame for your meeting. You can do this directly with your prospective customer or with his or her designated representative.

It's worth the effort to confirm. Why should you waste your valuable time on an appointment that is not going to happen? Wouldn't you be better off finding out in advance, rescheduling that appointment, and using the time for another, more valuable activity?

Here's how to do that. First, of course, always do it by telephone. Don't rely solely on e-mail. Perhaps you could do both. That's better! Why is that? Prospective customers, as a rule, will not do anything that requires too much extra effort to entertain a sales presentation, no matter how badly they may need or want what you sell—and that includes even opening an e-mail! Sorry, but that's just how it is. Don't expect an e-mail reply telling you that he or she needs to reschedule the meeting. Occasionally, a proactive prospective customer will either call or e-mail to confirm or, more likely, to cancel or reschedule. However, don't expect that. Such people are few and far between. Therefore, here's a "double confirmation" strategy.

How to Confirm an Appointment by E-Mail

First, you e-mail, several days in advance of the meeting:

To: Ms. Johnson

Subject: Tuesday's Meeting

Dear _____,

This short e-mail is to confirm our meeting on Tuesday, June 15. I'm extremely excited about seeing you and discovering ways we can help you _____.

I will, of course, call on Monday to confirm our appointment. I look forward to seeing you on Tuesday, June 15 at 10:00 a.m.

Bill Smith

Sales Representative, XYZ Corporation

Special Note: You can even do this with a handwritten note. Why handwritten? Sending a formal, typed note or letter is stuffy, cold, and reflects that you do this in a production-line manner. Therefore, try this same verbiage in a warm, personally written format. It works.

How to Confirm an Appointment by Phone

Second, you call, as you promised:

You hear: "Good morning. Ms. Johnson's office. This is Corrie. How may I help you?"

You say: "Good morning, Corrie. This is _____ with _____. I'm calling to confirm my appointment with Ms. Johnson for tomorrow at 10:00 a.m. I'll be there at 9:45 a.m. for our meeting scheduled from 10:00 a.m. to 11:00 a.m. Is that still the correct time and does everything appear to be on schedule?"

You hear: (A) "Yes, it is" or (B) "No, there's a problem."

If (A), you say: "Good, I'll see you tomorrow morning at 9:45. However, should something come up, please e-mail me at _____ or call me at _____. Thank you very much."

If (B), you say: "I'm sorry to hear that. However, I would like to reschedule, if that's OK. Can you schedule an appointment for me with Ms. Johnson or would you recommend that I talk directly with her?"

Based on the response, you will either reschedule with the assistant or talk with your prospective customer in order to reschedule.

Chapter 7
Multiple Strategies for Lead Generation and How to Make Them Work

Seminars and Workshops

There are some settings where seminar selling for lead generation has been very common. In fact, I was involved in my first seminar selling situation way back in 1973 and it's still popular today! Products or services such as financial planning, retirement planning, direct marketing/sales opportunities, personal/professional growth, home security, medical services, and pharmaceuticals, among others, use this strategy.

However, this can prove to be a great strategy for virtually any product or service. Here are a few tips:

- Develop a method for both attracting and enrolling participants. It could be to mail invitations to those who will be attending a trade show or convention where you might be presenting. It might be to invite them by phone. You can even make them hot by including some sort of response mechanism—and you'll know who is planning to attend and who is not.

- Deliver whatever information you promise. Never, ever use your seminar as an opportunity to sell, as counterintuitive as that may sound.
- Explain, up front, what you're going to do—and then do it. Don't deviate from your planned message!
- Present solid, usable, principles-based information relative to the use of what you sell and how that information will aid each and every participant.
- Never present too much information. For example, consider presenting only three fundamental ideas, no more, making your most critical points #1 and #3. People remember what they hear first and last and they can never remember many things.
- Never, ever forget the real reason why you're there—to secure names, addresses, phone numbers, and/or e-mail addresses of those who are interested in follow-up.
- Do not fail to follow up with those who express interest within 12 to 24 hours of the event. If you don't do that, you have wasted your effort!

Introducing Your Seminar/Workshop

"Welcome to this seminar. Our purpose here today/tonight is to provide you with the fundamentals that are so successful for people (or franchisees, entrepreneurs, et al.) like you. We're going to be discussing _____, _____, and _____. Please feel free to jot down any questions you may have and please hold them for the end of the program. We'll then ensure that each of your questions is answered fully. However, I guarantee that we will be finished no later than (time)."

Pre-Presentation Operations

You say: "The formal program will last about _____ minutes and be followed by a _____-minute question-and-answer period. At that point I will hand out a very carefully designed manual that will go through all of this in greater detail. Should you be interested in a follow-up meeting, I will also pass out a form for you to fill out and return to me. Should you not be interested, but perhaps know someone else who might be, you will see a section on that form to fill in his or her name, address, phone, and e-mail, should you be so inclined."

If you promise a manual, many people will stay through the program just to get it. Therefore, it must be relevant and valuable in and of itself.

You may want to add: "The manual I'll be handing out contains much more valuable information than I could ever provide in this program."

And: "Please feel free to use the restroom facilities at any time. They are located _____. Also, should you be interested, we have coffee and/or soft drinks available throughout the program (or at break time). Now, let's get started."

Delivery of Seminar Content

Here are a few tips about presenting:

- Deliver only data that explains *why*. Don't be so concerned with all the *hows* of your product. That will come later!
- Use examples of what you've done for other people just like your participants, but use them only as pure examples—not to sell and not by name. This is particularly true if you sell in a vertical market to competitors.
- Make your most startling point first and your most powerful point last. Remember that people tend to remember what they hear first and last.
- Be well prepared, practiced, and skillful with the technology you use. Use technology appropriately. For example, don't use a laptop screen for more than six people; use an LCD projector.
- *Always* start and end on time.
- Remember your purpose for being there (again)—to identify prospective customers for follow-up sales activity.

Question-and-Answer Session

You say: "As you'll recall, I asked you to hold any questions so that we can deal with all of them at one time. What is the first question?"

It's not unusual for people to be hesitant to be the first to pose a question. If you detect hesitation, say,

"One of the most common questions we often get is

_____."

Answer that planned question and solicit another from the group. If participants are still hesitant, say,

"Another common question is _____."

Answer that question and solicit questions again. If there are still no questions from the group, move to the closing segment.

Closing Segment

You say: "I'm now going to pass out the manual (tip sheet, etc.) that will go into what we have talked about here in more detail. I'll also pass out a form for you to fill out with your contact information, if you are interested in learning more about how this can apply directly to you. Then I'll give you a call in the next day or so and we'll be able to go from there. If you know others who might be interested, please put their names and contact information on the form and we'll invite them to another program just like this one."

Then: "If, for any reason, you're not interested immediately but would like to receive our (monthly/quarterly) update, newsletter, e-zine, special report, etc., simply check the box and we'll make sure you receive our regular updates. Please understand that you can opt off our list at any time."

Never send any of these tools without some mechanism that allows recipients to request more information, request an appointment, etc. (More about this later when we deal with nurture or cultivation prospecting.)

Remember: people will always buy on their time frame, not yours! It could be six months later. Anyone who responds and expresses interest is a hot prospective customer.

Then What?

Pass out the forms and then collect one from every participant—those who are not interested, those who are, those who supply referrals, and those who agree to be on your contact list. Then, say,

"Thank you very much for attending. I hope you've found our time together valuable and you've gotten some good ideas. Those of you who have expressed interest, I look forward to talking with you within the next day.

"I'll be here for the next _____ minutes to answer any questions you may have."

The Result

You now have all the participants broken into four distinct groups:

- Those who will expect to hear from you very soon
- Those who give you referrals
- Those who agree to be contacted regularly and respond to your ongoing offers
- Those who are not interested

Now, take the appropriate action with each type of prospective customer!

Users Conferences

If you're not using a users conference or—better yet, multiple conferences—to generate leads, you need to start. It is a fantastic way to encourage your current customers to buy more of your product or service. It is also a great way to further cement your relationships with your customers, vertically integrate other divisions, and have referrals attend the sessions and interface with your current customers. This strategy is extremely effective if you sell into multiple, noncompetitive industries, if your pricing is consistent, and if you have customers who don't compete in the same geographic area. Otherwise, proceed with caution.

Tips for Making Your Conference a Success

- Use the conference to introduce and promote upgrades, new products, or expanded services.
- Educate customers how to use or get the most from new and/or established products or services.
- Have customers present at the conference. Have them discuss their success stories, insights, breakthroughs, or unique applications of your product or service. (Be exceedingly careful with this if you sell into a tightly defined geographic or a highly competitive niche.)
- Consider having the conference at either your facility (if appropriate and to your advantage) or an exciting, different spot (if affordable).
- Give thought to giving awards to presenters and to others (Customer of the Year, Most Innovative Use of Your Product/Service, etc.).

How to Organize and Promote Your Event

Organization is essential. This event must be highly structured and operationally sound. Of course, the way you announce your conference and invite people to participate is essential to the success of the event. Here are some recommendations:

- Allow plenty of time (three to six months) between your promotion and the event. Most people need lots of time to plan and be available.
- Develop a campaign to promote the event. Consider using your data relative to your customers. Contact all of your current customers and highly qualified prospective customers via letter, card, invitation, personal phone calls, your newsletter or e-zine, e-mail, or personal visits.
- Ensure that no one is left off your list. Don't risk offending anyone.
- Consider inviting strong and qualified prospective customers and/or having customers/clients invite guests of their choice.
- Carefully select those customers/clients who will participate. Be sure they are able and willing. Contact these people personally and allow them to select the topics that they will address—e.g., how they use your product or service, best practices, case studies, users panels, expert tables, etc.
- Prepare a detailed outline, high-end brochure, or downloadable document.

- Make it easy to register for the event.
- Provide a number for participants to call in case of questions or issues, etc.
- Make sure that all details are handled: directions, rooms, reservations, meals, materials, audiovisual setup in rooms, events, awards, etc.
- Schedule time for networking (formal and informal) and for presentations—by customers, by your executives, by operations/support staff, and by sales staff.
- Salespeople must be present and able to spend time with their customers/clients and accounts.
- Follow-up is essential: certificates of attendance, incentive items, thank-you letters, etc.

These events are not easy to execute. Like anything else in life that is valuable, they require effort. However, don't be fearful. Try it. I guarantee you that it will be worth it!

Introducing Your Conference

You say: "Welcome to our _____ annual Users Conference. Our purpose at this conference is to allow you, our customers and potential customers, to get to know each other better. It's also designed to allow you to learn from one another, to share best practices, and to see how others maximize the use of our _____.

"As you know, the conference will last _____ days and will allow plenty of time for presentations, networking, and idea sharing.

"Now, I'd like to hand out our final agenda for your review."

Distribute the agenda and go through each item—logistics, meals, rest breaks, facility layout, etc. Ask if there are any questions about anything.

Speeches

Giving speeches can open up opportunities to prospect for hidden gold. However, be warned here. If you are not an experienced presenter or are unwilling to learn how to master this craft, this may be a strategy to avoid. A speech is far different from a seminar or workshop. It requires a stronger platform presence, a tested format, and a quicker hitting delivery.

But if you are able and willing, this is a masterful strategy—and perhaps the most powerful.

- Speeches establish you as an expert. The common perception is that only experts speak.
- Speeches give you economy of scale. How else could you be in front of a larger, focused group of prospective customers?
- Speeches allow you to present your ideas or strategies and make the case for your product or service.

Where should you be speaking about your product or service? There are lots of possibilities here for being in front of your customers and/or prospective customers. We will look at just four:

- Associations of which they are members
- Conventions that they attend
- Forums in which they participate
- Users conferences for their customers (the end users of your products)

How to Find Opportunities to Speak

How do you get the opportunity to speak? Ask your prospective customers or current customers if there are any trade groups, buying groups, associations, or related organizations to which they belong or any conventions, trade shows, or regularly scheduled meetings that they attend. Then, ask them if they have presenters at the programs. (This is, by the way, the same way to pursue seminars or workshops.) If they use speakers, learn who selects them and how you could go about discussing the possibility of presenting to them. Ask your contact to help you do that. One caveat here. You must say:

> "My presentation is not a commercial in any way. I will not, under any circumstances, without your approval, promote or sell my organization or any of our products or services. In fact, I will guarantee that."

This phrase is essential to the success or failure of this strategy.

Remember: this is not a sales presentation; it is a speech. You absolutely must provide valuable, vital insight that establishes you as an absolute expert in your field. Your product or service is not that important. What is important is you are positioned as a vital source of knowledge, expertise, and assistance. And, as in a seminar that is not product- or service-centered, violate this rule and you'll lose in many ways. Your sponsor will be embarrassed, you will never be invited back. You'll also be in for more headaches than you can ever imagine.

What to Title Your Speech

What should you speak about? Let's look at ten perfect phrases to use when titling your presentation:

1. "The Three Proven Ways to _____"
2. "Three Insider Tips to _____"
3. "Street-Smart, How-to-Do-It Ways to _____"
4. "How to Grow Your Business Faster and Easier: The Three Secrets"
5. "The Three Biggest Mistakes to Avoid in _____"
6. "How Most Companies (Practices, Banks, Manufacturers, etc.) Derail and How to Avoid Joining Them"
7. "Solving Our Industry's Biggest Dilemma: How to _____"
8. "How You Can Take Advantage of _____"
9. "The Success Formula: How to _____"
10. "Three Most Proven Ways to Fail as a _____ and How to Avoid Them"

You'll notice that with each of these titles there is a little "mystery" coupled with some sort of "secret," "insight," "formula," or things to "avoid." That's because people really want to be in on secrets, acquire greater knowledge, learn about a system for success, or avoid pain or aggravation. So, give them what they really want!

If that's the case, what do they really not want? That's simple. They don't want a sales pitch—especially if it's misrepresented as being a valuable, vital, and insightful presentation. **Be warned:** cross this line at your own peril. If you try to sell, this strategy fails.

Make your presentation based on sound, solid principles that lie behind the application of your product or service. Let people deduce why they need to pay attention to the general problems, issues, circumstances, or realities that your product or service addresses.

Here's an example. You sell air conditioning units. You are going to speak to an organization of plant managers. Your presentation is entitled "The Three Biggest Problems That Improperly Installed Air Conditioning Units Can Cause at Your Plant." If you address that topic with great insight, some of those people will want to deal with you (and, as a by-product, buy air conditioning units from you) based on your expertise, positioning, and knowledge. You're now an expert—not an air conditioner salesperson. And there is a big difference.

How to Arrange to Do a Presentation

You must first obtain key information from an advocate. You will need to know the person to contact, if the organization has a meeting scheduled, and if the person has the authority to engage a speaker or presenter.

Here's what you say: "Hello, Mr./Ms. _____? Do you have a minute or so that we might talk? My name is _____ with _____. A mutual friend of ours, _____ [your advocate], asked me to give you a call and I promised I would. He/she told me that you are responsible for programming at the upcoming meeting at _____ on _____. Is that correct?"

If it is not correct, say: "I'm wondering, if you are not the correct person, could you direct me to the person I should contact? Do you have his or her phone number and/or address? Do you mind if I tell this person that you have referred me?"

If it is correct, say: "Have you filled all of your slots for the meeting at _____ on _____?"

If so, ask about the next meeting.

If not, say: "I have been involved with this industry for _____. And during that time I have made observations and developed some unique insight into the ways that participants at your next meeting can be more successful and/or avoid certain problems. In fact, I have put together a short presentation entitled _____. It can be anywhere from ____ minutes to ____ minutes, depending on your available time.

"Even though I work with [your organization], my interests are far beyond just selling my product/service. Therefore, I want to reassure you that if you allow me to present these insights I will not, under any circumstances, use my presentation as a platform to even mention my organization, product, or service without your approval. In fact, if I do, you can simply ask me to leave—even if it's in the middle of my presentation. Would you like to learn more about this?"

If yes, now what?

You say: "I've got some descriptive material that I'd like to get to you. Do you prefer e-mail, fax, or hard copy?"

Then you prepare some sort of outline or program description that provides the following:

- Program title
- Reason(s) why the topic is important
- Outline of key points and subtitles
- Time frame(s)

Give the recipient a few days to review your material. Then call.

Say: "Hello, Mr./Ms. _____? This is _____ with _____. We talked a few days ago about the opportunity for me to make a presentation at the upcoming meeting at _____ on _____. Have you had a chance to review the material I sent you via (e-mail, fax, or mail)?"

If yes,

Say: "Good. Does it look like something you'd be interested in having at your meeting?"

If yes, handle the details relative to location, time, dress, audiovisual needs, and other logistics.

Then say, "As I told you, my presentation is not a commercial in any way. However, I find that people have questions and/or are interested in learning more about this topic. Do you mind if I _____?"

This action could be collecting cards from those interested, passing out an interest sheet, or signing up those interested in your newsletter or your nurturing program.

Remember: you have told this contact person that you will not do anything commercial without his or her approval. You are now seeking that approval. Frankly, this is your real end game, done at the close of your presentation. If there is any resistance to allowing you to do that, it only means that your presentation will have to be beyond great, because you will then be relying on people seeking you out on their own. The presentation still works—but only if you present a vital topic and do it extremely well.

If you receive a "no" when you ask if the person would be interested, ask one or more of the following questions:

- "Is there a topic that might be more appealing to you?"
- "Are you concerned that I might be too commercial?"
- "When do you have your next meeting scheduled?"

You are now in a position to deal with each of these issues. If you run into a dead end, simply move on; you don't have a qualified prospective customer. Try to find other associations or trade groups that you can contact.

Networking—It's Still Alive!

Entire books have been written about networking. So, let's just say this: if you are going to use this strategy, you must be a natural connector, a person who knows how to meet people, help other people meet people, and have the capacity, interest, aptitude, time, and energy to expend at events and activities.

Also, bear in mind that networking is valuable only if it positions you with the right prospective customers. Invest your valuable time where it will generate the best returns: finding and connecting the right people.

The groups through which you network will depend on what you sell. It may be charities and sponsored events. It may be trade shows. It may be associations. It may even be a "lead club" or a "tip club." You must choose wisely.

One of the keys to networking is to be legitimately interested in other people. The main tip here? It's really, really simple and disarmingly effective: don't tell them what you do until they ask. Instead, ask about them! Ask what they do! It's that simple.

Here are some examples of networking.

Social Event

Someone you know introduces you to a friend, Mary.

You say: "Mary, it's certainly nice to meet you. This is a nice event, isn't it?"

You'll get a response, probably something like "Yes, it is." You then ask questions such as these:

- "Do you live here in town?" If so, "How long have you lived here?" If not, "Where do you live?"
- "How long have you known _____ (host, sponsor, or event planner) or been a member of (organization)?"
- "What do you do?" (No matter what the person says, be interested! Ask follow-up questions.)
- "Tell me about yourself." (This should go on a long time, as you express interest—"Tell me more," "That's interesting," etc.—and ask follow-up questions.)

Only when the other person asks you what you do, give your Direct Value Statement:

"I (or we) assist clients (or customers) in the _____ industry (or business) to _____. We do this by _____."

If you're in front of the right person, he or she may be interested in what you do. However, caution! You're not there to sell. You're there to network. That means to gather names, contact information, help others do the same, and move on.

Should the person express an interest, it's important to remember the principle that works both here and in trade show prospecting—it's far better to receive than give.

Here's what that means. Imagine that the person is interested in what you have to offer. You say this: "If you'd like to pursue this, I'd certainly love to do so. Do you have a card?"

Don't just offer your card in the hope that you'll hear from that person. You won't! If you can, get his or her card. If not, get his or her number and/or e-mail and put that contact information on the back of one of your cards. Then give the person another one of your cards.

Ask, "Do you mind if I call you tomorrow or the next day so we might pursue this conversation?"

Again, a word of caution. Don't continue to sell! Don't look desperate! Don't get pushy! You want to stay casual, social, and at ease.

FOLLOW-UP E-MAIL: WHAT TO SAY

The next morning, you may want to send an e-mail indicating that you'll call. Here's a sample:

Good Morning _____;

It was most enjoyable meeting you at _____ last night. It was a great affair. _____ certainly did a great job of putting it together. I hope you had as good a time as I did.

As a follow-up to our conversation, I'd like to call you in the next day or so to pursue our conversation further. I have also included a link to our Web site, should you want to learn a little more about our products/services.

I'll call you later today or tomorrow about getting together. It was great to meet you.

FOLLOW-UP HANDWRITTEN NOTE: WHAT TO SAY

Their time frame may make it smart to alter this standard approach. If, during your networking conversation, you learned that this person is actively reviewing sources that supply what you do or is planning to do so, you may want to send him or her a note (handwritten, of course) that might be like this:

Dear _____;

It was most enjoyable meeting you at _____. From our conversation I understand that you are possibly interested in _____. I will, therefore, send you some descriptive information under separate cover that should get to you in a few days.

I want to drop you this personal note, though, to tell you that I certainly enjoyed talking with you and hope that you will be in a position to accept my phone call in the next week or so. That way we can mutually determine if there's a way we can help you.

My best personal wishes to you.

PHONE CALL FOLLOWING A NETWORKING EVENT: WHAT TO SAY

You are calling for an appointment after meeting your prospective customer at a networking event.

You hear: "Hello. Ken Froman's office. This is Heidi. How may I help you?"

You say: "Good morning, Heidi. My name is _____. I recently met Mr. Froman at [event]. He asked me to give him a call and I promised him I would. I'm wondering if you could connect us."

You hear: "Certainly."

You are connected.

You hear: "Hello, this is Ken Froman. May I help you?"

You say: "Hello, Mr. Froman (or Ken, if you used first names). This is _____. We met recently at [event]. As you may recall, I indicated that I'd call you and you suggested I do so. Do you have a few minutes right now?"

You hear: "No" or "Yes."

If no, make an appointment to call at a more convenient time. If yes,

You say: "Good. As you recall, I'm with _____. [Insert your Direct Value Statement.] Would it make sense for us to sit down and discuss how we might help you?"

If the response is negative, proceed to qualify the prospective customer further to determine if there is some possible way to meet.

If the response is unsure or tentative, you should also proceed to ask qualifying questions to have the prospective customer verbalize a problem you could possibly solve.

If the response is positive, schedule an appointment.

Referral Selling

This could be the most powerful and effective prospecting tool. However, there are three issues with it:

1. If you're just starting out in sales or haven't had sufficient time to develop a customer base, it's difficult—your referral base is just not large enough. It's that simple.
2. If you sell to a tightly niched base of customers who are competitors, you'll have difficulty getting one competitor to refer you to another.
3. If you don't provide high-quality, on-time delivery of your product or service or if your product or service is inferior, you may not have the confidence of your referral base.

However, if you don't have these challenges, referral selling is, by far, the absolute best prospecting method. But in order to use it successfully, you should consider these two points:

- You should develop a program that empowers your customers to want to refer you. (This is far beyond rewarding them; in fact, it's instead of giving rewards.)
- You should do it without either badgering your customers to do it or appearing to be desperate for business.

This type of prospecting works best if you have a method for staying in touch with your customers continuously. This could be with regular meetings/updates (if they are key accounts), mailings, newsletters, active involvement in associations to which they belong, incentive or promotional items, users conferences, product bulletins, and so on.

Here's an example. You are phoning a prospective customer who is a direct referral to you from someone who knows him or her.

You hear: "Good morning. Lester Jamison's office. This is Lori. How may I help you?"

You say: "Good morning, Lori. My name is _____ with _____. Jack Perry (person who made the referral), a mutual friend of Mr. Jamison's and mine, asked me to give him a call and I promised him I would."

You hear: "Let me check with Mr. Jamison."

Or

If you hear: "Mr. Jamison isn't in,"

Say: "I'm sorry that I can't talk with him. However, do you have his schedule so that I can be sure to talk directly with him?"

This is a strong lead. Don't let it get away! Get time frames and set up a firm telephone appointment with the gatekeeper.

If you hear: "Mr. Jamison isn't in, would you like to leave a message?"

Say: "How would you recommend I do that? Would it be better to leave a message with you or would you suggest that I leave a voice mail?"

If you leave a message with the gatekeeper or a voice-mail message, use the words "asked" and "promised," and remember that, as usual, your singular goal is to set up a phone conversation to establish a face-to-face selling situation.

If the gatekeeper says, "Let me check with Mr. Jamison," you should then hear, "I'll connect you" or "He wants to know what this is all about" or "He doesn't have time to talk with you now."

If you hear: "I'll connect you,"

You say: "Thank you very much."

You hear: "Good morning. This is Lester Jamison."

You say: "Good morning. As Lori may have told you, my name is _____. Jack Perry, a mutual friend, asked me to give you a call and I promised him I would."

You hear: "How is Jack?"

You say: "He's fine (or "He's still ill" or "He's getting better" or "He asked about you," whichever is appropriate) and he suggested contacting you, since we have been helpful to him in ways that may also be of interest to you."

You hear: "What is this all about?" or "What do you do?" or "How can I help you?"

You say: "[Insert your Direct Value Statement.]"

Never forget your sole goal, as in all prospecting calls, is to secure a face-to-face presentation. However, you may want to get permission to send materials and then follow up with another phone call.

If the gatekeeper says, "Mr. Jamison wants to know what this is all about,"

You say: "Please tell him that I have provided some valuable ideas (or services or solutions to some problems, etc.) to his friend, Mr. Perry, who feels very strongly that I should talk with Mr. Jamison."

As always, your sole goal is to gain an appointment. If your prospective customer requests that you send materials, do so. Although this can be a dodge or a stall, you have the power of a strong referral and should follow through. Plus, you never, ever want to get too pushy with any referral. It could cause problems with the person who made the referral. However, if you send the prospective customer anything, establish a firm time to call back to find out what he or she thinks about what you sent and to establish an appointment.

You may be able to get through to your prospective customer solely based upon your response to the gatekeeper. If that's the case, always remember that your sole, singular, and solitary goal is to gain an appointment.

If the gatekeeper says, "He doesn't have time to talk with you now," say one of two things.

You can say: "I can understand that. However, do you know if there's a time when he might be available?"

You can say: "Mr. Perry was very eager for me to talk with Mr. Jamison. Let me ask you this. Could I send something that Mr. Jamison might be able to review? If that's acceptable, I'll call in a week or so to see if he's had a chance to review it. Is that OK?"

In this case, it is perfectly acceptable to confirm the correct physical or e-mail address for sending materials, to ensure that there is no delay.

How do you actually ask for a referral? Here's one great way.

You say: "My organization expects me to earn as many referrals as I can. In fact, I frequently have to supply that referral list to my manager. I'm wondering, can you think of others, like you, who may have a need for our product/service?"

If you get a positive response to your request, get all the information you can—full address, correct title, phone number, e-mail address.

If you can't gather all of this information from your referral source, you may want to ask him or her how and where you can get that information.

Then ask, "Is it OK if I use your name?" or (better) "Would you mind contacting him/her so that he/she will be anticipating my call?"

Having the referral source actually contact a prospective customer gives you a tremendous advantage, for obvious reasons.

If your source agrees to make the contact, you need to then ask,

"Do you have any idea when you'll be able to contact _____? That way I'll know when to contact him/her. I certainly wouldn't want to catch him/her off guard or wait too long following your contact."

Trade Show Lead Generation

Trade shows give you great exposure to prospects. However, shows can be extremely expensive and even counterproductive if not handled correctly.

Determine Your Objectives

The first thing is to ensure that a certain show is appropriate for your needs. The second is to establish your primary objective(s) for being there. What are you trying to accomplish?

- Educate prospective customers?
- Establish or maintain a presence?
- Stay competitive?
- Introduce a product or a service to the market?
- Greet current customers?
- Make sales?
- Collect contact information?
- Use it as a platform for meeting with customers?
- Serve as a destination point to send participants from a seminar, speech, or workshop you do?

All of these are good and valid reasons for working a trade show. Always, always, always clearly define your objective for being there. And your objective will, in large measure, determine the words you will use at your exhibit! For example, making a sale is far different from merely educating prospective customers about your newest offering.

What to Do

Here are five rules for the whole trade-show experience, no matter what your objective. Then we'll get into some specific phrases to use.

Perfect Phrases for Lead Generation

1. Don't bunch up or gather in a cluster with your fellow salespeople. It is cold, threatening, and unwelcoming to participants.
2. Always assign roles to each member of your trade-show team—greeter, tour guide, or supplier (for brochures, etc.)—and rotate roles regularly.
3. Quickly qualify the seriously interested from the "pure looker," and then qualify each further.
4. Establish a traffic flow for your exhibit and maintain that flow.
5. Never forget why you're there—to achieve your primary objective.

At the Booth: What to Say

Position yourself at the front of your exhibit and stay on your feet. Never, ever sit down. Engage those who look at your exhibit or make eye contact with you.

Do not ask, "May I help you?" or "Are you enjoying the show?" or "Are you having a good show?"

Instead, ask questions that elicit responses other than "Yes" or "No." That means that you should ask questions like these:

- "How familiar are you with [your organization or product or service]?"
- "When is the last time you have used a product/service like ours?"
- "How long has it been since you've been updated on [your product/service]?"
- "How familiar are you with our most recent upgrades?"

Your goal is to elicit some sort of response. You're looking for any multi-word response—"It has been some time" or "Five years" or even "I've never heard of you." It makes no difference what they say. You're simply looking for some base on which to build.

Then, give a simple, short response like the following:

- "That's interesting."
- "Why do you say that?"
- "Let me ask you a few questions."
- "How much time do you have?"

That will give you an opportunity, a reason to ask more questions relative to qualifying your prospective customers quickly. The secret here is that one or two questions will tell you exactly where to go first in your exhibit, what to show them first, and even what literature to give them. It will tell you if they are highly qualified prospective customers or not. Granted, this takes quick judgment. However, at trade shows, speed is the key. Here are a few ways to get the information you need:

- "What type of time frame are you working with? How long have you been looking?"
- "Tell me about your business. How often do you have a need for [your product or service]?"
- "What is your goal for attending this show (to look, buy, shop, learn, gather data, etc.)?"

Based on what you hear, you now know how to proceed with your prospective customers. What are your options?

- Take them through the exhibit.
- Hand them off to someone else.
- Give them literature.
- Collect their personal data and give them your card.
- Make an appointment to see them during or following the show.
- Make a sale.
- Thank them and find other prospective customers.

Let's assume that you have a qualified and interested prospective customer. However, if you are selling a complex product that requires lots of education to understand, don't spend too much time showing too much: your time is too limited and so is theirs.

You might say this: "Since our time is so limited, I'd like to give you this descriptive literature and allow you time to read and more fully understand our [product or service]. I can meet with you after the show (or at dinner, lunch, etc.) to explain it more fully. Is that acceptable to you?"

Or you might say this: "I'd like to give you a quick tour of our booth. That way you can see what we're featuring. I've also got some descriptive material that will explain everything in greater detail. If you're interested, we can spend more time here or I can meet with you after the show (or at dinner, lunch, etc.). Is that acceptable to you?"

When you are taking your prospective customer through your exhibit, before you get too far into your tour, ask what is most essential to him or her. You don't want to show the wrong thing, communicate irrelevant features, or stress the wrong benefits of your product or service. Therefore, before you start, be sure to ask a few questions like these:

- "What is it that you're looking to accomplish?"
- "What are the biggest problems you're trying to solve?"
- "How important is (size, price, power, etc.) to you?"
- "What are you currently using? What do you like about it? What do you dislike?"
- "What are you looking for, if anything, that you haven't found?"

Based on the answers to these questions and more, you're ready to proceed. Bear in mind that this whole process, from the beginning to this point, should take no more than three to five minutes.

Here's the phrase that is essential: "Based on what you're telling me, I am going to recommend that we take a look at _____."

Now, show only those specific benefits of that specific product or service that will address what the prospective customer wants. Don't get into a full demonstration. Take just a few minutes and secure a follow-up meeting, phone call, or conference.

In order to do this, say, "Assuming that you like what you see, I'd like to make arrangements for us to get together so that we can pursue this further."

Then say, "Do you have your calendar with you?"

If yes, schedule a follow-up meeting for the show or afterward.

If no, say, "Do you have your business card? I'd like to contact you about a follow-up meeting."

If your prospective customer doesn't have a card, use a form or ask for exact contact information. Either way, say, "I'll contact you within the next _____ hours/days in order to arrange a meeting time, is that OK with you?"

You must get contact information from your prospective customer. Don't give your card and expect that he or she will contact you. Frankly, the chances of that happening are quite slim, at best.

Be sure to take notes about impressions, needs, wants, problems, promises you've made, etc. so that your follow-up will be appropriate and accurate. A great place to do that is on the back of the business card.

You will also want to classify the prospective customer in some objective way for follow-up purposes. Here's a great way to do that:

- AAA: Super Hot
- AA: Very Hot
- A: Hot
- B: Good
- C: Fair

It's essential that you remember not to spend too much time with any single prospective customer! Exhibit time is both too expensive and too limited for that. The goal here is the follow-up.

The only exception is if you are at a show where a lot of sales are made. If so, consummate a sale ... and then find more prospective customers and make more sales!

Working with Redemption Offers

Prospective customers driven to your booth following a seminar, a speech, or a workshop are familiar with you, your product or service, and your organization. Ideally, these prospective customers should have been given something at your seminar to redeem for something at your exhibit.

For example, they receive a printed card at the seminar to redeem at your exhibit for a confidential report or an insider tip sheet, perhaps an incentive item. You say, "Welcome. I see you attended our seminar/workshop. Thank you for attending. Let me get your [gift]." Then you say, "Let me ask you this: what part of the program did you find most valuable to you?"

You are now in a position to repeat the same process as outlined in the previous section. But here you are dealing with a prospective customer who has at least learned something about your product.

By the way, it's far smarter to provide participants with information on "how-to-do-it" materials than to offer some pure incentive item (caps, cups, etc.). You want them to learn more about how to apply your product or service as a solution, not just to show up to acquire one more incentive.

One More Point About Leaving Messages

In today's sales world you will encounter more and more opportunities to leave messages than you could ever use! As a consequence, you need to know how to leave a powerful, meaningful message. We discussed this before, but let's take another look.

It's not unusual for a prospective customer to have a secretary, an assistant, or a gatekeeper answering the phone. And if the prospective customer is not available, that person will invariably ask you if you would like to leave a voice-mail message.

What should you do?

You say: "Which would you recommend? The information I have to share with _____ is very important. Do you know when he/she will be retrieving messages? Would it be better if I left it with you?"

You hear: "Just leave a voice mail" or "I can take a message for you" or "Either way is fine with me."

If you must, leave the voice-mail message as explained in Chapter 3. However, it's highly recommended that you do your best to leave the message with a real, live person. In this process, you'll want to develop a person-to-person relationship with the person with whom you leave the message.

Be sure to thank the person for taking the message. Be as friendly and accommodating as possible. Again, here's the message to leave:

"Please tell Mr./Ms. _____ that I am _____

with _____. Our firm specializes in _____.
I was hoping that we might talk. My phone number is
_____. [Give it twice.] I'll be available all day.
However, if I don't hear from him/her by [date], I hope
that he/she will be in a position to accept my call."

This message is easy for the other person to transcribe quickly. As you'll note, this carefully crafted message contains this key data:

- Your name
- Your organization
- What you do
- Your purpose
- Your phone number
- Your goal
- Your availability
- Their option to return your call or accept a call from you
- Thank the person and hang up.

Don't expect a return call. You won't get one! However, you will have begun to build a relationship with the gatekeeper. He or she will remember you. In subsequent calls, develop strong internal advocacy with that person. Get into lengthier discussions, getting to know him or her better.

I have trained salespeople in this manner who tell me that the gatekeeper will tell them exactly when the prospective customer will be available, promise to hold all other calls at that time, and guarantee that the call will go through. It doesn't get any better than that, does it?

Nurture Prospecting

Although this approach has been around for some time, it has mainly been viewed as a direct marketing strategy. However, with the blurring of the lines between marketing and prospecting, it is now just as much a prospecting strategy as a marketing approach. This is particularly true with the digital tools available to salespeople for tracking and managing this type of process.

The philosophy is to initiate permission-based communication with your prospective customer. This can be done with cold, warm, or hot prospective customers. It's also extremely effective with current customers in order to sell them more of your products or services. It works equally well with referrals, trade show leads—anybody.

Why is that the case? Because all prospecting goes back to the basic premise of this book, that people buy when they're ready to buy, not when you need to make a sale. Therefore, the secret is for you to be in front of prospective customers when they are ready to buy!

The Process of Nurture Prospecting

Here's the process:

- Make contact.
- Qualify the prospective customer.
- Attempt to make an appointment to make a sale.
- Seek permission to stay in touch.
- Put valuable, useful information in front of your prospective customer regularly and consistently. (You can make each contact "hot" by including a response mechanism.)
- Contact your prospective customer at a strategic point.
- Attempt to make a sale.

- If you do not make a sale, seek permission to stay in touch.
- Continue to put valuable, useful information in front of your prospective customer regularly and consistently. (Again, you can make it "hot" by including a response mechanism.)
- Contact your prospective customer.
- Attempt to make a sale.
- Decide whether or not you want the process to continue.

This process will allow you to stay in front of your prospective customers, provide them valuable, useful information (more about that later), give them a chance to contact you, allow you to get in touch with them again, and so on. The result? When they have need of or want your product or service, who will they think of first? You.

A word of caution here. The material you send should not be overly commercial or solicitous. Instead, it needs to be valuable, vital information that they can use. Items such as pamphlets, booklets, research reports, case studies, white papers, insider tip sheets, and related information-rich tools are what you need to send (either by e-mail or regular mail). I strongly recommend e-mail: it's much more cost-effective.

Nurture Prospecting: How It Works

After you have had any of the conversations with any prospective customer as outlined with any strategy in this book and have determined that he or she is not prepared to buy, you simply say, "It appears as if you are not prepared to make a purchase decision (or proceed further) at this time. Is that correct?"

If the answer is "Yes. I'm just not ready,"

simply say, "Since that's the case, would you mind if I make arrangements for you to receive valuable information from time to time? It will keep you abreast of what is going on in [your industry]."

If the answer is "No, I wouldn't mind" or "Yes, I would like to receive some things,"

simply say, "Good. Do you prefer e-mail? Frankly, we've found it is faster, easier, and more efficient. What is your e-mail address? By the way, we never sell, rent, or release, in any way, any of our e-mail contracts. Could I please have yours?"

This is easy now. You have gotten permission to send materials until they say stop, opt out, buy, or go out of business!

If the answer is "No, I don't want to receive anything,"

simply say, "I understand. But do you mind if I contact you personally on an occasional basis to check in with you and determine if your needs or circumstance might change?"

At this point you need to put the prospect into your digital or manual tickler file and call him or her as often as necessary.

If they answer that they'd like to receive information, here is the first e-mail I'd suggest that you put in place:

Subject: Information We Discussed: [title of document]

Dear [first name],

Thanks for expressing interest in [your organization]. As you may recall, [Direct Value Statement]. However, there's more to us than just that. We regularly conduct research and work hard to be at the forefront of what's happening in your industry.

Here's a very specific report for your review [white paper, etc.]:

Click here to download: [title URL].

Sincerely,

[your name]

Reports

Now, what should your reports contain?

It is important that you and your organization appear as a "thought leader" for the market(s) that you serve. As a consequence, your documents should be developed by you and/or a "research division" of your organization. A great way to do that is to identify and help solve the biggest problem that your current and prospective customers have. If you are unable to do that, hire someone who can! Writers are available everywhere. Just find them. This sophisticated strategy of thought leadership will serve you well as you are positioned much better in the minds of your prospective customers. Here are a few beginnings of white paper titles you could consider:

- The 10 Ways to …
- The Hidden Secrets to …
- How to Avoid …
- The Insider Tips to …
- The Three Biggest Things You Need to Know in Order to …
- The Single Biggest Secret Behind …

As an example, here are just a few of the documents we use:

- The 10 Ways That Sales Managers Fail
- The Five Ways Sales Training Fails
- 21 Tips for Selecting a Sales Training Provider
- The Paradox of Urgency and Patience in Consultative Selling

Each of these reports is from five to 20 pages long. (If you'd like to see one of our in-depth reports, go to www.BrooksGroup.com/PhrasesWhitepaper.)

You can do the same … if you are knowledgeable, insightful, and interested in your product, service, or industry. You may want to include a downloadable, fax-back response mechanism with each of your documents as well. Here's an example of one that we use:

tbg

3810 North Elm Street, Ste. 202
Greensboro, NC 27455
(800) 633-7762
info@thebrooksgroup.com

Tell me more about The Brooks Group.
I'm interested in:

☐ Sales Training ☐ Speaking Services

☐ Sales Management Training ☐ Other

☐ Assessments

Simply fill out this form and **fax** it back to **(336) 282-5707**
or call The Brooks Group at **(800) 633-7762**

Name: _____

Company: _____

Title _____

Phone: _____

Email: _____@_____

Address: _____

City, State, Zip: _____

wk11

www.BrooksGroup.com | info@thebrooksgroup.com | (800) 633-7762

The System

Now let's look at the whole system. Remember that it could be a monthly, quarterly, or even bimonthly system. The choice is yours. Let's go!

- Phone conversation #1 as previously outlined
- Lead cultivation e-mail #1
- Lead cultivation e-mail #2
- Lead cultivation e-mail #3
- Phone conversation #2

Make contact in phone conversation #2 by saying, "Hello, _____. I hope you have been receiving the requested reports we have been sending you. Have you been receiving the information?"

Now, ask these questions:

- "Have you found it useful?"
- "What has been most useful?"
- "What would you like to learn more about?"
- "What topics have been most interesting to you?"
- "Is there a way we can help you?"

Determine if the prospective customer is inclined to discuss a purchase at this point.

If so, proceed with your usual sales process.

If not, ask, "Would you like to continue hearing from us?"

If no, delete from your list.
If yes, continue.

- Lead cultivation contact #4
- Lead cultivation contact #5

- Lead cultivation contact #6
- Phone conversation #3

Make contact for phone conversation #3 and say, "Hello, _____. I hope you have been receiving the informative material we have been sending you and that you had requested. Have you been receiving it?"

Now, ask these questions:

- "Have you found it useful?"
- "What has been most useful?"
- "What would you like to learn more about?"
- "What topics have been most interesting to you?"
- "Is there a way we can help you?"

Determine if your prospective customer is inclined to consider a purchase.

If so, proceed with the sales process.

If not, ask, "Would you like to continue hearing from us?"

If yes, continue your cultivation/nurturing process with that person.

If no, delete that prospective customer from your list.

Don't worry that you're saying the same thing on each phone contact. Your prospective customer won't recall what was said in previous calls! You can continue this process for as long as you'd like to do so.

And never forget: anytime your prospective customer returns any response form, he or she is saying, "Yes! Contact me!" Therefore, again, never, ever send any correspondence in this process without including a response mechanism.

Now, let's look at this process again from the perspective of having any prospective customer responding to you via fax, e-mail, phone, or any response mechanism you arrange.

You will send an e-mail (or letter) to your prospective customer:

Subject: Responding to your request [or another, equally good headline/subject]

Thank you for returning the form registering your interest in _____. I am looking forward to talking with you soon. Please accept my best wishes.

Truly yours.

[your name and title]

Now, follow up with a phone call.

You say: "Hello, _____. This is _____. I certainly appreciate your interest and hope that you have enjoyed those things we have forwarded to you. Do you have a few minutes that we might talk?"

If no, schedule a later phone conversation.

If yes, say, "It is good to talk with you. I hope you have been well."

Acknowledge the response. Then say, "I'd like to make arrangements for us to get together, if that's OK with you. But before we do that, I'd like to prepare some things to make our time together more valuable. In order to do that, do you mind if I ask you a few questions?"

- "Has anything changed since the last time we met?"
- "What, specifically, would you like to learn more about?"
- "What circumstances have led to your renewed interest?"

Determine their answers and then say, "I have some time available on my calendar. Do you have your calendar so that we can coordinate a time?"

Schedule your appointment and be sure to confirm it, as described in Chapter 6.

Confirming Appointments Based on Nurture Prospecting

As mentioned earlier in this book, never, ever go on any appointment unless you first confirm it with your prospective customer. In the business-to-business environment, this should be done no less than two or three days prior to your meeting. Business-to-consumer sales can have a shorter timeline.

What do you say?

"Hello, _____. This is [your name], with [your organization]. I'm calling to confirm our appointment for tomorrow at [time]. I'll arrive at [15 minutes in advance]. Are there any instructions I need to know in order to gain access to your office (home)?"

"I look forward to seeing you [tomorrow/day] at [time]. Thank you for your interest and I look forward to seeing you."

Thank-You and Follow-up Notes: What to Write

You should never, ever, have a meeting or even a phone conversation with any prospective customer without following that session with some sort of personal correspondence. And that correspondence should be in writing. Whether it is a handwritten note, a formal letter, or an e-mail depends upon the relationship you have built with the prospective customer.

You should send your note within 24 hours following the meeting, no later. As a general rule, the note should consist of three parts:

1. Thank the prospective customer for the meeting.
2. Recap the meeting.
3. Outline the next steps in the relationship.

Here's an example:

Dear Rob/Mr. Rogers (depending upon your relationship),

Thank you for the generous amount of time you spent with me yesterday. I thoroughly enjoyed our discussion.

I was extremely interested to learn about how you'd like to solve your delivery issues and discover ways that we can help you resolve them.

As we discussed, I will be pulling together some data and examples of how we have done this in the past and will call you next week to set up our next meeting.

Should you have any questions in the meantime, please feel free to give me a call at (555) 555-5555.

My best to you,

[your name and title]

Now, let's look at the note in a different way:

Dear (Name),

Thank you for _____. It was most _____. I was extremely _____ to learn about _____ and _____.

As we discussed, I will _____ and will _____ in order to _____.

Should you have any questions in the meantime, please feel free to _____.

All you have to do is to fill in the blanks with reference to each of the three components—the thank-you, the rehash of the discussion, and the next steps.

Another Type of Thank-You Note: What to Write

Another form of thank-you note that is critical to your relationship arsenal is the thank-you note that you must send to a person who provides you a reference or referral. Fail to do this at your own peril! Don't you like to be thanked for doing something for someone else? You can bet that your referral source feels the same way.

As a general rule, this note should consist of four parts:

1. Thank the referral and commit to contacting the prospective customer.
2. Provide an update of your progress with the prospective customer.
3. Update him or her on the next steps with the prospective customer.
4. Thank the referral again.

This, too, can be a formal message on your organization's letterhead, a handwritten note, or an e-mail. The format, again, depends on the relationship you have with that person. Here's a sample:

Dear Susan:

Thank you so much for referring Barb Horn to me. Please be assured that I will handle my relationship with her as carefully and professionally as I have handled my relationship with you.

I have contacted Ms. Horn and we are planning to get together next week at her office to pursue some ways that we may be able to assist her.

I will contact you following the meeting in order to bring you up to speed on the progress we make. Please accept my sincerest appreciation for allowing me to have the possibility of working with Ms. Horn and her organization.

My very best wishes to you.

Truly yours,

Bill Brooks

Now, let's look at it this way:

Dear _____,

Thank you so much for _____.
Please be assured that I will

_____

_____.

I have contacted _____ and we are planning to _____.

I will contact you _____
in order to _____. Please accept my sincerest appreciation for _____.

My very best to you.

Truly yours,

_____

Conclusion

This section has captured a great deal of the technology and research related to contemporary, 21st-century prospecting. However, never lose sight of the reality that it is not just what you say that matters; what really matters is how you say it.

Prospecting is all about deploying the right strategy, saying the right things, and then saying those things in the right way. And, frankly, communicating the right way to use tone, speed, and sincerity with words is a virtual impossibility with the written word. So, be careful: it's not only what you say but how you say it. And that's the winning difference!

Now, here's a challenge for you. Are you prepared to prospect in some positive, productive way every single day? And this question applies to you however sophisticated you may be, however complex your sales cycle, whatever the price point of your product or service, and whatever level of service your offering demands of you.

Why is that? Here we go again. The secret to selling is to be in front of a prospective customer when he or she is ready to buy, not when you need to make a sale.

It has certainly been a pleasure writing this section. I hope that you find its content as valuable to you as it has been to me. These are the very same strategies, tactics, and phrases that I personally use daily in my sales career. Our sales team uses the same tools—and we have trained tens of thousands of salespeople worldwide to use them as well. Now they're yours. Use them well.

Section Two

Perfect Phrases for the Sales Call

Hundreds of Ready-to-Use Phrases for Any Sale—From Prospect to Close

William T. Brooks

Contents

Introduction   **271**

Part One. The Basics of Selling in the 21st Century   **277**

Chapter 1. The Realities of 21st-Century Selling   **279**

1. The Secret to Selling Is Never in the Selling   279
2. To Sell Successfully, You Must Be in Front of a Qualified Prospect   280
3. You Must Position Yourself Correctly   280
4. There Is Less Margin for Error   281
5. Prospects Must Believe You Have Something Important to Say   281
6. Being Trusted Is More Important Than Being Liked   282
7. Prospects Are Busy   282
8. Prospects Will Buy to Solve their Problems, Not Yours   282
9. Prospects Will Try to Make Your Product or Service a Commodity   283

10. Prospects Will Want the Price Before You
Want to Give It   283
11. Establish the Value or It's All About Price   284
12. Relationships Have Changed   284
Understanding the Realities   284
Six Truths of Selling   285

Chapter 2. The Nine Sales You Must Make First   286
1. If You're Not Sold, No One Else Will Be Either   286
2. If You Have No Prospects, You Will Fail   288
3. Being Trusted Is More Essential Than Being Liked   290
4. The Sale Is All in the Questions   291
5. Selling Is About Providing Solutions   292
6. You Can Minimize Stalls, Objections, and
Delaying Strategies   294
7. Closing Is Not Just Using Closes   296
8. Promise a Lot—and Deliver Even More   297
9. You Must Master Special Situations   298

Chapter 3. Your Direct Value Statement   299
Sample Direct Value Statements   300
Using the Direct Value Statements   301

**Part Two. Scenarios for the Six Steps
of the Sale   303**

Chapter 4. Step 1. Investigate   305
Defeat Negative Self-Talk   305
Step 1. Investigate: Prospecting, Positioning,
and Pre-Call Planning   307
Appointment-Setting Scenarios   309
You Are Calling for an Appointment after Meeting Your
Prospect at an Event   310

You Are Calling a Prospect Who Is a Direct Referral
to You   312
You Are Responding to an Inquiry from the Prospect   316
You Have Sent Materials for Your Prospect to Review   317
You Have Not Sent Materials to Your Prospect and
Are Making a Cold Call   320
Leaving an Effective Voice-Mail Message   328
Confirming Your Appointment   330
Special Situations   332
Dislodging a Competitor   336

Chapter 5. Step 2. Meet Your Prospect   **339**
Statement of Intention and Primary
Bonding Statement   341

Chapter 6. Probe   **346**
Problem Resolution Questions   347
Agitation Questions   349
Solution- and Feeling-Based Questions   351
Needs-Based Questions   353
Feature-Benefit Questions   356
Objection-Testing Questions   358
Yes/No Questions   361
Level–1, –2, and –3 Questions   363
Silver Bullet Questions   365

Chapter 7. Step 4. Apply Your Solutions   **366**
Making Your Recommendation   368
Handling Premature Price Questions   370
Presenting Your Price   373
How to Guarantee That Your Price Will Never
Be Accepted   377
Making the Feature-Benefit Conversion   379
The Power of Course-Correction Questions   381

**Chapter 8. Step 5. Convince Your Prospect
of Your Claims**   **384**
    Getting Satisfied Customers to Help You Sell   389
    Overcoming Objections in the Real World   394

Chapter 9. Step 6. Tie It Up: Finalizing Transactions   **400**
    The Assumptive Close   402
    Cementing and Reinforcing the Sale   406
    Following up the Sale   407

**Part Three. Additional Sales Scenarios:
Three Types of Customers**   **409**

**Chapter 10. Super Sophisticated Selling: Entrepreneurs,
Corporate Executives, Purchasing Managers**   **411**

Selling to Entrepreneurs
How to Form a Special Instant Bond in Your
    First Interaction   414
How to Make Your Product or Service the Right Answer—
    No Matter What You Sell   418
How to Make Your Organization the Ideal Provider   422
How to Move Your Benefits to a Higher Level   425
How to Make Your Price, Rate, or Fee a True Bargain   428
Your Letters and Advertising   430
Words That Don't Work   432

Selling to Corporate Executives (Non-CEO)
How to Form a Special Instant Bond in Your
    First Interaction   434
How to Make Your Product or Service the Right Answer—
    No Matter What You Sell   438
How to Make Your Organization the Ideal Provider   440
How to Move Your Benefits to a Higher Level   444

Make Your Price, Rate, or Fee a True Bargain   446
How to Letters and Advertising   448
Words That Don't Work   450

Selling to a Purchasing Manager
How to Form a Special Instant Bond in Your
    First Interaction   452
How to Make Your Product or Service the Right Answer—
    No Matter What You Sell   456
How to Make Your Organization the Ideal Provider   461
How to Move your Benefits to a Higher Level   466
How to Make Your Price, Rate, or Fee a True Bargain   469
How to Letters and Advertising   471
Words That Don't Work   473

101 Universal Sales Truths   **475**

Introduction

Why This Section Works

The world of selling in the 21st century is far different from that of the last century. And there are lots of factors for that shift. International competition, technology, a shrinking world economy, intensified price pressure, the commoditization of products and services, and rapidly sped-up communication have all combined to make sales an even more demanding career than ever before. Let there be little doubt: the world of selling has certainly changed—and changed forever. In all likelihood, it will change even more as the future unfolds. And it will never be the same again.

What does that mean to you? Lots of things! Like:

- You have less time to get your prospects' attention.
- More and more salespeople are vying for the same prospects' and customers' business.
- Prospects' attention spans are shorter.
- You are facing more barriers that stand between you and your prospects.
- You need to differentiate yourself from everyone else who sells the same product or service you sell.

- Your margin for error is getting smaller and smaller virtually every single day.
- You must be willing to change, to grow, and to study your craft now more than ever before.

If you are to sell well, never forget that sales is all about persuasion. However, persuasion is *not* about verbosity or how long you can speak without either taking a breath or allowing your prospect to speak. Instead, it's all about how you can both efficiently and succinctly provide solutions that specifically address a prospect's unique set of problems. More importantly, it's how effectively you can transport your prospects from where they currently are to where they need or want to be as it relates to their issues, their problems, or the solutions or end results that they ideally would like to gain.

However, don't for one second believe that it's all about memorizing a set of canned responses. Instead, it's first understanding the *why* behind every *how*. It's gaining a complete understanding as to why certain strategies are effective in specific situations. Then, it is all about applying those very same strategies—*not* word for word, but concept by concept. Don't worry about repeating the phrases exactly. Instead, adapt the concept—understand and master the subtlety, the nuances, and the key words that are intended in each strategy. As long as you are close, you will be fine! Just being close is much better than never trying at all. Don't worry about perfection. See what works for you and then move closer and closer to the precise phraseology that is comfortable and natural for you and most effective with your prospects and customers.

In fact, as you read this section you'll see that I might refer to a strategy (primary bonding statement, statement of intention, etc.) and actually use different words and phrases for that strategy at different times in the same chapter. That's *not* a mistake—it's intentional. Except for one phrase (your Direct Value Statement), it's not about memorization—it's about *personalization*. Personalization means you actually *own* the words, phrases, and responses that you use. And there is a big, big difference between memorizing and personalizing!

Organization

Part One of this section consists of three chapters. The first chapter will present the 12 realities of 21st-century selling. It is devoted to providing you an overview of exactly why the contents of this section are so critical to your sales success in terms of the new realities of selling in this century.

Chapter 2 outlines the nine specific sales you will have to make to yourself *before* you can ever expect to sell your product or service to any prospect or customer.

The final chapter of Part One will demonstrate how you can design and deliver your own Direct Value Statement. I urge you to learn to do this word for word. It will serve you well in lots of situations. Fail to do this at your own risk. It's that important.

Part Two contains dozens of very specific, word-for-word scenarios divided among the six steps of the IMPACT Selling System®. These scenarios will give you the exact words to use when prospecting, seeking appointments, meeting customers, qualifying and asking questions, making effective presentations, proving your claims, creating value, presenting price, finalizing transactions, seeking referrals, overcoming objectives, and servicing accounts.

Part Two of the section may, at first glance, appear to be the most important to you. And it *is* important because it reveals the most accurate, precise words, approach, strategy, and philosophy for any situation with any prospect. However, don't underestimate the value of Part One, for it is there that you'll find the essential *whys* behind the *hows*. In the final analysis, they may be the real pearls.

Part Three will reveal a most powerful, one-of-a-kind set of tools that are being published for the very first time anywhere. Based on years of research, they will reveal the very simple, yet profound reality that prospects rarely buy what they need, that instead they always buy what they want!

In this part of the section you will find three unique research reports that will reveal the precise, exact words to use with four types of prospects—the entrepreneur, the corporate executive, and the purchasing manager. Those prospects were selected as a representative sample of the prospects to whom salespeople like you must sell. Whether you sell paint to factories, benefit plans to corporations, software to emerging businesses, or medical supplies to doctors, you'll find something relevant here for dealing more effectively with your prospects.

You will find words to use when describing the relationship that you will forge with each prospect (describing exactly the type of relationship he or she *wants* to have with a salesperson), the benefits of your product or service (describing them in the exact words he or she *wants* to hear), the features of your product or service (presented and positioned as he or she *wants* to buy it), your organization (presented exactly as he or she *wants* a provider to be), and your price, rate, or fee (described and positioned as he or she *wants* to perceive it).

Conclusion

This section is far more than a presentation of a sales philosophy. It is loaded with real-world, how-to-do-it ideas, phrases, tips, and insider secrets that can propel your sales career instantly.

However, please take heed of this heartfelt warning. Don't expect the words to jump off the page and work for you. You'll need to read, understand, practice, master, assimilate, and apply them, first in your mind and then with others in safe, nonthreatening environments before you try to use them in the high-risk world of selling. Trust me: they will work. However, they certainly won't work if you use them amateurishly, clumsily, casually, or with a false sense of confidence. Also, I will totally guarantee that if you do absolutely nothing they won't work at all. The choice is yours.

You'll need to invest the time required to understand each skill and then use the words and terms as often as possible in risk-free environments. This is one case where practice makes perfect—or at least as perfect as the demanding world of selling can be.

Acknowledgments

My heartfelt appreciation to Bonnie Joyce, who continually amazes me with her organizational and clerical skills. Her ability to develop clarity from my sometimes haphazard thoughts is astounding. Her unique ability to decipher my writing even more amazing!

I would also like to thank McGraw-Hill and especially John Woods, who conceived of this project and gave me the opportunity to attack it with the latitude and direction that was required.

Thanks to Bob Magnan of CWL for his expertise in editing the final manuscript.

A special thank-you to all of the staff at The Brooks Group who put up with my difficult, demanding behavior as projects like this tend to put lots of other priorities in the background.

Most of all, I'd like to thank my wife, Nancy. She has continually understood the difficulties and dynamics that the demanding career of speaking, writing, business building, client management, and all the rest put on a relationship. Very few people could have ever done that—and done it so marvelously for 30 years.

Part One

The Basics of Selling in the 21st Century

Chapter 1
The Realities of
21st-Century Selling

There are 12 realities that form the philosophical under-pinning as to why the phrases and terms outlined in this book really work. Why is that? Because sales is a dynamic science that, when practiced correctly, becomes an art form. And although it's constantly changing in tactics, its foundational principles remain constant.

As I suggested in this Section's Introduction, it is a fundamental truth that sales has changed significantly over the past decade or so. In fact, it has changed more in the last eight to 10 years than in the previous 20 to 30 years. Let's take a look at a few of the 21st-century principles that have emerged from those changes.

1. The Secret to Selling Is Never in the Selling

Reality: The secret to selling is never in the selling. Instead, it is always in the continuous act of prospecting.

Most salespeople fail because they lack a sufficient supply of qualified prospects. What does that tell you? That you need to consistently, intelligently, and capably prospect for business no matter how long you have been selling. It never stops. Whether you are vertically integrating an account or attacking an entire market segment, sales is always all about prospecting. And that's true whether you have been selling for two months or two years—or even 30 years or more like me!

2. To Sell Successfully, You Must Be in Front of a Qualified Prospect

Reality: To sell successfully, you must be in front of a qualified prospect when he or she is ready to buy, not when you need to make a sale.

It's all about being the best and most viable available option among many that prospects seek when it comes time for them to make a purchase decision. And there is a fundamental truth that they will make their buying decision on their time schedule, not yours. A major part of that secret is to invest your time intelligently and wisely. You must avoid at all costs merely spending, irresponsibly wasting, or just plain abusing your time with unqualified prospects. You need to expediently and efficiently identify the most promising prospects fast and move beyond those who are not qualified. Your only real asset is time and your only real advantage is how you invest your time and with whom you invest it.

3. You Must Position Yourself Correctly

Reality: You must position yourself, your organization, and your product or service correctly in the mind of the buyer.

Due to competitive pressures, a crowded market, and the commoditization of many products or services, you must differentiate what you do and how you do it from the rest of the pack. And this is becoming even more critical to long-term sales success. And, in the final analysis, how you position yourself will far outdistance how your organization, product, or service is positioned. And that's true no matter how large or small your organization's advertising and promotion budget may be.

4. There Is Less Margin for Error

Reality: There is less margin for error than ever.

This reality mandates that you must always show up on time, fully prepared, equipped with thorough knowledge of your prospects, what they are trying to solve, how they function, how and why they make decisions, and much, much more. Bottom line? Virtually all prospects have a plethora of options from which to choose.Unfortunately for you,you are only one of those choices among many.

As a consequence, you must not only be quick on your feet, but also have the skills to apply your product or service, know exactly how to impart that knowledge to your prospect, and know how you can leverage his or her understanding of it to your best advantage.

5. Prospects Must Believe You Have Something Important to Say

Reality: Prospects will grant appointments only to salespeople whom they perceive as having something important to say to them.

Coming across as desperate or ill-prepared will do nothing to help you maximize on this principle. On the other hand, knowing what to say, when to say it, and precisely how to position yourself will allow you to put it on your side.

Let there be no doubt. Silly, old-school things like aimless cold calling, using "tie-down questions," or memorizing scores of worn-out, old closes will only blow up in your face if that's primarily how you generate new business in this century.

6. Being Trusted Is More Important Than Being Liked

Reality: Being trusted supersedes being liked when selling.

Salespeople who master being trusted clearly outsell those who are merely glad-handers looking for another target of opportunity. All in all, a salesperson who is trustworthy and knows exactly how to demonstrate and communicate that trustworthiness in the very first transactional interaction with a prospect will outperform one who is just a smooth-talking "flash in the pan" at every turn. Which do you want to be? Which should you be? Which are you? What type of sales experience are your prospects and customers looking for and expecting? What type of experience do you actually give them?

7. Prospects Are Busy

Reality: Prospects are busy.

What does that mean to you? Simply that you need to know exactly how to get to the point of your presentation with the greatest speed and efficiency. To move from small talk to positive, effective sales talk with confidence, trust, and ease. Prospects just don't have time to invest in a long, drawn-out journey waiting for you to get to the point.

8. Prospects Will Buy to Solve Their Problems, Not Yours

Reality: Prospects will buy to solve their problems, not yours.

What might be your problem? To make a sale, earn a commission, win a contest, earn a bonus, keep your job, pay your bills, get a promotion, or look good to other people.

The truth is that none of these have anything to do with *their* problem! And just what might be *their* problem? To achieve greater efficiency, make money or a profit, keep their job, fix something that's broken, enhance their organization—or to solve whatever your product or service helps them solve.

9. Prospects Will Try to Make Your Product or Service a Commodity

Reality: Prospects will try to make your product or service a commodity.

Why will they do that? It's really quite simple. In the world of commoditization, price always rules. And prospects are always trying to get the best price. Therefore, if they can reduce whatever product or service you sell to being a commodity, they'll win! Your job is to keep that from happening. However, in order to do that, you must know exactly what, when, and how to deal with it. You need to be prepared to handle "I can get the same thing down the street"—and handle it well.

10. Prospects Will Want the Price Before You Want to Give It

Reality: Prospects will ask the price of your product or service before you're prepared to give it.

Premature price questions are far more the rule than the exception. And, once you offer a price either verbally or in writing, that is likely the only thing your prospect will remember about your product or service!

And if you offer it too soon you will not have created value. Why is that? Because you have not shown how you can satisfy a want, fulfill a need, solve a problem, or resolve an issue.

On the other hand, if you withhold it too long or too clumsily, you'll run the risk of alienating your prospect and creating an adversarial relationship.

Clearly, both of these options are wrong. So, what do you do? Hang on: you'll find out soon.

11. Establish the Value or It's All About Price

Reality: In the absence of value, every transaction will revolve around price.

Salespeople (including you) cannot presume that prospects perceive, understand, and comprehend the value of any offering without having it first interpreted for them. Price is such a dominant factor in today's crowded marketplace that the value you deliver must be so clear in the mind of the buyer that it supersedes his or her drive to seek a progressively lower and lower price.

12. Relationships Have Changed

Reality: The definition of relationships has changed forever.

It's true. Customers are not as loyal as they used to be. Couple that with younger and younger buyers coming into the marketplace who have learned to define relationships in terms of text messaging and Internet communications and the impending changes promise to be cataclysmic for the unprepared.

Those factors, the constant pressure to compare prices, and the emergence of new products, suppliers, and services into the marketplace on a wholesale basis all merge to tell us that the terrain that defines relationships has truly been transformed forever.

Understanding the Realities

All of these harsh realities mean that your fundamental philosophy of sales may need to be modified—as well as the very words, exact phrases, and specific utterances that you have been using. However, there are certain sales truths that have not changed and likely will never change.

For example, the pre-eminent role customers play in the relationship will never, ever change. In spite of this, there have been thousands of cases where a company or organization had the corner on a market and the people falsely believed that they didn't need to change, only to discover that, once their market changed without them and their customers had other choices, ultimately the customer was still in charge! And those customers decided to change suppliers—fast, furiously, and often.

Six Truths of Selling

Here are six truths that will never, ever change in the world of selling, no matter how much the landscape of sales may change:

1. Listening is still the best personal skill a salesperson can ever master.
2. Failing to get in front of the real decision maker is a fatal error.
3. If you can't close sales, you'll never be successful as a salesperson.
4. Successful selling requires a significant level of skill in time and self-management.
5. Great salespeople are simultaneously both competitive and resilient.
6. Sales is all about presence and persuasion.

This book is really all about #6. It's about how to create a strong, positive presence and simultaneously be more persuasive. More specifically, it will show you how to be "succinctly persuasive." How to avoid wasting words, time, and your prospect's attention.

Now, let's get to work!

Chapter 2
The Nine Sales
You Must Make First

Here are the nine specific points on which you will have to sell yourself before you can expect to sell your product or service to any prospect.

1. If You're Not Sold, No One Else Will Be Either

In the last century an entire body of work developed around the concept of "self-talk." That science said that each of us, in the final analysis, is nothing more than a manifestation of everything we have ever heard, read, or believed about ourselves. And that belief is further refined and defined by how we actually utter phrases (usually silently) to ourselves that reflect nothing more than those things we have heard others say, write, or otherwise communicate about us. That is called self-talk. And that self-talk will ultimately define your level of drive, achievement, and motivation. It really is an inside job ... and anchors your personal level of drive, achievement, and willingness to perform at peak levels.

For example, to one child a parent says, "You'll never be as successful as your sister" and a teacher declares, "You just aren't good in math," while to another child a parent says, "You will be great at leading others" and a teacher says, "You have a great deal of potential."

You can guess the result, can't you? The first two create self-doubt, a sense of inadequacy, and a lack of confidence. The latter two do just the opposite. And, in both cases, the children start repeating those very same phrases—good or bad—to themselves. And there is a direct relationship to performance.

But what does this have to do specifically with the profession of sales? More specifically, your view, belief, or the level of confidence you have in your product, service, or organization? In sales as a profession?

Have you ever heard someone say, "All salespeople are crooks" or "Salespeople are people who can't do anything else"? How about this one? "When are you going to get a real job?" Or this gem, "Just promise them anything. Sell it now and we'll worry about fixing it later" or "I know it's only version 1.0; we can always upgrade or improve it with later versions."

These types of comments plant seeds of doubt in us, forcing each and every one of us to wonder about our profession, our products or services, our abilities, our integrity, and a lot more. And it is essential that salespeople (you!) replace all of this negativity with a more positive bias or point of view.

And this can all start with some sort of affirmative, proactive self-talk that enables you to feel more positive, have a clearer and more valuable expectation of yourself and your products or services, and feel better about the organization you represent. To be excited and even grateful—yes, grateful—for what you do, how you do it, and what you have even been placed on this earth to do!

However, it is extremely difficult to use affirmative, proactive self-talk when you are overwhelmed with all types of negativity. What really matters, though, is the way you choose to respond to it, how you choose to frame it, how you choose to define who and what you are. And you do that with positive, productive self-talk. Powerful statements or affirmations that you drive into your subconscious. Phrases that deflect, defeat, and reverse the mounds of negativity that come your way about sales, success, your offerings, your self-management skills, and all the rest that salespeople face day after day.

There's no doubt about it. The first sale that any salesperson must make is to himself or herself. And the phrases that you use when talking to yourself are, in fact, the first set of phrases that you will really need to master. We'll deal with that shortly.

You likely opened this book hoping to deal with something else first. Perhaps how to deal with objections, stalls, or put-offs. But if you don't deal with your own sense of direction, self-worth, self-image, and self-belief first, all else will fail. That is precisely why the very first phrases that we will dig into will be the phrases you need to master in order to sell yourself on yourself and your future, your product or service, and the value that you deliver to your prospects and customers.

It's a basic reality of sales. If you're not sold, no one else will be, either.

2. If You Have No Prospects, You Will Fail

If you have no prospects you will fail—guaranteed! Prospecting is the key to your sales career.

The single, most fundamental reason why most salespeople fail, no matter what they sell, is that they lack a sufficient supply of qualified prospects to whom they can tell their story.

How about you? Have you ever examined your pipeline only to discover that you definitely have too few prospects? Or, perhaps you have a lot of prospects—but they really aren't qualified.

Who, then, are truly qualified prospects? In my experience, after over 30 years of selling and consulting in over 500 industries, truly qualified prospects have five common traits:

- They have a need for your product or service and legitimately want it to solve a problem, fill a gap, give them pleasure, or resolve an issue.
- They have the position, power, and legitimate authority to pay for it.
- They have a legitimate, self-defined sense of urgency to obtain it.
- They have some degree of trust in you, your product or service, and your organization.
- They are eagerly willing to listen to you.

Once you have identified those qualified prospects, you will have to deal with some very specific challenges or unique situations in trying to get face-to-face with them. We'll deal with each of these in detail later. However, at this point it is essential to stress the importance of the initial interaction that prospects have with you and/or anything about you. That means your voice, written communication, voice-mail messages, door-opening premium, or anything else that serves as the very first interaction between you and a prospect.

Every relationship you'll have with any prospect must start with some interaction. And that first interaction will define the level of receptivity with which that prospect will consider you and whatever you are selling. It will also, in large measure, define the level of trust that will forge your ongoing relationship. Therefore, the first interaction, with the right person, is an absolute essential for you to master. You must define it carefully, it must be accurate, you must think it through thoroughly, and you must execute it flawlessly and with confidence. Anything less is unacceptable and guaranteed to place you in the pile of also-rans who tried their hand at sales and were cast out because they were unable to gain the attention of the right people—the ones who can pay you for your products or services and would, if necessary, move heaven and earth to get what you're selling if you were to present it to them properly.

3. Being Trusted Is More Essential Than Being Liked

We talked about this in Chapter 1. Are you fundamentally an approval seeker? Do you say things that you believe allow your prospects to identify with you and you with them? Do you ask them about their collection of antique cars, framed autographs, stuffed fish, or family pictures?

If you do, you'll just be one more face in the crowd. What do you think the last dozen or so salespeople who have entered their office, place of business, or home asked them about? The same things?

How are you different? Asking prospects about the same things makes you the same. It makes you a walking, talking stereotype that fits the image and style of every salesperson for those prospects. And that's not good. It makes you nothing more than a "glad-handing approval seeker."

Let me ask you a question. If you had to deal with the same questions about the same things day in and day out, how would you feel? The typical prospect's response to the typical salesperson goes something like this: "They'll start with small talk and then, when they think I 'like' them, it's time for them to move to sales talk." Unfortunately, for most salespeople, the transition from small talk to sales talk is about as smooth as shifting gears in a pre-owned car with a defective transmission.

Later on we'll deal with the real secrets to avoiding making this first impression. At this point, though, it is critical that we discuss the psychology of this whole interaction.

You want to sell. And your prospect wants to avoid being sold ... or at least avoid paying your premium price. It's really that simple. And that's what sales is fundamentally all about. However, the prospect *may* be interested in buying. And that's not double-talk. What I mean is that prospects don't want to be sold. However, they may really want and even need what you are selling. And they want to buy from someone whom they trust, someone who inspires confidence. Quite simply, they merely want to believe that they will receive everything promised to them in exchange for a fair price.

Unfortunately, "glad-handing approval seekers" don't fit that expectation. They may be glib, friendly, and positive, but they don't necessarily come across as being totally trustworthy, 100% honorable, and completely professional.

On the other hand, a salesperson who matches the pace and attitude of the prospect, understands what that prospect really wants, allows the prospect to engage in small talk if he or she chooses to do so (but doesn't force it), and allows the process to move at the prospect's pace will generally sell better.

4. The Sale Is All in the Questions

A great deal of time will be devoted to this topic in this book. The reason? Sales is all about what you ask, not what you say. Unfortunately, most salespeople believe that it's all about the presentation, their ability to be persuasive, the smoothness of their delivery, and the "power of the close." All of this *is* important. However, what if it's the wrong presentation? What if it's a great presentation to the wrong person? What if it's persuasive, but it persuades someone to make a decision that's not in his or her best interest? What if it's a presentation that falls on deaf ears?

The questions start long before you ever get in front of a prospect. First, you question yourself—and answer the tough questions about the prospect, your presence, and more. Then, you need to ask yourself questions about your product or service. Next, you need to consider the questions your prospect is likely to ask you. And then the questions you'll need to ask your prospect, both before and when you present your product or service. And, ultimately, you'll ask your prospect to buy your product or service.

There are definite questions you must ask yourself as you prepare for your prospect. There are questions you need to know that are on your prospect's mind as you first approach him or her. There are questions to make sure your prospect is ready to hear your presentation. There are questions you'll need to ask to determine what your prospect will buy, when he or she will buy it, how, and under what conditions. There are questions to determine when and how to present your price, justify your case, and ultimately finalize the transaction. Then there are questions you'll need to ask your prospect in order to secure the purchase.

Yes, sales is all about questions. You know that you really can question your way to the sale, don't you? And it is far easier to do that than to talk your way into it. Another truth? It is not really difficult at all to talk your way out of a sale! Just ask lots of salespeople who do it everyday. They sell their product or service ... and then actually buy it back!

5. Selling Is About Providing Solutions

You're not selling products or services. You're offering solutions. Present what you sell so people want to buy.

Let me ask you a critical, foundational question. Do you know the subtle difference between a product-driven presentation and an application-based solution? As obvious as this might sound, lots of salespeople don't really know the difference. And many of those who do, unfortunately, fail to apply that knowledge in the real, rough-and-tumble world of selling.

Oh, they can philosophically discuss "meeting prospect's needs," "addressing customer concerns," or their "value proposition" with great ease. However, when it's time to make a targeted, prospect-centric presentation, they fall terribly short of the mark.

Earlier I mentioned salespeople who try to sell prospects something rather than allowing them to buy what they legitimately need, want, or would gain the most from acquiring. Have you ever been like that? If so, what drives you and others to do that? A contest? A higher commission? A bonus? Insufficient product knowledge relative to what the prospects really should have bought? Laziness? Pressure from the boss?

There are lots of reasons to do this wrong—and only one to do it right. And here it is. Your prospects and customers deserve the wisdom of your best, most thoughtful recommendation—a recommendation to help them maximize whatever they are trying to get from your product or service. And for you to fail in that responsibility for whatever personal reasons is simply a failure to understand the essence of *professional* selling.

And what is that essence? The secret to *professional* selling is to be in front of a qualified prospect when he or she is ready to buy and then to present your product or service in such a way that it solves his or her problem, addresses his or her need, or satisfies a want he or she may have. It's that simple.

However, simple isn't always easy, is it? Too many things get in the way. And, usually, we're the source or cause of a lot of those things. Here are just a few.Ego.Greed. A lack of confidence in ourselves or what we're selling. Failure to actively listen to the prospect. Believing that we know what's best for the prospect in spite of overwhelming evidence otherwise, making false assumptions about the prospect, the conditions, or the circumstances. And there are many more things that get in the way of professional selling.

Selling is really all about presenting your product or service persuasively within the context of how it addresses your prospect's stated, implied, or implicit need, want, or circumstance. And then basing your recommendation on fact and articulating it with persuasion and emotion to create a compelling story that allows your prospect to see, feel, understand, and value your solution. It really is that simple.

6. You Can Minimize Stalls, Objections, and Delaying Strategies

"Hey, you've forced me to resist!" Maybe no prospect has ever told you that in just so many words. Yet that feeling is behind stalls, objections, and delaying strategies.

We'll deal with all of these reactions later. Why? Because any book on sales has to have some of that "stuff" in it.However, you want the truth, don't you?

In most cases a prospect will object, stall, or use other delaying strategies only if you haven't built trust or you haven't asked the right questions or you've asked the right questions but haven't listened to the answers or you've presented the wrong solution or you've failed to create value that offset the perception of price or you've moved the prospect through the sales process too fast or your prospect just doesn't believe the claims you've made.

It's really that simple. So, if you want to eliminate such problems, deal with each of the aforementioned issues one at a time as you move through the sale. We'll see exactly how to do that shortly.

However, to presume that prospects won't object to things like price, terms, delivery, or conditions would be both irresponsible and naïve. Therefore, you need the tools and skills to contend with the experienced, trained buyer who absolutely believes that it always boils down to some sort of hand-to-hand (or at least verbal) combat. Yet it is possible to at least minimize the intensity of that combat by applying proper and professional selling strategies before the prospect begins to resist.

Never forget a few, critical things in your sales career. Success in sales is really all about prospecting, pre-call planning, properly positioning yourself and your product or service, building trust, asking the right questions, addressing your prospect's situation with an accurate understanding of what he or she wants to accomplish, creating value, and allowing your prospect to feel free to object to anything that causes concern or difficulty.

Are objections really a sign of interest? Maybe. At least you haven't been thrown out, yet, have you? If your prospect is going to take the time to protest and give you a chance to present your solution again, it would appear that he or she is at least willing to give you another chance. Perhaps the prospect has no other source, maybe someone told him or her to buy from you, or perhaps he or she feels as if you're the only reliable source. There are lots of reasons to object—and many others to buy. But just remember: at least the prospect hasn't thrown you out—yet.

So, seize the opportunity. Deal with whatever your prospect throws your way. But do it professionally, ethically, and confidently. Learn to manage objections. This book will show you precisely how to do that in a formulaic way.

7. Closing Is Not Just Using Closes

The key to finalizing transactions is to make prospects happy to buy from you—and then to get them to commit.

Making sales is all about asking people to take advantage of your offer. Remember: if you fail to ask your prospect to buy, you will have accomplished nothing. If you don't make some effort to gain closure, don't expect your prospect to take your product or service of his or her own volition. Closing is essential. No agreement, no sale. No decision to purchase equals a failed effort.

In the grand scheme of things, however, the value of learning scores of closing techniques, memorizing closing phrases, or mastering power closes is far overblown. If you have done everything to this point successfully, finalizing a sale is not, will not, and never should be a major difficulty. So this book will contain surprisingly few closes. In fact, only one.

The real secret is to make prospects actually happy to buy from you. It is an old, old, old but proven sales truth that people don't like to be sold. They like to buy. Your job is to make them happy to do that. But never forget: you'll have to ask them to make a decision to do it. And that takes knowledge, skill, tenacity, and frankly, some real old-fashioned courage. And nothing and nobody can give you that courage—not this book or any other, not I, not any motivational speaker, not any audio CD or DVD. You have to get that courage for yourself.

Courage comes from confidence. Confidence comes from preparation. So, it all goes back to preparation and knowledge. And this book *can* help you in that. Therefore, never forget that because closing sales really is an inside job, you are personally responsible for at least learning how to do it.

8. Promise a Lot—and Deliver Even More

Don't, even for one second, believe the old nonsense about "under-promising and overdelivering." To be successful in today's crushingly competitive selling environment you need to give some serious thought to adopting a different philosophy—one that can truly differentiate you from virtually every single competitor.

Here's that philosophy: "Promise a lot but work to deliver even more!"

That means that you actually have to do the things you have committed to doing. It also means that you must have the resources—the delivery, customer service, operational support, etc.—that enable you to do them.

It also means a lot more work on your part: more time, effort, energy, commitment, dedication, and personal follow-through. It means that you can't make a sale and just walk away. And that's true no matter what you sell—products, services, processes, or systems. It is totally incumbent upon you, and you alone, to ensure that your customers experience the level of service, confidence, use, and application that you have promised them. You can make the first sale without follow-up strategies—but just don't expect to sell to that prospect again. Make it easier for yourself to keep selling: deliver what you've promised . . . and more!

And never forget one very important thing: you are first and foremost your prospects' most critical link to your organization. When things go right, you have a great chance to sell them more. If things don't go well, you need to bear the brunt of their dismay. The onus is on you to win or lose prospects and to retain or lose customers. And those stakes are too high to risk by being lazy, lethargic, or irresponsible.

9. You Must Master Special Situations

There are many unique circumstances that you will have to master if you ever hope to be a super successful salesperson. And those circumstances center primarily around two specific issues—handling price and dislodging competitors who are already providing products or services to your prospect. Without a doubt, these two issues most often prove to be the most difficult for salespeople, no matter their level of experience or expertise.

The first, price, really requires an entire book to explore. In fact, I have co-authored just such a book that deals with this one complex issue. Suffice it to say at this point that your ease in handling the myriad questions and problems that revolve around price will be one of your major challenges. And here's why.

Sales is most fundamentally all about margin. Don't for one second believe that you can survive very long in the world of sales if you get into discounting to meet a competitor's price or in some other way eroding margin. Highly professional salespeople know that the secret to a long-term sales career is how well they deal with price issues and maintain margin despite the efforts of prospects to get them to reduce the price.

The second issue, dislodging a competitor, requires tact, patience, and skill. It involves one of the more subtle and precise skills you will ever have to master and also some precise information and questions that you will have to master in order to be able to expand the reach and increase the depth of your sales effort. Ironically, that skill is really far more a matter of pre-call planning and intelligent questioning than of persuasion.

One key truth should be both clear and implicit: your best customer is someone else's top prospect! So defend the high ground. And you should simultaneously make someone else's best customer your top prospect, too. That's just the way it is in sales, isn't it?

Chapter 3
Your Direct
Value Statement

W hat are the prospecting situations where you find yourself most often? They can likely be broken into the following categories:

- Face-to-face, formally or informally
- By telephone
- At tradeshows
- Through referrals from current customers
- Through referrals from people other than customers
- At networking events

In each of these situations you'll need to know the importance and use of your own, one-of-a-kind Direct Value Statement (DVS). This is a straightforward, succinct statement that clearly and declaratively communicates the fundamental reason why your organization exists and why you're selling its products or services. And it is likely the most important thing you'll learn in this book. Yet most salespeople never master the concept. In fact, surprisingly, some never even know about it.

Sample Direct Value Statements

- We assist our clients in the banking industry to improve their profitability. We do this by reducing their costs, improving product performance, and geometrically expanding their markets.

The DVS is such an important concept that we'll be spending some time showing you how to design your own. Why is your DVS so important? Because it succinctly (there's that word again!), clearly, and very precisely defines what you do and how you do it. Better yet, it defines clearly what you do and how you do it that benefits your customers … and identifies your core customers. It also plays a central role in virtually every prospecting situation in which you will ever find yourself. In fact, I refer to it in every prospecting scenario explained in this section.

No matter your business, it can always start with the same phrase:

"We assist clients (or. customers) in the _____ industry (or business) to _____. We do this by _____." However, in order to do that, it's important for you to really understand what end-result benefits you actually deliver to your customers. You also need to know what end-result benefits your prospects and customers actually want to gain, enjoy, achieve, or have.

Here are several examples:

- "We assist our clients (or customers) in the interior design industry to provide their clients a wide variety of cost-effective floor coverings. We do this by _____."

- "We assist our clients (or customers) in the real estate industry to pass their state real estate exams easier, faster, and the first time. We do this by _____."
- "We assist our clients (or customers) in the agricultural industry to grow greater yields from their land and enjoy greater profits. We do this by _____."

Using the Direct Value Statements

Your Direct Value Statement is extremely important to you. You can use it (as you'll see) for gaining appointments, meeting people, answering the question, "What do you do?" and in lots of other situations.

Again, the structure is always the same: "We assist our _____ in the _____ industry to _____. We do this by _____."

No matter what your business, venture, service, or industry, this statement will work for you. Therefore, I'd urge you to give some serious, serious thought to answering these four questions when developing your own Direct Value Statement.

- Do you work with individuals, organizations, enterprises, associations, or governments?
- Do you specialize in an industry? Market? Type of business?
- What do you help your customers to do? Reduce costs? Improve productivity? Reduce turnover? Maximize returns? Gain market share? Enhance stock value? Improve profits?
- How do you do that? By improving processes? Improving manufacturing yield? Providing upgraded equipment?

If you cannot communicate the fundamental reason why people or organizations choose to do business with you and how you do what you do, you will have a very serious problem in prospecting for customers. In fact, if you can't verbalize those things, you'll likely never even get your foot in the door.

In the final analysis, people will choose to do business with you in order to reduce or remove a problem, solve an issue, improve a situation, or enhance their position. They are vitally interested in securing solutions. That's really what it is all about.

Some more examples:

- "We assist our clients (or customers) in the communication industry to reduce personnel costs. We do this by offering screening and assessment services, hiring systems, and retention programs."
- "We assist veterinarians in rural markets to provide better care to large farm animals. We do this by having the largest research facility in the world with more scientists dedicated solely to large animal care."
- "We assist teachers in elementary schools to provide real-time experiences for their students. We do this by having over 300 real-world learning products available at discount prices that we market through home parties for teachers, sponsored by teachers."

  Your turn. Fill in the blanks of your value statement.
- We assist _____ [customers] in _____ [industry or occupation] to _____ [how you help]. We do this by _____ [your solution].

Of all the things that are explained in this book, this one single concept could very well be the most important to your sales career. Craft your DVS and use it over and over again. It will prove to be invaluable to you in gaining appointments with even the most difficult prospects.

Part Two

Scenarios for the Six Steps of the Sale

art Two presents scenarios that follow the six key steps of the sale, according to the IMPACT Selling System, as outlined below. These scenarios will provide the words to use when prospecting, seeking appointments, meeting prospects and customers, qualifying prospects and asking questions, making effective presentations, proving your claims, creating value, presenting price, finalizing transactions, seeking referrals, overcoming objections, and servicing accounts.

Nobody can provide the exact words for you, of course, because the right words must be appropriate to your products or services and must fit the specific situation with your prospect and his or her words. However, in these scenarios I provide phrases that use effective strategies and I explain how those strategies work, putting in italics words and phrases that are key to making the strategies work.

IMPACT Selling System[1]

There are six stept's in the IMPACT process system:

1. This complete system is described in detail in *Sales Techniques,* William T. Brooks (New York: McGraw-Hill, 2004).

Investigate—Prospecting, Positioning, Pre-Call Planning
- *Objective:* To pre-call plan, position yourself properly, and gain a face-to-face appointment with a qualified prospect

Meet—Building face-to-face trust and rapport
- *Objective:* To set the face-to-face sales process in motion

Probe—To have your prospect identify, verbalize, and discuss his or her needs, wants, and desires
- *Objective:* To determine what, when, how, and why your prospect will buy your product or service

Apply—To show your prospect how your product or service will solve his or her problem, fill a need, or satisfy a want he or she has verbalized
- *Objective:* To recommend and present your product or service in a way that clearly matches the solution your prospect is trying to achieve

Convince—To corroborate your claims
- *Objective:* To provide powerful social, statistical, or third-party proof of your claims

Tie it up—To finalize the transaction, cement, and reinforce the sale
- *Objective:* To empower your prospect to buy, solidifying the sale, servicing, and vertically integrating the new account

Clearly, appropriate phrases must fall within the context of each step. I would simply like for you to understand these words, phrases, and series of responses within the larger context of each step in which they are found. That's the foundation of Part Two.

Chapter 4
Step 1. Investigate

Before we get into the specifics of the Investigate step, there are some preliminaries to take up that will have relevance for all steps. Let's deal with them now.

Defeat Negative Self-Talk

We are starting this critical section of this book with the exact, precise words related to self-talk for one simple reason. I said earlier that it all starts with you. Remember the reality that we discussed in Chapter 2: "If you're not sold, no one else will be, either." Here's how to deal with that essential issue.

I recommend positive affirmations to convince yourself of your own capabilities, the importance of sales as a profession, and the value of your product, service, or organization. Choose one, two, or three of the phrases from each of the lists below and repeat it or them silently to yourself regularly, up to 30 times each, in the morning and in the evening, over an extended period of time, such as 30 days.

Defeat Self-Sabotage

This section will tell you exactly what to say personally and privately to yourself in order to defeat self-sabotaging comments you tend to make to yourself about yourself, such as "I'll never be wealthy" or "I'll never be successful" or "I'm not worthy of success."

Positive Affirmations

- I am a capable, confident, professional salesperson.
- I deserve to be successful.
- I am a person who achieves goals and I am fulfilled by what I do.

Defeat Negative Thoughts about Sales Profession

The following are statements that you can make to yourself to defeat negative comments relative to your perception of sales as a profession, such as "Sales is not highly regarded as a profession."

Positive Affirmations

- Sales is an honorable profession worthy of my best efforts.
- Sales is a profession that allows me to create great value for my customers.
- Without me, my customers' most important needs, wants, and desires could never be satisfied.

Defeat Negative Thoughts About Product/Service

Here are some things that you should say to yourself in order to defeat negative comments relative to your product or service, such as "My product isn't nearly as good as I am asked to represent it as being" or "Our price is way too high for what we offer."

Positive Affirmations

- My product/service is worth a lot more than I ask my prospects and customers to pay for it.
- My product/service is invaluable to my prospects and customers.

- In the absence of my product/service, my prospects or clients would not be as successful as they need to be.

Defeat Self-Talk about Your Organization

These are statements that you should make to yourself in order to defeat negative self-talk relative to your organization, such as "My employer doesn't deliver value to our customers."

Positive Affirmations

- My company and I work hard to ensure we always promise a lot and deliver more.
- My company is well respected and delivers even more than it promises.
- My employer is the best in our industry

Tip: Select one affirmation from each section (yourself, sales, product/service, and employer/organization), place each on a card that is visible to you at least twice daily, and silently repeat each one up to 30 times a day for 30 days. You'll be surprised at the result! But only if you really believe it will work and you do it daily.

Step 1. Investigate: Prospecting, Positioning, and Pre-Call Planning

Objective. To gather sufficient information about your market and individual prospects within it to enable you to make the best possible sales presentation.

There are four key roles that various people can play inside your prospect's organization:

- **Buffer**—the person whose job is to keep you out
- **User**—the person who will utilize your product or service

- **Check writer**—the person who will approve the purchase
- **Internal advocate**—the person in the organization who can help you

Early in the sales process the internal advocate is the most important person to you. Why is that? That is the person who can guide you through the difficulties that you will inevitably encounter. You will need to find a way to identify and get in front of this person. And, as you will see, the valuable information you can glean from this person will be extremely critical to you when you get in front of the check writer. The following are questions to which you must uncover the answers very early on in the sales process. You need to have the internal advocate provide specific answers to these questions:

- "What organization will I be competing against for this business?"
- "Who, by name, is the salesperson I will be competing against?"
- "How strong a relationship does that person have with the organization?"
- "How strong a relationship does his/her organization have?"
- "How long has he/she had those relationships?"
- "What do the buyers like most about the competition?"
- "What do they like least?"
- "What type of time frame is the organization working with to make a decision?"
- "What type of budget do they have in mind?"
- "What is their opinion of my company? Our product/service? Me?"
- "What do they look for in a salesperson?"
- "What is most important—price, quality, delivery, or service?"

- "What is the one thing that I could do to lose this sale?"
- "How is the organization formally structured?"
- "How does the organization go about making decisions?"
- "What is the likelihood of change or reorganization within the organization?"
- "How much depth will I need in the account to ensure that I stay vital?"
- "What is the single, most critical buying motive for the user? For the check writer?"

You need to develop such a deep sense of rapport and trust with your internal advocate that he or she will readily, openly, and easily provide you the answers to these questions.

Just who might this internal advocate be? It might be the buffer, the user, or even the check writer. Bottom line? This is a person, inside your targeted organization, who sincerely believes that your solution is the best, most ideal alternative for the organization to select.

Equipped with this information, you will be well prepared to move forward. Fail to ask these questions and you will be ill-equipped to know precisely how and exactly when to proceed.

Appointment-Setting Scenarios

These scenarios will be presented in order from the most effective to the least effective. All will be methods for gaining appointments by telephone. There are, of course, other ways (like drop-in cold-calling on an unsuspecting prospect). However, they are far less effective and of significantly less value.

You Are Calling for an Appointment after Meeting Your Prospect at an Event

Your prospect's gatekeeper answers the phone.

You hear: "Hello. Bart Decker's office. This is Heidi. How may I help you?"

You say: "Good morning, Heidi. I recently met Mr. Decker at [insert event]. He asked me to give him a call and I promised him I would. I'm wondering if you could connect us?"

You hear: "Certainly."

You hear: "Hello, this is Bart Decker. May I help you?"

You say: "Hello, Mr. Decker. This is _____. We met recently at the _____. As you may recall, I indicated that I'd call you and you suggested I do so. Do you have a few minutes right now?"

Two possibilities:

You hear: "No."

You say: "Can we make an appointment for a call at a more convenient time?"

or

You hear: "Yes."

  You say: "Good. As you recall, I'm with _____. [Insert your Direct Value Statement.] Would it make sense for us to sit down and discuss how we might help you further?"

Three possibilities:

You hear: "Yes."
You say: "Let's schedule an appointment."

or

You hear: "I'm not sure."

You say: [Proceed to ask qualifying questions to have the prospect verbalize a potential problem you can solve.]

or

You hear: "No."

You say: [Qualify the prospect further to determine if there is some possible way to meet.]

You Are Calling a Prospect Who Is a Direct Referral to You

This usually means someone who knows the prospect has referred you to the prospect.

Your prospect's assistant or secretary answers the phone.

You hear: "Good morning. Lester Jamison's office. This is Lori. How may I help you?"

You say: "Good morning, Lori. My name is _____ with _____. Jack Perry, a mutual friend of Mr. Jamison's and mine, *asked* me to give him a call and I *promised* him I would."

Three possibilities:

You hear: "Mr. Jamison isn't in."

You say: "I'm sorry that I can't talk with him. However, do you have his schedule so that I can be sure to talk directly with him?"

Obtain time frames and set up a firm telephone appointment with the gatekeeper. Remember: this is a powerful scenario—you are entering with a referral.

or

You hear: "Mr. Jamison isn't in. Would you like to leave a message?"

You say: "How would you recommend I do that? Would it be better to leave a message with you or would you suggest that I leave a voice mail?"

Note: In either case, re-emphasize the "asked"-"promised" phrase when you leave either a message or a voice mail.

Remember, also, that your singular goal is to set up a phone conversation to establish a face-to-face selling situation.

or

You hear: "Let me check with Mr. Jamison."

Three possibilities can occur:

You hear: "He doesn't have time to talk with you now."

You say: "I can understand that. However, do you know if there's a time when he might be available?"

or

You say: "Mr. Perry was very eager for me to talk with him. Let me ask you this. Could I drop something in the mail that he might be able to review? If that's acceptable, I'll call in a week or so to see if he's had a chance to review it. Is that OK?"

In this case, it is perfectly acceptable to confirm the correct address for sending materials to ensure that there is no delay in delivery.

or

You hear: "He wants to know what this is all about."

You say: "Please tell him that I have provided some valuable ideas to Mr. Perry, and he felt very strongly that I should talk with Mr. Jamison."

You may be able to get through to your prospect based upon your response to the gatekeeper. If that's the case, be sure to remember that your sole, singular goal is to gain an appointment with your prospect.

If you are requested to send materials, do so. However, try

to set a firm time to call again to determine your prospect's response to the materials and to make an appointment.

or

You hear: "I'll connect you."

You say: "Thank you very much."

You hear: "Good morning, this is Lester Jamison."

You say: "Good morning. As Lori may have told you, my name is _____. Jack Perry *asked* me to give you a call and I *promised* him I would."

You hear: "How is Jack?"

You say: "He's fine … and suggested to me that we have been helpful to him in some ways that may be of interest to you as well."

You hear: "What is this all about? *or* What do you do? *or* How can I help you?"

You say: "[Insert your Direct Value Statement.]"

Again, your sole goal is to secure a face-to-face presentation. You may be able to make an appointment right away based on the power of the referral source. If not, you may want to get permission to forward materials and follow up with another phone call.

You hear: "Hello. Bart Decker's office. This is Heidi. How may I help you?"

You say: "Good morning, Heidi. I recently met Mr. Decker at [insert event]. He *asked* me to give him a call, and I *promised* him I would. I'm wondering if you could connect us?"

You hear: "Certainly."

You hear: "Hello, this is Bart Decker. May I help you?"

  You say: "Hello, Mr. Decker. This is _____. We met recently at the _____. As you may recall, I indicated that I'd call you and you suggested I do so. Do you have a few minutes right now?"

Two possibilities:

You hear: "No."

You: Make an appointment to call at a more convenient time.

or

You hear: "Yes."

You say: "Good. As you recall, I'm with _____.

[Insert your Direct Value Statement.] Would it make sense for us to sit down and discuss how we might help you further?"

Three possible answers to this question:

You hear: "Yes."

You: [Schedule an appointment.]

or

You hear: "I'm not sure."

You: [Proceed to ask qualifying questions to have the prospect verbalize a potential problem you can solve.]

or

You hear: "No."

You: [Proceed to qualify the prospect further to turn the situation around and determine if there is some possible way to meet.]

You Are Responding to an Inquiry from the Prospect

Such inquiries may come from an e-mail response, a response to a mailing, or even a voice-mail message.

Your prospect answers the phone ...

You hear: "Hello, this is Doris Maloney."

You say: "Hello, Ms. Maloney. My name is _____ with _____. I'm calling you in response to your communication with us. As you may recall, you [insert action—called us, left us a message, sent in a response card, etc.] with reference to our [insert your product or service] ."

You hear: "Yes, I recall doing that."

You say: "Good. As you know, [insert your Direct Value Statement]. If you don't mind my asking, is there something in particular that I might be able to help you with?"

Your goal here is to get a question that you will answer and then use to lead you to other questions that the prospect wants to have solved.

Then your goal will be one of three: to set a face-to-face appointment, if relevant; to make a phone sales presentation, if appropriate; or to deduce that the prospect is not qualified.

You Have Sent Materials for Your Prospect to Review

Other than through a prior meeting or a client referral, this is a much more powerful way to approach prospects than through any unsolicited, whether direct phone or drop-in.

SITUATION #1

You encounter a very difficult, highly resistant gatekeeper.

You hear: "Good afternoon. Ms. Smithson's office. This is Barbara."

You say: "Good afternoon, Barbara. My name is _____ with _____. [Insert your Direct Value Statement.] I'm following up on some material I sent last week. I'm wondering if Ms. Smithson is available?"

You hear: "She doesn't take calls from people trying to sell her something."

You say: "I can understand that. However, I've got a *problem* and I need your *help*. Who, in your organization, handles decisions related to [insert your product or service]?"

You hear: "That would be Ms. Smithson. However, I know she won't take your call. She never does."

You say: "I do understand. However, maybe you could help me. Do you know if she received the materials I sent?"

Three possibilities:

You hear: "Yes, she has."

You say: "Great. If that's the case, I wonder if I could talk with her about her reaction to what I sent?"

or

You hear: "No, she hasn't." … or … "I don't know."

You say: "Let me ask you this. Could I go ahead and forward some new material to her? Perhaps I could follow-up next week to see if she had a chance to review it."

This situation, unfortunately, is not unusual. Many gatekeepers are given the primary duty of keeping you out, to serve as the buffer. Never forget: your goal is simple, straightforward, and clear—to get an appointment with the prospect. Period. Remember: never alienate the gatekeeper.

However, you may need to circumvent the gatekeeper by sending material to your prospect and then going directly to a voice-mail message, leaving a powerful, benefit-rich statement, hoping to either make your prospect eager to expect your next call or have your prospect tell the gatekeeper to anticipate your call.

SITUATION #2

You have previously forwarded materials for your prospect to review and are now calling to gain an appointment.

You hear: "Good afternoon. Mr. Price's office. This is Janet speaking. How may I help you?"

You say: "Hello, Janet. My name is _____ with _____. [Insert your Direct Value Statement.] I recently forwarded some materials to Mr. Price about our organization. Do you know if he has received them?"

Three possibilities:

You hear: "I don't know."

You say: "I sent it last week. I'm wondering if I could talk with Mr. Price to see if he has received it and had a chance to read it. Could you please connect us?"

or

You hear: "Yes, he has."

You say: "Do you know if he's had a chance to review it? If it's OK with you, I'd like to talk with him to see what he thought of what I sent to him. Could you please connect us?"

or

You hear: "No, he hasn't."

You say: "I understand. He's extremely busy. I sent it last week. Would you suggest that I resend it? Or do you think that he might have received it without your knowledge? I wonder if you might connect us so that I can track this down?"

Remember: your *sole* goal is to speak directly with your prospect in order to gain an appointment. The material you sent was to open the door, to provide a reason to have a discussion in order to gain an appointment.

Your secondary goal here, as in all of these scenarios, is to develop an internal advocate as early as possible. Quite often, that person is the gatekeeper. Here's another great phrase:

"Janet, I know that Mr. Price counts a great deal on you to keep things straight. I'm wondering if you might be able to help me …?"

Never forget: you need to maximize the opportunity for leverage. To leverage the materials you've sent and your contact with the gatekeeper to determine your prospect's receptivity and to gain access to the prospect in order to establish further dialogue.

You Have Not Yet Sent Materials to Your Prospect and Are Making a Cold Call

This is, by far, the weakest basis for any contact with any prospect at any time!

SITUATION #1

The gatekeeper answers the phone. Her response is positive and receptive. However, when you get to talk with your prospect, he or she shows some resistance and reluctance.

You hear: "Hello. Margaret Smith's office. This is Barbara. How may I help you?"

You say: "Hello, Barbara. My name is _____ with _____. I'm wondering if Ms. Smith is available."

You hear: "Yes, she is. May I ask you what this is in reference to?"

You say: "Certainly. As I said, my name is _____. I'm with _____. (Insert your Direct Value Statement.)"

You are connected.

You hear: "Hello. This is Margaret Smith."

You say: "Hello, Ms. Smith. As I told Barbara, my name is_____ with _____. [Insert your Direct Value Statement.] I was wondering if it might be possible for us to get together so that I could show you exactly how we could possibly do the same for you."

Pause and wait for a response.

You hear: "That sounds good. However, I'm not interested in spending a lot of time looking at what you have to offer right now."

You say: "I can understand that. My purpose, however, is not to sell you anything right now, anyway. I'd really like to have a chance to meet you personally, learn something about your situation, and, perhaps, give you some idea of what we do so that we might be a viable option for you at a time when you might be interested in moving forward."

You hear: "I might be willing to listen. However, don't expect me to buy anything."

You say: "I certainly don't. In fact, I promise that we will only begin a dialogue around taking a look at what we have. I'm wondering. Do you have your calendar available? Is there a time next week that's better than any other for us to get together?"

You hear: "How much time will this take?"

You say: "How much time could you spare? I promise I won't take any more time than you can give me."

Establish the time frame and confirm the day, time, and location. Be sure to reinforce that your meeting will take only as long as the prospect can set aside for it. Notice that you respond to a question ("How much time will this take?") with a question ("How much time can you spare?").

Don't believe that a prospect is or isn't interested in your product or service. Your goal is to deflect his or her belief that you will expect a purchase decision immediately. Your goal is to emphasize your interest in determining if you can help in any way and to introduce your product or service so he or she will consider it or at least be aware of it. Never forget that. And never violate that promise. If, however, your prospect becomes very interested during your visit, don't hesitate to move ahead as aggressively as necessary.

SITUATION #2

Your prospect's assistant/secretary answers the phone.

You hear: "Good morning. Ms. Johnson's office. This is Linda speaking. How may I help you?"

You say: "Hello, Linda. My name is _____, with_____. I've got a *problem* and I need you *help*."

Remember: gatekeepers are trained to provide assistance to people who seek it.

You hear: "How can I help you?"

You say: "Linda, my name is _____. [Insert your Direct Value Statement.] I would like to talk with Ms. Johnson or send her some information or leave a message with you or leave a voice-mail message for her.
Which method would you suggest?"

Work with the gatekeeper to achieve your one, single objective (an appointment), always soliciting that person's help in suggesting the best way to get your message to the decision maker.

It is essential that you earn this person's support so that you can broaden your base of internal advocacy within your prospect's organization.

SITUATION #3

The gatekeeper answers the phone and the response is positive and receptive.

You hear: "Margaret Smith's office. This is Barbara. How may I help you?"

You say: "Hello, Barbara. My name is _____ with _____. I'm wondering if Ms. Smith is available."

You hear: "Yes, she is. May I ask you what this is in reference to?"

You say: "Certainly. As I said, my name is _____. I'm with _____. [Insert your Direct Value Statement.]"

You are connected.

You hear: "Hello. This is Margaret Smith."

You say: "Hello, Ms. Smith. As I told Barbara, my name is _____ with _____. [Insert your Direct Value Statement.] I was wondering if it might be possible for us to schedule an appointment so that I could show you how we might possibly be able to do the same for you."

Pause and wait for a response.

You hear: "That sounds interesting."

You say: "I can promise you this. If what we have, in your opinion, won't work for you, I'll certainly understand and not take too much of your time. Does that make sense?"

You hear: "As long as you do that, I'll be happy to see you."

You say: "Good. Do you have your calendar handy? If so, let's go ahead and schedule an appointment. Is there a day next week that's particularly good for you?"

Agree on a time and date and schedule the appointment.

This situation is not as rare as you may think. There are times when you will be able to get a good, positive first meeting. It is essential, however, that you remember that your singular, solitary goal is always to get an appointment—not to spend a lot of time on the phone and/or make a presentation about your product or service and/or try to make a sale. One more time: your single, primary goal is to gain an appointment.

In many of these situations, you will note the overwhelming importance of your Direct Value Statement. You must prepare it carefully, and it is the *only* thing in this book that you must learn word for word. Use it at the most appropriate times and it will prove to be invaluable to you.

Should you receive questions with regard to your product or service, always defer them with the statement, "I can answer those questions when we get together. However, in order to answer them adequately, I'd like to ask you a few questions to see precisely how our solution can best be positioned to be of greatest value to you when we do get together."

Never forget: all phone calls are always about one thing—getting an appointment. You are not making a sales presentation on the phone.

SITUATION #4

The decision maker answers the phone.

You hear: "Good morning, this is John Johnson."

You say: "Mr. Johnson, how are you today? My name is_____ with _____. [Insert your Direct Value Statement.] The purpose of my call is to see if there is some way that we may be able to get together and have a discussion about some things that might be of mutual interest."

You hear: "I'm not interested in talking to anyone like you. I don't have the time, the interest, or the inclination."

You say: "I can understand that. I'm wondering, though, if I might be able to send you some material that you can react to and then I'll call, follow up, and see if there is some way that we *might* be able to establish a meeting. Does that sound like it might be acceptable to you?"

You hear: "Yes, that's OK. Just go ahead and send the material."

Make sure that you have the correct address. You can get this through an online service or additional research. Avoid having to ask the prospect for the address, especially if he or she is initially reluctant. The last thing you want to do is take more time, appear to be disorganized, and come across as just another cold caller.

You say: "I'll send you the material today. And if it's OK with you, I'll give you a call in a few days to make sure you have received it, and see if you've had a chance to review it. If it looks like it might be of some mutual interest, we might be able to go from there. Does that sound OK?"

You hear: "Yes, that's fine."

Your strategy is designed solely to get materials into your prospect's hands because it is very clear at this point that trying to talk him or her into a meeting would likely prove to be counterproductive. This process will also give you a reason to make a warm call at a later point as you follow up to ensure the prospect has received the materials and read them and to ask if he or she has any questions about them.

SITUATION #5

The decision maker answers the phone and you receive a positive response.

You hear: "Good afternoon. Howard Smith."

You say: "Mr. Smith, my name is _____ with _____. [Insert your Direct Value Statement.] The purpose of my call is to discover if you might have an interest in meeting with me to see if there is some way that we could possibly be of service to you."

You hear: "Well, tell me a little bit more about what it is that you sell."

You say: "We have worked with lots of organizations such as yours over the years and have found that once we are able to establish a relationship we've been able to assist them in unique and different ways. [Insert your Direct Value Statement.] However, in order to see if we might be able to be of some service to *you*, it's important that we have a face-to-face meeting. I'm wondering, is there a time next week that might be best for you?"

Your sole strategy here is to gain an appointment, no matter how positively responsive the prospect may be. Never place yourself in the position of trying to oversell. You'll note that you never attempt in this conversation to make a sales presentation. You simply talk about the benefits of your particular product or service and establish an appointment. The biggest mistake you can ever make here is to try to oversell a prospect who seems responsive.

SITUATION #6

The decision maker answers the phone and the response is somewhat neutral.

You hear: "Good afternoon. Betty Johnson."

You say: "Ms. Johnson, my name is _____ with _____. [Insert your Direct Value Statement.] The purpose of my call is to see if there is some way that we may be able to establish a mutually convenient time to sit down and determine if we might be of some service or value to you and your organization."

You hear: "Well, I'm not that familiar with your organization and don't know much about it. And, frankly, I'm not sure if we're in a position to make a decision at this point."

You say: "I can understand that. Very few of our clients are ever in the position to make a decision when we first contact them. However, I would like to send you some material that will give you a better understanding of who we are and what we offer. And then, if possible, I'd like to get back in touch with you in the next couple of days to determine if we might be able to pursue it further if the material looks interesting to you."

You hear: "Sure, that's OK. Go ahead and send the material."

It is important for you to make sure you have the proper address. Find it online or through some other source. Confirm with the prospect that you will call in a couple of days to set up an appointment for another meeting.

Leaving an Effective Voice-Mail Message

This strategy should be used whenever you leave a voice-mail message, regardless of how you ended up in voice mail!

You call and are only able to make contact through a voice-mail message.

You hear: "This is Mary Smith. I'm sorry that I'm not at my desk right now. Please leave a message and I'll get back with you at my earliest possible convenience."

You say: "My name is _____ with _____. [Insert your Direct Value Statement.] The purpose of my call is to see if there is some way that we might be able to be of some service or value to you. I certainly don't expect you to return my call. However, should you be so inclined, I would like to leave my number. [Leave your number, twice, slowly.] If I don't hear from you in a day or two, I will certainly give you a call to see if there is some way we might be able to get together."

Never expect your prospect to return a voice message! However, never oversell. Leave a message that is benefit-rich, one that explains in detail the benefits the prospect will receive when doing business with you—your DVS.

You will notice that you give your phone number twice. It is very important to do that because the person may not have a pen or pencil handy and can get one by the second time you provide the number. Be sure to give your number very slowly and clearly so that the prospect can understand it. You'll also notice that you are doing your best to establish a situation in which you will call that person back in a couple of days and he or she will be expecting your call.

You may even want to think about writing your own phone number down as you leave it verbally. Why is that? Simply this. Your prospect can't write any faster than you can! Try not to be one of those people who speak at a normal speed until they leave their phone number—and then they speed up! If you're like me, those are the numbers I delete. Forever. I'll bet you do, too. So will your prospect.

Confirming Your Appointment

Never, never, never go to any appointment unless you have first called to confirm the time, date, location, and time frame for your meeting. You can do this directly with your prospect or with his or her designated representative.

The reason for this? Why should you waste your valuable time going to an appointment that is not going to happen, that's been postponed or cancelled? Wouldn't you be better off rescheduling that appointment and doing another, more valuable activity in that time frame rather than showing up for nothing?

Here's how to do that. First, of course, always do it by telephone. Don't rely on e-mail. Why is that? Prospects, as a rule, will not do anything that requires much extra effort to entertain a sales presentation, no matter how badly they may need or want what you sell. I'm sorry if that's news to you, but that's just how it is. Don't expect a return e-mail telling you the meeting needs to be rescheduled. The only exception is the rare proactive prospect who will either call or e-mail to cancel or reschedule. However, don't rely on that. They are few and far between.

You hear: "Good morning. Ms. Johnson's office. This is Corrie. How may I help you?"

You say: "Good morning, Corrie. This is _____ with _____. I'm calling to confirm my appointment with Ms. Johnson for tomorrow at 10:00 a.m. I'll be there at 9:45. Our meeting is scheduled for 10:00 a.m. to 11:00 a.m. Is that correct and is everything still on schedule?"

Two possibilities:

You hear: "Yes, it is."

You say: "Good. I'll see you tomorrow morning at 9:45. Thank you very much."

or

You hear: "No, there's a problem."

You say: "I'm sorry to hear that. However, I would like to reschedule, if that's OK. Can you schedule an appointment for me with Ms. Johnson or would you recommend that I talk directly to her?"

Based on the response, you will either reschedule the appointment with the assistant or place a follow-up call directly to your prospect in order to reschedule your meeting.

Special Situations

At times you may be contacting a person whom you do not believe to be a fully qualified prospect.

In *any* of the previous prospecting scenarios, you ideally should be calling from a list of qualified prospects or have been referred to a prospect who was somewhat qualified. Unfortunately, however, that is not always the case.

Remember, as described earlier, the ideal prospect for you will have the following characteristics—or at least as many as possible.

1. The prospect has both a need and a want for your product or service—and is aware of that circumstance.
2. The prospect has both the authority and the ability to pay for it.
3. The prospect has a sense of urgency about solving a problem or fulfilling a need.
4. The prospect trusts both you and your organization.
5. The prospect is willing to listen to you.

Here's a suggestion. Don't just settle for #5. How do you do that? You ask the right questions and make the precise, right statements! You can evaluate the prospect on characteristics 1, 2, and 3 by asking specific questions *after* you tell the prospect who you are and issue your Direct Value Statement. Here's how it works:

You hear: "Good afternoon. Ms. Jackson's office. This is Robert speaking."

You say: "Good afternoon, Robert. My name is _____

with _____. [Insert your Direct Value Statement.] I'm wondering if I might be able to talk with Ms. Jackson about how we might be able to help your organization."

Two possibilities:

You hear: "I'm sorry she's not available."

You say: "Which would you recommend that I do, leave a voice-mail message or have you deliver a message to Ms. Jackson?"

If the recommendation is to leave a voice-mail message, do it as outlined earlier.

or

You hear: "Yes, she's available."

You say: "Good! May I be connected, please?"

You hear: "This is Jean Jackson."

You say: "Hello, Ms. Jackson. My name is _____ with _____. How are you?"

You hear: "I'm fine. How are you? How can I help you?"

You say: "I'm fine, too. Thanks. [Insert your Direct Value Statement]. I was wondering if we might be able to discuss the possibility of helping you and your organization as well."

Two possibilities:

You hear: "Fine."

You say: "That's good to hear. However, before we go ahead, do you mind if I ask you a few questions so that I might know exactly how to proceed?"

You will then ask a few of the following questions. Choose the three or four that are most relevant to you and your product or service.

- How familiar are you with our organization?
- How have you been handling any problems relative to [what your product or service solves]?
- How receptive would you be to looking at a possible alternative to your current situation?
- Who normally handles the decisions relative to [your product or service]?
  - Who else, other than you, of course, is involved in working with [what your product or service solves]?

The answers to these questions will help you assess how qualified the prospect is at this point. If you determine from the answers to these questions that you should go ahead:

You say: "It certainly sounds as if we might be able to help you. I'm wondering, could we go ahead and schedule an appointment to pursue this further? Which day this or next week would be best for you?"

Schedule an appointment. Call and confirm. Pre-call plan correctly and go to your meeting.

or

You hear: "I'm not interested."

You say: "I can understand why you might say that. Lots of our strongest customers haven't been interested initially due to timing, circumstances, or other conditions. Plus, I'm not really trying to sell you anything now. If you don't really need what we have, there's no sense in investing in it, anyway. Isn't that right?"

You hear: "That's right."

You say: "Do you mind if I ask you just a few questions to see exactly where you stand on a few things? It will only take a few seconds. I promise."

You hear: "No, I don't mind."

If that's the case, ask a few of the questions outlined in this section to determine whether the prospect has any issues you might be able to help him or her resolve. Then, do your best to schedule an appointment.

If the prospect expresses no interest, do your best to secure permission to contact him or her again at some exact time in the future, put him or her on an e-mail or mailing list, or talk with someone else within his or her organization to gather background information that may help you in case the situation or circumstance changes.

If you determine that the prospect is not really qualified, simply say that you appreciate his or her time, but from what you can gather, it really wouldn't be to "his or her advantage" to meet with you and that "perhaps someone else would be better suited." Thank the prospect for his or her time and move on to the next prospect.

Dislodging a Competitor

If you are prospecting in an attempt to dislodge a current supplier, the absolute worst thing you can ever do is to disparage the supplier in any way. There are lots of reasons for that. Among them is that it clearly implies that you believe the prospect has made either a bad decision to hire that competitor or an equally bad decision in keeping them. In either case, you'll lose!

Therefore, how do you dislodge without destroying your credibility? It starts, of course, in the Investigate step, where you will need to learn exactly what is going on with the current supplier. The source of information is, of course, your internal advocate.

You will need to learn from that internal advocate answers to the following questions before you *ever* get in front of your prospect:

- Who made the original decision to buy from your competitor?
- What were the factors that led to that decision?
- How, if at all, have those factors changed?
- How much loyalty is there to the current supplier?
- Who is the most loyal to them? Why?
- Who is the current salesperson?
- How well is this supplier respected?
- What does this supplier do well?
- What do they do poorly?
- What could be improved, if anything?
- How much interest is there in replacing this supplier?

- What sort of political risks would anyone take in replacing them?
- How receptive is the company to looking at an alternative source?

You will need to call and schedule an appointment with the right person. You will, of course, need to meet that prospect correctly, as explained in the next step. However, the real secret to this sale is in the Probe step!

You'll need to ask the right questions of the right people within your prospect's organization. Clearly, if there is no problem with the current supplier, if loyalty is strong, and if the supplier is providing superior quality or service, you'll be fighting an uphill battle. However, if you have been able to determine that there are some possible chinks in your competitor's armor, you may want to ask the following questions of your prospect in the Probe step:

- If you could change anything about your current supplier what would it be? Why do you say that?
- In looking at your current supplier's performance, how would you rate the following aspects on a scale of 1–10, with 10 being the highest?
  - On-time delivery?
  - Quality?
  - Service?
  - Price?
  - Cost?
  - Support?
  - Responsiveness?
  - Customer service?

- Ease of use?
- Other.

■ How receptive would you be to looking at an alternative source?

■ How receptive would you be to having us try a test or trial to see how well we could do?

■ What would determine, from that test, our level of success?

Clearly, the answers to these questions will tell you how possible it would be to dislodge the competitor. There is no sense in trying to do this if it doesn't seem realistic. However, if your pre-call planning research indicates that there is some degree of receptivity toward at least looking at another option, that is a good start.

You need to get in front of the right person and have him or her verbalize some degree of receptivity to change, an openness to pursue other options or to try some sort of trial or test.

You can then proceed to dislodge! However, proceed with caution. Expect your established competitor to respond. Prepare for the fight of your life. If there's not a fight, perhaps you should wonder why. Maybe they don't care about losing the account. What does that tell you?

Chapter 5
Step 2. Meet Your Prospect

Objective: To set the face-to-face sales process in motion

This is the interaction that launches the sales process. Let there be no doubt: this phase is critical to the sale. Why is that? Because it establishes the "primary perception" ... and you have merely 19–39 seconds to establish that perception as being either positive or negative. Here's how it works:

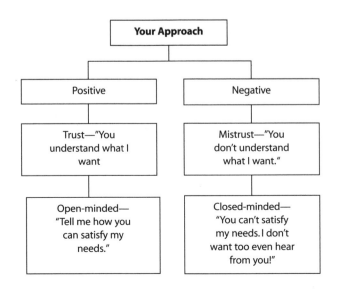

Let's take a look at the most common ways salespeople traditionally open the sale so that we can explain how the process we're going to explain is so very, very different.

1. Small talk ("That's a great pen. Do you collect pens?")
2. Product or service reference ("Our product has been featured on TV!")
3. Benefit claim ("We can reduce expenses by 30%.")
4. Tie-down or provocative question ("If I could show you how to double your productivity, you'd be interested, wouldn't you?")
5. Company reference ("We're the oldest.")
6. Quality claim ("We've been rated #1 in the industry.")

Here's some shocking news. Every one of these traditional ways to open the sale elicits either a negative or a neutral response on the part of prospects. Here's how they rank and the percentage of prospects who feel negative or neutral toward each approach:[1]

- Unsolicited small talk (95%)
  - Benefit claim (89%)
  - Product or service reference (85%)
  - Tie-down or provocative question (84%)
  - Company reference (74%)
  - Quality claim (71%)

So, what is the best way to open the sale?

1. *You're Working Too Hard to Make the Sale* (Greensboro, NC: GamePlan Press, 2005) by William T. Brooks and Tom Travisano.

Statement of Intention and Primary Bonding Statement

We're going to suggest a *statement of intention*—even though 78% of prospects feel either negative or neutral about statements of intention. However, this strategy, when immediately followed by a *primary bonding statement* (a statement that offsets any negativity or neutrality), is, in all likelihood, the least risky and is the most easily articulated. The bottom line is that you must say something!

However, remember that the exact phrasing of the statement of intention can reduce even further any potentially negative effect. So, here's how you open the meeting with your prospect:

You say: "Good morning, Mr. Gillette. I'm _____. It's certainly good to meet you. Thank you for this opportunity."

Then you insert a statement of intention:

You say: "If it's acceptable to you, I'd like to use this opportunity to meet you and for us, together, to determine if there's some way that my company and I might be able to be of service to you and your organization. Is that OK with you?"

You hear: "That's fine with me."
You say: "Good."

Then you insert a generic primary bonding statement:

You say: "Our real goal here is to help you get what you want. In order to help us do that, do you mind if I ask you a few questions?"

341

Part Three of this section will provide you the exact primary bonding statement to use with four specific prospect types. However, this generic bonding statement will work with all prospects. Use it!

You hear: "Fine."

You say: "I'd like to take a few notes to be sure that I have a record to refer back to. Is that OK with you?"

You hear: "That's OK with me."

That's it! That's all you have to say in order to initiate the sales process on a positive, productive note. Don't worry about looking for something in the prospect's home or office to discuss (such as mounted fish, paintings, or pictures). Don't be concerned with small talk *unless* it is initiated by the prospect. Then respond appropriately.

There is an important point to be made here. Remember: I said that prospects are bothered by *unsolicited* small talk. That means small talk that *you* initiate, not small talk that *they* initiate.

Your prospect might ask, for example, "How was the drive?" or "Did you have any trouble finding our place?" or "How long did it take you to get here?"

These comments are, clearly, attempts by the *prospect* to engage in small talk. You will, of course, respond and engage in conversation. For example:

You hear: "How was the drive?"

You say: "It was fine. However, the traffic was a little heavy on Route 45. Is that pretty common?"

In this scenario you will, of course, continue to discuss the traffic and whatever other topic comes up. However, your constant goal will be to steer the discussion (at the appropriate time, of course) back to the sequence of statement of intention, primary bonding statement, and permission to ask questions and record answers. And you must stay alert to any opportunity that will allow you to do that.

Remember: your sole goal in the Meet step is to set the face-to-face sales presentation in motion while ensuring that you create a positive primary perception. This is your agenda:

1. Tell your prospect why you're there.
2. Let your prospect know that you want to help him or her get what he or she wants (not what he or she needs).
3. Ensure that your prospect understands that you'll need to ask some questions and record the answers. Even with permission to proceed, your success in asking the right questions will hinge totally on your ability to ask even the most difficult questions in an empathetic and caring way, with the right words and tone.
4. Have the prospect acknowledge that he or she agrees with this agenda and wants to accomplish the same things.

In order to achieve this fourth objective, there is an excellent verbal strategy that virtually guarantees that your prospect will be comfortable and totally at ease and will answer your probing questions candidly and openly. Here it is:

You say: "If, in the course of our discussion, we mutually discover that I don't have anything that I can help you with, I can certainly recommend someone else who might be able to help you. Does that sound fair?"

You hear: "It certainly does."

You say: "Good! Then let's get started."

The secret here is for you to be totally committed to referring your prospect to someone else if you discover that your product or service doesn't address the specific issue that your prospect is trying to resolve.

Again, Part Three offers examples of precise, exact primary bonding statements to be used with four types of customers. The next best thing to using those carefully researched phrases is for you to use a generic bonding statement: "Our ultimate goal here is to help you get exactly what you want."

The key here is to understand this one simple truth:

Prospects eagerly buy what they need from salespeople who understand what they want.

That means that you must assure prospects that you'll help them get what they legitimately want.

Here are some examples of what prospects specifically want, based on their roles. Entrepreneurs want independence and freedom, purchasing managers want recognition and respect for what they do, and CFOs want no disruptions in their dat-to-day work flow.

It's critical for you to understand that saying to a prospect, "I'm here to meet your needs" falls on deaf ears, while, for example, "I'm here to help you achieve your goals while working behind the scenes" (the primary bonding statement for an HR director) elicits a fantastic, positive response. And you must accomplish this early in the face-to-face interaction—again, within 19–39 seconds.

Rest assured, however, that incorporating the simple phrase "help you get what you want" will usually be more than enough to gain the favor of lots of prospects who are tired of salespeople who dominate the conversation, overstay their welcome, or never get to the point.

Believe it or not, that is all there is to it. Don't make the Meet step more than it needs to be. It should be enough to launch you on what we call the "90% path."

Here's what that means. A negative primary perception gives you perhaps a 10% chance of success, while a positive primary perception gives you a greater than 90% chance of success. Which would you choose?

Now, let's go over the sequence, one more time:

You say: "Good morning, Ms. _____. I'm _____. It's certainly good to meet you. Thanks for the opportunity."

If it's acceptable to your prospect …

You say: "I'd like to use this opportunity today to meet you and for us, together, to determine if there's some way that we may be of service to you and your organization. Is that OK with you?" [statement of intention]

You say: "Our real goal here is to help you get what you want. [generic primary bonding statement] In order to do that, do you mind if I ask you a few questions? Is it OK if I take a few notes so that I have a record to refer to?"

You say: "If, in the course of our discussion, we mutually discover that I don't have anything I can help you with, I can certainly recommend someone else who might be able to help you. Does that sound fair?"

Now, you're in the Probe step.

Chapter 6
Step 3. Probe for Success

Objective: To have your prospect identify, verbalize, and discuss his or her needs, wants, and desires

Note the wording: this is the phase of the sale in which the prospect expresses his or her needs, desires, and wishes. And then you determine *what* he or she will buy, *how* he or she will buy it, *why* he or she will buy it, and *under what conditions* he or she will buy it. Never forget: different people buy the same things for different reasons—theirs and theirs alone. Not yours. Your goal is to uncover those very personal buying motives.

It's really no big secret that people buy for their reasons and not for yours. And that is the fundamental truth behind the Probe. However, the real winning secret behind the Probe is the questions that you ask in order to learn why they really would choose to buy your product or service.

This section will certainly provide you some of those questions. However, the level of success that your sales career will reach ultimately will be determined by your success in learning how to develop your own questions. So, you will now have that opportunity across a broad array of questions. We'll then take a look at a series of "silver bullet" questions that will help you sell better no matter what you sell or to whom you sell it.

Problem-Resolution Questions

In the final analysis, your prospects will buy your product or service to solve a problem, relieve a situation, or resolve an issue that they have. Period. For example:

- To improve cash flow
- To reduce overhead
- To increase sluggish sales
- To break out of a rut
- To stop being embarrassed by a situation

To understand how to use problem-resolution questions, you'll need to know exactly what problems, situations, difficulties, issues, or circumstances your prospect is likely to want to resolve, eliminate, reduce, or replace. You also need to know what issues your product or service helps them resolve.

So, here's what you do. Ask yourself this question: What problems or issues could this prospect possibly have that your product or service could help remove, relieve, or improve? List those problems on a piece of paper, numbering them from 1-10. Determine what questions you need to ask your prospect to determine if your prospect really does have the problems you've listed.

If you've done proper pre-call planning and research and you've learned from your internal advocate(s), you should ideally already know those problems. Even so, you still must pursue these questions. Why is that? Because it's all about getting the prospect to verbalize the problems, agree that he or she wants to solve them, and commit to a solution.

So, now you have a list of problems and questions. Here are some examples from four possible lists:

Potential Problem	Question
Reduce manufacturing waste	"How much, if any, manufacturing waste do you currently experience?"
Cost overruns	"How often, if ever, do you experience cost overruns?"
Poor physical conditioning	"How frequently, if ever, do you feel tired, run down, or have an overall sense of physical weakness?"
Inefficiency in kitchen	"How would you rate your ability to get things done quickly and efficiently in your kitchen?"

Agitation Questions

Just because someone has a problem, there's no proof that he or she is prepared to take action on it. Therefore, you need to determine exactly how much of a problem your prospect has and how strongly he or she feels about taking action on it.

To determine this, simply ask what I call *agitation questions* to follow up each problem-resolution question. For example:

You say: "How much manufacturing waste, if any, do you currently experience?"

You hear: "Quite a bit."

You say: "If you don't mind me asking, what is 'quite a bit'?" [agitation question]

You hear: "Enough to make a significant difference in our gross profit."

You say: "How big a problem is that to your profit picture? What will happen if it continues?" [agitation question]

As you can imagine, by asking these types of questions you'll learn lots of powerful things you'll be able to use later. Let's take a look at another example:

You say: "How would you rate your ability to get things done quickly and efficiently in your kitchen?"

You hear: "Well, we're certainly not as productive as we need to be."

You say: "What sort of problems does this create for your wait staff? Customers? How does it affect the number of tables you can turn each night? What does this mean to your bottom line? Turnover of wait staff? Training time, money, and energy? [agitation questions]

This scenario can be played out with any product, service, or offering. The reason? Most people are far more interested in alleviating problems than anything else. However, we're not done yet. There is a third leg to this stool—*solution- and feeling-based questions*.

Solution-and Feeling-Based Questions

These questions allow your prospects to tell you exactly how they feel about the current problem(s) and how prepared they are to solve the problem(s). The examples:

You say: "How do you feel about that?"

You hear: "Not good."

You say: "What steps, then, if any, have you taken to alleviate the problem?"

Customer explains some steps taken.

You say: "How do you feel about those things? How severely have they affected you so far? What happens if this continues?"

You hear: "I think it could be a problem. I have noticed some morale problems and some customer grumbling. Maybe I ought to start looking into it."

You say: "What steps, then, have you taken to alleviate the problem?"

You'll notice that we have taken the questions to three levels:

1. problem-resolution questions
2. agitation questions
3. solution- and feeling-based questions

This is a process that you can use to determine the level of pain from any problem for any prospect, with any product or service, and in any business-to-business or business-toconsumer situation.

Again, here's the formula:

■ What problems/pains do you have?

- To what extent is it causing you discomfort?
- How do you feel about it?
- What have you done thus far to solve it?

It's really that simple!

Needs-Based Questions

If you have not had a strong pre-call planning opportunity and haven't been able to determine through data, a third party, or even your prospect via a phone interview what specific problem your prospect is attempting to solve, you may want to start the Probe with *needs-based questions*.

The reason for this is that needs-based questions are not as potentially intrusive or penetrating as problem-resolution questions. Therefore, they are not nearly as dangerous or potentially volatile. On the other hand, they are not nearly as powerful or revealing. Let's take a look at how to develop needs-based questions.

First, write the name of your product or service on a piece of paper. Then, next to it list those needs that a prospect would likely have for your unique product or service. Some examples are listed below product by product or service by service:

Product or Service	Potential Need Product or Service Fills
A mortgage	To afford a home
An automobile	Transportation
Accounting services	Accurate tax information
Furniture	To decorate a home

In order to do this successfully, you'll need to list at least five to eight specific needs that your product or service can fulfill. Here's an example:

Product or Service	Potential Need Product or Service Fills
Heating and air conditioning repair and check-up service	• To keep equipment running efficiently • To ensure that equipment retains value • To keep property properly cooled • To keep certain objects in home properly cooled • To ensure that guests are comfortable

The next step is very simple. Convert those needs into questions. Using the previous service (air conditioning repair) as an example, here's how that would work.

To determine if the prospect has a need for keeping his or her equipment running efficiently, you might ask …

- "How long do you usually keep your original heating and air conditioning equipment?"
- "What experience have you had with equipment that is not maintained properly?"

To determine if the prospect has a need for the equipment to keep its value, you might ask …

- "How familiar are you with the costs of a complete system overhaul? Replacement costs? How long do you plan to live in your home?"

To determine if the prospect has a need to keep his or her property properly cooled, you might ask …

- "How often do you find your home/office uncomfortable?"

To determine if the prospect has a need to keep certain objects properly cooled, you might ask …

■ "What objects, if any, do you have in your home/office that must be kept at 68° or cooler?"

To determine if the prospect has a need to be sure guests are comfortable, you might ask …

■ "How often do you entertain out-of-town guests? Have dinner parties?"
■ "If so, where do you do so? Inside or outside?"

These are, of course, merely examples for reference. However, they should help you a great deal if you would just follow the suggested format.

Feature-Benefit Questions

Would you agree that if a benefit that your product or service provides is of no value to your prospect, the feature that drives that benefit is totally worthless to them—no matter what you think of the feature?

If you don't agree, you probably should! The secret, therefore, is to ask questions to determine if your prospect needs a specific benefit that your product or service provides and then present your product or service within those defined parameters.

Let's take a look at how this works.

Product or Service	Feature	Benefit
Flat-screen TV	2" thick	Takes up less floor space
Question: "How important is it for you to maximize your available floor space?"		
Floral delivery service	Same-day service	Flowers when and where you need them
Question: "How often do you need flowers delivered on short notice?"		
Gas generator	Automatic starting	Gives you peace of mind when power is lost
Question: "How many times a year do you lose power in your home and need immediate electricity?"		

In order for you to master this questioning skill, you will simply need to list your products or services, determine the-unique set of benefits that each provides, and then prepare questions that answer this one, single question:

What do I need to ask my prospect in order to determine if he or she needs each benefit?

Objection-Testing Questions

In "old school" selling, salespeople were taught to learn "canned responses" to the most common objections that they would hear. And because it is so "old school," none of them will be included in this book! Over the years lots of books have been written on exactly what words to use when certain objections are heard. If you believe that that approach still works, you may want to find some of those old books— they're still around. And most are in mint condition because they haven't been read or used!

It's like the old joke about the prisoners who weren't allowed to speak to one another. However, they would occasionally yell out numbers. Apparently, each number was a joke. One prisoner would yell out "36!" and another would laugh. Then another would yell out "42!" and laughter would ring out again. Apparently, it was a special code—not unlike a sales code for overcoming objections or closing a sale. The "think it over response" or "the Ben Franklin response," for example, were two such memorized strategies. The promise? Just call up the right one and you'll be successful! However, not in today's competitive market. I guarantee that.

Let's take a different approach. We'll take a look at common objections and develop a method for managing those objections and all others through a series of *objection-testing questions* that you can ask in the Probe. The purpose of these questions is to determine two things:

- whether an objection will ever come up
- precisely how to craft your presentation to deal with that objection when you apply your solution

Let's start with this sequence:

You hear: "I want to think about it." [objection]

You say: "What process do you use when making decisions like this?" [objection-testing question]

or

You say: "What kind of a time frame are you working with to make this decision?" [objection-testing question]

Think about this for a moment. If you ask either or both of those questions, won't you have a better, clearer idea of whether or not your prospect will tell you, later on, that he or she wants "to think about it"? Better yet, if you know that your prospect likes to give extensive thought to decisions, doesn't that tell you exactly how to proceed? Faster or slower, decisively or deliberately, with a simple presentation or multiple presentations? How your prospects answer those two, simple questions ensures that you'll never hear, "I want to think about it" ever again!

Now, let's look at other common objections and some questions you can ask to either avoid them completely or, at least, be able to anticipate them.

You hear: "I want to talk this over with _____." [objection]

You say: "Who else, other than you, of course, is involved in this decision?" [objection-testing question]

or

You hear: "Your price is too high." [objection]

You say: "What kind of a budget range are you working with?" [objection-testing question]

or

You say: "What role does price play in your decision?" [objection-testing question]

or

You say: "Which is more essential in your decision—price, quality, or delivery?" [objection-testing question]

You hear: "I'm happy with my current supplier." [objection]

You say: "If you could change anything about your current supplier, what would it be?" [objection-testing question]

You hear: "I'm not ready to make any type of decision." [objection]

You say: "What type of time frame do you have in mind for making this decision?" [objection-testing question]

You hear: "I need to talk with some other suppliers." [objection]

You say: "How broad a search are you conducting for this purchase?" [objection-testing question]

or

You say: "How far along are you? How many potential suppliers, if any, are you planning to talk with?" [objection-testing question]

These testing questions will allow you to anticipate potential objections, prepare your presentation to deal with them, or position yourself to feel confident that they may never, ever come up with this prospect.

Yes/No Questions

Yes, there is a role for *yes/no questions*! Their role? To seek clear, accurate delineation of a position, circumstance, situation, condition, decision, or point of view. However, to be truly valuable, they should ideally be followed immediately by clarification questions. Here are some examples:

You say: "Are you pleased with your current level of productivity?"

You hear: "No."

You say: "That's interesting. If you don't mind my asking, why do you feel that way?"

You'll notice that the follow-up or clarification questions start with a statement, such as "That's interesting." The purpose of that type of statement is to demonstrate understanding and empathy or to neutralize the response. Some more examples?

You say: "Is your current situation going to continue?"

You hear: "Yes."

You say: "If you don't mind my asking, what impact will that have on your ongoing plan? Are you planning to continue manufacturing that product?"

You hear: "No."

You say: "That's surprising, but not something I didn't expect to hear. But let me ask you this, if you do decide to discontinue it, what plans do you have for replacement?"

The statement can be a complete sentence or the preface to a clarification question. Either way will work. The ideal format, however, is to use the yes/no question as a springboard to further clarification. This example shows how to take the questioning down several layers, three layers in this case.

You say: "Are you planning to expand your fleet?"

You hear: "No, I'm not."

You say: "That's intriguing. What's driving that decision?" [level 1]

You hear: "We're concerned that the economy is going to weaken."

You say: "I can understand that. What impact, if any, do you think that will have on the rest of your business?" [level 2]

You hear: "I believe that it will ultimately affect our subsidiaries as well."

You say: "If that's the case, what impact do you believe that will have with reference to expanding your outsourcing needs?" [level 3]

Here's the formula:

- Yes/No question
- Statement or phrase
- Clarification question—level 1
- Clarification question—level 2
- Clarification question—level 3

Level–1, –2, and –3 Questions

These types of questions can be used to gain depth with any type of question, not just yes/no questions. After all, it's essential for you to have as much understanding of problems, situations, issues, and circumstances as humanly possible before you present your solution, isn't it?

Here's how to use *level–1, –2, and –3 questions*. You simply follow up any question with questions like these:

- "That's interesting. Tell me more."
- "Why do you say that?"
- "Could you expand on that a little?"
- "What are the ramifications of that?"
- "How would that work for you?"
- "What further steps would you take?"

An example:

> *You say:* "What is your biggest, single challenge right now?"
>
> *You hear:* "Staying competitive in the market."
>
> *You say:* "If you don't mind my asking, what is really driving that competition?" [level 1]
>
> *You hear:* "Lower-priced competitors. Frankly, they're just driving us to our knees."
>
> *You say:* "I understand. Who is your absolute toughest competitor?" [level 2]
>
> *You hear:* "It's not really one competitor. It's everybody."
>
> *You say:* "If you don't mind my asking, what do you mean by 'everybody'?" [level 3]

Hopefully, you can see that you could go to Level 4, 5, 6, 7, or higher! The secret? It's really nothing more than a conversation. Remember: it's not a monologue! How about another example?

You say: "What is the single most important issue facing you with reference to a purchase like this?"

You hear: "That's easy. It's the down payment."

You say: "I see. But let me ask you this. What role does the down payment play in your decision?" [level 1]

You hear: "Well, what do you require?"

You say: "That depends on a number of factors. But I'd like to ask you this, if I might. How important is the length of the loan to you?" [level 2]

You hear: "I haven't really thought about that."

You say: "That's OK—and not unusual. Don't feel badly about that. Most people haven't really thought about that. However, maybe this question would help. What do you plan to do with the property in eight to 10 years?" [level 3]

You hear: "Why is that important?"

You say: "That will play a big role in the decisions you'll be making relative to building equity. However, if you're not sure about that, I'd like to ask you this .... [level 4]

This example should show you exactly how to respond to whatever you hear, transition it to another question, and continually get more information relative to developing a solution for your prospect.

Silver Bullet Questions

Silver bullet questions are ones that you can ask most any prospect, no matter the product or service you sell. I urge you to take them and use them. Mix them with the other eight types of questions we've discussed—and you'll be well on your way!

- "What are some of the major challenges/changes within your company/department/industry in the past 6/12/18 months?"
- "What impact have these had on your profits/morale/market share, etc.?"
- "What, if anything, are you looking for from an organization like ours that you haven't found?"
- "What do you like most about your current supplier?"
- "What, if anything, would you like to see them improve or change?"
- "What kind of budget range, if any, are you working within?"
- "What kind of a time frame, if any, do you have in mind?"
- "What have you seen that's particularly appealed to you?"
- "What process do you use to make this type of decision?"
- "Who else, other than you, of course, is involved in this decision?"
- "What is it in your current situation that you absolutely do not want to see changed?"
- "If you could change anything about your current situation, what would it be?"
- "What is the single thing that's most important to you about this type of decision?"
- "If we were able to solve your problem what would this mean to your organization?"
- "What would it mean to you personally?"

Chapter 7
Step 4. Apply Your Solution

Objective: To recommend and present your product or service in a way that clearly matches the solution your prospect is trying to achieve

The purpose of this step of the sale is to show the prospect precisely how your recommended product or service meets his or her specific needs, solves a problem, or delivers a specific benefit. This is far more than merely demonstrating your product or service. Instead, it is applying it as a solution. There's a big difference between the two.

Here's how to transition from probing to applying:

You say: "I understand you're looking for improved efficiency, reduced costs, and maximizing your technology. Is that correct?"

You will have listened carefully to what your prospect has told you that he or she is trying to accomplish, solve, eliminate, seek, or resolve. However, you will have gotten to this point only if you have been able to identify at least three specific solutions that you can provide to your prospect. Five would be even stronger. It is critical that you do not move to this point unless you have uncovered specifically strong solutions to recommend to your prospect.

Three possibilities:

You hear: "Yes, that's correct."

You say: "Based on that, I'd like to recommend …" or

You hear: "No, that's not accurate."

You say: "I'm sorry. What is it that I missed (or misunderstood)?" or

You hear: "Yes, but I'd also like to _____."

You say: "I understand. Is there anything else that you'd like to pursue before we proceed?"

If you have consumed a significant amount of time in the Probe step, you may want to suggest that you establish a specific time at a later date to return and make your presentation. If so, you must establish a mutually acceptable time, date, and location for that next meeting.

However, if the opportunity is right and time is available to do so, you may want to go ahead and begin your presentation.

Making Your Recommendation

When you are prepared to recommend a solution to your prospect, be absolutely sure to present it only within the scope of the specific parameters that your prospect has verbalized for the problem that he or she is trying to resolve. This is true whether you are presenting a tangible product, a professional service, or a software solution. Remember: you have previously described your understanding of what your prospect is attempting to accomplish. Now, however, you will prioritize those things as follows.

You say: "I understand you're looking to solve _____. Is that correct?"

Two possibilities:

You hear: "No, that's not correct."

You say: "I'm sorry that I missed that. So, please help me. Could you confirm for me what is the most important thing you're looking for?"

You then reprioritize your presentation, dealing with the number-one priority first and then ask your prospect to reconfirm number two, number three, number four, etc.

or

You hear: "Yes, that's right."

You say: "Based on what you're trying to accomplish first, let me tell you what I'm going to recommend to address that issue."

Now, present your product or service in such a way that it addresses specifically your prospect's number-one, most pressing issue. For example: "As you can see, the speed of this machine will reduce your downtime by 25%. Let me show you how it works ...." You then confirm the prospect's second, third, and fourth priorities and work your way through each benefit or feature.

Handling Premature Price Questions

Of all the issues that you will ever face in the sales process, the premature price question is not only the most problematic, but also the most common. I have placed it here in the Apply step because it has to go somewhere. However, don't be shocked if it comes much earlier.

This question can arise in several places. It could come while you are prospecting and seeking an appointment, when you are meeting with the prospect, or here in the Apply step before you have been able to create sufficient value for your product or service. That's because, like you, your prospect doesn't want to invest too much time in something that will not go anywhere. This could involve price, order levels required, delivery dates, or even more.

No matter when this question arises or why, if it is asked prematurely, don't answer it! You must always deal with it as outlined in this section.

The problem? If you appear elusive or evasive or if you handle this whole thing clumsily, you are guaranteed to lose the sale. Therefore, you need to know how to handle the inevitable with accuracy.

First, what are the most likely questions you'll hear? They all deal with price, but come in the following formats:

- "How much does it cost?"
- "What's your best price?"
- "Give me a ballpark price."
- "How much is that one over there?"
- "What's the minimum order required?"
- "Do you have any up charges?"

No matter what the specific question, you need to be able

to handle the issue. There are two basic strategies:

- The delay
- The range

THE DELAY STRATEGY

You hear: "How much is it?"

You say: "We've got a full range of prices. However, before we deal with that, let's make sure that it's exactly the right thing for you. Does that make sense?"

Two possibilities:

You hear: "Fine."

Proceed to ask sufficient probing questions to enable you to identify the three to five specific needs or issues you can help your prospect resolve.

or

You hear: "No, I want to know the price."

Go to the range strategy.

THE RANGE STRATEGY

You hear: "How much is it?"

You say: "We've got a full range of prices. However, before we can even deal with that, let's make sure that it's exactly the right thing for you, does that make sense?"

You hear: "No, I want to know the price."

You say: "We've got a range, anywhere from _____ to _____. No doubt you'll be somewhere in between. However, before we can be more specific, I'll need to know more about what you're trying to accomplish. Once I know that, I'll give you the exact price. Does that sound fair?"

When you present your range, it is critical to present a bottom price that is, realistically, the lowest possible, acceptable price that you can accept. That's because the low price is likely the only thing your prospect will ever remember about your presentation! Therefore, fail to use this strategy at your own peril!

In most cases, you will then proceed to say, "In order to determine that exact price, do you mind if I ask you a few questions?"

In almost all cases, this will satisfy your prospect. However, you will need to provide your prospect the range of prices you promised and not be afraid to do so.

Presenting Your Price

Make no doubt about it: knowing when and precisely how to present your price is essential to your success in sales. Present your price only after you have created sufficient value to offset the perception of cost and emotional turmoil. Let's deal with that issue now.

THE STACKING STRATEGY

The best way to do this is by applying the stacking strategy.

You say: "Before I give you our price, I'd like to make sure that you understand everything that it includes. Is that OK with you?"

You hear: "That's fine with me."

You say: "Good. Then let's get started."

Everything that will be presented here is for illustrative purposes only. You will, of course, need to substitute your specific information where appropriate.

You say: "You indicated that you wanted a supplier that could deliver on time, guaranteed. Our price includes that guaranteed on-time delivery and if we don't do that, you'll receive a 10% discount. You also wanted the full warranty, dedicated technicians, 24-hour service, and the latest software. Our price does, of course, include all of that. Your major concern was color consistency. Our price also includes our upgraded color-matching system. Our price includes all of this for $5.00 per unit in lots of up to 1,000 per order. But that's not all; we also provide full data backup, easy-to-read billing, and a dedicated account representative to handle any issues that may arise. How does that sound?"

Let's take a graphic look at how we just worked the stacking strategy.

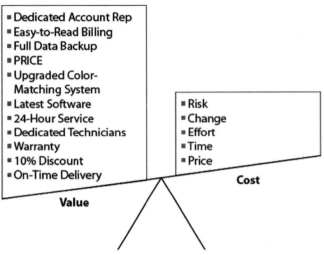

Clearly, the features to be gained outweigh the cost, don't they? However, you can achieve this only by stacking the features—those attributes that clearly outweigh the cost, effort, time, risk, and other issues that, together, constitute the cost of your offering in the mind of your prospect.

Now, let's make it even better!

You say: "Before I give you our price, I'd like to make sure that you understand everything that it includes. Is that OK with you?"

You hear: "That's fine with me."

You say: "Good, let's get started. You indicated that you wanted a supplier that could give you peace of mind relative to on-time delivery. We can do that on a guaranteed basis. We will, in fact, even make it more attractive with a

10% refund if we fail to satisfy your delivery concern. We will also provide you our no-risk warranty and technicians who know your account intimately whom you can contact 24 hours a day, seven days a week. Our latest software with all upgrades that are easier than ever to understand, a concern you had, will also be included at no extra cost. Your price for all of this is only $5.00 per unit, in easy-to-order at-store lots of 1,000. But that's not all. To ensure that you have no data problems, it also includes backup for all data, delivering documents that contain easy-to-follow instructions and your own account representative who will be assigned to handle your most complex, yet essential issues. How does that sound?"

You'll notice how we "upgraded" the presentation of price by listing benefits instead of features. Now, our formula looks like this:

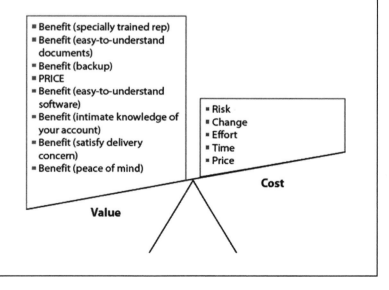

Clearly, we have outweighed any perception of cost by listing the benefits and "burying" the price between those benefits. Compare that with the following:

You hear: "What's your best price?"

You say: "$5.00 per unit in lots of 1,000."

What do you think you'll hear? How about this?

You hear: "$5.00? And I have to order 1,000 at a time? Are you crazy?"

In spite of your best efforts, you are still likely to hear some sort of price objection. Therefore, we need to further discuss how to present your price.

How to Guarantee That Your Price Will Never Be Accepted

There is often great wisdom in knowing exactly what not to do in certain situations. One of those is knowing how not to present your price.

First, avoid at all costs any of the self-defeating, even stupid statements that salespeople make when presenting price, such as the following:

- "I'll give you my best price."
- "I'll really sharpen my pencil on this one for you."
- "We really want your business, so tell me where I need to be."
- "Do you have your seatbelt on?"

Each and every one of these statements is guaranteed to have your prospect drive you to your knees. What do they all communicate? One thing—that you yourself don't even believe in your price. That you feel that your price is too high and, if your prospect will balk, hesitate, or complain, you will panic, retreat, seek a lower price, and do whatever you need to do in order to secure an order.

The other, surefire giveaway is for you to place some sort of modifier on your price as you present it. Some examples?

- "Our regular price is …."
- "Our standard price is …."
- "Our quoted price is …."

What do you believe your prospect will deduce from that? That his or her price will be lower, that's what! That you are negotiable on your price.

The best way to present your price is to say, "Our price is …" However, when that price is stacked between benefits, you clearly have created a situation where you have maximized the value that is represented in your price.

Very few factors in the sale are more important to your ultimate success than when and how you present your price, so learn how to do it with confidence and power.

Making the Feature-Benefit Conversion

Remember in the Probe step I suggested that you ask feature/ benefit questions to determine which of the features of your product or service would fit seamlessly into your product or service recommendation and presentation. Here's how to present your solution to your prospect based on those findings.

> **You say:** "You've indicated that long-lasting wear was important to you, isn't that right?"
>
> **You hear:** "Yes, I did."
>
> **You say:** "Let me explain the construction of our X–19 Model, the one I've recommended to you. As you can see it's triple coated and is made of heavy-gauge steel. The triple coating means that it will last longer than any competitor's model. The heavy-gauge shell means that it will withstand more intense pressure than any product on the market. Does that sound like the kind of thing you're looking for?"
>
> **You hear:** "Yes, it does."

Here's another example:

> **You say:** "You indicated that the assignment of a senior copywriter was important to you. You also wanted to run a test of the copy before the full-blown mailing goes out. Isn't that right? Our senior copywriters each have at least 10 years of experience. That means that each and every one has done at least 500 projects like yours. And, in our case, if they don't have a 95% success rate, they don't stay here! By the same token, each of them has done at least 1,000 split-copy tests in their career. That means lots of

tested, proven experience will be on your team. Does that sound like the kind of experience you're looking for?"

You hear: "It sure does."

The Power of Course-Correction Questions

When you are presenting your solution, it's essential that you are confident that it's 100%, totally on target relative to solving your prospect's most pressing problems, addressing an issue, or resolving a dilemma. In order to do that, you need to know just exactly where you stand throughout your presentation.

Here's how to do that. As you present your solution, stop and ask your prospect exactly how on or off target your solution is. You do that by asking *course-correction questions*. Examples?

- "How does this look?"
- "Are we on target?"
- "Does this look like something you can use?"
- "Does this make sense?"
- "How are we doing?"
- "What do you think?"
- "Can you see yourself using this?"

You will hear one of three answers when you ask these questions.

Three possibilities:

You hear: "Yes, I like it."

If your prospect's response is positive, that means that your presentation is on target. Keep going!

or

You hear: "No, I don't."

You say: "Why do you say that? How did I miss the target?"

You hear: "I don't like the color."

You say: "What color would work better for you?"

You hear: "Do you have it in red?"

You say: "Of course we do. Let me show the same thing in red. How does this look?"

You hear: "That's much better."

Here's another example:

You say: "How does this look?"

You hear: "I think it's too complicated for our application."

You say: "What part is too complicated?"

You hear: "We don't need all of the upgrade options."

You say: "Which specific options, if any, do you feel would be most helpful to you?"

You hear: "Maybe just the Phase I and Phase II options."

You say: "That's fine. Let me show you how it works with just those options.How does it look now?"

You hear: "That's much better."

The strategy in this scenario consists of doing four things:

- You ask a course-correction question.
- You respond to your prospect's answer.
- You present an alternative solution.
- You ask another course-correction question to determine if you have correctly realigned your solution.

It is essential to remember to stop frequently during your presentation to make totally sure that you are 100% on target. The only way to do that is to ask course-correction questions and then act according to the response.

or

You hear: "I'm not sure."

You say: "What is it that you're not sure about?"

You hear: "I'm not sure about the upgrade option."

You say: "I can understand that. But if you don't mind my asking, what is it about it that makes you unsure?"

You hear: "It's the cost of the upgrade. I don't think it's worth it."

You say: "I understand. However, let me tell you what makes it such a great opportunity at the price we're offering...."

This is the formula:

- Ask what the prospect is concerned or unsure about.
- Listen to his or her answer.
- Display empathy and then ask a question that allows the prospect to tell you exactly why he or she is concerned or unsure.
- Listen to his or her answer.
- Deal with the issue or concern.
- End your response with a course-correction question, such as "Does this clarify your issue?" or "Does this resolve your concern?"

These questions are tools that are essential to your sales success. Interestingly enough, however, most salespeople fail to employ them. And if you fail to employ them, it could prove fatal to your sale.

Chapter 8
Step 5. Convince Your Prospect of Your Claims

Objective: To provide powerful social, stastical, or third-party proof of your claims

There is a basic fundamental truth in sales. People expect salespeople to make claims for their products or services. However, they are impressed when someone else does. Once you have adequately presented your product or service, created great value for it, and ensured that your presentation is 100% on target for your prospect, here's the next step.

You say: "Now, let me show you what other people (or organizations) very much like you have to say about our _____ [product, service, company, warranty, delivery, etc.]."

At this point, you will want to consider offering one or more of three ways for your prospect to experience corroboration of your claims.

For example, if your prospect shows concern or disbelief over quality or product issues you have claimed:

You say: "Let me show what _____, the leading trade journal in your industry, has to say about our quality."

or

You say: "Let me show you how we rank in the latest research by Consumer Reports (or some other relevant, respected, third-party evaluation)."

Put the hard copy of the report data directly in their hands. Let them read it for themselves. Then you follow up:

You say: "You can see why we're so highly rated by those who research and rank products/services like ours, can't you?"

If your prospect has shown concern over the credibility of your statements:

You say: "Let me show you some letters that we have received from some of the people we do business with, people/companies just like you."

At this point, show them letters from satisfied users of your product or service that you have prepared (highlighting key phrases, if possible) that help to corroborate your claims. Allow them to read, touch, and keep these letters. Then you follow up:

You say: "Hopefully, you can see the reaction to what we provide. Do these comments satisfy any concern you may have relative to [quality, delivery, service, price, etc.]?"

Three possibilities:

You hear: "Yes, it does."

You have moved one step closer to the sale. In fact, you may want to take a closing action at this point (Step 6, Tie It Up).

or

You hear: "No, not really."

or

You hear: "I'm not sure."

If the prospect is not satisfied, you should proceed to the next level:

You: "Would you like to speak to one of our customers/ clients? That way you can pose your question or have your concern answered personally by someone who, clearly, has nothing to gain. If that's what you'd prefer to do, here is a list of _____ (six is an ideal number) people who have agreed to talk with anyone like you who might have a question. Would you like to do that?"

Two possibilities:

You hear: "Yes, I would."

You say: "That's good. Is there a person, or several people, on the list that you'd prefer to call? The reason why I am asking that is that I want to be sure to alert them to expect your call. We do this as a courtesy to them so that they can anticipate your call and be prepared for it. Is that OK with you?"

You hear: "That's fine."

You say: "Do you have any idea when you might be calling them so that I can give them an idea as to the timing?"

You hear: "Within the next week or so."

You say: "Good. Now, which one or ones do you prefer to call?"

Once you have determined who will be called and when, you continue:

You say: "You should have all of your calls completed by _____. Is that correct? Would you prefer that I call you a day or so after that, or should I wait for your call?"

Get an answer. In either case, you need to be moving closer to finalizing the sale.

or

You hear: "No, that's not necessary."

You may want to do one of two things.
Two possibilities:

You say: "OK, then, does everything look acceptable to you?"
or

You say: "What further evidence, if any, do you need to move ahead?"

In either case, you are now forcing your prospect's hand. You will determine if he or she is prepared to buy, is stalling, or needs more evidence.

We will consider the third possibility in a moment.

If it seems that the prospect is prepared to buy or is stalling, you need to move to finalize the sale. (Details on just how to do that are outlined in Step 6, Tie It Up.) Here's how you determine whether the prospect is prepared to buy or not.

You say: "Why do you say that?"

Two possibilities:

You hear: "I'm ready to move ahead."

It's time to take a closing action at this point (Step 6, Tie It Up).

or

You hear: "I would rather find out for myself."

You say: "Would you like to experience the product/service yourself?"

You hear: "Yes, I would."

You say: "We have lots of customers/clients who like to do that. When that's the case, we often run tests, trials, or beta tests. Let me tell you how that works."

Now, set up the test and determine what parameters will be used to define success. Assume that once those parameters have been met, it's time for you to assume the sale.

Getting Satisfied Customers to Help You Sell

In the real world of selling, lots of clients or customers will readily agree to have their name on a list to be contacted if only you ask them to do so. And how do you ask customers to indicate their level of satisfaction with your product or service?

Some people will not help you unless you ask them to do so. Those eager enough to do it on their own are few and far between. So in order to more fully and carefully prepare the tools you'll need to convince your prospects that your claims are true, you'll need to know how to secure words of approval from your satisfied customers.

Let's talk about what to say, when to say it, and how to secure the documentation you need. You'll need one or more of basically three types:

- A written document indicating satisfaction
- A name, contact information, and type of product or service provided, to be placed on a list agreeing to be called
- A willingness to supply you the name and information you'll need to make contact with potential prospects

The exact time to approach someone about this is very easy to understand. It's when you have earned the right to do so. Period. However, there is one exception to that rule. When your customer says, "You're really great!" or something to that effect, you need to take advantage of that opportunity—even if you feel that you have more work to do in order to feel that you have fully satisfied them. The real truth? They must be satisfied enough to verbalize their pleasure. That's all.

You hear: "I really like your _____."

You say: "Could you put that in writing?"

You hear: "Of course."

You say: "Would you like me to suggest some verbiage that you might use or would you prefer to phrase it in your exact words?"

Two possibilities:

You hear: "Yes, help me."

You then agree to help.

or

You hear: "I'd prefer to use my own words."

In either case, you're fine. However, you're not done yet. You need to establish a specific time frame for receipt of the letter.

You say: "How soon do you think I might expect the letter? I don't want to inconvenience you, but the sooner I can get it, the better!"

You hear: "When would you like it?"

You say: "I'd like it by _____. Is that acceptable?"

You hear: "That's fine."

or

You hear: "No, but by _____ would be better."

Either way, you're in good shape. The goal? To get a letter indicating the level of satisfaction they have with what you've provided.

What should you do with the letter? Here are several suggestions:

- Make copies of the original and use it in your sales presentation.
- Scan it for downloading as you need it and use it in either a digital or a hard-copy format.
- Underline or highlight key words that reflect end results similar to what your prospect is trying to achieve. You can do this digitally or by hand.

Another strategy is to have a prepared list of happy, satisfied customers whom prospects can contact if they choose to do so. Here's how to secure those who are most willing to be on the list.

You say: "Would you mind if I placed your name, contact information, and type of product/service we provided to you on a list for other prospective customers to review?"

Two possibilities:

You hear: "Yes, that's OK with me."

You say: "I will promise you this: if anyone does want to contact you, I will tell them that, as a matter of courtesy to you, I will inform you so that you will be able to anticipate their call. Does all of this sound OK?"

You hear: "That's fine."

You say: "Good. I also promise that I'll only keep your name on the list for a short period of time. That way you won't have to worry about it. In fact, I'll even contact you when it's time for me to remove you from the list. What do you think?"

or

You hear: "No, I don't want to do that."

You say: "I understand. However, is there any specific reason why you wouldn't be interested?"

Based on their response, you may want to either resolve the concern or get your customer to agree to just a letter of recommendation.

If the initial response to your request is negative, you may also want to consider this approach:

You say: "That's fine, I understand. However, if someone does want to talk with you, is that OK?"

Then proceed accordingly.

Many prospects will ask for a list and never call anyone, anyway. They just want to be sure that you have a list of satisfied customers!

However, when a prospect indicates that he or she will be contacting someone, you need to contact your customer and inform him or her that a prospect will be calling. Here's how that conversation usually goes:

You say: "Hello, Terry. This is _____. How are you?"

You hear: "Hi, _____. How are you?"

You say: "I'm great. The reason for my call is that one of our prospective customers, Bob Jones with XYZ Corporation, indicated that he'd like to talk with you. Is that OK?"

Here's the most interesting part. If you have placed highly satisfied prospects on the list, they will ask you this simple, straightforward question nearly 100% of the time:

You hear: "What do you want me to say?"

Your answer? Tell them to truthfully, of course, frame their response within the context of how you want to help your prospect address a need, handle a problem, or overcome an objective or your prospect wants corroboration of your claims from an independent third party—your happy, satisfied customer. And your customers will do that—as long as you have earned the right for them to be totally, 100% enthusiastic about you, your product or service, and your organization.

Overcoming Objections in the Real World

It's a fundamental truth that highly successful salespeople don't encounter many objections. That's because they generally uncover the most likely objections in the Probe step with objection-testing questions and then present their solution in a way that eliminates reasons for objections.

However, it is critical in a book of this type to cover at least the most common objections that salespeople will encounter no matter what product or service they sell. What are they?

- "I want to think about it."
- "I need to talk to _____ [my boss, spouse, partner, associate, attorney, accountant, advisor, etc.]"
- "Your price is too high."
- "I don't see any reason to change [suppliers, vendors, etc.]"

We deal with each one in a moment. However, first we need to deal with the specific dialogue that you'll need to use in order to transition into the exact formula for managing each.

Your prospect raises any of the four most common objections—or any of hundreds of others. (After all, it's the formula or pattern you'll need to master, not dealing with a specific objection.)

You say: "I understand why you might say that. Is there anything else that causes you concern at this point?"

Now, wait for an answer.

This response will do the following:

- It will neutralize any negativity.

- It will clearly show that you understand that your prospect might have a concern.
- It will uncover any other issue that may be causing your prospect to have an objection while isolating any specific objection(s).
- It will show that you really do want to know the reason(s) behind his or her response and deal with it.

Now, let's look at each objection and a specific response to each.

FIRST COMMON OBJECTION

You hear: "I want to think about it."

You say: "I can understand why you might say that. Is there anything else that would cause you concern at this point?"

You hear: "No, not really. I just don't make decisions like this so quickly."

You say: "I understand. What type of time frame would you like to have to think this over?"

or

You say: "I understand. What is it that you'd like to think about?"

or

You say: "I understand. What is it you'd like to think about and what type of time frame would you like to have to think it over?"

In each of these cases you are doing the following:

- You emphasize that you really do understand your prospect's concern.

- You give your prospect an opportunity to verbalize any other concern.
- You ask a question that will allow you to present your solution one more time.

For example:

You say: "Let me emphasize that making a decision now certainly does not obligate you for the future. Let me explain."

or

You say: "Let me stress that the time frame you select, will, of course, be one of your choosing. So, let me ask you this: what other information do you need?"

SECOND COMMON OBJECTION

Now, let's look at the second most common objection, "I need to talk to _____."

You hear: "I need to talk to my accountant about this."

You say: "I can understand that. Is there anything else other than talking to your accountant that concerns you at this point?"

You hear: "No, not really. But I do need to run this by him."

You say: "If you don't mind my asking, what is it that you would like to discuss with him?"

You will solicit the specific issue or question and either do your best to answer it for the prospect or offer to meet with the other person to help with this issue. Remember: you sell your product or service and can discuss it more effectively with the other person than your prospect ever could. However, you really should have discovered this objection earlier, shouldn't you?

THIRD COMMON OBJECTION

How about the third most common objection, "Your price is too high"?

> **You hear:** "Your price is too high."

> **You say:** "I can understand why you might say that. Is there anything other than price that concerns you at this point?"

> **You hear:** "No. It's just the price."

> **You say:** "If you don't mind my asking, what is it about the price that concerns you?"

> **You hear:** "I just don't see any reason to spend that much money."

> **You say:** "Let me explain to you why our price is where it is."

You again recap the benefits the prospect will receive, how your product or service is superior, why your price is higher, or, if possible with your product or service, how you could remove certain components in order to meet the prospect's price demands.

FOURTH COMMON OBJECTION

Finally, the fourth objection, "I don't see any reason to change."

> **You hear:** "I don't see any reason to change."

> **You say:** "I can understand why you might say that. Is there anything else that concerns you at this point?"

> **You hear:** "No."

> **You say:** "If you don't mind my asking, if you could change, modify, alter, or improve anything at all about your current supplier, what would it be?"

Your goal is to isolate this as the only objection (as you do in each and every case) and then determine if there is any single issue that is less than 100%, totally acceptable to the prospect with regard to the current supplier, vendor, or source.

OTHER OBJECTIONS

In each example here, when you ask, "Is there anything else that causes you concern?" the response is "No." Unfortunately, in the real world, that may not be the case. Let's look at an example:

You say: "Is there anything else that causes you concern?"

You hear: "Yes, there is."

You say: "What is that?"

You hear: "I'm also concerned about the terms, warranty, and delivery schedule."

You say: "Is there anything else that concerns you?"

You hear: "No."

You say: "So, what I understand you to say is that the price, terms, warranty, and delivery are the only issues, is that right?"

You hear: "Correct."

You say: "Let's deal with each, if it's OK. Which would you like to deal with first?"

You hear: "The price."

Deal with the price issue first. Then ask your prospect which issue to deal with next. Be sure that you satisfy his or her concern with each issue, in order. Do this by asking, "Does this answer your question about _____?"

When you are confident that you have dealt with each issue to your prospect's satisfaction, you are now prepared to move closer to finalizing the transaction.

The largest, single issue relative to objections is to know that they should never arise. You should identify them either in pre-call planning through your internal advocate, identified in the Probe, or eliminate them in your presentation by circumventing them with a properly designed recommendation.

However, if objections come up, here's the formula for dealing with them.

- Give your prospect verbal approval to have an objection.
- Ask if there are other concerns.
- Identify and isolate each issue.
- Deal with each issue, one at a time, being sure that each is resolved before you move on to the next objection.
- Don't be deterred from moving ahead with the sale.

Never forget that a "stall" simply means that your prospect wants to slow down the process, not feeling prepared to forge ahead with the sale, whereas objections are true issues that you need to resolve before you can move on with the sale.

Chapter 9
Step 6. Tie It Up:
Finalizing Transactions

Objective: To empower your prospect to buy, solidifying the sale, servicing, and vertically integrating the new account

In this step you ask the prospect to buy, negotiate an agreement, finalize, reinforce, and then cement the sale. You also service your new customer in ways that guarantee more sales, strong referrals, and an ongoing, productive relationship.

Without securing a commitment, you will not have a sale, of course. And, after all, isn't that your real purpose for being in front of the prospect?

However, it's important for you to understand that finalizing the transaction depends on everything you do in the first five steps—starting with proper prospecting, positioning, and precall planning and then gaining and securing trust with your prospect, asking the right questions, making a strong and correct recommendation, and ensuring that your prospect believes your claims about your product or service and your organization and believes that both can help your prospect achieve what he or she wants.

Now that you've gone through the first five steps successfully, it's crucial to know exactly what you should say now to get to consummating the sale.

In spite of a strong temptation to provide you with a plethora of ways to finalize the sale, I believe that you need to understand, master, and apply one single, powerful way to make a sale. It is far better to have one proven strategy and be able to use it correctly than it is to memorize a series of complicated maneuvers that, in the real world, you'll never actually use.

The Assumptive Close

What is that one single, powerful strategy? It's the *assumptive close*. It is called that because you are assuming that your prospect will buy and you are either making a straightforward statement or asking a simple question. And this close has been around for years and years.

Here are some examples of assumptive closes as statements:

- "Let me show you how we can get started."
- "Let me send you a letter of agreement."
- "Let's take care of the paperwork."
- "I'll set you up for delivery on Tuesday."

Here are some assumptive closes in the form of a question:

- "When would you like to get started?"
- "Can we go ahead and take care of the paperwork in order to get started?"
- "May I set delivery for Tuesday?"

In each one of these cases, whether you use a statement or a question, you imply that you assume your prospect will buy your product or service.

Again, however, in the real world, either of these methods will elicit one of three responses—"Yes," "No," or "I'm not sure." Now, let's take a look at how you would handle each of these responses.

You say: "Let me show you how we can get started."

You hear: "OK."

You say: "Let's take care of the paperwork now and you can sign it. We can then get the order process set up."

You are now in business. Of course, in the real world you would use the specific verbiage related to your situation for handling the details of initiating the sale of your specific product or service (letter of agreement, purchase order, delivery schedule, etc.).

Another example:

> **You say:** "Would you like to get started?"
>
> **You hear:** "Yes, let's go ahead."
>
> **You say:** "Good. Here's where we need your signature in order to get everything started."

However, you may not always receive such a positive response. If the response is negative, what do you do? What do you actually say?

> **You say:** "Can we go ahead and take care of the paperwork in order to get started?"
>
> **You hear:** "No, I don't think so."
>
> **You say:** "What is it that would cause you not to go ahead?"
>
> **You hear:** "I need to discuss it with my wife."
>
> **You say:** "Is that your only concern, the only thing that would cause you not to go ahead with this?"

Let's examine what just happened. You utilized the assumptive close only to discover that your assumption was incorrect! However, that is certainly not the end of the world.

Now you need to isolate your prospect's concern or objection ("What is it that would cause you not to go ahead?") and uncover any other reason ("Is that your only concern …?").

Once you have isolated the problem and either identified

it as the only one or identified others, your next task is to try to resolve it to your prospect's satisfaction.

You say: "If we can solve this issue to your satisfaction, can I presume that we will be able to go ahead?"

You will hear either "Yes" or "No." You then need to proceed accordingly. Here's how it works:

You ask: "Now, what, exactly, is your concern about _____?"

You hear: "I'm concerned about the warranty" or "I'm still concerned about spending that much money."

You say: "As I understand it, if your concern about _____ can be resolved, everything else looks OK. Is that right?"

You hear: "Yes, I think so."

You say: "I understand. Let's deal with your concern about _____."

You will now work to resolve your prospect's concern by re-applying your solution in terms that resolve, solve, or eradicate that concern. During this process, be sure to ask coursecorrection questions consistently ("Does this answer your concern?" or "How does this look?" or "Does this look more acceptable?").

When you have resolved any concern(s) to your prospect's satisfaction, you will again use some form of the assumptive close.

You say: "If this solves your problem with _____, can we go ahead and get started?" or "If this answers your concern, let's get started."

At this point, say absolutely nothing. Don't respond, utter

a word, or say anything! Your prospect will either say "Yes," "No," or "I'm not sure." If the answer is "Yes," you've made a sale. If the answer is "No," you'll need to re-apply the same formula as just described one more time. If the answer is "I'm not sure," you'll need to ask, "What is it that you're not sure about?" Then, you'll deal, one more time, with the issue or concern and repeat the same process.

This is a very important process to master. Never lose sight of the fact that if you are unable to deal with objections and finalize transactions you'll never be successful in sales. It's just that simple.

If you hear your prospect say, "I'm not sure" after you ask an assumptive question or issue an assumptive statement, you simply need to ask this question, "What is it that you're not sure about?" Whatever they say, you'll need to respond with "I can understand that. What do we have to do to resolve that issue so that we can move ahead with this?"

Now, you can easily go ahead and resolve the issue(s) so that the sale can be consummated.

Cementing and Reinforcing the Sale

Make no mistake about it. Sales are consummated only when and if your prospect's check clears the bank! Never, ever believe that you can make a sale, no matter what the size, and then pack your bag and leave.

It's critical that you understand the mindset of most buyers, no matter what they've bought. Thoughts like these run through their minds:

- "Did I do the right thing?"
- "Did I buy too much? Too little?"
- "How will I defend this to my boss?"
- "Did I pay too much?"
- "Should I have looked elsewhere?"

Then be sure to say things to cement and reinforce the sale:

You say: "I'm sure glad that you decided to go ahead with _____. It really is our best-performing model. You're really going to like it."

or

You say: "You'll feel real confident going forward, knowing that you have the extended warranty. I'm really glad that you decided to do that."

or

You say: "You made the right choice. Congratulations!"

Remember: you are reinforcing and cementing the sale in order to counter the thoughts of concern that can creep into your prospect's mind. Prospects generally don't verbalize these concerns, so you'll never know if they really feel like this. Simply assume that they feel like that and be sure to reinforce and cement the sale every single time.

Following up the Sale

These strategies are essential to your success with your new customer on a long-term basis. Do you want to sell him or her more of your product or service? Do you want to use him or her as a referral source? If the answer to either of these questions is yes, then this is an important section for you to understand and master.

After you cement and reinforce the sale, you'll need to be very clear about what happens next. For example:

You say: "I'll call you tomorrow to confirm that the delivery schedule has been finalized for next week."

or

You say: "I'm going to leave here and go back to the office and make arrangements for Jane, our customer service manager, to contact you tomorrow morning."

or

You say: "I'll be calling you no later than Thursday to reconfirm the details and guarantee proper shipment."

Bottom line? You must articulate some sort of action you are going to take, when you'll do it, and what that means to your new customer. Fail to do this at your own peril. Why? Because you need to start proving to your new customer, right now, that you are proactive, dependable, and capable of ensuring his or her satisfaction. Trust me: this will empower you significantly with your customers—and prove to them that you are truly interested in far more than collecting a commission, making a sale, or winning a contest.

Upselling your new customer at this point is much easier than you might think. After all, the tough part—the initial sale—is over, isn't it? That's often a good time to sell other products or services related to that sale. Upselling is happening all around us. Have you ever bought a dress and then the salesperson suggested shoes to go with that dress? How about a suit and you ended up buying a shirt and tie with it?

All you need to do is suggest an additional component or logical extension to your product or service. You might ask a question, like this:

> ***You say:*** "Have you given some thought to adding the extended warranty?"

You might make a statement and follow it with a question, like this:.

> ***You say:*** "Most of our customers take advantage of the help desk option. Would you like to do that?"

In any case, as counterintuitive as it may appear, upselling immediately after making a sale is far easier than waiting to do so. Try it. You'll be surprised how easy it really is.

FINAL THOUGHTS

These scenarios for the six steps of the IMPACT sales process should provide you with the perfect phrases you need to prospect, seek appointments, meet prospects and customers, qualify prospects and ask questions, make effective presentations, prove your claims, create value, present price, finalize transactions, seek referrals, overcome objectives, and service accounts. Now, in Chapter 10, Super Sophisticated Selling, we'll get into some very precise words, phrases, and strategies that work with specific types of prospects and customers.

Part Three

Additional Sales Scenarios: Three Types of Customers

Chapter 10
Super Sophisticated Selling:
Entrepreneurs, Corporate Executives,
Purchasing Managers

There are universal sales truths, principles, and concepts—and there are also some very precise words, phrases, and strategies that appeal to each specific type of prospect or customer. And that is very, very sophisticated selling.

This differentiation centers on a unique concept presented earlier in this section—a concept that most salespeople never understand, let alone master. Here it is:

Prospects don't always buy what they need. They always, however, buy what they want.

Here's the difference: Needs are …

- Product-specific
- Rational
- Above the surface
- Based on fact

Wants, on the other hand, are …

- Product-neutral

- Emotional
- Below the surface
- Based on perception

As a consequence, here's the principle:

Salespeople who can present their product or service (a need) in the way that their prospect wants to perceive it will be more likely to make the sale.

Let's put it another way:

Prospects are more likely to buy what they need from salespeople who understand what they really want.

This final chapter will deal with how you can do this with three specific types of prospects:

- Entrepreneurs
- Corporate executives (not CEOs)
- Purchasing managers

These three were selected because they represent a cross section of prospect or customer types. Each was selected from our library of Special Reports that are listed and available for order through our Web site, **www.thewordsthatsell.com**.

In every case, there are five specific wants that every prospect has, no matter what your product or service might be. Your job is to describe and position each of them before you actually present them. These are those five specific wants:

- **Primary Want:** The type of relationship that the prospect wants to have with a salesperson, supplier, or vendor.
- **Product or Service Want:** The way that the prospect wants to perceive the product or service he or she seeks.
- **Benefit Want:** The perception of the benefits that a prospect wants to receive in any product or service.

- **Provider Want:** The type of ideal provider that a prospect wants to do business with in securing a product or service.
- **Price Want:** How the prospect wants to perceive the ideal price.

What does all of this mean? That you need to properly position, describe, and articulate in absolute terms each of these wants (primary, product/service, benefit, provider, and price) to the prospect before you actually verbalize them in terms based on needs.

Let's talk more about how this works.

For example, to an entrepreneur the most important thing about any product or service is that it must be "practical, streetsmart, and designed for their unique situation." And it makes no difference what the product or service might be! Here's how you'd present your product or service, for example, to an entrepreneur:

"Before I get real specific about our service and how it works, let me first say that it's street-smart, practical, and designed for your unique situation. Now, let me describe it to you in detail ..."

The purchasing manager wants to see any product or service as being "easy to understand, solid and safe, not technically challenging." So, how would you present your product or service to this type of prospect? Here it is:

"Before I get real specific about my product and how it works, let me first say that it's easy to understand, is a solid and safe purchase, and doesn't require a lot of technical education. Now, let me describe it to you in detail ..."

Got the picture? Now, let's look at three specific prospects:

- Entrepreneurs (pages 414–433)
- Corporate executives who aren't CEOs (pages 434–451)
- Purchasing managers (pages 452–474)

Selling to Entrepreneurs: How to Form a Special Instant Bond in Your First Interaction

PRIMARY WANT

To form a strong bond with this type of prospect, your presentation must begin with a description of what he or she really wants out of having a relationship with you. This specific bonding statement can replace the generic bonding statement outlined in Part Two when selling to an entrepreneur.

To do this, you'll need to initially engage your prospect using phrases like the following:

- "Being in charge"
- "Calling your own shots"
- "Personal independence"
- "Being your own person"
- "Making the business run your way"
- "Doing whatever you want to do, whenever you want to do it"
- "Having complete control over your business"

EXAMPLE OF A PRIMARY BONDING STATEMENT

- "Independence, freedom, and calling your own shots is probably why you started your business in the first place. We know that. To see if we can help you achieve even more of that, do you mind if I ask you a few questions?"

WHY THESE WORDS WORK

Surprisingly, most entrepreneurs aren't trying to build financial empires for themselves. Most of them went into business to achieve a far different goal—a steady, respectable paycheck without having to put up with a boss.

Material in this and following examples copyright North American Sales Research Institute, 2005. Used with permission.

These prospects could never accept a position in a large organization, no matter how prestigious or well paying it might be. And if they ever do, they resent it and yearn to return to their entrepreneurial roots before too long.

If there's a fact about this type of prospect that rings most true, it's that they're virtually unemployable.

Why is that? Entrepreneurs generally resent any form of authority that's exerted over them. In fact, they lack the single characteristic every employee must have ... being willing to obey the orders of a superior, even when they think the superior is wrong.

On top of that, entrepreneurs would never sit still for doing the things that employees are expected to do, like:

- Reporting their results
- Explaining their actions
- Justifying their decisions
- Appearing at times and places "on demand"
- Cooperating with a superior whose capabilities they believe aren't any greater than their own, and are probably inferior
- Accepting other people's decision-making authority

Being a cooperative employee runs against the very fiber of their being. As a result, their desire for personal independence—more than any other impulse—drove entrepreneurs to start their own businesses.

The impulse wasn't profit or riches. It was freedom.

That's an important distinction because it actually tells you the best way to approach this prospect ... and the approach you should avoid.

You can summarize almost all the approaches that most salespeople use with entrepreneurs in two words: profitability and growth. In other words, they promise either a better bottom line or a bigger business. A few promise both. And either or both are badly off target.

"Profitability" is nothing more than an intellectual abstraction for most entrepreneurs. They can't really "feel it." It has no emotional urgency, value, or meaning for them.

Of course, they'll always nod in agreement and make the right comments when the subject of profitability comes up. But it doesn't motivate them.

They relate more readily and eagerly to the amount of money they have in a checking account or the cash register at the end of every day, or week, or month.

Cash position has always mattered far more to entrepreneurs than profits ever could. It represents a reality they can easily understand and respect. When compared with the realworld significance of cash, profits seem empty and theoretical ... merely an entry on a financial statement.

"Growth" raises the fear that they'll lose control over their businesses, a fear that comes from a perception that's fundamental to how entrepreneurs approach their business.

They fear that a major increase in the size of the business will outstrip their ability to manage it.

You need to understand that entrepreneurs rarely use any kind of coherent management strategy. They're more likely to manage in a very hands-on way. That's why they have difficulty handling managerial challenges that they can't handle both directly and personally.

If a decision has to be made regarding inventory control, for example, they have to "go and see for themselves" before deciding.

If their receivables department is having trouble collecting an overdue account? They'll say, "Give me the phone, I'll talk to 'em."

When they don't like the way the product is being shipped, they'll run down to the loading dock and show the people down there how to do it right, the way they did it when they were doing it themselves.

Managing a business is much more an act of physical labor than of intellectual insight for them. So, they manage by direct, personal intervention rather than through memos, policies, or standards.

That, by the way, is one reason why they're so unwilling to delegate and why they do it so badly. Nothing of real importance is ever written down and passed on to employees so they can learn how to do their jobs satisfactorily. The result is a group of employees who are underinformed, undertrained, and undermotivated.

And, of course, nobody in his or her right mind would delegate to people who are underinformed, undertrained, and undermotivated. Of course, the fact that the entrepreneur made those people that way always seems to escape his or her attention.

Selling to Entrepreneurs: How to Make Your Product or Service the Right Answer— No Matter What You Sell

PRODUCT OR SERVICE WANT

To gain the best chance of having an entrepreneur believe and accept any product/service claim, you must carefully position your product or service before you start to describe it.

And you should position it by using words and phrases such as these:

- "Designed specifically for your unique situation"
- "Practical"
- "Street-smart"
- "Nothing theoretical or abstract about it"
- "Won't put any demands on your time"
- "Won't strain your resources"

EXAMPLE OF A PRODUCT- OR SERVICE-POSITIONING STATEMENT

- "Before we discuss our product/service, let me stress that it is practical and street-smart. It's also been carefully designed for your unique business situation."

WHY THESE WORDS WORK

Entrepreneurs are strongly attracted to products and services that they perceive have been designed specifically for their unique situations. If they had their "druthers," entrepreneurs wouldn't buy a single product or service that wasn't designed and developed precisely—100%—for their specific business, industry, application, or competitive environment.

I once heard of an entrepreneur in the St. Louis area, who said, "I only buy from companies that do business on the Missouri side." He was referring, of course, to the Missouri side of the Mississippi River. According to him, companies "over on the Illinois side," as he put it, do business in a totally different way. Therefore, he couldn't possibly buy from a vendor who was unable to accommodate the difference between the two sides.

By the way, when asked for a specific definition of the difference between the two sides, he couldn't provide one. However, he was still fully convinced that there was a difference!

Entrepreneurs have that obsession because they don't like to make what I'll call a "conceptual leap."

In other words, they don't eagerly make the move from the general to the specific, or from one application to another, or from one industry to another. And they usually resist adapting any broad, general concept to their own situation.

As a consequence, they're always suspicious that salespeople are trying to make them force a square peg into a round hole.

As a result, salespeople often hear entrepreneurs condemn their product or service by saying, "That doesn't apply to me" or "My business is different, it's unique." Actually, what they're really saying is "I'm unique, but you don't make me feel that way." Never forget: the owner and the business are practically one and the same.

Surprisingly, the actual words "specific to his or her unique situation" will even have different meanings for different entrepreneurs.

Those words are really a matter of perception. They might simply mean that your product or service was designed for an entrepreneurial type of business, or an owner-operated business, or a small business. If you pay close enough attention, the prospect will tell you which one he or she wants to hear.

When a product or service is perceived as "practical, street-smart, and not theoretical," most entrepreneurs believe that it will do all three of the following:

- It will eliminate complexity from their lives.
- It won't strain the company's resources.
- It won't put additional demands on their own personal time.

Entrepreneurs have no patience for complexity because it interferes with the hands-on, quick-action performance they consider so vital to their personal independence.

When things are too complex and ambiguous, the path is open for the abstract. And entrepreneurs don't trust anything abstract because it's theoretical, in contrast to anything they think of as concrete. And theoretical just doesn't work in their world.

Anything that's theoretical is automatically "ivory tower," academic, or intellectual. And because it lacks the basic strength that comes from being "street-smart," it doesn't have any no-nonsense, hard-nosed practicality.

An entrepreneur draws a clear distinction between "the street "and the rest of the world. And only "the street" has the desirable virtue of being uncomplicated, down-to-earth, and easy to understand.

That's why entrepreneurs can be so frustratingly resistant to learning anything but hard information that deals with "how to." Anything that relates to "why" is of very little interest to them.

Their bias can be summarized in the statement: "Don't tell me why, just tell me how." Or "Don't tell me about the theory behind it, just tell me how to use it."

As far as entrepreneurs are concerned, stopping and thinking—which is what theory and ambiguity make them do—is a colossal waste of time. It gets in the way of doing.

And nothing must be allowed to stop that. Nothing must get in the way of action.

Entrepreneurs always seem to be running … from one fire to another, from one crisis to another, from one challenge to another. There's always a tension right below the surface when you talk with them.

And what are they usually tense about? Burning through their resources.

And it doesn't matter how rich in resources the business might be. They can't help but have either one of two perceptions about their resources—they're either completely insufficient or just barely adequate to do the job.

Earlier, I referred to the almost mystical relationship between entrepreneurs and their businesses. I said that owners and their businesses are practically one and the same. Therefore, an entrepreneur's idea of resources is personal, very, very personal.

If you listen carefully enough, you'll often hear them say things like "I pay my bills." Although they mean that the business pays its bills, they can't stop themselves from speaking in the first person—"They owe me money" is synonymous with "They owe my company money."

And since resources often take on personal significance, they mean (over and above anything else) their own time.

This next statement is essential for you to understand. Even though the decision maker might not ever get personally involved in the use of your product or service, it still must be perceived as not placing any additional demands on his or her time.

Nothing that passes in and out of the doors of that business is thought of in anything but the most personal of terms.

Selling to Entrepreneurs: How to Make Your Organization the Ideal Provider

PROVIDER WANT

To gain the best chance of having the entrepreneur accept your organization as an ideal provider, as with the other four wants, you must first position it before you start to describe it.

Describe your organization in the following ways:

- "We're flexible."
- "We're responsive."
- "We're accommodating/willing to make accommodations."
- "We never try to put a square peg in a round hole."
- "We recognize your uniqueness."
- "We're thorough."
- "We follow through on everything."
- "We cover all the bases for you."
- "We're willing to do whatever it takes."
- "We make sure every detail is covered."

EXAMPLE OF A PROVIDER-POSITIONING STATEMENT

- "Let me tell you a little about our company. We pride our-selves on being flexible, responsible, accountable, and thorough. We follow through on everything. We cover all the bases for you so that you don't have to."

WHY THESE WORDS WORK

An entrepreneur's desire for flexibility from you is a reflection of two other needs—personal independence and products/ services that are designed specifically for his or her unique situation.

Small and medium-size businesses outnumber giant companies by as much as 45-to-l. Yet, entrepreneurs perceive that almost every element of society favors the large companies and institutions—university courses, professional and consulting services, taxes, trade shows, seminars, books, research data, legislation, health insurance, periodicals, and just about everything else that teaches, explains, or reveals anything that has any value. And when they look at the structure of that world, they perceive a rigid, unyielding indifference.

And the world is just too big and powerful for them to bend to their will, too impersonal to care about them, and too consumed by what's of no interest or value to them. It won't yield to their needs or, for that matter, even pay attention to them. And they resent that.

Therefore, they want to do business only with a provider who considers them important enough to warrant flexibility or, if you will, very special treatment.

To be the ideal provider, you must be willing to make accommodations to what entrepreneurs consider their own unique requirements. Surprisingly, you won't have to actually be that flexible or even make that many exceptions. You simply have to be perceived as being willing to do so. And that is the secret! And essential for you to understand.

Remember: the need for personal independence is a statement to the effect that "I'm different from all the others, so I should get unique treatment." They're not claiming to be better than everyone else, only different from them.

That overriding sense of uniqueness—of having special needs—is the main source of this type of prospect's highly suspicious attitude toward most people who sell them anything.

You may have noticed that they often begin the sales cycle with the assumption that the salesperson doesn't understand them and is "just trying to sell me something." And, as mentioned earlier, that's usually a square peg for a round hole.

Again, if entrepreneurs are going to perceive that your product or service was designed specifically for them, they also must perceive that you took all the necessary steps to make it the right way. That's why they always demand that you be more thorough and disciplined than they are. This is what might be called a "would have" or "should have" situation.

When they blame their chaos on the lack of resources—again, their most common complaint—they want to be assured that you did everything they would have done if they had sufficient resources to make sure that your product or service is right for them. In other words, they would have done their own due diligence, allegedly, if they had the time and money to do it. That's the "would have" side.

On the "should have" side, a few entrepreneurs are honest enough to admit that their lack of discipline has nothing to do with resources. In those rare cases, they want to know that you did what they should have done.

Being thorough, therefore, means you'll protect them from either uncontrollable conditions ("what they would have done") or from themselves ("what they should have done"). In fact, the typical situation reflects some of both.

Although they are often short on resources, they're also notorious for not being thorough and they rarely follow through ... even when ample resources are available.

That well-deserved reputation is a major contributor to their need for independence. As said before, they show a range of traits that really do make them virtually unemployable.

Selling to Entrepreneurs: How to Move Your Benefits to a Higher Level

BENEFIT WANT

Like the other wants, in order to gain the best chance of having an entrepreneur believe and accept your benefit claims, you must first position them before you start to describe them.

Describe your benefits as delivering the following benefits:

- "Order (in the business)"
- "Control"
- "Allowing you to be in control automatically"
- "Order that reflects your personal wishes"
- "No more chaos"
- "An ability for you to never tolerate disorder again"

EXAMPLE OF A BENEFIT-POSITIONING STATEMENT

- "Our product/service will give you a lot more order and control. Any chaos will be reduced ... and that way you'll have a lot more automatic control without direct involvement on your part."

WHY THESE WORDS WORK

If there's a word that reminds most entrepreneurs of their businesses, that word is "chaos."

Every senior executive in every large company must learn to deal with a certain amount of disorganization and tolerate it. Entrepreneurs, on the other hand, can't deal with it and can't tolerate it, either. Not a pretty picture, is it?

When they try to deal with chaos, they become victims of their own management style. If you recall, for them running a business is an act of physical labor rather than one of intellectual insight so they manage by direct, personal intervention.

Consequently, they experience an exhausting drain on their energies whenever they wear the manager's hat. Being in charge wears them down mentally; overcoming the disorder in the business is a challenge they'd do just about anything to avoid.

If they accept the challenge, they know they're going to be totally exhausted. But if they don't accept it, they have to tolerate it. And tolerating chaos is just as terrible an experience as trying to eliminate it.

Executives who are not entrepreneurial view the companies where they work as their place of employment. Entrepreneurs, however, consider it practically their home, the place where their very existence is on the line every day. It's where the drama of their lives is acted out from minute to minute.

Their fate ultimately rests on everything that happens within those walls. It's where their identity, value, and purpose are being tested constantly. And, as mentioned earlier, they consider themselves and the business to be almost the same entity.

The need entrepreneurs have for order is to believe that their lives aren't being squandered. After all, their business and life are one and the same. And they don't want to squander either one. However, because they deeply dread the challenges associated with their personal-intervention management style, they'd rather get control of the business in a different way— automatically.

They perceive that business problems are attributable to people—to themselves and their employees—which is why they tend to explain problems and failures in total human terms.

Since being in business is such an intensely personal experience for them, it's not surprising that successes and reverses are almost always seen as the result of human performance, good or bad.

Blind, impersonal forces like marketplace dynamics might interest academics and other ivory-tower types, but they're just idle speculation to an entrepreneur. If a problem persists, people have to change the way they work in order to solve it. Period.

However, in starting their businesses, they made the statement that they have no interest in changing themselves. They are what they are and are stubbornly proud of it, even when they criticize themselves.

At the same time, they've grudgingly reached the conclusion that their employees won't change either or they don't know how to change their employees or they can't summon up the energy to make the effort.

One solution is to give the assignment to another person. But, when that happens, entrepreneurs immediately put themselves back in power as soon as the person makes a decision they don't like.

Because they could never surrender genuine control of the business to anyone else, except when they're ready to pass it to their hand-picked successors, order must come in some kind of automatic way, so that the owner doesn't have to intervene or change people's behavior. In effect, it just happens—and it happens the way the entrepreneur wants it to.

It doesn't take a great leap of logic to reach the point toward which all of the evidence points—that entrepreneurs want their businesses to reflect their personal identities.

These prospects draw such personal value and identity from the business that it becomes an extension of themselves. It's as much a part of them as are their children. And, like all parents, they want their offspring to show something of themselves.

In no way is this an ego trip or anything as shallow as that. It's a matter of personal survival.

Selling to Entrepreneurs: How to Make Your Price, Rate, or Fee a True Bargain

PRICE, RATE, OR FEE WANT

One more time, as with the other wants, for the best chance of having the entrepreneur accept your price, rate, or fee, you must first position it before you ever quote it.

How you should position your price, rate, or fee before you present it:

- "It costs the same as ... "
- "It doesn't cost any more than ... "

EXAMPLE OF A PRICE-, RATE-, OR FEE-POSITIONING STATEMENT

- "Before we discuss price/rate/fee, let me stress that it won't cost any more than what you'd make from three additional sales. I'd also like to make sure you understand everything it includes ..."

WHY THESE WORDS WORK

Many types of prospects are likely to talk endlessly about things like cost-effectiveness, but the entrepreneur is one of the few who's really serious about it.

The reason for that is simple: no matter how large the business becomes, entrepreneurs always perceive that buying anything means taking the money out of their own pockets.

Earlier, it was indicated that running a company is an intensely personal experience for entrepreneurs. Consequently, they consider the company's cash their personal money, just as they consider the furniture as being their furniture, the equipment as being their equipment, and so on.

They must perceive the ideal product or service as being worth the money and producing a tangible benefit on a virtual one-to-one basis for each dollar spent. And the best way to describe that is through graphic terms. In other words, choose a symbol that's familiar to your entrepreneurial prospect and use it as a model against which he or she can compare the price (e.g., "It costs the same as a set of tires"). For example, "Before I present our price, I'd like to make sure you understand everything it includes. The truth is that it will cost no more than three additional sales. Let me explain …"

Selling to Entrepreneurs: Letters and Advertising

IN A LETTER

Dear _____,

Form a Special Instant Bond: There's nothing like being your own person, . . . doing whatever you want to do, whenever you want to do it.

Make Your Product or Service the Right Answer: To help you get there, a product or service has to be specific to your unique situation. It should also be practical and very streetsmart.

Make Your Organization the Ideal Provider: But, even the best product or service won't do you much good unless it comes from people who are willing to do whatever it takes to make sure every detail is covered.

Move Your Benefits to a Higher Level: Then, you'll have control over your business that totally reflects your personal wishes.

Make Your Price, Rate, or Fee a True Bargain: And whatever you buy should never cost more than _____. [See the section above on positioning your price, rate, or fee.]

I believe you'll find that [your product or service] and [company] can provide all of those things for you. But you, of course, should be free to make that decision for yourself.

[Now, state your purpose for writing the letter, what you want the prospect to do (a call to action), communicate your normal sales message, and finish the letter.]

IN THE FORM OF ADVERTISING COPY
BEING YOUR OWN PERSON

There's nothing like being your own person, . . . doing whatever you want to do, whenever you want to do it.

To help you get there, a product or service has to be specific to your unique situation. It also should be practical and very street-smart.

But, even the best product or service won't do you much good unless it comes from people who are willing to do whatever it takes to make sure every detail is covered.

Then, you'll have control over your business that totally reflects your personal wishes. And whatever you buy should never cost more than _____. (See the section above on positioning your price, rate, or fee.)

I believe you'll find that (your product or service) and (company) can be all that for you. But, you should be free to make that decision for yourself.

[Communicate your normal marketing message, state what you want the prospect to do (a call to action), and finish the ad.]

Important: Always put the Words That Sell in generic terms, as if you were describing "universal standards." Remember: their purpose is positioning. Once you communicate them, you can then use whatever words you normally use to tell the prospect about your product or service, your benefits, your company, and your price.

Selling to Entrepreneurs: Words That Don't Work

Avoid at all costs using these words and phrases to describe yourself, your organization, or your product or service.

However, feel free to use them to describe your competitors! Do so and you'll never have to criticize them in front of the prospect (which you should never, ever do in any circumstance anyway), if you know how to describe your competitors with the Words That Don't Work:

- "Organization"
- "Sophisticated"
- "Employee"
- "Theoretical"
- "Standardized"
- "Uniform"
- "The same for everyone"
- "Structured"
- "Procedures"
- "Growth"
- "Profitability"

EXAMPLE

- "XYZ (your competitor) is a <u>sophisticated organization</u>. Everything they do is based on a <u>standardized</u> format that comes from their highly structured research. What they do is <u>the same for everyone</u>. They accomplish this with <u>procedures</u> designed to help their customers have greater <u>profitability</u>. Their <u>uniform</u> approach appeals most to <u>employees</u>."

WHY THESE WORDS DON'T WORK

What do you think? It sounds like they're great—but not to this prospect! You'll notice that you're not saying one single negative word about your competitor? Of course, you don't want to say these things if they're not true. However, all of these words will work regardless of what you sell. Remember, though: use them with integrity!

Selling to Corporate Executives (Non-CEO): How to Form a Special Instant Bond in Your First Interaction

PRIMARY WANT

To form a strong, initial trust with this prospect, your presentation must begin with a description of what he or she really wants out of having a relationship with you. This specific bonding statement can replace the generic bonding statement outlined in Part Two when selling to a corporate executive.

In the Meet step you will want to use words like these:

- "Teamwork"
- "Not sticking your neck out"
- "Staying in the mainstream"
- "Sensible responsibilities"
- "Being involved in all the important decisions"
- "Advancing steadily"
- "Protecting yourself from unwarranted intrusions"
- "Keeping everything on a safe course"
- "Insulating yourself"

EXAMPLE OF A PRIMARY BONDING STATEMENT

- "Teamwork is critical to what you do and part of that is keeping you as involved as you want to be in making decisions. After all, advancing steadily is important. To see if we can help you achieve more of those things, do you mind if I ask you a few questions?"

Remember: this can and will substitute for the generic bonding statement. However, this specific statement is good for use only with a corporate executive.

WHY THESE WORDS WORK

The typical corporate executive wants to be thought of as a team player who is "comfortably anonymous" and never singled out for extraordinary responsibilities.

At the same time, he or she doesn't want to be left out of important processes and decisions, either. Sound contradictory? Not really.

Few corporate executives have the necessary ambition or critical political skills to keep advancing their careers carefully and purposefully to the very top of the pyramid, although some of them can come fairly close. As a result, they usually end their careers anywhere between middle management and a vice presidency or a directorship.

For corporate executives, therefore, the notion of teamwork and being a team player is vitally important. They have an inordinate need for "collective participation" because within the confines of the group is a comforting and protective anonymity, not from others within the company but from the outside world.

It's revealing that CEOs and other high-ranking corporate officers are actually easier to reach on the phone than the typical corporate executive. This is because this breed of prospect has become an expert at hiding from the world inside the bureaucracy.

Becoming a vice president or a director isn't, however, what I meant by "extraordinary responsibilities." Even though most corporate executives don't reach those levels, there's still nothing all that extraordinary about it.

An "extraordinary responsibility" would be taking on the task of contributing a significant improvement to the company's profit margin, achieving a dramatic turnaround of some sort, or developing an entirely new way of implementing a work process.

In other words, it's a challenge that is far out of the mainstream of normal corporate life ... with a lot riding on the outcome. Even their careers. And corporate executives really don't want to have that much riding on what they do.

At the same time, they don't want to be excluded from what they perceive to be "important processes and decisions."

Today, consensus is a crucial tool for CEOs. They won't move ahead with a decision until everyone who's involved has "signed off on it" or "had input into it." And among the people who have to sign off are the legions of corporate executives.

While they have an aversion to standing out in any exposed way—which is what an extraordinary responsibility will require—they're extremely sensitive to being left out of activities in which they believe they should be included.

In fact, given the consensus style of management practiced by virtually all CEOs, corporate executives have been conditioned to think in those terms. They expect to be included.

And if they are not, their world gets turned upside-down and they become disoriented. It simply does not "feel right."

An interesting drama takes place when a corporate executive perceives that he or she has been omitted from an important decision-making process or project. Deviating from his or her usual cooperative, "don't rock the boat" style, the offended party can easily become the very obstacle with which you'll have to deal.

Corporate executives are not, in fact, above issuing threats that they will sabotage a project unless they are consulted on it, which certainly is exceptional behavior for someone who wants to be such a team player.

But that is exactly the point. Being excluded from the process shows that they are not "well-thought-of team players." And that is exactly what they don't want to happen.

The protocol that is part of their protective anonymity has been violated and, as a result, the familiar and comfortable way of doing things is stripped away.

Many corporate executives will instantly reverse themselves and become supportively cooperative at the very moment they are included in the process. And from then on, they will often have so little to contribute to the actual decision-making process that you might wonder what all the fuss was about. The fuss, in fact, was not about wanting to insert exciting ideas into the process. It was really all about being included, as a good team player should be.

Selling to Corporate Executives (Non-CEO): How to Make Your Product or Service the Right Answer—No Matter What You Sell

PRODUCT OR SERVICE WANT

As with all five wants, to gain the best chance of having a corporate executive believe and accept your product or service claims, you must precisely position it before you ever start to describe it.

Position your product or service by using phrases such as the following:

- "Supports what you have already accomplished"
- "Is not a departure from what you are doing"
- "Right in line with the direction you are taking"

EXAMPLE OF A PRODUCT- OR SERVICE-POSITIONING STATEMENT

- "Before I present our product/service let me stress that it really does support what you have already accomplished and is not a departure at all from what you are already doing."

WHY THESE WORDS WORK

If you approach a typical entrepreneur with a product or service that promises "more of the same," you are likely to be in for a major surprise. Independent business owners are known for making radical changes because they are forever struggling with the conditions that cause them to lose sleep every night. As a result, "more of the same"—or nothing more than a slight course correction—is rarely satisfying for the typical entrepreneur.

On the other hand, that slight course correction is about all the corporate executive can cope with.

When an entrepreneur admits to having wasted the company's resources on some form of foolishness, he or she does not have to fear the displeasure of a superior, because there isn't one. Entrepreneurs do not need, therefore, to be personally validated by every product and service they buy.

For senior executives, however, that is precisely the issue. It is the equivalent of professional suicide (i.e., not being a highly regarded team player) to openly admit that their error in judgment has cost the company money, reputation, or whatever.

Radical shifts in direction are simply not a part of this prospect's universe, because shifts invalidate whatever the executive has worked so hard to sustain. Instead, every new purchase must be justified as one more complementary step, another building block that fits in neatly with all the previous steps and blocks.

Even in those rare situations in which a product or service represents a substantial departure from past practices, you will find corporate executives concocting all sorts of elaborate reasons to prove that it is not really such a departure. In fact, their ability to torture reality sufficiently to satisfy this requirement is really nothing short of awesome.

Selling to Corporate Executives (Non-CEO): How to Make Your Organization the Ideal Provider

PROVIDER WANT

Again, to gain the best chance of having the corporate executive (non-CEO) accept your organization as an ideal provider, you must position it before you start to describe it.

Describe your organization in these terms:

- "Team players"
- "Widely accepted"
- "Blend in well with everyone"
- "Committed to a team approach"

EXAMPLE OF A PROVIDER-POSITIONING STATEMENT

- "Let me tell you a little about our company. We pride ourselves on being team players who blend in well with everyone. We operate under that total team concept and, as a consequence, are widely accepted within all of our customers'/clients'organizations."

WHY THESE WORDS WORK

Your organization has to be acceptable to the corporate executive's superiors, peers, and subordinates.

Whenever you approach corporate executives, keep uppermost in your mind that you have been allowed to enter the "inner sanctum." And that private work environment is a highly private world into which few are allowed to encroach.

For example, salespeople often find that it takes months to just get an appointment with a corporate executive. Because of that, they make the mistake of concluding that he or she is a "tough sell" whose schedule is crammed with important meetings and other monumentally important events.

The opposite is almost always true.

It is shocking for most salespeople to learn that corporate executives actually fill their days with a bare minimum of critical work, instead spending excessive amounts of time to generate imperceptible results or no results at all.

During the research for this report, to cite one example, we watched a corporate executive spend nearly an entire morning drafting a single, three-page letter!

Their lunches are usually leisurely. Meetings are frequent, wordy, and unnecessarily long. Telephone conversations are often just as social as they are professional. Office banter and chitchat go on to a degree that would drive most entrepreneurs into an uncontrollable fury because they sign the paychecks and want nonstop work in return. But this is a totally different culture.

The reason these prospects can be so chronically and frustratingly inaccessible has nothing to do with their workloads. Instead, it has everything to do with their need for insulation.

The truth is that they are nervous about letting outsiders in and will do almost anything to avoid it. Every outsider, every provider they bring in is a reflection on themselves.

But there is a huge paradox here:

Corporate executives crave anonymity, which causes them to avoid making a large number of decisions. After all, the fewer decisions you make, the less chance both you and those decisions will stand out in any negative way. Yet, because they make so few truly important decisions, each one they make takes on an exceptional significance, ... merely because it is such a rarity!

One such decision is the selection of a provider—you.

That is why salespeople who represent small and/or less well-known companies are so frequently disappointed when corporate executives decide to go with "old tried and true," providers with the big names and fabled reputations—the "least-risk vendor" scenario. Even if their solutions are subpar, ineffectual, and overpriced. They appear to be safe and easily defensible. And that is one of the reasons why strong brands can breed poor sales skills!

And despite what you might believe, the decision had little to do with features, benefits, price, or any of the other conventional issues. It was, more often than not, strictly a matter of which provider would have the better chance of being the most acceptable to everyone who's involved.

And "everyone" implies a four-way perspective. Corporate executives are convinced that a provider must pass muster in "four directions:"

1. Upward (with superiors)
2. To the right (with peers "on one side")
3. To the left (with peers "on the other side")
4. Downward (with subordinates)

Since the team concept is so fundamental to these prospects, an objection from any of the four directions can kill your potential sale … or put it squarely into the revenue stream of "old tried and true." Again, no matter how expensive, overpriced, or ineffectual what you're selling might really be!

Another aspect of this four-way concern is the shifting loyalty most corporate executives have toward providers. These prospects can be boundlessly enthusiastic about doing business with you, only to instantly reverse their opinion if "flak" comes from any of the four directions.

For that matter, it is not even valid to use the word "loyalty," since the relationship most corporate executives have with their providers is better described as a "marriage of convenience." The relationship will only take on a tone of permanence if and when the provider establishes itself over a very long period of time. Until then, however, the provider is only as good as the latest opinion rendered by a superior, a peer, or a subordinate.

And that's only because that's how real, "dedicated team players" do it.

Selling to Corporate Executives (Non-CEO): How to Move Your Benefits to a Higher Level

BENEFIT WANT

To gain the best chance of having a corporate executive believe and accept your benefit claims, you must position those claims before you describe them to the corporate executive.

Describe your benefits as delivering the following benefits:

- "Nothing you have to defend or explain"
- "Nothing you have to apologize for"
- "Results everyone accepts"
- "The outcome everyone accepts"

EXAMPLE OF A BENEFIT-POSITIONING STATEMENT

- "Our product/service is nothing that you will have to defend or explain. It will deliver the results and outcomes that everyone will accept."

WHY THESE WORDS WORK

Corporate executives are deathly afraid of being embarrassed in front of their coworkers and never want to be forced to defend an unpopular decision—or, worse yet, apologize for it. Any of those events could set their careers back for years or even derail them completely.

I even heard one of these prospects agree that a service I was selling was superior in every way to the one they had previously purchased. However, she had championed that decision and actually told me that, if she recommended changing to our service, it would be "career suicide." Needless to say, I never made the sale. And I didn't expect to, once I saw how totally consumed this buyer was with "career insurance." Even at the risk of continuing to purchase an inferior service!

Given their insulation from the world outside their company's doors, corporate executives have a very unusual opinion of what the word "results" means. Unfortunately, it has little to do with the actual impact a company's product or service has on the customer.

Most prospects of this type are, surprisingly, emotionally and intellectually disassociated from that important aspect of the company's activities. They don't "feel" any genuine commitment, therefore, to such traditional notions as market share, customer satisfaction, "the bottom line," and so on. Oh, they can verbalize it with the best of them—but they don't really "feel" it. These concepts have an aura of unreality for them because their real world is insulated, defined by the boundaries of their departments and by the groups immediately surrounding them. They will, however, readily and fluently talk about "market share," "bottom line," "shareholder value," and all the rest. After all, using the right buzzwords makes them members of the team, doesn't it?

For them, the word which salespeople tend to use a bit too often—"results"—means that they could be embarrassed and/or forced to explain their decisions. Another bad word? "Accountability." In relation to you, both mean the buying decision. And, although accountability really is a watchword in business today, it is far more a word to use than an action to take or a process to implement.

There is an old saying: "Victory has a thousand fathers; defeat is an orphan."

With amazing skill and dexterity, corporate executives will widely distance themselves from an embarrassing decision ... even if they are the ones who made it! In their environment, no one can afford to take that kind of heat.

Selling to Corporate Executives (Non-CEO): How to Make Your Price, Rate, or Fee a True Bargain

PRICE WANT

Remember: as with all wants, to gain the best chance of having a corporate executive accept your price, rate, or fee, you must first position it before you start to quote it.

How should you position your price before you present it to this prospect?

- "Priced within the mainstream"
- "In line with the industry"

EXAMPLE OF A PRICE-, RATE-, OR FEE-POSITIONING STATEMENT

- "Before I give you the exact price/rate/fee, let me stress that it is absolutely in line with the industry and is certainly priced within the mainstream. I'd also like to be sure that you know everything it includes …."

WHY THESE WORDS WORK

Your price, rate, or fee must be perceived as being close to that of your competition.

And, with this prospect, pricing your product or service substantially higher than your competition's is a recipe for disaster.

Not even the most courageous corporate executive—not even the one who is completely enchanted with you—will be able to comfortably pay what others could perceive as an inflated price in their world.

You must understand, however, that the reason has nothing to do with saving their employer any money, because there is very little motivation among these decision makers for that sort of thing. A budget is, after all, just a budget. It's not their money. Although they can be depended upon to say all the right things about cost savings and so on, that is just so many words.

In their world, not paying an inflated price, rate, or fee is strictly a matter of the personal credibility of a team player.

Selling to Corporate Executives (Non-CEO): Letters and Advertising

IN A LETTER

Dear _____,

Form a Special Instant Bond: You should be able to stay in the mainstream—with sensible responsibilities—while being involved in all the important decisions, as you keep everything on a safe course.

Make Your Product or Service the Right Answer: That requires products and services to support what you've already accomplished because they are right in line with the direction you are taking.

Make Your Organization the Ideal Provider: It also requires good team players who are widely accepted for blending in well with everyone.

Move Your Benefits to a Higher Level: When you get that, there's nothing you have to defend or apologize for because the results are what everyone expects.

Make Your Price, Rate, or Fee a True Bargain: On top of that, they expect a price, rate, or fee that is in line with the industry. I like to think that [your product or service] and [company] can provide all of those things for you. But you, of course, should be free to make that decision for yourself.

[Now, state your purpose for writing the letter, what you want the prospect to do (a call to action), communicate your normal sales message, and finish the letter.]

IN THE FORM OF ADVERTISING COPY

STAYING IN THE MAINSTREAM

You should be able to stay in the mainstream—with sensible responsibilities—while being involved in all the important decisions, as you keep everything on a safe course.

That requires products and services to support what you have already accomplished because they are right in line with the direction you are taking.

It also requires good team players who are widely accepted for blending in well with everyone.

When you get that, there is nothing you have to defend or apologize for because the results are what everyone expects. On top of that, they expect a price, rate, or fee that is in line with the industry.

We like to think that (your product or service) and (company) can both be all that for you. But, you should be free to make that decision for yourself.

[Communicate your usual marketing message, state what you want the prospect to do (a call to action), and finish the ad.]

Important: Always put the Words That Sell in generic terms, as if you were describing "universal standards." Remember: their purpose is positioning. Once you communicate them, you can then use whatever words you usually use to tell the prospect about your product or service, your benefits, your organization, and your price.

Selling to Corporate Executives (Non-CEO): Words That Don't Work

Avoid at all costs using these words and phrases to describe yourself, your company, or your product or service.

However, feel free to use them to describe your competitors! Do so and you'll never have to criticize them in front of the prospect (which you should never, ever do in any circumstance anyway), if you know how to describe your competitors with the Words That Don't Work:

- "Accountability"
- "Plot an unusual course"
- "Considerable responsibilities"
- "Keep your door open to everyone"
- "Be out in front"
- "Lead the pack"
- "A departure"
- "Shift direction"
- "Change from the ground up"
- "Substantial change"
- "Defend"
- "Explain"
- "Surprising results"
- "Unexpected"

EXAMPLE

- "XYZ is a great organization. They are very good at <u>introducing change from the ground floor up.</u> They like to help people like you get out in front and <u>plot unusual courses</u>. There's a lot of <u>accountability</u> related to what they do."

Remember: Don't say things that aren't true! However, if these words express, in fact, what your competitor does, describe them in this way.

Selling to Purchasing Managers: How to Form a Special Instant Bond in Your First Interaction

PRIMARY WANT

To form a strong bond with this prospect, your presentation must begin with a description of what he or she really wants out of having a relationship with you. This specific bonding statement can replace the generic bonding statement outlined in Part Two when selling to a purchasing manager.

Initially engage your prospect using phrases like these:

- "Getting recognition"
- "Being respected for what you do"
- "Getting credit"
- "You probably do a lot more than you get credit for"
- "Gaining respect"
- "You're doing important work"
- "Making a big contribution"
- "You're important to your company's success"

EXAMPLE OF A SPECIFIC PRIMARY BONDING STATEMENT

- "You make significant contributions with the difficult decisions you make. And that's important work. In order for us to be sure that we can help you continue to do that, do you mind if I ask you a few questions?"

Remember: you will have first issued your statement of intention by saying, "My purpose is to have a chance to meet you and ask you a few questions."

WHY THESE WORDS WORK

The typical purchasing manager wants to be considered by senior management as being equal to the company's "line" personnel and to receive the same kind of respect, recognition, and validation as those people garner (and the purchasing manager doesn't believe that he or she is receiving).

Never forget: these prospects are "staff," a status that differentiates them from their coworkers in the "line" divisions and departments.

The dominant bias in most companies is that line people are more important than staff people because line people are supposedly "the best and the brightest" the company has.

In a manufacturing firm, for example, the line divisions are Sales and Manufacturing (or Production). They're considered "line to the product" because one of them builds it and the other sells it.

All the other divisions and departments—Purchasing, Human Resources, and so on—are "staff" because they support and service the line divisions/departments.

Due to this bias, purchasing managers are often actually resented because:

- They supposedly work safely "behind the lines," where they're insulated from the dangers "in the trenches."
- They're considered only marginally important.
- They're not thought of as competent.
- They don't get credit for making a significant contribution to the company's success.

As a result, most of them have very little influence with their user departments.

Salespeople often have the frustrating experience of getting purchasing managers excited about their product or service, only to have the actual user fail to even show up for a meeting to discuss it! Has that happened to you? It has certainly happened to me—more than once!

Purchasing managers know that that bias is lurking beneath almost every contact they have with the line divisions. In response, they either strive to overcome it or retreat behind a wall of self-protective defensiveness. And since defensiveness is more typical, it's not unusual for you to find them becoming "territorial."

Given this lack of support and confidence from varied user groups, purchasing managers are often put in the role of the "go-between." They essentially "run back and forth" between the user group and the salesperson, trying to please the former and driving the latter to distraction.

As a consequence, they can be frustrating for you to deal with even because their own user departments usually fail to even deal with them properly. So, they're often unsure about what to buy or the conditions under which to buy it.

Users rarely take the time to inform purchasing managers of anything but the most rudimentary facts around what they need. And users generally transfer any buying authority to the purchasing department on issues of no perceived importance.

"If it meets the specs, I don't care who you buy it from" is a comment purchasing managers report hearing frequently from their users. It communicates a lot between the lines because another way to say it is "I made the important decision. Now, you can make the unimportant one."

It's not unusual for salespeople to perceive purchasing managers as being excessively demanding or even unreasonable.

Specifically, salespeople often claim that many purchasing managers are so obsessed with price that they seem to place little value on quality or value.

Many purchasing managers are known for their almost single-minded focus on price. However, it's quite often just a misperception that purchasing managers are ordered to buy at the lowest available price. However, there is ample evidence to prove that something else is going on.

Here are some research results. Over 62% of the purchasing managers studied in so-called "lowest-price" environments admitted to legally adjusting their specifications/calculations in order to award a favored provider whose price wasn't the lowest. In another study, on-time delivery superseded price as the major buying criteria.

Other typical reasons for purchase have to do with the issues such as useful product life, anticipated benefits, compatibility, upgrade ability, and a number of other factors that could "fudge" the issue of price.

When asked what makes a provider "favored," the factors that appeared again and again were "sincerity," "making the purchasing manager feel respectable and important," "a lack of technical obsession," and "patience."

On the other hand, when purchasing managers don't perceive a salesperson as being that way, these prospects can become rigidly demanding on such issues as price and delivery. They might also conduct quite rigorous facility inspections and use some sort of supplier equipment checklist as a fierce measuring stick.

In other words, if you can't satisfy the purchasing managers' need for importance, they're going to create their own by becoming "tough" buyers. And that's your fault!

Selling to Purchasing Managers: How to Make Your Product or Service the Right Answer—No Matter What You Sell

PRODUCT OR SERVICE WANT

Like with all prospects, to gain the best chance of having a purchasing manager believe and accept your product or service claims, you must position them before you start to describe them.

Position your product or service with these phrases:

- "Easy to understand"
- "A solid and safe purchase"
- "Doesn't require a lot of technical education"
- "Not technically challenging"

EXAMPLE OF A PRODUCT- OR SERVICE-POSITIONING STATEMENT

- "Before I present our product/service, let me stress that it is easy to understand, is not technically challenging, and certainly represents a solid and safe purchase."

WHY THESE WORDS WORK

These prospects frequently feel vulnerable and highly self-conscious, as words such as "sincere" and "patient" demonstrate.

And much of what they both want and fear has to do with their being "nontechnical."

That means that, despite whatever knowledge they might have of technical products and services, they can't really understand all the particular ones they're buying.

For example, a purchasing manager might know a lot about how PC boards are manufactured, which is an obviously technical application. Yet, she might be assigned to purchasing narrow-pipe components (e.g., tube connectors) and know nothing about them. So she is "technical" when it comes to buying PC boards but very "nontechnical" when she has to buy narrow-pipe components.

Of course, it's usually more common for purchasing managers to understand a little about PC boards and components, but not enough to qualify as technical experts.

However, they're in a position of power — because they can issue purchase orders—even though they're definitely "nontechnical." It's absolutely crucial, therefore, that purchasing managers perceive any product or service they buy as being "easy to understand."

However, even if your product or service is, in reality, easy to understand, don't assume that you have no challenge here. What your product or service actually is has little to do with how it's perceived.

Keep this in mind: when perception and reality conflict, perception always wins—and it wins hands down, every single time. Far too many salespeople make the mistake of assuming that the realities associated with their products and services will automatically match the decision maker's perceptions. That is rarely, rarely the case.

Not only are most purchasing managers branded with the label of "nontechnical," they're also well aware of it. And they resent it.

But to be completely candid about it, only the rarest purchasing managers make a strong effort to correct the situation.

The typical purchasing manager has amazingly little desire to learn everything he or she can about the products and services to be purchased. In fact, most purchasing managers actually resist most attempts to educate them beyond the most basic levels.

One of the reasons for that resistance is the reality that the purchasing profession has undergone a dramatic change over the past 15 or 20 years.

There was a time when most purchasing managers considered purchasing to be their careers. They studied it, studied the products and services they were supposed to buy, and acted in every other way as a professional usually acts.

Fifteen to 10 years ago, however, the balance shifted from the traditional purchasing manager to a more "modern" type— those who consider the position to be nothing more than a "résumé stop" on the way to something better.

The real fact is that today's average purchasing manager doesn't have nearly the same depth of intellectual curiosity or technical knowledge as his or her predecessor had decades ago.

Another common reason for the general resistance among purchasing managers toward education is just plain emotional fatigue. They're tired of seeing themselves struggling behind the knowledge curve, which is exactly their reaction when you take a stab at educating them.

In the old way of selling, the salesperson buried the prospect under an avalanche of whatever "techno speak" was common to the application. Buzzwords and dense jargon flew around in a confusing swarm that left this prospect with the depressing belief: "I won't ever be able to learn this stuff."

On top of that, the only time most salespeople even made an attempt at education was when they were desperate. They sensed that the sale was slipping away—or the purchasing managers might have told them outright that it was "no sale"— and they reacted by verbally assaulting the prospect with all sorts of technical information about their product or service.

In the typical scenario, the purchasing manager was using price as the excuse for not buying and the salesperson responded with a torrent that followed this logic: "We charge more than our competitors because ... (techno speak)."

This, of course, was the last thing this type of prospect wanted to hear and, as a consequence, didn't pay attention anyway. But even today, purchasing managers, like all other prospect types, use price as an excuse—not always, but usually—for not buying.

By the way, don't be misled by the term "techno speak." You could be selling anything from computer programming services to pencils and there will always be some "techno speak" (sometimes called jargon) in your industry.

So, the "education" a purchasing manager got from a typical salesperson was really a relentless browbeating, a desperate and self-interested reaction to a missed sales opportunity.

However, even today, for this prospect, the ideal product or service would be so simple that it would require no education whatsoever, technical or otherwise. And if your product or service fits that mold, you're automatically way ahead of the game.

But if it doesn't, you must face the challenge head-on. And, except for the very simplest products and services, a certain degree of education is unavoidable. Purchasing managers know it and accept it.

Make certain at least that purchasing managers perceive your product or service as not overly technically challenging or requiring significant education. Even if you have the world's most complex product or service, your prospect must perceive it otherwise. Creating that perception will make whatever education is actually required much easier for you to deliver and for the purchasing manager to accept.

Selling to Purchasing Managers: How to Make Your Organization the Ideal Provider

PROVIDER WANT

To gain the best chance of having a purchasing manager accept your organization as an ideal provider, you must position it, too, before you start to describe it.

You need to position your organization with these words:

- "Sincere"
- "Nonjudgmental"
- "Patient"
- "Not technically obsessed with your product or service"
- "More interested in your customers than in what they're selling"
- "Don't attach any strings to a relationship with you"
- "People"

EXAMPLE OF A PROVIDER-POSITIONING STATEMENT

- "Let me tell you a little bit about our company. We pride ourselves in being patient, not technically obsessed with what we sell, and far more interested in our customers than in what we sell."

WHY THESE WORDS WORK

For reasons that are both real and perceived, purchasing managers consider most salespeople as being less than sincere. Much of that perception has been formed historically as a result of the tactics used by salespeople, some of which have been identified in this report.

The purchasing manager's desire for sincerity is, in fact, a reflection of his or her feeling of vulnerability and the fear that he or she really isn't up to the task.

Remember: most prospects who deal from any position of strength rarely worry about how sincere you are.

However, that's an advantage most purchasing managers don't usually have. And because they often "don't really know what they're buying," they have nothing much to rely on but a salesperson's sincerity.

Purchasing managers perceive most suppliers as "conditional" in that the provider's interest in them varies according to the situation, thus putting conditions on the relationship. In other words, the provider demonstrates interest only when there's a sale to be made.

This purchasing manager needs to believe that you see him or her as being more important and valuable to you than simply being a "buying machine." The purchasing manager can't think of your interest in him or her as being based solely upon a sale being made.

You must also be nonjudgmental. Here you have prospects who already feel judged enough by the people they work with. And they certainly don't want or need another person in their lives who seems judgmental.

In other parts of this report, I've addressed the issue of the decision maker being "nontechnical." And if I seem to be hammering away at it, please forgive me. It happens to be a crucial issue, one that affects every aspect of your relationship with purchasing managers.

Be careful that you are not perceived as being technically obsessed with your product or service, even if that product or service is easy to understand and capable of being bought safely without much technical education.

You already know that being "nontechnical" is a badge of dishonor for most purchasing managers, a source of their "corporate inferiority complex."

Remember: diminished self-perception stems in part from their realization that they're "staff." According to many of their coworkers, that makes them somehow less important than the people in "line" departments.

That bias is reinforced even further by the reality that purchasing managers are considered "nontechnical."

And no one in any technical environment—not user groups, no one—ever uses that expression in anything but the most derisive and disapproving tones.

And as if they don't hear enough of it from inside their companies, purchasing managers are also reminded of it by their suppliers. Of course, the supplier never makes an open issue out of it, but the perception comes across loud and clear.

As I said before, the typical provider can't resist the urge to "educate" purchasing managers about the esoteric complexities of their product or service, which they rarely do for the decision maker's benefit.

Salespeople resort to the "education tactic" whenever they sense a wall of resistance over issues like price, delivery, and so on. By trumpeting the technical virtues of whatever they're selling, they hope to overcome any problems with regard to those other issues. And it just doesn't work.

Worse yet, it aggravates the prospect's deep sense of inferiority and intensifies his or her resistance to making a buying decision that is going to please the provider.

Therefore, you must avoid creating the impression of being "technically obsessed."

Being exposed to providers who, in the words of a purchasing manager, "are in love with their own products" makes the nontechnical purchasing manager extremely uncomfortable.

A provider speaks a language the decision maker can't even understand, is enchanted with things of no interest to the decision maker, and shows impatience when the decision maker "doesn't get it."

Your patience with the purchasing manager is yet another vital ingredient in the relationship. It's related to everything I've said up to this point about his or her being nontechnical and uninterested in a thorough education about a product, service, or supplier.

Most purchasing managers want some education, if for no other reason than that it's simply unavoidable. However, it has to occur under specific conditions, according to certain guidelines:

1. **Simple terms**—The education must be expressed in simple and easy-to-grasp terms, but not be so rudimentary as to be insulting. You must strike a very delicate balance in this regard.
2. **Not related to sales**—You should never offer the education when you're trying to make or save a sale. In other words, it can't be perceived as an attempt to use technical information the way most providers use it.
3. **Gradual**—The education must be delivered in small "packets" over an extended span of time. And if you're in doubt, err on the side of making the packet smaller and making the time span longer.
4. **Minimal**—Don't be overly ambitious. These prospects have no desire to be technical wizards. They simply want and need to know enough so they can avoid embarrassing themselves with glaring mistakes.

Always refer to your organization as "people." That one, single word could turn out to be one of the most important of all.

It's important for you to "personalize" yourself and your organization for these prospects. You'll score a major positioning victory if you can create the perception that you're actually a group of people and your competitors are merely companies or organizations.

Almost anything that's depersonalized makes the purchasing manager feel uncomfortable. People, on the other hand, are something he or she can easily understand.

Selling to Purchasing Managers: How to Move Your Benefits to a Higher Level

BENEFIT WANT

To gain the best chance of having a purchasing manager believe and accept your benefit claims, you must position them before you ever start to describe them.

Describe your benefits as delivering the following:

- "Things that should run smoothly for you"
- "Quietly"
- "No crises"
- "Decisions that are certain and sure"

EXAMPLE OF A BENEFIT-POSITIONING STATEMENT

- "Our product/service will allow things to run smoothly for you. I guarantee that you can make decisions that are certain and sure."

WHY THESE WORDS WORK

It's far more common for this type of prospect to be recognized for poor performance rather than good.

In the 21st-century self-preservation corporate game of assigning blame to anyone but oneself, user departments have mastered quite well the tactic of shifting all the accountability for mistakes to the purchasing manager.

So, for example, when a provider doesn't deliver on time, it was the purchasing manager who selected them. A bad purchase is never hung on the user's door. It's always dropped right at the feet of the purchasing department.

Underlying this almost exclusive concentration on negative recognition is the corporate bias I mentioned before.

If you start with the assumption that the purchasing manager does "no-brainer" glorified clerical work, two unfavorable conclusions automatically fall into place:

1. Performing a mindless task well doesn't deserve praise because no extraordinary effort or talent is required.
2. Mistakes are practically unforgivable because the supposedly unchallenging nature of their work puts human error beyond the realm of acceptability.

In other words, success will go unnoticed while mistakes draw an unbelievable amount of fire.

One of the responses you hear most often when speaking with purchasing managers is the desire to "avoid making mistakes."

They need a tremendous amount of decision-making certainty. That means that making the right decision ensures satisfying the user group. But make sure you understand what that means.

Unfortunately, purchasing managers take much of their personal value from the user group's satisfaction with their performance. Unfortunately, that sense of satisfaction is almost never expressed, unless you define "expressed" as the absence of complaining.

Don't, for a single moment, believe that you can reverse a trend that has existed for decades. In other words, your product or service won't cause user groups to suddenly begin heaping praise on the purchasing department.

But what you can hope for—and what the purchasing manager is willing to settle for—are "quiet" working conditions. Given the pressures these prospects are subjected to, it's understandable that they want quiet working conditions. But this need has an even deeper significance than that.

To someone who's accustomed to hearing complaints, silence from the user department is the equivalent of approval. It may not be the ideal reaction, but it's better than what they're used to hearing.

Selling to Purchasing Managers: How to Make Your Price, Rate, or Fee a True Bargain

PRICE WANT

To gain the best chance of having a purchasing manager accept your price, rate, or fee, you must position it before you start to describe it.

Here's how you should position your price, rate, or fee before you present it:

- "Directly related to the benefits you'll receive"
- "Justified by the benefits"
- "Easily translated into the benefits you get"

EXAMPLE OF A PRICE-, RATE-, OR FEE-POSITIONING STATEMENT

- "As I give you my price/rate/fee, please bear in mind that it is directly related to the benefits you'll receive. In fact, it will be more than justified by those benefits. I'd also like to make sure that you understand everything it includes … ."

WHY THESE WORDS WORK

Of all the prospect types, purchasing managers probably have the most notorious reputation for price-sensitivity.

In reality, they personally care very little about how much you charge for your product or service. It matters only when it becomes a cause of controversy between or among themselves, their superiors, and/or the finance department.

If you recall from the case study mentioned earlier, purchasing managers will often actually go out of their way to do business with the providers they favor. But that's possible only when your price, rate, or fee—if it's higher than what your competitors are charging—can be translated into benefits. In other words, the purchasing manager has to be able to say, "Even though they charge more, I still chose them because ..."

Selling to Purchasing Managers: Letters and Advertising

IN A LETTER

Dear _____,

Form a Special Instant Bond: You should get respect for what you do, and you probably do a lot more than you get credit for—important work that makes a big contribution to your company's success.

Make Your Product or Service the Right Answer: You can improve that situation with products and services that are safe purchases because they're easy to understand and don't require a lot of technical education.

Make Your Organization the Ideal Provider: It takes special people to come out with a product or service like that, people who are more interested in the customer than in what they're selling.

Move Your Benefits to a Higher Level: With teammates like that, things will run smoothly for you—quietly, with no crises.

Make Your Price, Rate, or Fee a True Bargain: Then, the price, rate, or fee can be easily translated into the benefits you get.

I like to think that [your product or service] and [company] can provide all of those things for you. But you, of course, should be free to make that decision for yourself.

[Now, state your purpose for writing the letter, what you want the prospect to do (a call to action), communicate your normal sales message, and finish the letter.]

IN THE FORM OF ADVERTISING COPY
YOU'RE DOING IMPORTANT WORKS

You should get respect for what you do, and you probably do a lot more than you get credit for—important work that makes a big contribution to your company's success.

You can improve that situation with products and services that are safe purchases because they're easy to understand and don't require a lot of technical education.

It takes special people to come out with a product or service like that, people who are more interested in the customer than in what they're selling.

With teammates like that, things will run smoothly for you—quietly, with no crises.

Then, the price can be easily translated into the benefits you get.

We like to think that (your product or service) and (company) itself can be all that for you. But, you should be free to make that decision for yourself.

[Communicate your normal marketing message, state what you want the prospect to do (a call to action), and finish the ad.]

Important: Always put the Words That Sell in generic terms, as if you were describing "universal standards." Remember: their purpose is positioning. Once you communicate them, you can then use whatever words you usually use to tell the prospect about your product or service, your benefits, your organization, and your price.

Selling to Purchasing Managers: Words That Don't Work

Avoid at all costs using these words and phrases to describe yourself, your organization, or your product or service.

However, feel free to use them to describe your competitors! Do so and you'll never have to criticize them in front of the prospect (which you should never, ever do in any circumstance anyway), if you know how to describe your competitors with the Words That Don't Work:

- "Challenging"
- "Highly technical"
- "Technology"
- "Technological"
- "Complex"
- "Make a judgment"
- "Education"
- "No-brainer"
- "Conditional"
- "Systematology"
- "Non-interactive"
- "Independent"
- "Requires study"

EXAMPLE

- "XYZ has a very <u>technical product</u>. It requires a lot of education to fully understand it. It is somewhat <u>complex</u>; therefore, purchasing it <u>requires study</u>."

WHY THESE WORDS DON'T WORK

You are not saying anything bad about your competition by saying this. However, you are describing them in words that are not strong, positive words to this prospect.

However, remember not to use these words or phrases loosely, carelessly, or without regard for the facts. Don't use them if they're not true. Always sell with integrity.

101 Universal Sales Truths*

1. Prospects pay attention to people they believe have something important to say to them.
2. People buy for their own reasons, not for yours or mine.
3. Different people buy the same product or service for different reasons.
4. When a salesperson and a customer get locked into a war of the wills, the salesperson always loses.
5. Buying is basically an emotional response no matter what you're selling.
6. Being the sort of salesperson people enjoy doing business with is an invaluable asset.
7. If you don't close sales, you won't make a living as a salesperson.
8. Prospects must believe you before they'll buy from you! And that's a lot tougher to do than you think it is.
9. You can only convince others of what you yourself believe.
10. The more you believe in yourself, the easier it is to get others to believe what you say.
11. A strong, positive self-concept is the most valuable personal attribute any salesperson can have.

*These come from *The Universal Sales Truths*, Bill Brooks (Greensboro, NC:Game Plan Press, 2002).

12. When you believe, you can make others believe. When you don't, no one else will, either.
13. Your customer will never believe in the value of your product or service any more strongly than you do!
14. The seller determines the cost of the product or service, but only the buyer can determine its true value.
15. People pay a lot more attention to what you *are* than to what you *say*!
16. Show people what they *need* most in a way they *want* to see it, and they will move heaven and earth to get it!
17. People are always too busy to waste time doing anything they don't really want to do!
18. It is always easier to sell to a prospect's perceived need than to create need in the prospect's mind!
19. All values are equal until someone points out the difference!
20. The secret to successful selling is not in the selling at all. Instead, it is in the accurate, consistent science of prospecting.
21. The vital part of any sale is seldom the close but what takes place before the sales interview even begins.
22. The better the job of finding qualified prospects you do, the higher your closing average will be!
23. The most productive sentence in any salesperson's vocabulary always ends with a question mark!
24. Treat prospecting as the lifeblood of your sales career—because it is.
25. You never know when your prospect's motivation to buy will suddenly and dramatically escalate.
26. The only certain way to ensure that you, your organization, or your product are thought of first is through frequent, repetitious contact.

27. Constantly search for a person who can give you a referral for each prospect or … better yet … make the initial contact for you.

28. Unless you get people to lower their mental/emotional defenses and let you in, eliminate tension and establish trust, build rapport and start a successful sales dialogue, you cannot move forward to make the sale.

29. The best way to serve your own interest is to put the needs and desires of your customer first!

30. To deliver value to the prospect, you must see yourself primarily as a value resource for the prospect!

31. To be a value resource for the prospect, you must first discover what your prospect perceives as value!

32. Never interrupt a prospect. However, you need to be interruptible!

33. Get your whole body involved in listening and show that you are paying attention. Look the person squarely in the eye and use facial expressions and gestures to show that you hear and understand what's being said.

34. All values are considered equal in the absence of a values interpreter.

35. The fatal flaw in selling occurs when you are so focused on what you want to happen that you lose sight of what the prospect wants to happen.

36. To a prospect, any price is too high until he or she understands the value of your product or service.

37. Always tailor your presentation to the prospect's needs and wants … not to yours.

38. All sales degenerate into a struggle over price in the absence of a value interpreter!

39. Avoid making price an issue yourself.

40. All values are considered equal until someone points out the difference!
41. What people believe strongly enough, they act upon!
42. Never make a claim you can't back up with facts.
43. It makes little difference what you believe to be true unless you can prove it to your prospect.
44. Prospects expect salespeople to make claims for what they are selling, but they are impressed when someone else makes or endorses those claims.
45. As trust in you and confidence in the value of what you are offering rise, fear of buying disappears.
46. Always assure buyers of the wisdom of their choices.
47. Concentrate on results, not on activities.
48. True, long-lasting enthusiasm is born on the inside.
49. Enthusiasm grows when you focus on solutions and opportunities instead of problems and circumstances.
50. Most of the things that can go wrong in sales happen when a salesperson's mouth is open.
51. There are four areas where you can focus: self, company, product, or customer. If you focus on the first three, your customer is outnumbered three to one.
52. To be a top sales professional enjoying long-range success, you must be an intelligent investor of your time, talent, resources, and energies.
53. Marketing strategy is what gets you to the customer's door in the best possible light. Sales strategy is what you do when you are inside.
54. You may have to take whatever comes your way in life, but you have to go after what you want in order to be a sales winner.
55. Price alone is rarely a key factor in buying decisions. Instead, the key factor in any buying decision is the perceived value to be gained by the buyer.

56. In a crowded marketplace, all other things being equal, the one with the most information who knows how to use it wins.
57. Let your questions do the selling for you.
58. Listen people into buying instead of talking your way out of the sale.
59. Get your prospects to openly share how they feel about what they have seen and heard so you will always know where you stand.
60. Your attitude toward sales as a profession determines your selling actions.
61. When selling, connect with your own deepest values and never settle to invest a moment in anything less.
62. Salespeople who only do what they feel like doing today are bound to spend the rest of their lives unable to do what they really feel like doing.
63. Trust produces an open mind and mistrust produces a closed mind. If you gain trust, the decision maker says, "Tell me how you can satisfy my needs" (open mind). If you achieve mistrust, the decision maker says, "You can't satisfy my needs" (closed mind).
64. You have to address the decision maker's emotions before you address his or her intellect. A hungry stomach cannot hear.
65. When the average decision maker doesn't buy, he or she remembers fewer than 10 words spoken verbatim by the salesperson during the presentation.
66. The average decision maker spends only between nine and 20 seconds reviewing written sales materials.The average decision maker spends only between four and 11 seconds reviewing a print ad.

67. The typical objection is the rational justification for an emotional decision that was made long before the objection is expressed.

68. An objection is almost always an indication that the decision maker has a closed mind. Therefore, the objection usually has nothing to do with what caused the emotional resistance.

69. Most decision makers are more interested in the person they're buying from than in the thing they're buying.

70. Never position yourself, your organization, or what you're selling on the basis of a feature or a benefit.

71. Successful selling amounts to making the decision maker feel good, and being in the room when he or she does.

72. More than 80% of all salespeople talk more than is necessary to secure a sale.

73. Goals define the way you shape your own life.

74. The two main ingredients for enthusiasm are being captivated by an ideal and a deep conviction that you can achieve it.

75. Compete against the achievement of your sales objectives, not against the successes of others or their expectations of you.

76. Dwell on your past sales successes. View past failures only as lessons learned.

77. A selling career is a continuous series of opportunities. The way we handle those opportunities is the way we handle our career.

78. Associate with positive, successful people and you will be more positive and successful.

79. The secret to selling is to be in front of qualified prospects when they're ready to buy, not when you need to make a sale.

80. Take an organized approach to prospecting ... but never at the expense of activity.

81. Never violate the formal structure of an organization ... but master an understanding of the informal.

82. You only have a matter of seconds to establish your credibility and convince a prospect that time spent with you will be valuable.

83. Without trust you can only sell price. With trust you can sell value.

84. Focus on what the prospect is saying ... not what he or she is going to say or what you're going to say.

85. When presenting price, always avoid cushioning statements like "Here we go ...," "Are you ready for this?" or "Are you sitting down?"

86. Never use "setup" statements like:"Tell me where we need to be ...," "The list price is ...," or "I want your business so ... ."

87. Always ensure that value exceeds price and then, and only then, present your price as related strictly to value.

88. Finalizing agreement and closing sales is a consequence of what has happened early in the sale rather than something the sale builds toward.

89. Selling is a science that, when practiced correctly, can become an art.

90. The fear of loss is as powerful as the joy of gain.

91. The jump from character (what you are) to reputation (what people think you are) is much smaller than many salespeople would like to believe.

92. Once you discover what your prospect perceives his or her most pressing need to be, build your whole presentation around that need.

93. Value-based salespeople always concern themselves first and foremost with how the prospect perceives his or her needs.

94. Uncover your prospect's needs, as he or she perceives them, and then enable him or her to meet those needs through what you are selling.

95. Canned sales presentations are insulting to today's educated and alert consumers, many of them professional buyers.

96. Lack of qualified prospects is the greatest single cause of failure among salespeople. Prospecting is the toughest part of selling.

97. Good prospecting is a matter of developing a solid game plan that works well for you and following that game plan to the letter.

98. There is a vast difference between self-centeredness and serving your own best interest.

99. If all you want to talk about is yourself—your interests, products, features, or organization—don't be surprised if you encounter strong sales resistance from the outset.

100. What allows salespeople to be differentiated from a vending machine is that salespeople have an opportunity to meet the widely varied and specific needs of each customer they serve.

101. Listening is a skill that can be learned and can also be continuously improved, but most of us have never been trained to listen. For example, which do we do most during the day: read or listen?

Section Three

Perfect Phrases for Customer Service

Hundreds of Tools, Techniques, and Scripts for Handling Any Situation

Robert Bacal

Contents

Introduction   **491**

Acknowledgments   **494**

Part One. Succeeding at Customer Service   **495**

Chapter 1. Basics of Customer Service   **497**

What's in It for Me?   498
Different Kinds of Customers   500
First Things First—Dispelling an Important
    Customer Service Myth   502
Understanding What Customers Want   503
About This Section   507

Chapter 2. Customer Service Tools and Techniques   **510**

Above and Beyond the Call of Duty   513
Acknowledge Customer's Needs   513
Acknowledging Without Encouraging   514
Active Listening   514
Admitting Mistakes   515
Allowing Venting   515

Apologize   516
Appropriate Nonverbals   516
Appropriate Smiles   516
Arranging Follow-Up   517
Assurances of Effort   517
Assurances of Results   518
Audience Removal   518
Bonus Buyoff   518
Broken Record   518
Closing Interactions Positively   519
Common Courtesy   519
Completing Follow-Up   520
Contact Security/Authorities/Management   520
Disengaging   521
Distraction   522
Empathy Statements   522
Expediting   523
Expert Recommendations   523
Explain Reasoning or Actions   523
Face-Saving Out   524
Finding Agreement Points   525
Finishing Off/Following Up   525
Isolate/Detach Customer   525
Leveling   525
Managing Height Differentials/Nonverbals   526
Managing Interpersonal Distance   526
Not Taking the Bait   528
Offering Choices/Empowering   528
Plain Language   529
Preemptive Strike   529
Privacy and Confidentiality   530

Probing Questions   530

Pros and Cons   531

Providing Alternatives   531

Providing a Customer Takeaway   532

Providing Explanations   532

Questioning Instead of Stating   533

Referral to Supervisor   533

Referral to Third Party   534

Refocus   535

Setting Limits   535

Some People Think That (Neutral Mode)   537

Stop Sign—Nonverbal   537

Suggest an Alternative to Waiting   538

Summarize the Conversation   538

Telephone Silence   539

Thank-Yous   540

Timeout   540

Use Customer's Name   540

Use of Timing with Angry Customers   541

Verbal Softeners   541

Voice Tone—Emphatic   542

When Question   542

You're Right!   543

Part Two. Dealing with Specific Customer Situations   545

1. When You Are Late or Know You Will Be Late   547

2. When a Customer Is in a Hurry   550

3. When a Customer Jumps Ahead in a Line of Waiting Customers   552

4. When a Customer Asks to Be Served Ahead of Other Waiting Customers   554

5. When a Customer Interrupts a Discussion Between the Employee and Another Customer   556
6. When a Customer Has a Negative Attitude About Your Company Due to Past Experiences   558
7. When You Need to Explain a Company Policy or Procedure   561
8. When a Customer Might Be Mistrustful   564
9. When the Customer Has Been Through Voicemail Hell   567
10. When a Customer Is Experiencing a Language Barrier   570
11. When the Customer Has Been "Buck-Passed"   573
12. When a Customer Needs to Follow a Sequence of Actions   575
13. When the Customer Insults Your Competence   577
14. When a Customer Won't Stop Talking on the Phone   579
15. When the Customer Swears or Yells in Person #1   581
16. When the Customer Swears or Yells in Person #2   584
17. When a Customer Won't Stop Talking and Is Getting Abusive on the Phone #1   587
18. When a Customer Won't Stop Talking and Is Getting Abusive on the Phone #2   590
19. When a Customer Has Been Waiting in a Line   593
20. When You Don't Have the Answer   595
21. When Nobody Handy Has the Answer   599
22. When You Need to Place a Caller on Hold   602
23. When You Need to Route a Customer Phone Call   605
24. When You Lack the Authority to …   608
25. When a Customer Threatens to Go over Your Head   610
26. When a Customer Demands to Speak with Your Supervisor   612
27. When a Customer Demands to Speak with Your Supervisor, Who Isn't Available   615

28. When a Customer Threatens to Complain
     to the Press   617
29. When a Customer Demands to Speak to the "Person in
     Charge"   620
30. When a Customer Makes an Embarrassing Mistake   624
31. When a Customer Withholds Information Due
     to Privacy Concerns   627
32. When a Customer Threatens Bodily Harm
     or Property Damage   630
33. When a Customer Is Confused About What He
     or She Wants or Needs   634
34. When a Customer Makes a Racist Remark   637
35. When a Customer Makes a Sexist Remark   640
36. When a Customer Refuses to Leave   643
37. When a Customer Accuses You of Racism   646
38. When a Customer Plays One Employee off
     Another ("So-and-So Said")   649
39. When a Customer Might Be Stealing   653
40. When a Customer Is Playing to an Audience
     of Other Customers   655
41. When a Customer Exhibits Passive-Aggressive
     Behavior   658
42. When a Customer Uses Nonverbal Attempts
     to Intimidate   661
43. When a Customer Makes Persistent and Frequent
     Phone Calls   664
44. When Someone Else Is Not Responding
     (No Callback)   667
45. When You Need to Clarify Commitments   671
46. When a Customer Wants Information You Are
     Not Allowed to Give   674

47. When a Customer Makes a Suggestion
    to Improve Service   676
48. When You Can't Find a Customer's Reservation/
    Appointment   679
49. When Your Are Following Up on a Customer
    Complaint   682
50. Properly Identifying the Internal Customer   685
51. When an Internal Customer Isn't Following Procedures
    to Request Service   688
52. When the Customer Wants Something That Won't
    Fill His Need   691
53. When You Want Feedback from the Customer   694
54. When a Customer Complains About Red Tape and
    Paperwork   697
55. When You Need to Respond to a Customer Complaint
    Made in Writing   700
56. When a Reservation/Appointment Is Lost and You
    Cannot Meet the Commitment   703
57. When Customers Are Waiting in a Waiting Room   706
58. When a Customer Complains About a
    Known Problem   709
59. When a Customer Asks Inappropriate Questions   711
60. When a Customer Tries an Unacceptable Merchandise
    Return   713

Introduction

I want to share a little known secret about the value of delivering good service to customers. Yes, it's good for business and the organization. Yes, you may derive a lot of satisfaction by doing a customer service job well. No question. But what's the most compelling reason to learn about, and deliver good customer service? It's this. When you deliver good customer service to your customers, you experience less stress, and less hassle and grief from customers. They argue less. They're much less likely to insult, and they're less demanding. They don't threaten you when they get upset ("I'll have your job!").

You can save huge amounts of time. One dissatisfied customer may take up to 10 or 20 times more of your time than a satisfied one. And the time spent with the dissatisfied customer is usually not all that much fun. Customer service skills help you keep your happy customers happy, help prevent customers from becoming unhappy and taking out their frustrations on you, and help you deal effectively and quickly with customers who are upset and unhappy.

This section gives you the tools to interact with customers more effectively, so that the company, the customer, and you, the person dealing with the customer, all benefit. It's a different kind of discussion about customer service. It's not full of principles or platitudes, or handy customer service slogans. It focuses on *doing*. What should you *do* with a customer who is swearing at you? What do you *do* to prevent customers who have waited a long time from getting really angry? What do you *do* to provide advice to customers so it will be heard and appreciated? This section will answer these questions, and many other ones about customer service situations—specifically and precisely. This section is about *solutions*.

Organization

Part One of this section has two chapters. In Chapter 1, we'll cover some basics of customer service, so you can increase your understanding of what customers want from you, and the things that cause customers to hit the roof. We'll also talk about various types of customers (internal, external, paying and non-paying), and we'll explain how you can best use this book.

Chapter 2 describes dozens of very specific customer service techniques. The explanations will help you decide when to use what techniques and in what customer situations. The pages in that part of the book are shaded black so you can easily refer to them for specific techniques, which are given in alphabetical order.

Part Two, and the most important, covers 60 common and not-so-common customer service situations and tells you specifically how you can deal with them. I do this by

- describing the situation
- listing the techniques to use in this situation

- presenting a dialogue to show you exactly what to say and do
- explaining the reasoning behind the use of the techniques
- providing a few hints and tips to help you use the techniques properly

Even if we have not included all of the situations you deal with on the job, you will be able to extrapolate the examples to other situations you do face. I think that regardless of whether you work in retail, the hospitality industry, government, or as a call-in customer service rep, the situations covered in this part will be very useful to you.

Conclusion

Far too much customer service training and far too many customer service books tell you only what you already know. Do you really need to be told *again* that you should smile? Or shake hands? No. But you might find it useful to know when it's a *bad* idea to smile at a customer. You'll learn that from this book.

So, here's the bottom line about this book: you may come across a few things you already know. But you'll also come across a number of techniques you probably haven't thought about. If you work at using these techniques properly, and focus on *doing* things differently with customers, you are going to be better at your job, be clearly better at customer service than others who don't understand these techniques, and help your employer and yourself be more successful. And along the way, save yourself a lot of hassle and a lot of grief.

The Customer Service Zone Web Site

I've created a Web site called the *Customer Service Zone*, where you will be able to find hundreds of articles on customer service. Use of the site is free of charge. We have great plans for the site, including using it to add more customer service techniques, and more customer service dialogues you can learn from. We may even have a forum where you can ask questions and share your customer service expertise. To visit, go to **www.customerservicezone.com**. By visiting, you can continue to learn and develop your customer service skills.

Acknowledgments

I continue to be grateful to McGraw-Hill for providing the opportunity for my writings to exist. Specifically, I'd like to thank Mary Glenn for her help in defining the focus of this discussion.

As usual, John Woods and Bob Magnan of CWL Publishing Enterprises have helped make this book what it is. Bob has edited all my books, and as always has carried out his job on this one with great patience and skill.

Finally, my wife, Nancy has to put up with all the angst and craziness from me that always accompanies a writing project. Thank you for taking on additional responsibilities so I could concentrate on getting this project done.

Part One

Succeeding at Customer Service

Chapter 1
Basics of Customer Service

There must be a billion words written about customer service. Advice abounds, from the banal and obvious (smile when you talk on the phone) to complex and difficult suggestions about how to "create a corporate culture of excellent customer service."

Amidst all of the words, simple or fancy, is hidden a basic truth about customer service: the person who interacts directly with the customer determines whether that customer perceives that he or she is receiving poor customer service, excellent service, or something in between. If you serve customers directly, *you* have the power to affect their perceptions. That customer contact is where "the rubber meets the road."

If you provide service to customers, your words and behaviors are the tools you use to create a positive customer perception of you and the company you work for. Whether you are a novice working with customers or a seasoned pro, what you do and say will affect how customers see you. You can't help it. Customers will form opinions, so you might as well learn how to create positive opinions. But you need to know how to do that.

That's what this section is for—to teach you about the dozens and dozens of techniques you can use when interacting with customers so they will walk away with positive feelings about the experience. You'll learn about very specific things you can do or say in all kinds of customer interactions. You'll learn how to deal with difficult customers. You'll learn how to approach customers and how to get information from them so you can do your job. You'll learn to deal with customer service problems quickly, efficiently, and professionally. Best of all, the techniques in this section will fit your needs, whether you serve burgers, staff the desk in a hotel, help people in health care environments, or even work in government.

This discussion will tell you exactly what to do and say and it will provide you with numerous examples so you can use customer service techniques effectively.

Let's get started!

What's in It for Me?

Why should you be concerned with providing excellent customer service? You don't own the company. You may not get paid more for providing excellent customer service. So, what's in it for you?

There are three powerful reasons for learning to provide great customer service: greater job satisfaction, reduced stress and hassle, and enhanced job success.

First, very few people can derive any job satisfaction when they feel that the time they spend at work is "wasted." Most of us need to feel useful and productive—to make a difference, whether it's helping a fast food customer make healthier food choices or dispensing legal advice. When you provide high-quality customer service, you feel that you are making that difference and can derive pride in your work.

When you do a good job with a customer, such as calming down someone who is angry and complaining, you feel good about having achieved something. But perhaps more important than your own perceptions is the customer's perceptions, when you do a good job with a customer and he or she tells you what you have achieved. That feedback really helps you feel good about yourself and the job you're doing. Doing a good job and taking pride in your customer service accomplishments is a way to prevent job burnout.

Second, learning to deliver quality customer service will save you a lot of stress and hassle. When you learn and use customer service skills, you are far less likely to get into protracted, unpleasant, and upsetting interactions with a customer. You make yourself less of a target for customer wrath. That's because customer service skills help keep customers from becoming angry and help reduce the length and intensity of the anger when and if difficult customer service situations occur.

Third, learning and using quality customer service techniques helps form the perceptions of those who may be able to help your career—supervisors, managers, and even potential employers. Using them makes you look good to everyone: that's critical in getting promoted, receiving pay raises, and getting new job opportunities. Managers and supervisors tend to notice when customers ask for you specifically because you do such a good job or contact them to provide positive comments about how you've helped.

Of course, you may have other reasons to want to provide the best customer service possible. You may want to contribute to the success of your employer. You may like the feeling of having other employees look up to you as a good model. Or you may even benefit directly if you work on a commission basis; people who are good at customer service do earn more.

Regardless of your reasons, you can learn how to use quality customer service techniques and serve your customers better.

In the rest of this chapter, we'll provide an overview of customer service principles and issues and explain how to use this book. In the next chapter, we'll describe 60 techniques you should be using. The rest of the discussion is dedicated to showing you how to use those techniques.

Different Kinds of Customers

Before we continue, we should clarify what the word "customer" means.

You are probably familiar with our starting definition: *the customer is the person who pays for goods or services that you provide.* This definition works in some contexts, but not all. It breaks down in situations where money does not directly change hands. For example, people often interact with government, public schools, and other organizations: they receive goods or services from them, but do not pay anything directly to them. We need to change our definition so that people who interact with these organizations fall under our definition of customer, since they, too, deserve high-quality customer service, even if they are not paying directly.

Here's a better definition: *the customer is the person next in line who receives your output (service, products).* That person may purchase goods or services directly or receive output you create or deliver without direct payment. The person may be outside your company, but this definition also includes anyone within the company who receives output from you.

Let's be more specific. There are four basic types of customer. Regardless of type, each customer deserves to receive top-quality customer service. Also, regardless of the type of customer, you and your organization will benefit by providing top-quality customer service.

First, there are *external paying customers*. These are the people who pay to eat in a restaurant, pay for health care and legal advice, or pay to stay in a hotel.

Second, there are *internal customers*. These are people who receive output (services, products, information) that you create or provide, but who are in the same organization. Internal customers may sometimes be billed via interdepartmental charge systems or there may be no payment system in place. For example, human resources staff involved in hiring employees are, in effect, working on behalf of internal customers (the managers of the work units needing new employees). The technician who maintains company computers is working for internal customers (the people who use the computers he or she maintains).

Third, there are *external nonpaying customers*. These customers receive services, goods, or other outputs but do not pay directly for them. For example, the tourist who visits a traveler's information kiosk by the highway may receive tourist information (outputs) and maps (goods), but is not paying directly. That tourist is a customer. Another example is the parent who attends the parent-teacher meeting at the local public school: he or she receives outputs and services from the teacher, but does not pay the teacher directly. That parent needs to be treated like a customer, too.

That brings us to the fourth type of customer, *regulated customers.* Government organizations often interact with people in ways that are not oriented toward providing something to individuals, but are instead toward regulating them for the common good. It might seem like people regulated by the government through licenses, zoning regulations, permits, and other controls are really not customers. But we want to include them, because even though government is regulating them, they still deserve the best possible levels of customer service. Including this group under the term "customer" reminds us (and, hopefully, government employees) that even when employees are telling people what to do or what they are allowed to do, they need to do so applying principles of customer service.

First Things First—Dispelling an Important Customer Service Myth

We need to address the single most popular false idea about customer service. No doubt you've heard the phrase, "The customer is always right." It's a great slogan, credited to H. Gordon Selfridge, who passed away in 1947. Unfortunately, it's wrong and misleading.

Clearly the customer is not always right. Customers make unreasonable requests and sometimes have unreasonable expectations. Sometimes customers play fast and loose with the truth. Customers may not understand your company and what you can and can't do for them.

Practically speaking, you can't operate under the assumption that the customer is always right. You can't give each customer what he or she asks for.

So, can we come up with a phrase or two that realistically describe how we should treat customers? Yes. Here are two short phrases that fit the bill.

- The customer always deserves to be treated as if he or she is important and his or her opinions, needs, and wants are worthy of listening to.
- The customer deserves to receive maximum effort on the part of those serving him or her, even when the customer's expectations, wants, and needs may be impractical.

Since the customer isn't "always right" and it's often not possible to give the customer what he or she wants, what are the implications for customer service?

It's simple. Customers have other important wants and needs. Even in situations where you can't do what the customer asks, you *can* contribute to the customer's development of a positive impression about *how* he or she is treated. That's what we've captured in the two phrases above. We need to focus not only on *what* we provide to the customer, but on *how* we provide it. That's the key to realistic excellent customer service. To do that, you need to understand these other wants and needs—and that's where we are going to go next.

Understanding What Customers Want

One thing about the customer service techniques you are going to learn: you can't succeed with them by memorizing them or using them in every situation. The key to customer service is doing the right thing at the right time.

To be able to choose the right techniques and to use them effectively, you have to understand what customers want. Knowing this will help you make sense of the techniques you'll be looking at. Below is a list of the most important customer wants and needs. When you address these, you create positive customer perceptions about you and your company, which means fewer arguments, fewer hassles, and better customer relationships.

- problem solved
- effort
- acknowledgment and understanding
- choices and options
- positive surprises
- consistency, reliability, and predictability
- value (not necessarily best price)
- reasonable simplicity
- speed
- confidentiality
- sense of importance

Customers want their *problem solved*. They want to get what they want from you, whether it's a product, service, or other output. This is the customer service "want" that most people are familiar with. However, it's not always possible to give the customer what he or she wants, which is where the rest of the "wants" come in. Even if you can't solve the customer's problem, you can create positive perceptions by addressing the other, less obvious customer wants.

Customers expect that you (and your company) will *make an effort* to address their problems, concerns, and needs, even if you can't give them what they want. Customers respect effort, often pay attention to effort above and beyond the call of duty, and will turn on you (create hassles) if they sense that you are not making an effort. Many of the techniques you will learn later in this section work because they demonstrate "effort above and beyond the call of duty."

Customers want and expect to have their wants, needs, expectations, feelings, and words *acknowledged and understood*. That means listening and proving to the customer that you have "got" what he or she is saying. Customers who feel understood and acknowledged feel important; that's a vital part of good customer relationships.

Customers also want to feel they have *choices and options* and are not trapped by you or your company. They want to feel they are making the decisions and that you are helping them, rather than the other way around. When customers feel helpless or powerless, they tend to more likely become frustrated, angry, and aggressive.

Customers also appreciate *"positive surprises."* Positive surprises are things you may do that go above and beyond their hopes and expectations (going the extra *five* miles). They include offering discounts or providing some other benefit that is normally not available to them. Positive surprises are most useful when dealing with difficult or angry customers.

Consistency, reliability, and predictability are also important customer wants. Customers expect that you will treat them in a consistent way and that you will do what you say you will do each and every time. By acting in accordance with these wants, you provide the customer with a sense of security and confidence in you personally and in the company. This builds loyalty.

Customers also expect *value* for their investments of time and money. What's interesting here is that while money (price) is part of the value equation, it is only a part. When customers look at value, they also take into account how they are treated, the quality and expertise of the advice they receive from you to help them make decisions, and a number of other factors. You may not be able to affect the price of services or products you provide, but you can add value by helping the customer in other ways.

Reasonable simplicity is also an important customer want. These days many people are overwhelmed by a complex world. If you complicate the customers' world or make them jump through a number of hoops, they will become frustrated and angry. One of your customer service roles should be to make things easier for the customer, not more complicated, without oversimplifying or treating the customers in a condescending way.

Speed and prompt service are also important wants on the part of customers. At minimum, they want you to make the effort to help them quickly and efficiently. They also expect that you will not create situations that have them waiting around unnecessarily. While you may not always be able to control how fast a customer is served, you can convey a sense that you are working at top speed.

Confidentiality is an important aspect of customer service. Clearly customers want you to keep their sensitive information to yourself, but it goes further than that. Customers may also want some degree of privacy even when talking to you about what may seem to be a mundane or nonsensitive issue. Customers may feel uncomfortable if there are other staff or other customers crowding around them.

We've left the most important need for last. Customers need the sense that *they are important*. Many of the above wants tie into this. Listening to and acknowledging customers demonstrates that you believe they are important. So does arranging for pleasant surprises or making an effort. Many of the specific phrases and techniques you are going to learn tie directly into helping the customer feel important.

About This Section

There is no "right" way to use this section, so you'll need to find what works for you. We end this chapter by explaining the format of the discussion, providing some suggestions about how to get the most out of it, and discussing how this section can be used to help others learn the customer service skills described in it.

Format

This section is broken into three parts. The first consists of this chapter, which provides an overview of some essential aspects of customer service. The second part provides brief summaries of the specific and practical customer service skills you will be learning.

The third part is the real heart of the discussion. In the third part, you will see customer service skills in action and in context. We will describe a particular customer service situation and indicate which techniques are being demonstrated in the example. You will then see a brief dialogue that describes what the customer says and does and how the employee in the example deals with the situation by applying the specific customer service skills. After each dialogue you will find an explanation that will help you understand why the employee chose to use these specific techniques and how they work.

We will also provide hints and tips and cross-reference to other dialogues that may relate to the particular example.

How to Get the Most from This Section

Some people will prefer to read this section from start to finish, which can be effective. We suggest that you read the first and second parts carefully before you move on to the specific dialogues and examples, since doing so will help you make sense of the specific applications of the techniques.

However, you may prefer to browse or to look for specific solutions to specific customer service situations that are particularly relevant to you. That's fine, too.

If you would like to be systematic and organized about learning customer service techniques, you might want to cover one example a day. Each day you can spend five minutes on a particular example, then try to use the techniques in your work. You can learn in small bits, which keeps you from being overwhelmed.

Hints

We have tried to include dialogues and examples from many professions and job types. The specific techniques for customer service are universal and apply across almost all customer situations. Even if the examples do not pertain directly to the kind of work you do, you'll learn how the techniques in the examples can and should be used. So, don't be put off if the example isn't quite perfect for your job. Adapt it as necessary.

When you are looking at the techniques and examples, keep in mind the links to the customer wants described in this chapter. Think about how the techniques can be used to help the customer understand that you believe he or she is important and that you are making an effort. That will help you understand the proper use of the techniques.

For Those Wanting to Help Others Learn Customer Service Skills

Managers, supervisors, and trainers may want to use this section as a basis for training others in customer service skills. Learners need not be exposed to the entire section at one time or in one training session; individual skills can be covered quickly, even in short lunch time meetings or staff meetings.

We are planning to produce a free, short guide for those who want to use this section to train others in the skills discussed here. At this time, we don't have a release date. It will be made available in electronic form from our customer service support site at www.customerservicezone.com. Even those not considering training others may want to visit this free site, since it contains numerous resources you may find useful in enhancing your own customer service skills.

Time to look at the tools of customer service—the things you can do and say to deal effectively with customer service situations that run from the basic and simple to the very challenging and difficult.

Chapter 2
Customer Service Tools
and Techniques

There are tools and techniques for every trade and profession. Carpenters have their hammers, saws, screwdrivers, and scores of other tools and techniques for using them. Plumbers have their pipe wrenches and pipe cutters and benders and the rest. Other professionals—accountants, doctors, psychologists, and so on—also have tools and techniques. Those involved in customer service are no different, although they use less tangible tools than carpenters and plumbers. The tools and techniques of effective customer service have to do with what employees say and do with reference to each customer.

Top-notch customer service employees know how to use each specific tool and how to match tools to specific situations. When you understand the tools available and understand the basics of customer service from the introduction, you'll be able to choose the *right* tools for each customer service "job."

In this section, we are going to describe and explain each of the major customer service tools at your disposal. Since customer service involves human interactions that are not always predictable, using these tools cannot always guarantee the positive result we might want. However, using these tools increases the chances of a successful interaction with each customer, whether that customer is currently happy or is angry and upset.

Since Part Two contains numerous examples of how to use the customer service techniques and tools, the descriptions in this section will be relatively short. You will find that in real life it won't always be easy to determine whether a "perfect phrase" is part of one customer strategy or another. That's because some phrases can actually fit more than one response and because some of the strategies overlap. Don't worry about what a strategy is called. Try to understand how the strategy might work and how you might use it or modify it to improve customer service.

Strategies are presented in alphabetical order.

Customer Service Tools and Techniques

Above and Beyond the Call of Duty   513
Acknowledge Customer's Needs   513
Acknowledging Without Encouraging   514
Active Listening   514
Admitting Mistakes   515
Allowing Venting   515
Apologize   516
Appropriate Nonverbals   516
Appropriate Smiles   516
Arranging Follow-Up   517
Assurances of Effort   517
Assurances of Results   518
Audience Removal   518
Bonus Buyoff   518

Broken Record   518

Closing Interactions Positively   519

Common Courtesy   519

Completing Follow-Up   520

Contact Security/Authorities/Management   520

Disengaging   521

Distraction   522

Empathy Statements   522

Expediting   523

Expert Recommendations   523

Explain Reasoning or Actions   523

Face-Saving Out   524

Finding Agreement Points   525

Finishing Off/Following Up   525

Isolate/Detach Customer   525

Leveling   525

Managing Height Differentials/Nonverbals   526

Managing Interpersonal Distance   526

Not Taking the Bait   528

Offering Choices/Empowering   528

Plain Language   529

Preemptive Strike   529

Privacy and Confidentiality   530

Probing Questions   530

Pros and Cons   531

Providing Alternatives   531

Providing a Customer Takeaway   532

Providing Explanations   532

Questioning Instead of Stating   533

Referral to Supervisor   533

Referral to Third Party   534
Refocus   535
Setting Limits   535
Some People Think That (Neutral Mode)   537
Stop Sign—Nonverbal   537
Suggest an Alternative to Waiting   538
Summarize the Conversation   538
Telephone Silence   539
Thank-Yous   540
Timeout   540
Use Customer's Name   540
Use of Timing with Angry Customers   541
Verbal Softeners   541
Voice Tone—Emphatic   542
When Question   542
You're Right!   543

Above and Beyond the Call of Duty

Going above and beyond the call of duty means doing something that is not required of you as part of your job or obligations to your customer. It means doing something special or extra. Customers, even difficult ones, often display extreme gratitude and loyalty when you can show them that they are so important that they are worth going beyond what is required. And that's one of the secrets to good customer service—demonstrating through your actions that your customer is important and special.

Acknowledge Customer's Needs

When a customer sees that you are making an effort to understand his or her needs (even if you can't meet them), it is more likely the customer will view you positively. Acknowledging needs may involve rephrasing something the customer has said to you (e.g., "I understand that you want to get the best value for your money") or it may involve responding to something you observe about the customer (e.g., "I can see that you must be in a hurry").

Acknowledging Without Encouraging

When you deal with an angry or difficult customer, it's important to prove to him or her that you understand the facts surrounding the situation that is upsetting and the feelings the customer is experiencing. The catch is that "what you focus on, you get more of"—and you don't want to encourage the customer to continue being difficult or continue angry behavior that interferes with helping the customer. Acknowledging Without Encouraging really involves the combination of two techniques.

The first set involves using both empathy statements and refocus statements together. First, you acknowledge the feelings in a short sentence and, without stopping, you refocus or steer the conversation back to the problem and away from the customer's emotions.

Similarly, you can do the same thing around demonstrating your understanding of the facts of the customer's situation by combining active listening with refocusing. Reflect back your understanding of the customer's situation and then refocus back to problem solving.

The important thing to remember is the principle. You need to acknowledge the facts of the situation and the emotions, but you don't want to dwell on them. Focusing on them results in longer interactions that tend to be more emotional.

Active Listening

Active listening proves to the customer that you are paying

attention and that you believe that the customer and what he or she has to say are important. Active listening involves rephrasing the key points of what the customer has said and reflecting them back to the customer, often in the form of a question. For example: "So, you're saying that you're sure there are parts missing from the product and you want a complete refund. Is that right?"

Admitting Mistakes

People in general and, of course, customers in particular tend to respect those who are honest and open about mistakes and errors and who take responsibility rather than avoiding it. When mistakes occur, it is often good strategy to admit to the mistake, whether you made it personally or the company you represent made it. Even if you are not completely sure where the problem occurred and who made a mistake, it's possible to admit the *possibility* of a mistake. This avoids unnecessarily provoking a customer by representing yourself or the company as infallible.

The key thing in admitting mistakes is to do so in a very short sentence and then move on to *solving* whatever problem exists.

Allowing Venting

You are probably familiar with the concept of venting. By allowing the customer to let off steam uninterrupted, the idea is that the customer will eventually calm down on his or her own. While this may work, you should know there are two types of people. Venters are people who will calm down if allowed to let off steam. Obsessors, however, will get angrier and angrier the more they talk about their upset or grievances.

If you allow a person to vent, and find s/he is getting more and more agitated, more active measures are needed, such as empathy statements, attempts to refocus, neutral mode, and so on.

Apologize

A *sincere* apology can help calm a customer, particularly when you or your company has made an error. You can apologize on behalf of your company. Keep in mind that tendering an apology does not necessarily mean that you are admitting culpability. As with admitting a mistake, your apology should be "short and sweet," followed by refocusing on solving the problem or addressing the customer's needs.

Perfunctory or insincere apologies are worse than saying nothing and anger customers. Also, due to a general overuse of the words "I'm sorry," apologies are not as powerful as you might think. They should always be used along with other techniques.

Appropriate Nonverbals

Nonverbals are body language. Customers tend to decide whether you are interested in them and want to help them based on whether you look at them when you speak (or listen), whether you stand or sit in an attentive posture, and even if you fidget or look like you are in a hurry to get rid of them.

Appropriate Smiles

Most customer service training stresses the importance of smiling. There's no question that a warm smile is valuable. However, and it's a big "however," smiles (and other facial expressions) must fit the situation. For example, if a customer is exceedingly upset about how she has been treated, smiling at the customer might be seen as smirking, adding fuel to the fire. That's why smiles need to be appropriate to the situation and the customer's state of mind. Smiling at the wrong time can send the message that you aren't taking the customer seriously.

Arranging Follow-Up

Not all customer problems can be addressed immediately. Many situations call for some form of follow-up or additional communication. For example, if you don't have an answer to a customer's question, you might arrange to find out and call the customer back within a few minutes. Proper follow-up tells the customer he or she is important to you.

Arranging follow-up should include three things: explaining what you will do between now and the actual follow-up, giving a specific time by which you will get back to the customer; and offering a choice as to the form and timing of the follow-up (e.g., you call back, you send an e-mail, the customer calls you). Needless to say, when you arrange a follow-up, you *must* be able to fulfill your promise—and you must do so.

Assurances of Effort

When customers don't feel you are making an effort, they get angry. On the flip side, when customers feel you are making an effort above and beyond the call of duty, they are less likely to target you for angry behavior if they can't get what they want.

An assurance of effort is a statement that tells the customer you will do your best to meet *his or her* needs. For example: "I can see you are in a hurry and I'm going to do my best to get this wrapped up in a few minutes."

Notice that an assurance of effort is different from an assurance of results. You can always assure the customer that you will try, even if you do not yet know if you can give the customer what he or she wants.

Assurances of Results

An assurance of results is a stronger statement than an assurance of effort: it promises that the customer will have his or her problem resolved. An assurance of effort doesn't promise results, so it can be used in almost any situation. Assurances of results should be made only when you can legitimately guarantee the results you are promising.

Audience Removal

Some angry customers will "play to the audience" in public situations where others are present. You can tell whether this is happening by observing whether the customer seems to be looking to other customers or other bystanders for approval or to be addressing them. Removing the audience involves arranging for the customer to be served away from the audience, usually in an office space or somewhere away from the audience. Here's an example of how to do it: "Mr. Jones, I'm sure you'd prefer that your privacy is protected, so let's go to the office and we can continue there."

Bonus Buyoff

This technique involves offering something of value to the customer as compensation for inconvenience or other problems. The offer need not be of significant monetary value, since the point is to be perceived as making an effort. It is used primarily when the organization has made an error, but it can also be used when an error has not been made and the employee wants to make a goodwill gesture.

Broken Record

This technique is used primarily with customers who won't work with you to solve their problems. Its intent is to send the message: We're not going to continue the conversation until we deal with the specific issue that I want to deal with.

It involves repeating the same message, but in different words, until the customer starts to work with you. For example: "You have several options. [Describe them.] Which would you prefer?"

If the customer ignores this, you repeat the message, but in different words: "You can [option one] or [option two]. Do you have a preference?"

The same message can be broken recorded four or five times, until the customer finally chooses one.

It can also be used for expressing empathy, with a customer who is too angry to engage in specific problem solving.

Closing Interactions Positively

A relatively simple technique to end conversations, closing interactions positively usually involves offering pleasantries (e.g., "Thanks for coming in" or "I appreciate your patience and apologize for the delay"). You want to end each interaction, even if it's difficult, on a positive note.

Common Courtesy

Common courtesy refers to a number of behaviors that are based on consideration and polite behavior standards in your country or area. They're basic and you probably know what they are, but it's essential not to lose sight of the importance of using "please" and "thank you," creating an environment for your customer/guest that is inviting, and using civil language. You can add your own ideas to what constitutes common courtesy for the people you serve.

Even with such simple techniques, there are one or two important points to keep in mind. When employees involved in customer service are under stress or rushed, they tend to stop using common courtesy. It's a natural mistake. In trying to address the customer's needs quickly (being task oriented), it's easy to forget that the process (how you interact with the customer) is important. You need to use common courtesy even when you are rushing to meet the needs of your customer, unless it's an emergency situation (e.g., a health emergency) where common courtesy may delay critical actions (e.g., calling 911 for expert help).

Also, remember that when you most need to use common courtesy is in the situations where you least feel like it. Difficult and obnoxious customers tend to push employees to respond rudely or at least curtly. Unfortunately, when you neglect common courtesy, problems escalate, so it's in your interests to be polite and courteous, even with the people you feel don't deserve it. It isn't about who deserves common courtesy, but what will work and reduce the time you waste.

Completing Follow-Up

Obviously, when you have arranged for follow-up, you need to complete the follow-up. There may also be situations where a colleague or your boss asks you to follow up on something. It's a simple process. Contact the individual. Identify yourself. Explain *why* you are following up. Request any information you need. Respond to the customer's problem/issue as needed.

Contact Security/Authorities/Management

Most employees are not trained in security, self-defense, or other methods for dealing with a violent, highly disruptive, or potentially violent customer. If it's not your job, it's not your job. Don't take on the responsibilities of security or the police. When you are faced with any situation that may be violent or pose a security threat, contact security personnel, management, and/or the police. If your company has a policy on this issue, follow it. Do not chase customers or attempt to apprehend them. This strategy also applies in situations where someone has made some sort of threat to you personally or to the company. At minimum, notify your manager immediately. Remember that safety is your first priority—for yourself, your colleagues, and other customers.

Disengaging

Disengaging is a technique that is most often used with a difficult or aggressive customer. It has several purposes: it serves to temporarily halt a conversation that is getting increasingly emotional and unpleasant and it is used if a conversation is going around in circles.

Disengaging means taking a break from the interaction to allow both parties to calm down or think more clearly so that, when the conversation resumes, it's more like a "fresh start." When you are in a situation in which the conversation is not likely to result in success, it's possible to offer a reason to stop and resume in a minute or two or after an even longer interlude. For example, you might say, "Mr. Smith, let me take a minute to check your file," and then suspend the conversation while you go check. You can also take the more direct approach, as follows: "Mr. Smith, maybe we both need a break so we can approach this fresh. How about if we resume this discussion tomorrow? We can set up a time that's convenient." This technique can be used in person and on the phone.

Disengaging is similar to using a timeout. A timeout is used to allow the customer to calm down by giving him or her an opportunity alone. Disengaging does not require the customer to be alone, but relies on the suspension of the conversation for its power.

Distraction

This technique is used with angry customers to shift their attention away from their anger and away from expressing their anger at you. It's designed to break the anger cycle. It works like this: direct the customer's attention to a physical object with words and with a gesture, so the customer needs to break eye contact with you. Here's an example: "If you'll take a look at the computer screen [swivel monitor and point to a specific spot on the monitor], you'll see that we have your policy expiry date as November 6. That's where the problem is."

Any physical object—brochures, forms, signs—can be used, but the object should have some relevance to the issue being discussed.

Empathy Statements

Empathy statements are used as primary responses to any situation where the customer is upset or frustrated or even might become frustrated or angry in the future. They are intended to prove to the customer that you understand his or her emotional state or why he or she is feeling that way. You need not agree with the reason why a customer is angry, but you need to acknowledge that the customer is angry. Here are some examples:

- "It seems like you are pretty upset by the delay."
- "I know it can be frustrating to have to complete these forms."

■ "You must have been pretty upset to find out the product didn't work."

Here's the key to effective empathy statements. Be specific. Name the emotion (anger, frustration, upset) and identify the source of the emotion (the delay, the forms, the product failure). Avoid general statements like "I see where you are coming from."

Expediting

Expediting means "making things go faster." In other words, give the impression that you are doing things to speed up whatever process the customer is trying to get done. You can convey this by talking more quickly and more emphatically, while clearing away barriers that may be slowing down progress toward getting what the customer wants.

Expert Recommendations

Customers don't always know what they want or need or they may be confused about what to do next. One of the roles of someone in customer service involves providing expert advice or recommendation about product selection or about the most efficient way for the customer to accomplish what he or she wants. Before giving advice or recommendation, it's always good to ask the customer if he or she would like you to provide it. Here's a key point. When you give advice or make product recommendation, explain *why* you think a specific product or action would be best for the customer. Provide pros and cons, a balanced recommendation.

Explain Reasoning or Actions

It's easy to assume that a customer will understand why you're doing something or why you're saying what you're saying. That's a mistake. The customer is not going to be familiar with your company, policies, and procedures, or at least not as familiar as you are.

Explain what you're doing for the customer and *why* you're doing it. Customers want to understand what is going on and may become frustrated or even frightened when they don't understand. Here's a simple example: "I'm going to [explain action] so that you'll be entered in the computer, so next time you come in things will be much faster."

Face-Saving Out

Embarrassing or humiliating a customer is always a bad thing, even in situations where the customer has made a stupid mistake or is angry and unpleasant. Providing a face-saving out is a technique to avoid embarrassing a customer, blaming a customer, or pointing out a customer error or deficiency.

The best way to explain is through example. Let's say a customer appears not to understand what an employee has told him and, even though the employee has given him written material to help him understand, he is still not getting it. The employee could say, "Well, if you read the material you were given, you would understand." That has potential to show up the customer, particularly if that person may have difficulty with reading comprehension. Instead, the employee can offer a face-saving out as follows: "Perhaps the written material isn't very clear or I haven't explained myself well, so let me see if I can talk you through this, since it can get complicated." This removes the blame component by moving responsibility to the employee, while trying not to point out any reading comprehension problems the customer might have.

Finding Agreement Points

When the customer sees you as being "on the same side," he or she is much less likely to strike out at you in anger. One common technique often used in hostage negotiations to create a sense of "we're in it together" is to look for things the customer says that you can agree with. Even expressing agreements on small points, like the weather or other topics not related to why you are talking to the customer, can create a better sense of rapport.

Finishing Off/Following Up

Related to "Arranging Follow-Up," described earlier in this section, following up or finishing off is the process of getting back to a customer to tie up loose ends, confirm that a problem has been solved, or obtain feedback from the customer. When contacting a customer to follow up, it's standard to introduce yourself, explain why you are making the contact, and ask permission to continue or ask if this is a good time. Following up is an extremely important method of showing the customer that he or she is valued and his or her opinions and satisfaction matter.

Isolate/Detach Customer

Isolating or detaching the customer is another name for a process that removes the audience effect (when the customer plays to other customers or bystanders) and provides an opportunity for the customer to think more calmly about the situation and how he or she is behaving. The key issue is to provide time for the customer to think and reflect. See "Timeout" for more details.

Leveling

Leveling involves being honest and forthright without blaming and without strong emotion. It is fairly similar to what some call *assertive communication*. It may involve expressing your feelings about a customer's comments in a calm way or pointing out a customer error in a nonblaming way. It's not a primary customer service technique, except in situations where you have a long-term relationship with a customer that you want to both keep and build. It's best used with customers you know well and you know will respond positively to open and honest communication. Not recommended for customers you do not know well.

Managing Height Differentials/Nonverbals

This involves a family of actions you can take when a customer is intruding into your personal space or using a height advantage and/or body language to intimidate or put you off balance. If you are standing and the customer moves into your space, pivot so you are at a 90-degree angle and not face to face. If you are seated and the customer is standing, it's best to stand. (Get up slowly and calmly.) Often coupled with the distraction technique, the idea is to create a comfort zone for yourself and to move the emphasis from a confrontational position (face to face) to a more cooperative one. With customers who use height differentials and enter your personal space, it's better to use these indirect techniques to manage the situation than to make it an issue by focusing on the space issue verbally.

Managing Interpersonal Distance

We all have comfort zones about our interpersonal space. When a person is too close, it can cause us to feel simply uncomfortable or even threatened and intimidated. All of those feelings make it more difficult to serve the customer. While customers will sometimes enter your interpersonal space intentionally (i.e., getting in your face) because they are angry or frustrated, it may also be unintentional.

Interpersonal space boundaries are both cultural and individual. Some cultures tend to have small interpersonal space (people get closer when they talk); within cultures, individuals differ. What may be uncomfortable for you may be comfortable for the other.

Be that as it may, you need to manage interpersonal distance so you are comfortable. You also want to be aware of the space boundaries of your customers. Don't get too close. If the customer moves backwards or looks away for no apparent reason, you should increase your distance.

If the customer is too close to you, you can use the "90-degree angle" techniques outlined in "Managing Height Differentials/Nonverbals." You can increase distance by directing the person's attention to something (a product or information) that requires the customer to move away from you. Or, of course, you can step away. If you step away, you should do so in a way that sends the message you are stepping toward something and not away from the client. Walk toward a product you are pointing to or to a file you pick up. It's a subtle difference. When you seem to be stepping toward something, it seems less obvious to the customer that you are stepping away from him or her. That's less likely to make interpersonal distance a focal point for your conversation.

Whenever possible, do not make an issue of interpersonal space by referring to it directly and verbally. You really don't want to spend any of your time and the customer's time talking about who is standing where. The exception occurs in some contexts, such as law enforcement situations and where you are concerned about your physical safety and nothing else works.

However, if you do feel physically threatened, your priority would be to extract yourself immediately.

Not Taking the Bait

One of the simplest techniques, and one of the most important when dealing with an angry customer, not taking the bait means not responding to insults, comments, innuendo, or other angry or abusive comments made by a customer. Typically, you can respond indirectly (using empathy statements) but not respond directly. The key thing to understand is that if you focus on or even simply acknowledge a customer's unpleasant comments, you are going to spend much more time arguing and talking about those comments than you would if you simply ignored them or responded to them with empathy statements. An essential tactic, not taking the bait requires some self-discipline. Remind yourself that the unpleasant customer shouldn't be allowed to upset you or ruin your day, an hour of it, or even a minute. Don't lower yourself to the level of an insulting customer.

Offering Choices/Empowering

One of the major reasons why customers get upset is that they often feel helpless and buffeted by policies, procedures, red tape, and other things they perceive are beyond their control. You can counter this feeling by offering choices to customers whenever possible. By offering them choices, you also show respect for their wishes and help them exert some positive control over the discussions, how and when they occur, and related issues. Even simple things, like offering someone a choice of coffee or tea, can help to create rapport and prevent conflict escalation.

Plain Language

It's easy to forget that our customers do not necessarily understand the jargon, acronyms, and terms that we use every day and take for granted. Using plain language involves translating our language into language that the customer can understand.

For example, a computer technician might use the term "LCD" to refer to a liquid crystal display computer monitor with other technicians, but this term may be totally foreign to most casual computer users. Some will know it, but some will not, so it's good to anticipate that not everyone will understand the term. The technician might translate it into "computer monitor," which is a more familiar term. In addition, the technician should be prepared to explain even that term in simple language. For example, "the computer monitor is the device that you look at when you use the computer." In this example, the technician would use the latter explanation only if the customer seemed to not understand "computer monitor," so as not to insult the customer's knowledge and intelligence.

Another example: A human resource professional might be comfortable using terms like "401(k)" "compensation," and "spousal benefits," but those terms may not be completely clear to an employee. So, the HR employee could replace "401(k)" with "company retirement account," "compensation" with "salary," and "spousal benefits" with "medical insurance for your wife and children." The idea is to focus on clarity and simplicity without being patronizing and to remember to communicate for the benefit of the customer, not yourself.

Preemptive Strike

The term "preemptive strike" is borrowed from the military. In customer service it means anticipating a problem a customer might have and addressing or acknowledging it before the customer brings it up. For example, if a customer has been waiting a long time, you can apologize for the wait or use an empathy statement to show you understand that the customer has been waiting a long time and that he or she is frustrated, rather than wait for the customer to start complaining. By mentioning the problem first, you demonstrate you both understand and are concerned about the customer's feelings. This technique can go a long way to prevent interactions from escalating.

Privacy and Confidentiality

Customers may be concerned about keeping their business and their conversations private, so others don't know about them. When dealing with any details a customer might want kept between the two of you, make sure you do so in an environment where you cannot be overheard *and* make it clear to the customer that you are taking steps to protect his or her privacy and confidentiality. Here's a tip. Some customers want to ensure that their information remains private, even if the information is not what most of us would consider personal. Offer and reassure about privacy and confidentiality, even in situations that might not seem to demand it.

Probing Questions

This technique refers to the use of a series of questions to help clarify a customer's needs, feelings, and wants and the facts of his or her situation. Probing questions are simple ones that cover one issue at a time so as not to overwhelm the customer. The main difference between probing questions and other questions is that a probing question is directly related to the answer the customer provides to the previous question. Probing questions invite the customer to clarify or add to his or her previous response.

For example, "What brought you in today?" is a question. An alternative is to break this down by first saying, "I see you are browsing the plasma television sets. Are you interested in more information about them?" If the customer says yes, the employee probes deeper by asking, "Did you have an interest in a particular size of television?" The interaction may continue this way, with the employee asking simple questions in a series, basing each on the response to earlier questions.

Apart from this being an important tool for getting good information from a customer, it shows that you are listening, since you're basing each question on the specifics of a customer response.

Pros and Cons

Customers see you as more credible or believable when you present both sides of something, like the pros and cons of products. For example, when describing a particular product, it's much better to include both its strengths and its weaknesses relative to other products, rather than to present only its strengths or only its weaknesses. The same applies when explaining any options a customer might have to choose from. Keep in mind that when you present a one-sided view, the customer will wonder why you are presenting what may appear to be an unbalanced perspective and will question or suspect your motives.

Providing Alternatives

Similar to "providing choices/empowering," this is a simple technique to present possible alternative products, services, or actions that might apply to the customer's situation. For example, "You can contact me by phone or e-mail, whatever is more convenient" provides two alternatives to the customer. What's the difference between offering choices, as described earlier, and offering alternatives? When you offer choices, you usually ask the customer which alternatives he or she wants to pursue. Providing alternatives demonstrates your interest in ensuring that the customer understands his or her options.

Providing a Customer Takeaway

Providing a customer takeaway involves giving something physical to the customer to take away. For example, you might provide a brochure, product information, a phone number written down that a customer needs, or a list of steps for a customer to solve a problem. When you provide a takeaway, you are not forcing the customer to rely on his or her memory and the customer can refer to it if needed. If you don't have printed material available, you can write down notes for the customer to take away. This is often seen by customers as being helpful beyond their expectations, which is a good thing. Takeaways can also be brief summaries of a conversation.

Providing Explanations

You may be surprised at the idea that employees tend to take for granted that customers understand what the employees are saying. But it happens all the time. Providing explanations means exactly what you'd think it means: you explain. Here's an example. Let's say a customer wants to return some underwear, but your store does not accept such returns for hygienic reasons. You could assume the reasoning is obvious, which would be a mistake, or you could explain the reasoning by talking about why your store has that policy, referencing any laws that might apply or that the policy exists to protect every customer.

When you educate a customer, that person usually becomes a better customer, easier to serve, and more loyal.

Questioning Instead of Stating

Questions can sometimes be used to soften a statement or command. Let's say a customer has a complaint about something. You could say, "Go down the hall and speak to our customer service branch." But that statement sounds harsh, because it's a command. People don't like to be ordered around. So, you can use a question to soften the situation like this: "Were you aware that you can speak to our customer service branch and they'll be able to help you?" In effect you are saying almost exactly the same thing, but the question form comes across as much more cooperative and avoids giving the impression that you are ordering the customer around.

Referral to Supervisor

There are situations when you are unable to help a customer further because you lack the authority or information to do so. There are other situations where a customer, usually angry, will likely respond more politely if he or she can talk with someone perceived as having more status in the organization—a manager or supervisor. We know that when a customer talks with a supervisor or someone else with more status he or she tends to behave more civilly than with someone seen as having less status.

Whether you cannot help due to lack of authority and information or whether you feel the customer will respond more positively with a supervisor, the techniques used are the same. First, ask or confirm that the customer wants to speak with the supervisor. Second, contact the supervisor and explain the situation to him or her. Normally you would provide the supervisor with the customer's name, the problem or issue, and the customer's general state of mind. This step ensures that the supervisor isn't blindsided, eliminates any need for the customer to explain the entire situation, and allows the supervisor to take control of the interaction when he or she makes contact with the customer.

Finally, the supervisor is "connected" with the customer. This might involve the supervisor introducing himself or herself as follows: "Hi, I'm Ms. Jones, and I understand you have some concerns about your billing." Whether the supervisor initiates contact in person or on the phone, the procedure should be the same.

It's absolutely important that you and your supervisor are on the same wavelength on referrals. Some supervisors don't ever want to have customers referred to them, some are willing under certain circumstances, and others are much more open. You need to know what *your* supervisor expects—and the time to find out is not when you have an angry customer waiting. Ask your supervisor when it's OK to refer customers and how he or she wants the process handled. Then abide by those wishes.

Referral to Third Party

This technique is very similar to "referral to supervisor," except that the person who will receive the customer isn't a supervisor, but someone else in the organization, often a coworker. Third-party referrals are useful when someone else may know more about the subject at hand than you do or when you believe that someone else, because of his or her personal style or approach, might work more effectively with a specific customer. Referral to a third party can also be used when a supervisor is not available.

The process works exactly the same, except that you present the third party as someone who is expert or knowledgeable, to enhance his or her perceived status. For example: "You might prefer to talk to John Angus. He's the person who knows the most about [subject of interest to customer]." Again, ensure that you inform the third party about the customer's situation before he or she interacts with the customer.

Refocus

Refocusing a conversation means bringing it back to the original issue or topic. Let's say an angry customer has a complaint about a product or service. He starts off talking about the problem, but then starts making critical remarks about the company or about you personally. Those comments and discussing them in depth are not going to help the customer resolve his concern. What you do is couple an empathy statement with a refocus statement as follows. "I can see you are angry about the product problem. Let's get back to what we can do to help you. I can suggest a few things that might help." What you want to do is shift the customer's attention away from his anger, and to something more constructive.

Setting Limits

You set limits in situations where a customer is acting in nonconstructive ways. The customer might be raising his or her voice, swearing, or making repeated nuisance phone calls. In order to help the customer (and keep your sanity), you need to encourage the customer to stop the inappropriate or destructive behavior. There are several parts to setting limits.

The setting limits process begins with an "if … then" statement. In that statement you are going to identify as specifically as possible what behavior you want to stop. You are also going to identify the consequence that will occur if the customer does not stop. It sounds like this: "If you do not stop swearing, I'm going to have to end this conversation." Here, the behavior is "swearing" and the consequence is "end this conversation."

But you aren't finished yet. The next step is to provide a choice statement. So after the "if … then" step, you add, "It's up to you whether you'd like to continue."

This step is included because we want the customer to understand that he gets to decide whether to stop swearing (and continue the conversation) or continue swearing (and end the conversation). By framing it as a choice for the customer, the consequence seems less like something the employee does *to* the customer and less like a punishment.

You must handle the entire process of setting limits and enforcing them calmly, so it does not seem like the process is personal.

If the customer abides by the limit, then the conversation can continue. If the customer continues to swear or argue, then the conversation must be terminated. Here's what you would say on the phone. "I'm going to end this conversation now. You are welcome to call back at some other time." You include the last sentence to tell the customer that you will be glad to help at some other time—provided that he stops swearing. Once you've indicated you are ending the conversation, you will do so unless the customer offers a clear apology or commitment to abide by the limit you set.

Before using limits to end interactions, you should be clear about your organization's policies and wishes regarding what constitutes reasonable grounds for ending an interaction or refusing further service. Also remember that setting and enforcing limits should be a last resort: use it only after other techniques have failed to encourage the customer to act more constructively.

Some People Think That (Neutral Mode)

Neutral mode is an indirect way to acknowledge something a customer has said without agreeing with it or disagreeing with it. That's why it's called neutral mode. Because it's an unusual, novel, or unexpected response, the technique tends to interrupt the flow of anger or emotion and causes the customer to stop and think. This provides the employee with an opening to use other techniques.

This technique has a specific form. If you change it much, it doesn't work as well. It goes like this: "Some people do think that [rephrase what the customer said in a straightforward, dispassionate way]."

Let's say a customer is going on and on about how inefficient government is. The employee, wanting to interrupt the flow, or rant, says, "You know, some people do feel that government isn't as efficient as it might be."

Notice that the employee didn't say "wastes money" or "squanders money" or any other stronger, emotionally laden words. That's important. Always rephrase in a neutral, unemotional way.

When the technique works, the customer will respond with a short sentence or two, then stop. Then the employee uses other techniques to intervene and get control over the conversation. The two most important techniques coupled with "neutral mode" are "Empathy Statements" and "Refocus."

Stop Sign—Nonverbal

Do you need to get an in-person customer to stop and listen? You can use the nonverbal stop sign to indicate you'd like to say something. The technique is simple, but you need to execute it just right. Hold up your hand toward the customer, with the palm facing half toward the floor and half toward the customer. In other words, your hand should be at about a 45-degree angle. Ensure that you are far enough away from the customer that there will be no risk of physical contact. Keep your hand no higher than the customer's chest level, not in his or her face.

This technique should *not* be used with any customer who appears potentially violent. Also, the stop sign should be raised slowly, not abruptly, and it can be coupled with a simple verbal request (e.g., "Hold on a sec.").

Suggest an Alternative to Waiting

This technique is an extension of the "Providing Alternatives" technique mentioned earlier. When customers are waiting, let's say in a doctor's waiting room, the longer they wait, the angrier they get. One reason is they don't know what to do. Do they have to stay in the waiting room or risk losing their places? Can they go somewhere and come back? Is there time to grab a cup of coffee?

If you are in charge of the waiting room, it's good to both explain the reasons for the delay and suggest what customers might do while they wait. Or, indicate they can reschedule if waiting is a problem. A very useful example goes like this: "For those of you with appointments after three o'clock, feel free to step out for a coffee break or snack in the restaurant next door. Just be sure to be back within a half-hour of your scheduled appointment and you won't lose your spot."

Summarize the Conversation

A simple technique used either in the middle or at the end of a conversation, this involves doing a quick recap of the critical parts of the discussion. Summarize any important details and particularly any specific commitments you and/or your customer have made during the conversation.

Summarizing shows that you are paying attention, but there's a more important reason to use it. It's not uncommon during conversations for both parties to believe that they understand what is being said in exactly the same way. But they may not. If misunderstandings are not caught, serious problems can arise. Summarizing allows you to confirm with the customer that both you and he or she understand what has been said in the same way.

Summarizing verbally can be accompanied by providing the customer with a takeaway—a written summary of the conversation.

Telephone Silence

It's sometimes hard to get someone on the phone to be quiet and listen to you, so you can offer help. Some people talk incessantly when they are upset, angry, frustrated, or frightened. One of the best ways to get a customer to stop talking over the phone is to say absolutely nothing. No words. No "Uh-huh." Nothing. What will happen is that the customer will stop and ask, "Hello, hello, are you there?" and then wait for a response from you. That gives you an opening to use other techniques and get some control over the conversation.

If you have a mute button, that works even better, because it blocks out all sounds, including background noise. Do *not* put a customer on hold in this situation. Putting a customer on hold means you cannot hear them or know when they have stopped talking so you can jump into the gap to take some control of the conversation. The mute button allows you to hear the customer, but the customer cannot hear you or any background noise.

Thank-Yous

One of the most obvious and simple techniques needs little explanation. Everyone likes to be thanked. Thank people. One tip: don't just say, "Thank you"—be more specific. For example, "Thank you for being so patient" or "Thank you for visiting our company."

Timeout

You might be familiar with timeouts in relation to children who are acting out. The principles are similar for adults: the timeout can provide a cooling-off period for customers who are upset or angry, particularly if their anger is getting in the way of providing help to them. Basically, you provide some sensible reason why the customer should wait on his or her own for a minute or two, preferably in a locale away from other people. For example, if you were in an office with a customer, you could say, "I need to check to make sure what I'm saying is accurate. Let me do that. It will just take a minute." Then exit, leaving the customer alone. Return in a minute or two.

Most angry customers are regular people who are upset and acting aggressively only temporarily. When you give them the chance to think about what they are doing, they will often apologize to you and act more constructively.

It's important to keep the timeout short. If it goes past a few minutes, that may provide an additional reason for the customer to remain angry or even for the anger to escalate. It's also important to understand that timeouts, at least for adults, are *not* punitive. They are meant to provide time to think.

Use Customer's Name

Another simple technique requires little explanation, using the customer's name personalizes the service you provide and indicates you think the customer is important enough to remember his or her name. There's another advantage: it indirectly suggests the customer is not anonymous. Anonymity tends to increase aggression.

It is sometimes difficult to know how to address a customer. With a woman, do you use Ms., Mrs., or Miss? When do you use a first name? The best way to find out is to ask how a customer would prefer to be addressed. First names are best used with customers you know well.

Use of Timing with Angry Customers

We've included this technique because timing is so important when dealing with angry customers. It's not a technique so much as something you should be aware of. Angry people are often not ready or even able to think logically or in an organized way. If you try to solve a customer's problem when he or she is not ready, it won't work.

First, deal with the customer's feelings using various acknowledgment and empathy techniques. Only when the customer is acting less upset should you move on (refocus) to solve the specific problem.

Here's a tip. You will know you are problem-solving too early if the customer ignores your attempts and you have to repeat yourself because he or she isn't hearing you.

Verbal Softeners

People don't respond well to language that sounds absolute, authoritarian, or harsh. For example, "We never make those kinds of mistakes" is very categorical and likely to antagonize even mild-mannered customers. Here's another way of putting it: "It's unlikely we've made a mistake." The word "unlikely" is a verbal softener. Other softeners include *perhaps, sometimes, it's possible,* and *occasionally.*

Here's another example, in a situation where the employee believes the customer has made a mistake. He could say, "Clearly, you've made a mistake." That would be bad. He could soften the sentence by saying, "Perhaps you've misinterpreted something here." "Perhaps" is the softener, but notice we've also replaced the word "mistake" with "misinterpreted," a less harsh word.

Verbal softeners are exceedingly valuable tools to help you appear more cooperative and likeable to customers and to prevent conflict from arising from the use of harsh language.

Voice Tone—Emphatic

You can use an emphatic voice tone to convey that you are strongly committed to helping the customer. For example, let's say a customer has been telling you that he's late for an appointment and is double-parked and needs to be served quickly. You can respond in a laidback way, but it's better to respond more emphatically—*I understand, I will get this done for you!* Note the emphasis on "will." Emphatic voice tones work best when they match the tone and energy that the customer is using.

When Question

The "when question" is a cousin of "neutral mode." Its function is to force the customer to think, thereby interrupting the flow of angry or aggressive speech aimed at you. It works on the same principle. The "when question" is an unusual or novel question and it's closed-ended so it tends to elicit short answers, which are what you want. It also has a specific form that goes like this:

"When did you start thinking that [summarize in a neutral way a key point from what the customer said]?"

When this works properly, the customer will respond with a specific time or incident and then stop. That gives you the opening you need so you can use other techniques.

So, let's say the customer is accusing you of not caring. He says: "If you gave a damn about me, you'd take care of me properly."

The employee replies, "When did you start feeling you weren't getting the service you wanted?"

The customer answers, "The first time I came in here," and then stops talking.

The employee uses that opening to empathize and try to refocus the customer back to the issue and back to more constructive behavior.

It's very important, once again, to not repeat any hot or emotional words the customer uses. For example, it would not work if the employee said, "When did you start thinking I didn't give a damn about you?"

You're Right!

The "you're right!" technique is a cousin of "neutral mode," the "when question," and "finding agreement points." It serves to surprise an angry customer, since the last thing he or she expects in the middle of a rant is for you to say "You're right!" You'll find that emphatic use of this phrase will result in the customer not knowing what to say next. That provides an opening for you to use other techniques.

The "you're right!" method is more emphatic than "finding agreement points."

Part Two

**Dealing with Specific
Customer Situations**

1. When You Are Late or Know You Will Be Late

THE SITUATION

Being late for an appointment or meeting with a customer is not a good thing, but there are situations where you are delayed a) due to circumstances beyond your control or b) because you needed to do something for the benefit of the customer. Here are some tips on how to handle situations where you know you will be late or you actually arrive late.

TECHNIQUES USED

- Apologize (1)
- Explain Reasoning or Actions (2)
- Empathy Statements (3)
- Offering Choices/Empowering (4)
- Providing Alternatives (5)
- Thank-Yous (6)

DIALOGUE

The employee realizes he is going to be at least 10 minutes late for a meeting with his customers because there was a delay in printing material that is needed for the meeting. The employee contacts the customer by phone.

Employee: Mr. Jones, I'm really sorry. (1) It looks like I'm going to be about 10 minutes late to arrive because there's been a delay in printing out the contracts we need to look at during the meeting. (2) I'm printing them out now and shouldn't be later than 3 p.m. (2)

Customer: Well, I've got the VP of Finance coming and I can't have him sitting around waiting. I have to tell you I'm not impressed.

Employee: I can understand you are disappointed. (3) I had to decide whether to delay coming over until the contracts are done or to come on time without the contracts. (2) It seems like the best use of time, but if you want to reschedule or if there's any way to make this more convenient, I'm flexible. (4)

Customer: No, that's fine.

Employee: If you want to go over the other reports while you're waiting, maybe we can shorten the meeting. (5)

Customer: That's a good idea.

When the employee finally arrives, this is what he says.

Employee: I have to apologize to all of you, (1) and especially to Mr. Smith (VP of Finance), for being late, and thank you for your patience. (6) [He then explains the reason for arriving late.] (2)

EXPLANATIONS

Most of the techniques used in this example are straightforward. The use of apologies (1), thank-yous (6), and empathy statements (3) doesn't need additional explanation.

Here's what's important. Even though the delay is "only" 10 minutes, the employee notifies the customer of the delay and provides an explanation of why he will be late. (2) Notification, even when you will only be a few minutes late, is always a good thing, because it demonstrates your concern for the customer and his or her time. If you look at (4), you will see the use of offering a choice to the customer. He is offering an "out" so that if the customer needs to reschedule or cancel the meeting, he can do so using the opening the employee provides.

In (5), the employee offers an alternative or suggestion as to how the customer might use the 10-minute delay to his advantage, recognizing that the delay shouldn't create "dead time" for the others attending the meeting.

Finally, when the employee arrives, you can see a repeat of the techniques the employee used when notifying the customer of the delay. The employee decides to explain why he is late just in case the people attending the meeting were not informed of the reason for the delay.

HINTS

If you are late without good reason (e.g., oversleeping, error in planning), it's probably best to give only a limited and general explanation, such as "I was unavoidably detained," or to be honest and admit your mistake. The more established and positive your relationships with the customer, the more honest you can be.

See Also: 9. When the Customer Has Been Through Voicemail Hell, 11. When the Customer Has Been "Buck-Passed"

2. When a Customer Is in a Hurry

THE SITUATION

In this day and age, people and customers are often in a hurry to conduct their business and move on. How can you interact with a customer who is in a hurry in a way that reflects that you understand the customer's need for speed?

TECHNIQUES USED

- Voice Tone—Emphatic (1)
- Assurances of Results (2)

DIALOGUE

A customer arrives at an airline counter to check in for her flight and is clearly flustered, out of breath, and in a hurry.

Customer: Oh lord, I don't want to miss my flight, my car broke down, and oh goodness ....

Employee: We'll get you on your flight. (2) [She looks at the ticket the customer presents.] No problem. You still have 15 minutes to get to the gate (1, 2). Bags to check? (1)

Customer: Just the one.

Employee: Seat preference, aisle or window? (1)

Customer: Window.

EXPLANATIONS

Since the customer is clearly flustered, the employee first reassures the customer that she won't miss her flight in (2). In addition to that simple reassurance, the employee informs the customer that she still has 15 minutes to get to the gate. That's reassuring information.

What really works well here is the use of a tone of voice that matches the situation. The employee uses a very firm, emphatic tone of voice (1), but also speaks more quickly than normal and in shorter sentences than she would with someone who is not feeling so time-pressured. Why? By speaking in a way that conveys urgency, she is communicating to the customer that she understands the customer's situation and is modifying her behavior to address the customer's need.

HINTS

The way you speak (speed, intensity, length) is important in conveying the right message to a customer. The key is to modify how you speak to fit the context. In this example, the employee speaks more quickly, more intensely, and in short bursts to reflect the urgency of the situation. In a funeral home, this way of speaking would be completely inappropriate. A slower, calmer, and more empathetic tone would fit.

See Also: 3. When a Customer Jumps Ahead in a Line of Waiting Customers, 4. When a Customer Asks to Be Served Ahead of Other Waiting Customers

3. When a Customer Jumps Ahead in a Line of Waiting Customers

THE SITUATION

One of the most frustrating things for customers is when someone pushes ahead of them in a line and for the employee to serve the more aggressive customer first, ignoring the fact that the aggressive customer has pushed in. To ignore the situation almost ensures that the customer being delayed is going to blame the employee for the aggressive customer's rude or oblivious behavior.

TECHNIQUES USED

- Verbal Softeners (1)
- Face-Saving Out (2)

DIALOGUE

This situation could occur in any context where people line up for service—grocery stores, other retail establishments, banks, hotels, restaurants. There's a line of five people waiting to be served and a sixth person steps into the middle of the line. Before any of the other customers say anything, the employee intervenes.

Employee: [to the customer who has pushed in] Perhaps you didn't notice that the line actually ends after this gentleman. (1) If you could move to the end, I'll be glad to serve you in turn.

Customer: Oh, I'm sorry. I didn't see that.

Employee: No problem. It's easy to miss. (2)

EXPLANATIONS

In this situation it's important to point out that the customer has jumped the line without doing anything that might humiliate or embarrass him or her. In (1) the employee uses a very gentle way of letting the customer know about the line, careful not to accuse the customer. The word "perhaps" is a good example of a verbal softener. Notice the difference in tone between what the employee said and the following: "Hey, you jumped the line. Get back to the end." Quite different.

In (2), you can see an example of a similar technique, providing a face-saving out. Since the customer has apologized, the employee can soften any embarrassment by making it OK, indicating that it's a mistake that's easy to make. That ends the interaction on a positive note.

HINTS

It's important that an employee who deals with situations where customers line up make a conscious effort to monitor the line in order to address "pushing-in" issues before another customer does. You don't want two customers arguing about something that is ultimately your responsibility.

When a customer cuts in, you can't know whether it is an intentional act of rudeness and inconsideration or simply a result of inattention. For this reason, you should always give the benefit of the doubt. To accuse a customer of pushing in intentionally is almost always guaranteed to start an argument. Even if you have a strong suspicion it was intentional, you must start with a gentle approach.

See Also: 2. When a Customer Is in a Hurry, 5. When a Customer Interrupts a Discussion Between tbe Employee and Another Customer

4. When a Customer Asks to Be Served Ahead of Other Waiting Customers

THE SITUATION

Here's a situation you may have encountered if you work in a retail environment. A customer in a line up at the cash register asks whether she can be served without waiting, because she is either in a hurry, or feels that her small number of items somehow justifies moving ahead of people with many more items to be processed at the check-out. Denying the request may incur the ire of the customer requesting the "speed-up" while accommodating the request may alienate the people ahead of her in the line. What do you do?

TECHNIQUES USED

■ Offering Choices/Empowering (1)

DIALOGUE

Four people are waiting in line at a grocery store. The first three people have full baskets while the fourth person has only three items. The customer with the fewest items gets your attention and asks if she can go first.

Customer: I'm in a real hurry and I only have a few items, so can I go ahead of these people?

Employee: Since these people have been waiting longer and might also be in a rush, it's really up to them. (1) If they don't mind, I can take you first. Otherwise, the wait is only a few minutes.

Customer: [to others in the line] Does anyone mind if I go ahead of you?

EXPLANATIONS

The cashier could have made a judgment call in this situation and simply made the decision himself, but that would have put the cashier in the middle—really between a rock and a hard place. Instead, the employee turns the responsibility for the decision back to where it belongs—to the people who might be inconvenienced. He provides the opportunity for the customer in a hurry to ask the others (1), if she chooses to do so. It's then up to the other customers. Not only is that the fairest way to deal with this situation, but it also sends the message that the customers who have been waiting are important to the employee.

HINTS

Notice that the cashier doesn't volunteer to ask the other customers himself. He puts the onus (and the choice) to do so on the customer who wants to be served first. Another reason for doing it this way is that it helps the other customers see the employee as neutral on this issue.

In situations like this, the employee needs to have a unanimous "vote" in order to break with procedure. A majority vote is not enough to change the order/procedure.

See Also: 2. When a Customer Is in a Hurry

5. When a Customer Interrupts a Discussion Between the Employee and Another Customer

THE SITUATION

You may face a situation where you are helping one customer and a second customer rushes up and interrupts your conversation. It may appear that you are caught between a rock and a hard place, since if you serve the first customer, the second may become annoyed, and if you serve the second one, the first customer, quite justifiably, may feel you are not treating him or her as important. In this situation we'll describe a single technique—the "stop sign—nonverbal" tactic.

TECHNIQUES USED

- Stop Sign—Nonverbal (1)

DIALOGUE

In a retail store, the employee has been talking with a primary customer for three or four minutes. All of a sudden, a second customer rushes up and interrupts the conversation.

Second Customer: Excuse me, but can you tell me who I need to talk to about returning some merchandise?

Employee: [turns to the second customer, makes eye contact, and holds up hand at about a 45-degree angle toward the second customer] I can help you in just a moment or you can go to the service desk. [The employee then breaks eye contact and returns to the first customer.] (1)

EXPLANATIONS

The first priority is always the customer with whom you're interacting. The key is to limit your interaction with the interrupting customer, so it's as brief as possible. That's why the employee uses a very short sentence and then immediately returns his attention to the first customer, indicating this by shifting eye contact. Note also that the employee, in his short sentence with the second customer, offers an option—wait or go to the service desk.

HINTS

Generally, you should not address the needs of the interrupting customer even if you can address them quickly, because it sends a message that the first customer is less important.

As an additional technique, if you feel you can address the second customer's concerns quickly, you could ask the first customer for permission to do so as follows: "Do you mind if I help this fellow out while you look at the items you are interested in? It will only take 30 seconds or so."

See Also: 2. When a Customer Is in a Hurry, 3. When a Customer Jumps Ahead in a Line of Waiting Customers

6. When a Customer Has a Negative Attitude About Your Company Due to Past Experiences

THE SITUATION

You may come across a situation where your customer comes in with a "chip on his shoulder" because he believes he has been treated badly in the past or has heard from others that your organization doesn't treat people well. This tends to happen more often in government and public sector environments (e.g., schools) because, unlike in the private sector, the customer cannot simply go somewhere else. The person needs to deal with the specific organization and the organization needs to provide service. How do you deal with the customer with negative preconceptions, whether justified or not?

TECHNIQUES USED
- Active Listening (1)
- Not Taking the Bait (2)
- Some People Think That (neutral mode) (3)
- Assurances of Effort (4)
- Refocus (5)

DIALOGUE

This situation occurs in a government office. The customer can't choose to take his business elsewhere and clearly has some negative preconceptions.

Customer: OK. I need to get these building permits done, and I don't want you guys to jerk me around like you usually do or run me through reams of red tape. I don't have the time.

Employee: It sounds to me like you want to get these permits done as quickly as possible, right? (1, 2)

Customer: Damn right. You know, nobody likes dealing with you guys. It's always a major hassle, and you screw it up half the time.

Employee: Some people get impatient with the process. (3) Let's see if I can surprise you. (4) Since you want to get this done fast, let's get to it. (5) I know you've done this before, so you probably have the information you need for the permits? (5)

EXPLANATIONS

Before we go through the specifics, what attitude is the employee demonstrating? Is it defensive? Or is the employee seeing this situation as a challenge he can win, turning around the negative attitude? Clearly, it's the latter. It's important that you do not feel defensive, argue, or react in negative ways.

Take a look at the first employee response. The employee wants to show concern, demonstrate she has heard the customer's comments, but not encourage the customer to rant and rave about the government organization. She does this by using a listening response (1) and by not taking the bait, and arguing with the customer to get him to change his mind about government.

The employee continues to acknowledge the concerns without encouraging in-depth focusing on his negative impressions by using a "when" question, sometimes called neutral mode ("Some people think that ") (3). This shows that she is paying attention, without encouraging argument.

In (4) she indicates that she will try to offer a better experience (assurances of effort). Then in (5) she makes the important transition away from the negative feelings to address the reason why the customer has come in—the permits. That's refocusing.

HINTS

As with all situations in which the customer is angry or prepared to be angry, it's important to acknowledge (show you hear and understand) "where the customer is coming from," without necessarily agreeing or disagreeing. However, you don't want to spend more time than is necessary on the feelings or the past. Acknowledge, then refocus on the task at hand.

Apart from refocusing from anger to the task, also refocus (move the conversation) from what's happened in the past to what's in front of the both of you—the here and now. Since customers usually want something now, it's to their benefit to stop focusing on the bad things they think have been done to them in the past and focus on getting things done in the present. That makes it easy to make the case for talking about the present and what you can do now for the customer.

See Also: 8. When a Customer Might Be Mistrustful, 54. When a Customer Complains About Red Tape and Paperwork

7. When You Need to Explain a Company Policy or Procedure

THE SITUATION

In an ideal world, your customers would already understand your policies and procedures and be willing to abide by them. But we don't live in an ideal world.

Whether it's a policy regarding returns of merchandize in the retail sector or a policy regarding who can receive specific government services, it's often the case that customers don't understand why those policies and procedures are in place. A customer who doesn't understand the purpose of a policy is much more likely to become angry if he or she sees the policy as interfering with getting what he or she wants. If you can explain the policy and the reasoning behind it so the customer understands, you are much less likely to receive flak about the policy.

TECHNIQUES USED

- Preemptive Strike (1)
- Plain Language (2)
- Providing a Customer Takeaway (3)

DIALOGUE

This example occurs in a government office, although similar situations could occur in any other sector. The customer is asked to furnish some information so his application can be processed. Unless the customer provides the information, his application can't be processed, because the policy requires this information. We join the conversation after the customer has made his original request.

Employee: I know this is going to be frustrating, but in order to process your application, we need to have some proof of identity, really two pieces of I.D. (1) One needs to have your picture on it. We also need proof of residence.

Customer: Darn right, it's frustrating. Why are you putting me through all these hoops? It's just typical of bureaucracy that I have to fill in umpteen forms and give you all kinds of personal information.

Employee: Maybe it would help if I explain why we need this information. Then it will make more sense. The major reason we ask for this information is to make sure that nobody can steal your identity and make an application using your identity. That's why we need positive proof so we are absolutely sure that nobody can do that. It's for everyone's protection. (2)

Customer: Well, OK. What exactly do you accept?

Employee: We accept a number of documents and I have a pamphlet that lists acceptable identification that you can keep. But let's go over the documents you can use. (3)

EXPLANATIONS

In this example, the employee knows that customers tend to resent having to provide the necessary documents. To cushion the blow, the employee uses the preemptive strike (1) to acknowledge that the customer may feel upset about the requirements. The premise here is that it's better for the employee to broach the subject of frustration, rather than wait for the customer to do so first.

Notice how the employee explains the purpose of the requirement. She explains it (2) in very plain language and from the point of view of the customer. When explaining policy, it's best to highlight how the policy benefits the customer and to avoid sounding bureaucratic.

In (3) she offers some printed material to the customer, a "takeaway." Why? So the customer doesn't have to rely only on his memory for critical information. The customer will be able to use this material to prepare if he has to come back. Also, note that the employee goes over the takeaway with the customer and doesn't rely on him actually reading the document.

HINTS

When explaining policy, it's best not to quote a specific policy number, clause, or detail from a policy manual. Policies and procedures are usually not written with the customer in mind and the language can be excessively bureaucratic. Also, it tends to suggest that your focus is on policies and procedures rather than people.

Rephrase the policy in plain language.

If you don't know the rationale behind a policy or procedure, you can offer to find out for the customer.

See Also: 54. When a Customer Complains About Red Tape and Paperwork, 60. When a Customer Tries an Unacceptable Merchandise Return

8. When a Customer Might Be Mistrustful

THE SITUATION

A customer who mistrusts you is going to be a difficult customer. Some professions or fields tend to garner more mistrust than others, primarily because the customer lacks the information to determine if you are serving him or her, or being self-serving. The techniques in this example are designed to build customer confidence in your honesty.

TECHNIQUES USED

- Explain Reasoning or Actions (1)
- Acknowledge Customer's Needs (2)
- Pros and Cons (3)
- Expert Recommendations (4)

DIALOGUE

In this example, a car mechanic is explaining the problems found with the customer's vehicle. The employee realizes the customer might mistrust what he's saying and takes action to build confidence.

Employee: As part of our normal vehicle check, we do a 45-point inspection in addition to looking at the reason why you brought the car in. We should talk about some of the other things you might want to address. (1)

Customer: [sounds dubious] OK.

Employee: Since you mentioned trouble with your brakes, that was the first thing we looked at. We found that the brake pads are 90% worn on the front. We also noticed you have a small oil leak. (1)

Customer: [Puts hand on chin, shakes head]

Employee: I'm thinking you want to keep repair costs down, since this is an older vehicle (2). So, I'd suggest that we replace the brake pads because [explains safety reasons] (4). Regarding the oil leak, to tell you the truth it's probably not worth repairing it. The advantage to addressing the leak is that you may save a bit of money on oil. (3) The disadvantage is that repairing the leak will involve taking the engine apart to replace a gasket. That's expensive. In any event, most older vehicles leak some oil. (3)

So, I'd suggest we do the brakes and keep an eye on the leak. If it gets worse down the road, we can discuss it again. (4)

EXPLANATIONS

The idea here is that the mechanic is presenting himself as working on behalf of the customer and not trying to pad the bill. First, he explains the process by which he identified the oil leak (1). Next, he proves to the customer that he understands his concerns and needs by acknowledging those needs (2).

The most important part of this interaction lies with presenting pros and cons from the customer's point of view (3). By presenting reasons why it may not be worthwhile to address the oil leak, the employee shows that he is acting in the interests of the customer, while leaving the door open for the customer to decide to have it repaired.

Finally, we see the employee offer his expert opinions about what should be done.

HINTS

Don't assume that a customer understands the pros and cons of various options. Often they don't and they want your expert (and honest, balanced) opinion.

Presenting both pros and cons is critical to developing customer confidence in your honesty.

See Also: 6. When a Customer Has a Negative Attitude About Your Company Due to Past Experiences, 7. When You Need to Explain a Company Policy or Procedure

9. When the Customer Has Been Through Voicemail Hell

THE SITUATION

These days most companies use some form of voicemail or automated phone system. Unfortunately, these systems are not always well thought out, resulting in situations where a customer can be routed around and around without having his or her needs met in a timely and simple manner. How can you deal with an irate customer who has had the misfortune of spending frustrating time navigating a voicemail or automated system and has now connected with you?

TECHNIQUES USED

- Assurances of Effort (1)
- Apologize (2)
- You're Right! (3)
- Offering Choices/Empowering (4)
- Broken Record (5)
- Refocus (6)

DIALOGUE

In this situation the customer is trying to get help with a computer problem he's experiencing. He's been through a number of "phone menus" and has been unable to reach a human or voicemail. (The mailbox is full.) He finally figures out how to speak to a live human being—you—and he's exceedingly annoyed.

Customer: What the heck is wrong with you people? I've been going around and around in your voicemail system and I haven't been able to even leave a voicemail so I can get some help. I should be able to contact you without having to spend all my money on long-distance charges.

Employee: I am going to help you (1) and I apologize if you've been having problems with our phone system. (2) You're right that this shouldn't happen. (3) Since you've already spent so much time on the phone, can I ask you a few questions so I can help? (4, 6)

Customer: Damn right this shouldn't happen! I need help and I need it right away, and I don't deserve to be going around in circles.

Employee: You're right. (2, 5) I'm sure you want that help *now*, so let me ask you some questions. Are you calling about a technical problem with a computer? (4, 6)

Customer: Yes.

Employee: OK. If you give me the make and model number and the nature of the problem, I can transfer you directly to a live person who can help.

EXPLANATIONS

This interaction follows a tried-and-true pattern for dealing with irate customers. The first goal is to defuse the customer's anger. Once the customer has calmed down a little bit, the employee moves the customer away from the secondary issue (frustration with the phone system) and back to the reason the customer called (technical problem).

The defusing process uses a succession of techniques, including assurances the employee will help (1), an apology (2), and the "you're right" technique (3).

As is often the case, the customer doesn't respond immediately and constructively, so the employee uses the broken record technique several times (4, 6).

Pay special attention to the use of refocus techniques. The refocus (4, 6) is used to focus the customer away from his anger and back to the reason why he called. In this case, the employee uses questions for this purpose and asks for permission to help the customer (4, 6) (offering choices/empowerment).

HINTS

When interacting with an angry customer, you will almost always have to defuse (deal with the anger) before you can move on to why the person is calling (the initial issue). That's because angry people are not ready to problem-solve. So, the first step is to use defusing techniques *first*.

The refocus technique is a key element for making the transition from focusing on anger to focusing on the needs of the customer. If a refocus statement or question does not work initially, it can be repeated (broken record), using different words.

Needless to say, it's absolutely critical that the customer not be returned to the "voicemail from hell" system, only to repeat the frustrating experience. When rescuing someone from the voicemail nightmare, find a way to avoid sending the person back to the voicemail (e.g., take a paper message, arrange a follow-up callback manually).

See Also: 11. When a Customer Has Been "Buck-Passed," 14. When a Customer Won't Stop Talking on the Phone

10. When a Customer Is Experiencing a Language Barrier

THE SITUATION

One of the biggest challenges in customer service involves dealing with a customer who has trouble understanding how you talk or is difficult to understand. While you'd think this happens primarily when dealing with someone born in another country and whose mother tongue is different from yours, it can also happen when people with different accents are talking.

TECHNIQUES USED

- Plain Language (1)
- Probing Questions (2)
- Summarize the Conversation (3)

DIALOGUE

In this example, the customer appears to be having difficulty making his needs understood because his native tongue is other than English. In addition, he seems to be having difficulty understanding what the employee is saying.

Customer: [asks employee a question that employee does not understand]

Employee: [talks slowly, calmly] I'm not sure I know how to help. Do you want help with insurance? (1, 2)

Customer: Yes, insurance.

Employee: OK, good. Car insurance? (1, 2)

Customer: No, no car.

Employee: House insurance? (1, 2)

Customer: Yes, yes.

Employee: OK. You own a house and you need insurance? (1, 3)

EXPLANATIONS

There is no easy solution to language barriers. Obviously the best solution is to connect the customer with someone who can speak his or her language or who might be better at understanding the specific accent, but that's not always practical.

In this example the strategy is clear. Throughout, the employee uses some plain language strategies (1). In particular, he breaks down the conversation into smaller "bits" and short sentences and questions. Here's why. A person struggling to understand another language has a lot to think about. It helps if he or she has to think about only one small thing at a time.

You can also see the use of probing questions (2), which in this case are short and can be answered with either a yes or a no. Again, this is to try to make the communication process simpler.

In (3) you can see the employee summarizing the conversation so far. In effect, he is checking with the customer to verify that they are both understanding the conversation.

HINTS

Perhaps the most important aspect of dealing with a language barrier is patience. Remember that it's frustrating for both of you, but that it's *your* job to make sure the communication works. Avoid any and all signs of frustration.

Don't speak more loudly. When there is a language barrier, people tend to yell, which would make you look completely foolish, startle the other person, and possibly even antagonize him or her.

Speak more slowly and clearly, using shorter sentences and questions. Don't overload the person.

If you get stuck and can't get beyond the barrier, it may be that one of your colleagues may be better at communicating with that specific customer. People have different ears for language and accents, so someone else might be able to help the customer more effectively. If you think that might work, involve someone else in the situation.

See Also: 7. When You Need to Explain a Company Policy or Procedure

11. When the Customer Has Been "Buck-Passed"

THE SITUATION

Customers who have talked to three or four people and have not had any success getting help get angry and frustrated, because they feel employees are passing the buck. Unfortunately, they may aim their aggression at you, even though you don't have control over what other employees have done. What do you do?

TECHNIQUES USED

- Empathy Statements (1)
- Finding Agreement Points (2)
- Voice Tone—Emphatic (3)
- Assurances of Effort (4)

DIALOGUE

In this example, which could occur in person or on the phone, the customer is very upset because he has contacted or visited four government employees in three departments, only to find that none of them was the right person. What's worse is that each employee has referred him to the wrong person.

Customer: Someone in the Waterworks department sent me here and told me you could help me get my water reconnected and my account fixed, and I'm telling you, this better be the last stop I have to make, because I've been sent pillar to post and [starts going on and on].

Employee: I agree that this should never happen. (2) You shouldn't have to be spending all this time finding the right person to talk to and I can understand how frustrated you must be. (1)

Customer: Yeah, well, so can you help me?

Employee: Yes, I can. (3) Here's what I can do for you. (3) I'm not sure I can do everything you need, but what I *can* do is contact anyone else who needs to be involved and get things moving before you leave this office. That's what I'm going to do my best to accomplish. I will help you get this done. (4)

EXPLANATIONS

The employee responses can be used in situations where the employee knows that he or she can actually solve the customer's problem. They can also be used if the employee feels that he or she cannot solve the entire problem. What's key here is that the employee is making a commitment to the customer to get things moving *now*. Notice the employee's use of empathy up front (1) and the strong agreement sentence in (2). Also pay attention to the use of an emphatic tone of voice (3). Saying, "Yes, I can help you" in a strong voice that promises commitment is going to be much more effective than a flat or indifferent tone of voice.

HINTS

Never make commitments that you may not be able to keep.

In a buck-passing situation where you aren't the right person to help the customer, make the effort to find out who the customer needs to see. A lot of times buck-passing occurs because employees simply don't want to take the time to get an answer for the customer.

See Also: 9. When the Customer Has Been Through Voicemail Hell, 20. When You Don't Have the Answer, 23. When You Need to Route a Customer Phone Call

12. When a Customer Needs to Follow a Sequence of Actions

THE SITUATION

There are some situations where a customer needs to follow a sequence of steps or actions in order to get something accomplished. For example, purchasing a house involves a series of steps, which would include selling the current house, finding a new house, engaging a lawyer, and arranging for a mortgage. Customers don't always know the sequence that is most advantageous. One role you can play is to help them navigate the sequence of steps. Here's how.

TECHNIQUES USED

- Empathy Statements (1)
- Assurances of Results (2)
- Providing Explanations (3)
- Providing a Customer Takeaway (4)

DIALOGUE

In this example, the customer is a first-time house-buyer working with a real estate agent for the first time.

Customer: Sheesh, I didn't know there was so much red tape and rigmarole involved with buying a house. It's a pretty scary, involved process.

Employee: It does seem overwhelming if you haven't gone through it before (1). I can help you get this organized, and I can tell you that it's almost always easier than it sounds, and we'll get through this (2).
    Here's what I'm going to do. I have some printed information that will explain all the steps. Let's go over that material: I'll go through it step by step and you can

ask questions. (3) [The employee brings out the printed material and goes through it with the customer, answering the questions.] (4)

EXPLANATIONS

Once again we see that the first step is to use an empathy statement. (1) In this case, the employee does this to help the customer understand that feeling overwhelmed is a "normal" reaction. She then emphasizes that the process is easier than it looks and it will all work out. (3)

Finally, she provides a customer takeaway that maps out the steps the customer needs to follow *and* covers each of the steps in a face-to-face conversation.

If there is no printed takeaway, the employee can make some simple notes by hand to summarize the conversation so the customer can take those notes with him and use them as a guide.

HINTS

It's useful to make notes to give to the customer even if there is printed material. At least mark the important points with a highlighter.

Takeaways should be simple and clear. They are best used as summaries of the face-to-face interactions between customer and employee.

Do not assume that your customer will understand or even read any written material you provide. You need to walk customers through the materials.

See Also: 7. When You Need to Explain a Company Policy or Procedure

13. When the Customer Insults Your Competence

THE SITUATION

Angry or frustrated customers sometimes vent or aim their anger about the situation at the most available person. That target could be you. One of the common attacks or insults has to do with the employee's competence or intelligence. How you handle this kind of situation means the difference between turning the situation into something positive and constructive and creating major hassles and upset for everyone. Here's how to deal with these insults.

TECHNIQUES USED

- Allow Venting (1)
- Empathy Statements (2)
- Not Taking the Bait (3)
- Refocus (4)

DIALOGUE

In this dialogue the customer is upset and chooses to make comments about the employee's competence and intelligence.

Customer: What the hell is wrong with you? Are you too stupid to understand what I'm trying to tell you? Or is it you just don't give a damn?

Employee: I can see you are concerned and I'd like to help. (1, 2, 3)

Customer: Damn right! I'm fed up having to deal with idiots like you.

Employee: I'd like to try to help you, but I need to ask a few questions. Let's see what we can do to get you what you need. (4)

EXPLANATIONS

The most important part of this example involves what the employee does *not* do. Although the insults are offensive, the employee realizes that if she reacts to them, the discussion will worsen into a flat-out argument, which won't help the customer and doesn't benefit the employee. So, she does not take the bait. (3) She focuses on showing the customer she understands he is upset using empathy (2) and also gives the customer some leeway to vent his frustration. (1)

After the customer has vented and not succeeded in getting the employee to jump at the bait, the employee tries to move the conversation away from the customer's anger and back to the reason why the customer contacted her. This refocusing (4) is intended to get back to the primary concern, issue, or problem.

HINTS

To help you not react to insults, keep in mind that the customer is, in effect, a stranger and should not be allowed to control your emotional reactions. And remember: you don't *have* to react with anger.

Keep in mind that if you end up in an argument, you are going to lose, since you don't have the freedom to unload on a customer, without running the risk of censure from your company.

It may not seem fair that you can't strike back—and it's not. If you take the bait, you end up suffering the consequences, in terms of stress, time, energy, and your reputation.

See Also: 25. When a Customer Threatens to Go over Your Head, 34. When a Customer Makes a Racist Remark

14. When a Customer Won't Stop Talking on the Phone

THE SITUATION

Sometimes customers will phone for help with a problem but are upset and do not allow you to respond to their concerns or even to help them. In this example, we'll try to get the customer to stop talking long enough so we can begin the helping process.

TECHNIQUES USED

- Telephone Silence (1)
- Empathy Statements (2)
- Assurances of Effort (3)
- Refocus (4)
- Offering Choices/Empowering (5)

DIALOGUE

The customer wants some help with an issue and has been talking on the phone with an employee almost continuously for two or three minutes.

Customer: … What kind of organization are you running here? I expect to get answers to my questions immediately, and when I call you just give me the runaround … [continues to talk].

Employee: [says nothing—no uh-huhs, nothing at all] (1)

Customer: And another thing … [continues for a time]. … Hello, are you there?

Employee: Yes, I'm here. It sounds like you are pretty upset (2), and I'm going to help you right now (3). I need to get a bit more information from you so I can help, so is it OK if I ask you a few questions? (4, 5)

Customer: Well, OK.

Employee: I only have a few questions. First, can you give me your account number?

EXPLANATIONS

You can't help someone unless you get the information you need, and you can't get that if the person is talking *at* you or rambling all over the place. In this example, the employee simply stops responding completely (1) until the customer is no longer sure if the employee is still there. (This works only on the phone.) When the person stops his constant stream of talk to ask whether the employee is there, it creates an opening for the employee to move the conversation back to whatever the customer has called about.

Note that the employee also wants to show the customer that his concerns and feelings are important (by using an empathy statement) (2) and to assure the customer that help will be offered immediately (3). He then refocuses (4) the conversation back to exploring the actual problem. This is done by asking permission or giving the person a choice. (5)

HINTS

- Keep using a calm tone of voice.
- Don't continually try to interrupt the customer, because that tends to cause him or her to start over or redouble the talk.
- Refrain from any signs of impatience, like sighing.

See Also: 17. When a Customer Won't Stop Talking and Is Getting Abusive on the Phone #1, 18. When a Customer Won't Stop Talking and Is Getting Abusive on the Phone #2

15. When the Customer Swears or Yells in Person #1

THE SITUATION

While most customers are able to control their behavior to keep it within acceptable bounds, some customers, when they are angry, may swear and yell, or otherwise "act out." Obviously this is an extremely upsetting situation for most employees, and it also interferes with the employee's ability to do his or her job. It's hard to help someone who is yelling at you, and not paying any attention to what you are saying. In situations like this, your first goal is NOT to try to address the specifics of the customer's problem, but to use techniques to halt the inappropriate behavior. We are going to be using some advanced techniques to stop the customer's ranting, and get the customer to listen to, and respond to our efforts to help.

TECHNIQUES USED

- Some People Think That (Neutral Mode) (1)
- Finding Agreement Points (2)
- Empathy Statements (3)
- Assurances of Effort (4)

DIALOGUE

In this situation the customer is upset because he received a parking ticket that he feels is unwarranted. He visits the town clerk (which is where tickets are paid), and starts to yell and swear at the clerk at the counter.

Customer: What the [bleep] is going on here? One of your stupid meter maids gave me a ticket for parking near a hydrant and I wasn't within ten feet of the goddamn thing. I'm not paying this thing, and I want you to cancel the [bleep] thing *now*. [customer appears to be starting a long rant without stopping]

Employee: Some people feel that their tickets aren't deserved. (1)

Customer: Darn right. I'm one of them. I'm fed up.

Employee: I agree. You don't feel your ticket is deserved. (2)

Customer: So, what are you going to do about it?

Employee: Obviously you are upset about this. (3) You may not be aware that we have a way for you to appeal the ticket if you like.

Customer: Yeah? How?

Employee: I'll do my best to explain your options, so you won't be liable for an infraction you didn't commit. (4)

Customer: OK.

EXPLANATIONS

When the customer starts raising his voice, and using swear words the employee realizes that until the customer calms down and begins to listen to the employee, nothing at all can be accomplished. So, he uses "some people think… or neutral mode" to try to break into the conversation. The reason this technique works (when it does), is that it's an unexpected response that the customer doesn't have a ready made answer for. Unexpected responses tend to derail rants. Notice also that the neutral mode response is short. That's because an angry customer isn't going to "hear" a long response.

The customer responds by indicating he is "one of

them." But what's important is the customer has become more attentive and is in the process of stopping the rant. The employee responds with an agreement point in (2). Notice that the employee isn't agreeing or disagreeing with whether the ticket is warranted or not, but is simply agreeing to the fact that the customer feels unfairly treated. Again, it's a short response.

The customer, while not happy, now behaves in a more constructive and acceptable way, which signals the employee that he can move the conversation to what the customer can do to dispute the ticket. First, the employee uses an empathy statement (3), and follows up with assuring the customer that he will make an effort to help. (4)

HINTS

When you act and speak as if you and the angry customer are on the same side, there's a tendency for angry customers to calm down, and stop yelling at you, since they don't see you as much as an "enemy."

Remember, with angry customers, you can't address their specific concern (in this case the ticket) until such time as the customer is calm enough to listen, and behave constructively to help solve his own problem.

With angry customers, look to engineer agreement. Look for things the customer says that you can agree with that will not put you in an awkward situation. Finding agreement points is such a powerful technique that it is often used by hostage negotiators.

See Also: 13. When the Customer Insults Your Competence, 16. When the Customer Swears or Yells in Person #2

16. When the Customer Swears or Yells in Person #2

THE SITUATION

In the previous example you saw one way of dealing with an extremely angry customer. It showed the importance of derailing customer rants, or inappropriate behavior. In this alternate example, you'll see how other techniques can be used for this purpose. We'll use the same situation as in the last example.

TECHNIQUES USED

- Distraction (1)
- Empathy Statements (2)
- Finding Agreement Points (3)
- Refocus (4)

DIALOGUE

As in the previous example, the customer is upset because he received a parking ticket that he feels is unwarranted. He visits the town clerk (which is where tickets are paid), and starts to yell and swear at the clerk at the counter.

Customer: What the [bleep] is going on here? One of your stupid meter maids gave me a ticket for parking near a hydrant and I wasn't within ten feet of the goddamn thing. I'm not paying this thing, and I want you to cancel the [bleep] thing *now*. I have children to take care of and a job where I don't get paid if I'm not there, so don't waste my time here…[customer appears to be starting a long rant without stopping].

Employee: How many children do you have? (1)

Customer: Well, three. What does that have to do with my [bleep] ticket?

Employee: I know it's a challenge enough to have to take care of children and go to a job everyday. (2)

Customer: Damn right it is.

Employee: Yes. It is. (3) Let's go back to the ticket, to see what we can do to provide you with an avenue to appeal. (4)

Customer: OK.

EXPLANATIONS

In this situation the employee uses Distraction—specifically a technique called "topic grab" (1). It is used to try to derail an angry customer by providing an unexpected response. In this situation, the employee "grabs" the reference to the customer's concerns about childcare, and asks the customer how many children he has. When the customer responds with a specific and short response, control of the conversation returns to the employee.

The employee responds with an empathy statement (2), followed by finding an agreement point. (3) Notice the artistry involved in creating a point of agreement. In (2) the employee offers an empathy statement, which the customer agrees with. In (3), the employee reaffirms the agreement, creating a sense that the customer and employee are on the same side.

Finally, the employee makes the transition from dealing with the customer's angry feelings, to dealing with the specific issue of the ticket and what the customer can do. This is done with a refocus statement. (4)

HINTS

The topic grab must be based on something the customer has said. You can't choose something at random, but must use something the customer has referred to that really has no connection to the customer's problem. Your topic grab question or statement must be short.

If the customer refuses to answer your topic grab, and responds with something like "It's none of your business," then you simply agree with *that* response "You're right, it really isn't. Let's see what we can do with the ticket." If the customer responds, and then stops to let you speak, the technique has done its job. Then you use the opening to refocus.

See Also: 15. When the Customer Swears or Yells in Person #1, 17. When a Customer Won't Stop Talking and Is Getting Abusive on the Phone #1

17. When a Customer Won't Stop Talking and Is Getting Abusive on the Phone #1

THE SITUATION

Generally, people tend to be somewhat more aggressive on the phone than when talking in person. Sometimes a customer calls and begins an angry "rant," which includes insults, swearing, or other abusive behavior. It's best to try to derail the rant gently. But if the main technique in the previous situation (telephone silence) doesn't work, a firmer approach is needed. In this example, you want to stop the person so you can help and send the message that you will help but not unless the person stops swearing or otherwise ceases the offending behaviors.

TECHNIQUES USED

- Empathy Statements (1)
- Setting Limits (2)
- Offering Choices/Empowering (3)
- Assurances of Effort (4)
- Broken Record (5)

DIALOGUE

The customer wants some help with an issue and has been talking with the employee on the phone almost continuously for two or three minutes. In the last minute or two, the customer has started swearing and calling the employee names. In the example below, you'll see how to set limits on the caller's behavior to try to encourage him or her to stop the negative talk that is offensive to you and interferes with your ability to help.

Customer: What are you, a ******** idiot? I'm fed up with you people, and I'm fed up with you. You don't seem to know your ***** from a hole in the ground.

Employee: Sir, I understand you are upset (1), but if you continue to yell and swear, I'll have to end the conversation. (2) It's up to you whether you would like to continue. (3)

Customer: I'd like you to get my damned check. Is that too much to ask?

Employee: I'll certainly try to help you with this (4), but I need your promise that you won't yell or swear at me. (5) Is that OK? (3)

Customer: Yeah, OK [reluctant]. Let's continue.

Employee: OK, good. I need to ask a few questions.

EXPLANATIONS

Notice that the employee began her response with an empathy statement (1) to soften the impact of setting limits later. She sets some limits that are specific and clear, sending the message that if the customer swears or yells, she will terminate the phone call. (2) It's important when setting limits to be as specific as possible and avoid general comments like "If you don't calm down…" or "If you aren't prepared to be civil . . . ." Describe the specific problematic behaviors.

Pay special attention to the statement used in the limit setting—"It's up to you whether you would like to continue." We want to send the message that the customer is in control of whether the conversation continues and that the employee won't be punishing the customer or doing something *to* him or her. You want it to be clear that it is the customer's choice as to whether the conversation continues.

You can also see the use of several other techniques here. The employee uses reassurance (4) that she will indeed help, provided the customer stops yelling and swearing, and she completes the limit-setting process by using the broken record technique (5) to encourage the customer to make a specific commitment to stop the destructive behavior. She follows the repetition with a question—"Is that OK?" She uses this question to reinforce the idea that she is interested in the agreement of the customer and that they can work together.

In this case, setting limits works. But there are two other possibilities to consider. The first is that the customer continues to yell and swear. The second is that the customer agrees to stop, but then steps over the agreed-upon limits. We'll look at these in the next two situations.

HINTS

Setting limits isn't threatening or warning. Use a matter-of-fact voice because you are simply stating a fact. Use the same voice and tone you would use to say, "If you go out in the rain without an umbrella, you are going to get wet."

Within reason, you can draw your own lines regarding what is acceptable and unacceptable customer behavior, subject to the expectations of your employer. It is useful to allow some wiggle room for customers, because, on occasion, brief unpleasant outbursts will cease on their own and you can get on to helping the customer.

See Also: 14. When a Customer Won't Stop Talking on the Phone, 18. When a Customer Won't Stop Talking and Is Getting Abusive on the Phone #2

18. When a Customer Won't Stop Talking and Is Getting Abusive on the Phone #2

THE SITUATION

In the last example you saw how setting limits can encourage a customer to stop negative behavior. But what happens if it doesn't work? In this example, we'll illustrate how to complete the limit-setting and limit-enforcing process. We'll simply extend the dialogue from the previous example.

TECHNIQUES USED
- Empathy Statements (1)
- Setting Limits (2)
- Offering Choices/Empowering (3)
- Setting Limits (4)

DIALOGUE

In this dialogue, the employee informs a customer of some behavior limits and the customer immediately steps past those limits.

Customer: What are you, an ******** idiot? I'm fed up with you people, and I'm fed up with you. You don't seem to know your *** from a hole in the ground.

Employee: Sir, I understand you are upset (1), but if you continue to yell and swear, I'll have to end the conversation. (2) It's up to you whether you would like to continue. (3)

Customer: I'd like you to get my damned check. Is that too much to ask, you stupid !x#!!* bleep?

Employee: I'm going to end this call. You are welcome to call back at some other time. (4)

Customer: [continues to swear]

Employee: [gently hangs up the phone]

EXPLANATIONS

This dialogue is identical to the one in the previous example, until the point where the customer ignores the limits and continues to swear and yell. The employee realizes that the customer is not likely to become less obnoxious right now and she can do little to help the customer until he stops the offending behavior. Having decided to end the call, she indicates her intention (4) and then says, "You are welcome to call back." She adds the latter invitation because she doesn't want to refuse service to the customer or be accused of hanging up. It's also an offer of a small bone to the customer.

It's generally not acceptable to simply hang up without a word. Hanging up without notice is also more likely to encourage the customer to call back, even angrier than before.

You can use the enforcing limits technique in a delayed fashion. Sometimes a customer will agree to abide by the limits you set, behave well for a minute or two, and then lose his or her temper and escalate into bad behavior. In that situation, you can repeat (broken record) the limit or begin the process of termination.

HINTS

Don't view hanging up or enforcing limits as punishment that's personal. All you are doing is trying to get control of the situation and encourage the person to stop the bad behavior *so you can help.*

Again, use a calm, matter-of-fact tone of voice.

Make sure you understand your organization's policy

about ending unpleasant customer interactions. Companies vary in terms of what they want employees to do in these situations.

Once you set a limit and indicate you are enforcing it (ending the conversation), the only thing that should keep you on the phone is a sincere, almost desperate apology. Ignore any grudging apologies and continue to end the conversation.

Don't set limits you aren't prepared and able to enforce. If you do, you lose all control and credibility.

Don't set limits and decide *not* to enforce them when required. Same reason as above.

See Also: 14. When a Customer Won't Stop Talking on the Phone, 17. When a Customer Won't Stop Talking and Is Getting Abusive on the Phone #1

19. When a Customer Has Been Waiting in a Line

THE SITUATION

In an ideal world, customers should be served immediately, without any waiting. But we don't work in an ideal world. Often the need for a customer to wait is a result of decisions made elsewhere in the organization, something you probably don't control. Is there a way of providing the best possible customer service when customers have to wait and reducing the possibility that the waiting customer will take out his or her frustration on you? Yes, there is.

TECHNIQUES USED

- Empathy Statements (1)
- Preemptive Strike (2)
- Assurances of Results (3)

DIALOGUE

In this example, the customer has been waiting to be served, either in a line or in a waiting area. This kind of situation occurs often in retail and in doctors' and dentists' offices, even when the customer has an appointment time. This dialogue highlights the importance of recognizing the customer's frustration before he or she has the chance to vent on the employee.

The employee notices that the line of customers waiting to be served has grown considerably over the last few minutes and that people in the line are showing signs of impatience—fidgeting, looking at their watches, sighing. This is what happens as the next person waiting approaches the service area.

Employee: I'm sorry you've had to wait (1) and I'm going to make sure you can finish up here as quickly as possible. (2, 3) What can I help you with?

EXPLANATION

This is called the preemptive strike: it works to defuse frustration and anger before the anger is expressed. It removes the incentive for the customer to complain and vent, since you have already acknowledged the customer's frustration. It paves the way for fast service.

You can add to this by providing an explanation of the reason for the delay, if you deem it helpful to the customer. For example, "I'm sorry you've had to wait, but the doctor had to deal with an emergency and is running late."

It's absolutely essential to the success of this technique that you speak first, before the customer has a chance to launch into a complaint. This helps you control the interaction and shortens the time needed, since you receive less lengthy complaints about delays.

HINTS

Speaking first allows you to gain control of the interaction and cuts down the amount of venting a customer may feel like doing about having to wait.

When things are behind schedule, consider making an announcement to the entire group of customers waiting and inform them of the approximate length of their wait.

See Also: 3. When a Customer Jumps Ahead in a Line of Waiting Customers, 5. When a Customer Interrupts a Discussion Between the Employee and Another Customer

THE SITUATION

It's almost impossible to have all of the answers to all possible questions customers may throw at you. When a customer asks you a question and you are unsure of the answer or simply don't know, you have two options—handle it the right way or the wrong way. The wrong way is to fake it, out of embarrassment, in the belief that the customer will think you stupid if you admit you don't know. The right way is to tell the customer you don't know, *but* to make a commitment to the customer to find out, either by researching and getting back to him or her or referring the customer to someone who will know.

If you fake it, you will find customers who will expose your ignorance for you. That's not a good feeling—and it's also bad business.

TECHNIQUES USED
- Acknowledge Customer's Needs (1)
- Offering Choices/Empowering (2)
- Referral to Third Party (3)
- Arranging Follow-Up (4)
- Suggest an Alternative to Waiting (5)

DIALOGUE

In this dialogue you will see several techniques strung together to address the situation where an employee does not have the answer to a customer's question. First, the employee tries to find the answer; then, when that does not succeed, the employee refers to a third party who does know the answer.

Customer: I'm looking at these DVD players, and I can't figure out why the prices are so different. Could you explain the differences between them?

Employee: I can see that you really need the right information and I want to make sure I don't give you inaccurate information. (1) Let me see if I can find the brochures so we can figure this out. It might take a minute or two. Is that OK? (2)

Customer: Sure, no problem.

Employee: If you want to browse some of the other items, I can look for the answers and get back to you when I've got something. (5)

Customer: That would be great.

The employee can't find the material and moves to plan B.

Employee: I think the best thing is for me to find John, who is really the DVD expert here. If anyone can help, it would be him. (3) If you have the time, I can do that now, or I can get back to you, or whatever works for you. (2)

Customer: I really can't wait right now, because I have a few other things to do. If I come back in 20 minutes, can I speak to John?

Employee: Yes, that would work well, and then you don't have to wait. I'll tell John to expect you, so just ask for him when you come in. (4)

EXPLANATIONS

The employee responds to the customer by acknowledging that the question is important to the customer, showing his concern for the customer's needs. (1) Before he leaves to find the information, he explains what he is doing and asks the customer if it's OK (2), an example of offering choices and empowering the customer.

In (5) the employee makes a suggestion—that rather than standing around waiting, the customer might prefer to browse some of the other items. Not only is this exceedingly considerate, but it's also a good way to encourage the customer to consider purchasing other items as well.

Unfortunately, the search for the brochures fails and the employee refers the customer to a third party (3). Note that the employee makes a special effort to describe John as the expert, which reassures the customer that the information he will eventually get from John will be accurate and useful and, best of all, worth waiting for. The employee also, once again, offers some choices by saying, "If you have the time, I can do that now . . ."

When the customer indicates he can't wait, the employee arranges for a follow-up (4).

There are some central themes here. We want to convey to the customer that we treat his or her need for information seriously and will do everything we can to provide that information, while inconveniencing him or her as little as possible. Throughout this dialogue, there's a sense that the employee is flexible and desires to go the extra mile. This turns a potentially embarrassing situation (lack of knowledge about merchandise) into a positive, an opportunity to demonstrate superior customer service skills and attitude.

HINTS

A customer who is waiting and doing nothing is a customer who will become annoyed and/or leave. Reduce waits as much as possible and offer something for the customer to do during waits (e.g., have coffee, browse other items, return in 10 minutes).

When referring to a third party, make absolutely sure the third party has the answers before making the referral. The best way to do that is to ask the third party before completing the handoff. The third party you refer to should be the last party the customer needs to talk with.

Keep the customer informed. Never walk away without explaining. Never say something like "Hold on a sec" and then walk off.

See Also: 21. When Nobody Handy Has the Answer, 24. When You Lack the Authority to ...

21. When Nobody Handy Has the Answer

THE SITUATION

Customers sometimes ask questions that nobody available can answer with confidence and authority. Such questions might be about a product's features or about a particular policy or procedure that has been developed in another part of the organization, and the customer service staff hasn't heard about it. If you don't know an answer and those around you don't know the answer, the question is still important to the customer. So, in the spirit of customer service, you still have an obligation to hunt down the answer.

TECHNIQUES USED

- Acknowledge Customer's Needs (1)
- Assurances of Effort (2)
- Offering Choices/Empowering (3)
- Arranging Follow-Up (4)
- Completing Follow-Up (5)

DIALOGUE

In this example, the customer asks for clarification of a particular policy about which the employee has not been informed. We join the dialogue at a point where the employee has concluded that he doesn't know the answer and neither do his colleagues and his immediate manager.

Employee: I can see that you feel it's important to have your question answered (1) and I'm going to do my best to get you an answer. (2) It will probably take me a day or two to find out and, when I do, I'd like to get back to you. What's the most convenient way to contact you with the answer? (3)

Customer: How about if I leave you my phone number and you can call and leave me a message?

Employee: I can do that. If you give me your number, I'll get back to you within 48 hours, one way or the other, so you won't be waiting and wondering. Does that work for you? (3, 4)

Customer: OK. I'll look forward to your call.

The employee then hunts down the answer. Regardless of whether he finds a definitive answer or not, he must respond within the 48 hours. If he has the answer, he phones to provide it. If he can't find the answer within the time period, then he phones as follows.

Employee: Mr. Jones, I wanted to get back to you about your inquiry. I haven't been able to get an answer for you, but I can refer you to someone who might know or you can call me to let me know if you want me to keep trying. (5, 3)

EXPLANATIONS

As with the dialogue in the previous situation, the employee makes sure to acknowledge that the question is important to the customer and to make sure the customer feels he has some choice and control. (1, 2) Then the employee arranges to go the extra mile by committing *personally* to follow up by trying to find the answer (3). The employee confirms the details of the follow-up and a time line/deadline by which he promises to contact the customer, whether he finds the answer or not. (4) Finally, you can see the actual follow-up process. (5)

What's important here is that the employee makes a personal commitment to help and the employee keeps that commitment and informs the customer.

HINTS

Never make a commitment to follow up that you may not be able to keep.

Keep your commitments each and every time. No excuses.

See Also: 20. When You Don't Have the Answer, 24. When You Lack the Authority to …

22. When You Need to Place a Caller on Hold

THE SITUATION

If you deal with any significant number of phone calls from customers, you will be in situations where you need to place a caller on hold. While nobody likes to be put on hold, the good news is that most callers are used to it, since it's become the norm. They are less likely to be annoyed if you handle the process professionally.

TECHNIQUES USED

- Explain Reasoning or Actions (1)
- Offering Choices/Empowering (2)
- Finishing Off/Following Up (3)
- Apologize (4)

DIALOGUE

In this situation the caller wishes to talk with the general manager of the company, who is currently on the phone with someone else, but is expected to be available shortly.

Employee: Mr. James is on the phone with another customer right now, but should be available in a few minutes. (1)

Customer: I'll wait. I need to speak with him as soon as possible.

Employee: OK, I can put you on hold and transfer you when he's available or we can call you back as soon as he's free. Did you still want to hold? (2)

Customer: Yes. I'll hold.

Employee: OK. I'll keep an eye on the lines and transfer you as soon as possible. (1) [puts customer on hold]

About one minute later, the employee checks back with the customer.

Employee: Hello. Mr. James is still on the other line. Did you still want to hold? (2)

Customer: Yes.

Finally, when Mr. James becomes available, the employee informs the customer as follows.

Employee: Hi. Good news. Mr. James is free. I apologize for the wait (4) and I'm connecting you right away. (2, 3)

EXPLANATIONS

What are the most important aspects of the employee's behavior here?

First, the employee informs the caller and explains the situation (1), rather than simply saying, "He's unavailable" and hitting the hold button. There are two reasons for this. One is to show the customer that he is important enough to merit an explanation. The other is to give enough information to the caller so he can make a decision about whether he wishes to be put on hold, call back, or pursue some other possibility.

Second, the employee allows the caller to make the choice as to whether he will be put on hold or not. (2) It is never advisable to put a caller on hold without both explaining why and giving the caller the choice. It may not always be possible to inform and offer a choice, particularly in a very busy switchboard environment, but it's worth trying.

The third important element is the follow-up. (3) It's important to check back with callers on hold to acknowledge that you know they are still waiting and to inquire if they'd like to receive a call back instead of waiting on hold. Notice also that the final sentence is an example of "finishing up." Rather than simply connecting the caller, the employee creates a sense of closure by telling the caller that Mr. James is available and that the employee is connecting them.

HINTS

Keep in mind that someone waiting on hold tends to experience time differently. One minute of wait time on hold might feel like four or five minutes of wait time in person. That's one reason why it's important to break up the wait time, by following up as possible.

See Also: 9. When the Customer Has Been Through Voicemail Hell , 23. When You Need to Route a Customer Phone Call

23. When You Need to Route a Customer Phone Call

THE SITUATION

Customers don't always know who they need to speak to or even the specific department they need to contact. When a customer calls and isn't clear about who to speak to, your job is to get enough information to route the phone call to the right place the first time, so the customer can be served quickly.

TECHNIQUES USED

- Offering Choices/Empowering (1)
- Probing Questions (2)
- Active Listening (3)

DIALOGUE

In this example, the customer is calling about some issue with her check, but the employee is not immediately clear on the specific issue and therefore the person or department that needs to be involved.

Customer: I need to speak to someone about my check.

Employee: I want to make sure I direct you to the right person the first time, so can I ask you a few questions? (1)

Customer: Sure.

Employee: OK, are you calling because there's a problem with your check? (2)

Customer: No, I'm just looking for information about how I can change my tax deductions.

Employee: So, you want to know what paperwork you need to complete to make sure the tax deducted is more accurate. Is that what you need? (3)

Customer: Yes, exactly.

Employee: Good. You need to speak to Jan in payroll. I can transfer your call or give you the number to phone direct, whatever is more convenient. What works best for you? (4)

EXPLANATIONS

The employee needs to get enough information to route the call to the correct person. To get that information, the employee uses probing questions (2). Notice that the employee asks permission to do this in order to demonstrate to the customer that she is important (1).

If necessary, the employee would ask a longer series of questions.

In (3) the employee uses reflective listening to verify or confirm that he and the customer are on the same wavelength and that he understands what the customer wants.

Once the employee is confident he has enough information to direct the call, he indicates the specific person that the caller needs to contact and offers two options—transferring her to Jan or giving her the direct phone number so she can phone Jan at her convenience (4).

HINTS

When transferring a call, it's always good to inform the party receiving the transfer about the nature of the caller's needs or problem.

It's worth spending a few more seconds finding out what the customer needs before directing the call. When you direct a customer to the right place the first time, everyone wins. The customer feels valued and impressed with your competence and your coworkers and other employees spend their time more productively.

See Also: 22. When You Need to Place a Caller on Hold, 11. When the Customer Has Been "Buck-Passed"

24. When You Lack the Authority to ...

THE SITUATION

You have probably been in situations where a customer asks you to do something for which you do not have sufficient authority. It might be as simple as reversing a transaction at a cash register, processing a return, or making an exception to a company policy or procedure. Here's how to handle this kind of situation.

TECHNIQUES USED

- Finding Agreement Points (1)
- Offering Choices/Empowering (2)
- Referral to Supervisor (3)

DIALOGUE

The customer approaches the employee and requests that she make an exception to a long-standing rule. However, she lacks the authority to violate the rule.

Customer: I don't see why I can't do [the thing prohibited by the policy]. It seems pretty reasonable and I'm sure I'm not the first to ask.

Employee: It does sound reasonable, (1) but I don't have the authority to say yes or no. The person who can approve that is the departmental manager, Mr. Smith. Do you want me to see if Mr. Smith is available? (2)

Customer: Sure.

Employee: OK. It will take a minute or two. [goes off to arrange the referral]

Employee: [returns to customer] Mr. Smith is available. To save you some time, I've explained to him what you are asking, so you won't have to repeat it, and I'm sure he'll help if he can. (3)

EXPLANATIONS

In this example, you see the employee actively trying to find agreement points (1). By agreeing with the customer that the request is reasonable, the employee helps the customer perceive that both of them are "on the same side."

The main technique used here is "referral to supervisor." The employee kicks off the referral process by asking the customer if he wants to talk to the supervisor about this issue. (2) Providing this choice allows the customer to decide for himself whether he wants to spend the time to talk with the supervisor or simply let the issue drop.

At the end of the referral process, it's important to communicate with the supervisor so he or she is prepared to deal with the customer in an informed way and knows in advance of any possible problem situation.

HINTS

When you lack the authority to fulfill a request *and* you also know the request is completely unreasonable and will be refused, it is still a good idea to arrange for the customer to speak with the decision maker. Customers tend to act more favorably when their request is refused by someone higher up (a supervisor or a manager).

As with any referrals, it's important that you and the supervisor are on the same wavelength regarding when it is appropriate or not appropriate to make the referral.

See Also: 26. When a Customer Demands to Speak with Your Supervisor, 20. When You Don't Have the Answer

25. When a Customer Threatens to Go over Your Head

THE SITUATION

Angry customers may threaten to go over your head, demand to speak with your supervisor or manager, or even try to intimidate you by demanding to speak with the "person in charge." The angry customer may want to talk with someone higher up because he or she believes that person will be better able to solve his or her problem *or* because he or she may be trying to intimidate or scare you into giving in to his or her demands.

TECHNIQUES USED

- Empathy Statements (1)
- Offering Choices/Empowering (2)

DIALOGUE

The customer is upset because the employee can't or won't do what the customer is asking.

Customer: If I don't get what I want, I'm going to go to your manager and your president, and then we'll see who is right.

Employee: I know you are unhappy about [topic of conversation] (1). If you believe it's best to talk to my manager, I can certainly help with that. Do you want me to help you arrange to talk to her? (2)

There are two common customer responses to this. The first is to back off from the threat, having realized the employee won't be intimidated. The second is to take the employee's offer. If the customer backs off, the employee turns the discussion back to the issue. If the customer continues to

demand to talk to "the boss," the employee makes the effort
to help the customer discuss the issue with the manager.
(See Referral to Third Party technique for details.)

EXPLANATIONS

Once again, we see the employee using an empathy statement (1) to show the customer that his feelings are
understood and acknowledged.

In the second part of the response, the employee does
not resist or try to convince the customer *not* to contact
someone higher up, but instead offers to help the customer do so, using options/empowerment to do so (2).
There are two reasons why the employee uses this technique. The obvious one is that the customer is within his
rights to ask to speak with the manager and the employee
is simply acknowledging that and helping the customer
do this. The second is that if the customer is bluffing for
effect or to intimidate, providing that option will often
convince the customer to give up that line of attack, since
the employee does not seem to be intimidated.

HINTS

Different organizations and managers have different rules
about making arrangements for a customer to talk with a
manager or senior official. Find out what they are before
using these techniques.

Offering to help tells the customer you won't be
intimidated by threats and won't be manipulated. When
in doubt, offer help.

See Also: 26. When a Customer Demands to Speak with Your
Supervisor, 28. When a Customer Threatens to Complain to
the Press

26. When a Customer Demands to Speak with Your Supervisor

THE SITUATION

One of the most common requests a frustrated customer makes is to speak with your supervisor or manager. A customer who demands to speak with your supervisor may be trying to intimidate you or may have a concern he or she feels will be best handled at the level above you. Customers who ask for such access may not even be frustrated, but believe that dealing with someone with more power is a faster, more efficient way to get what they want.

TECHNIQUES USED

- Probing Questions (1)
- Assurances of Effort (2)
- Not Taking the Bait (3)
- Referral to Supervisor (4)

DIALOGUE

In this example, the customer asks to speak to the supervisor right off the bat.

Customer: I want to speak to your supervisor.

Employee: I'll be happy to help you talk to Mrs. Jones (2), who is my manager, but is there anything I can do? (1) It might save you some time.

Customer: [sullenly] No. I don't want to speak to you. I'm tired of speaking to people who don't know what they are doing.

Employee: OK. I'll check to see if she's free, but it would help if I could tell her what you'd like to speak to her about. (3, 1)

Customer: Just tell her I want to talk about the poor service here.

Customer: OK. It will just take a minute. If you want to take a seat, I'll be back in a minute or two.

[The employee goes to the supervisor's office.]

Employee: Mrs. Jones, I have a customer who is demanding to speak to you about "poor service." Are you free? (4)

Supervisor: Sure, I'll come out and bring him or her to my office. [The employee and the supervisor approach the customer.]

Supervisor: Hi, I'm Mrs. Jones. I understand you wanted to speak to me about some service issues. If you'd like to come with me, we can talk where we won't be interrupted [gestures to customer to follow]. (4)

EXPLANATIONS

Since the customer asks to see the supervisor right off the bat, the employee doesn't know why this request is being made. So her first approach is designed to identify the "why," and to determine if the employee can be of assistance. To do that she asks one or two probing questions (1), while at the same time assuring the customer that the employee will make the effort to connect the customer to the supervisor. (2)

The employee quickly understands that this customer isn't going to provide any additional information. Note that the employee refuses to take the bait (3) when the customer says: "I'm tired of speaking to people who don't know what they are doing." In essence she simply ignores this backhanded swipe.

The second and third parts of the conversation show the mechanics of the referral to the supervisor. (4) In the second part, the employee explains the situation very briefly to the supervisor. In the third part, the supervisor and employee go to the customer. What's important here is that the supervisor takes control over the interaction immediately: she introduces herself, rather than the employee doing the introductions. You can see that, as part of the introduction, the supervisor says, "I understand you wanted to speak to me about some service issues." Why? To show that the employee has told her why the customer wants to speak with her and she is ready to discuss the issue.

HINTS

As an employee, you should know when your supervisor considers it appropriate to refer a customer to him or her and when it is not. If you are not clear about what your supervisor expects, ask.

While you may want to offer your services to help, instead of referring the customer to your supervisor, it's important to do this in a nondefensive way. Don't appear to be trying to dissuade the customer from speaking to the supervisor.

See Also: 25. When a Customer Threatens to Go over Your Head, 27. When a Customer Demands to Speak to Your Supervisor, Who Isn't Available

27. When a Customer Demands to Speak with Your Supervisor, Who Isn't Available

THE SITUATION

Your supervisor may not be immediately available when a customer demands to speak with him or her. Or maybe your supervisor really dislikes talking with customers and has made it clear that he or she doesn't want to do so. You have several options for dealing with these situations, but we're going to focus on an alternative—referring the customer to one of your peers.

TECHNIQUES USED

- Referral to Third Party (1)
- Acknowledge Customer's Needs (2)
- Offering Choices/Empowering (3)

DIALOGUE

In this example, the customer is upset because the merchandise he purchased seems to be defective.

Customer: This is the second time this week that I've gotten stuck with defective merchandise from you, and I'm fed up. I want to speak to your supervisor, and I want to speak to him now.

Employee: I can see that you want this resolved right away. (2) My supervisor isn't available right now, and I don't want to delay you, so I have a suggestion. John Jackson is an expert in this product line; if anyone can help you with this, he's your guy. (1) I know he's available, so if you like I can arrange for you to speak with him right now. If that doesn't work out, we can set up a time for you to speak with the manager. How does that sound? (3)

Customer: OK. I'll try that.

The employee then goes off to explain the situation to John. He returns to the customer with John, who introduces himself, making sure to demonstrate to the customer that he and the first employee have made an effort to discuss the customer's complaint.

John: I think I understand your problem. Let's see if we can get it solved for you.

EXPLANATIONS

The core element of this interaction is how the employee offers the referral. (1) The employee introduces the possibility of talking to John by highlighting his expertise about the customer's specific problem. In other words, he explains why talking to John will address the customer's problem—the faulty product. In reality, John may not have any more knowledge than the first employee, but by presenting John as an expert (which he is), the employee increases the chances the customer will respond positively to the offer and the interaction with John.

Notice also that the employee acknowledges the customer's need to get this resolved quickly (2) and leaves the decision to the customer by offering choices. (3)

HINTS

Never lie to a customer. If, for example, John knew absolutely nothing about the product in question, but was presented as an expert, no good would come from the referral.

As with referring to a supervisor, both the referring employee and the "expert" need to have arranged this referral process beforehand.

See Also: 26. When a Customer Demands to Speak to Your Supervisor, 29. When a Customer Demands to Speak to the "Person in Charge"

THE SITUATION

Occasionally, an angry or frustrated customer may threaten to "go to the press" about how he or she has been treated by you and your company. Sometimes this is simply an empty threat intended to pressure you into doing what the customer wants. In other situations, it may be a genuine reflection of how upset he or she is. Here's a way to handle this situation.

TECHNIQUES USED

- Not Taking the Bait (1)
- Broken Record (2)
- Offering Choices/Empowering (3)

DIALOGUE

The customer has been dealing with the organization for a long time about a specific issue. Despite the organization's best attempts to solve the problem, the customer rejects any compromise solution offered. In a phone call, the customer threatens to complain to the press.

Customer: I've been trying to solve this problem for three solid months and I'm absolutely fed up. I think you need to be exposed for what you are and, by golly, I'm going to do it unless you do what I'm asking. I'm going to contact [newspaper name] and tell them everything. Then we'll see who wins.

Employee: That's certainly your right. (1, 2, 3) We'd prefer to come to an agreement with you, and I can suggest you speak to our VP of Finance, but it's really up to you which path you want to take. (3) Do you want me to arrange a discussion with the VP? (3)

Customer: Don't waste my time. If I don't get what I want, I'm going to the newspaper.

Employee: As I said, that's completely up to you. (3) If that's the case, then I guess we don't have anything else to discuss.

EXPLANATIONS

There's a theme that runs through this example. At no point in the conversation does the employee come across as defensive or overly concerned about the prospect of the customer going to the press. This is an example of not taking the bait. (1) By treating the threat as non-threatening, he removes the power of the threat. Notice also that, while suggesting a preference for resolving the problem with the customer, the employee is not trying to directly dissuade the customer from carrying out the threat. Not taking the bait sends the message that the threat isn't going to work, in effect calling the customer's bluff.

The employee actively recognizes that the customer has the right to contact the press and recognizes this as an option for the customer. He emphasizes this by using the broken record technique (2).

HINTS

While no company or employee wants to appear in a negative light in the press, there is no guarantee that the press will agree with a customer who thinks he is being mistreated. In other words, the threat more often than not is not going to cause any problem.

The key thing to keep in mind is that you cannot fight head to head in a situation like this. Don't appear to be put off balance by the threat and don't try to convince the customer not to contact the press. That is much more likely to cause the customer to carry out the threat.

See Also: 25. When a Customer Threatens to Go over Your Head, 29. When a Customer Demands to Speak to the "Person in Charge"

29. When a Customer Demands to Speak to the "Person in Charge"

THE SITUATION

Customers who feel—(rightly or wrongly)—that they are not getting what they want or not being treated the way they want sometimes demand to speak to the "person in charge," usually someone at the top of the organization. This could be a CEO, a vice president, or someone of equivalent rank and status. Often that person is not "on premises" and is not easily accessible to customers. Before discussing the best way of dealing with this situation, it's good to know that some percentage of people making such demands are sincere in wanting to talk to the person in charge. Others, however, use the demand to pressure, intimidate, or manipulate employees in the hope that they would rather give in than have to deal with a complaint registered with the executive. So, how do you handle this kind of situation?

TECHNIQUES USED

- Empathy Statements (1)
- Offering Choices/Empowering (2)
- Explain Reasoning or Actions (3)
- Providing a Customer Takeaway (4)
- Closing Interactions Positively (5)

DIALOGUE

In this example, the customer is upset because her auto insurance company has offered her much lower compensation for damage to her vehicle than she wanted. After the employee informs her of the settlement offer, she becomes exceedingly angry and, after arguing her case unsuccessfully, starts demanding to talk with the president of the insurance company, who is actually located in another city.

Customer: I've been paying these ridiculous premiums for over 20 years, and this is just the third time I've ever made a claim, and you're trying to screw me. I'm through wasting my time with you underlings. I want to speak to the president and I want to speak to him now.

Employee: It's clear you're disappointed in the figures, Mrs. Jones, and I can understand you want to speak to someone you think might be able to help. (1)

Customer: Damn right! And you aren't going to help much. So, let me speak to the president.

Employee: That would be Maria Pollock, the president of Loveme Insurance. If you want to go that route, instead of something that might be faster and easier for you, I'd be glad to help you get in touch with her. Before I do that, do you want to consider other options first? (2)

Customer: No, I don't want any "options." I want this Maria Pollock person.

Employee: OK. That's up to you. Maria Pollock is located at the head office in Lubbock. (3) You have a few options that I can help you with. You can phone her office, send her a fax, or write a letter outlining your concerns. If you tell me what you'd prefer, I can give you the information. (2, 3)

Customer: I want to speak to her *now*, right *now*.

Employee: OK. I understand you want fast action. (1) I'm going to write the president's name and toll-free number down for you, along with your file/incident number and related information. [while talking, writes down information] That way you won't have to pay for long distance and you'll have the information you'll need when you speak to her office. [hands information to customer] (4)

Customer: Why can't you just call now and give me the phone?

Employee: I'm sure you would prefer to have some privacy for your conversation and be able to call at your convenience.

Customer: Well, OK.

Employee: If you decide you'd like additional help, please feel free to get in touch with me. And also if you'd let me know how it goes, I would appreciate that. Anything else we need to do right now? (5)

Customer: No, I guess not.

Employee: OK. I'm sorry we couldn't come to some agreement. Good luck! (5)

EXPLANATIONS

There is an important theme that runs through the employee's responses here—nondefensiveness. It's essential that the employee not appear to be threatened by the demand. The best way to send a message of nondefensiveness is to be helpful to the person making the demand.

The employee first responds with an empathy statement (1), showing that she understands where the customer is coming from. After the customer reiterates her desire to speak with the president, the employee explains where the president is located and suggests that there might be other options that would work better for the customer. The employee could have specified the options (e.g., contacting the local manager, lodging an appeal, etc.), but decided to hint at them so as not to appear defensive. Since the customer remained adamant, the employee shifted to helping the customer contact the president by explaining options and providing information (2, 3).

The employee used some other techniques, ranging from another empathy statement to providing a takeaway to help the customer contact the president. The employee ends the conversation by offering further help and closing the conversation on a positive and nondefensive note (5).

HINTS

While we can never know for sure, the odds that a customer will actually take the time to follow through on his or her demand are relatively small. Employees still need to take such a demand seriously.

You may know that when the customer contacts the president's office, the chances of actually speaking with the president might be quite small, at least at first. Or you may know that the president's office is simply going to kick the problem back down the hierarchy. It's best to allow the customer to discover that himself or herself, rather than to point it out at the time the demand is made. If you say something like "Well, the president is very busy and it may take weeks to get a response," you'll simply come across as defensive. Provide other options beneficial to the customer in a light-handed way, but don't try to discourage him or her from contacting the executive.

See Also: 25. When a Customer Threatens to Go over Your Head, 28. When a Customer Threatens to Complain to the Press

30. When a Customer Makes an Embarrassing Mistake

THE SITUATION

Customers aren't always right. In fact, sometimes customers can be embarrassingly wrong. It may be tempting, particularly with a rude or annoying customer who blames his or her mistake on you, to point out the stupid mistake and put the customer in his or her place. While this is a great and common desire or fantasy, it's poor customer service and bad business. So how do you handle a situation where it's pretty clear the customer has made a very embarrassing error?

TECHNIQUES USED

- Empathy Statements (1)
- Bonus Buyoff (2)
- Refocus (3)
- Providing Alternatives (4)
- Face-Saving Out (5)

DIALOGUE

This situation takes place in a chain motel lobby, where four or five patrons are awaiting service. The obviously tired customer next in line announces that he has a reservation. The employee checks and can find no record of the reservation for that date, but does find a reservation for the next weekend. Since the motel is full, the employee cannot provide a room. In this situation, the employee, while annoyed at the customer's aggressiveness, decides that there is nothing to be gained by embarrassing the customer, particularly in front of the other patrons.

Customer: What kind of dip [bleep] place is this? I made a reservation, and now what? You lose it and now what am I supposed to do?

Employee: I know this is frustrating and you've obviously been traveling all day and want to relax. (1) I'm showing that you do have a reservation for next weekend and I'm thinking that, one way or another, something has gone awry here. (5) Since we don't have any rooms available right now, let's see what we can do. (3)

Customer: Next weekend? What the hell are you talking about?

Employee: Let's not worry about what's gone wrong right now, but let's find you a place to stay. (3) We have another motel about a mile from here. I'll see if we can book you there. (4) Is that OK?

Customer: Well, OK. But I'm still not happy about this.

Employee: Tell you what, I'll see if I can get you a discount or an upgrade at the other motel. (2)

EXPLANATIONS

The employee's front-line response is to use an empathy statement (1) to indicate she understands the customer is tired and anxious to find a place to stay.

The most important part of this dialogue involves two techniques—refocusing and providing a face-saving out. You can see in the responses marked (3) that while the customer seems to want to complain and blame, the employee refocuses the conversation on what is really the issue, finding the customer a place to stay. Even with an angry customer who has made a mistake, the logic for doing so is compelling. The second technique, providing a face-saving out, is shown where the employee says, "Something has gone awry" rather than suggesting that the customer has confused the dates and thus caused his own misfortune. That's because it doesn't matter *who* made the mistake; even if the employee *knows* the error lies with the customer, there's no reason to point it out— especially since, when a customer feels embarrassed or humiliated, one response is to strike out in anger at the employee.

Once the employee refocuses on the real issue, she goes the extra mile to arrange a room elsewhere and even offers a discount as a form of bonus buyoff, even though it's the customer who made the mistake. (2)

HINTS

While it's tempting to force an annoying customer to acknowledge the error lies with him or her, there's no benefit in doing so. Embarrassed people often strike out. That means the interaction takes longer and can become more and more unpleasant. That's not good for the customer, for you, or the other customers who are waiting in line.

Another reason to avoid embarrassing a customer who has seemingly made an error is that you may not be absolutely sure the mistake lies only with the customer. It's better to stay away from the "blame game," because whether the customer is at fault or you are, you will lose.

See Also: 33. When a Customer Is Confused About What He or She Wants or Needs, 46. When a Customer Wants Information You Are Not Allowed to Give

31. When a Customer Withholds Information Due to Privacy Concerns

THE SITUATION

Some people are very protective of their personal information, even to the point where they may refuse to provide information to you that may be essential or helpful in determining the best way to provide assistance. For example, a person might call a doctor's office to make an appointment and not want to tell the receptionist the nature of the medical problem. We can all understand someone wanting to keep personal details limited to as few people as possible. Surprisingly, some people are so "private" that they may not want a retail store clerk to know what size of trousers they wear. How do you handle these situations professionally and without causing embarrassment?

TECHNIQUES USED

- Offering Choices/Empowering (1)
- Face-Saving Out (2)

DIALOGUE

A rather large man is browsing the suits in a mid-scale men's clothing store. He's looking at suits that are clearly not going to fit him. After greeting the customer and identifying that the customer wants to purchase a new suit, the employee continues.

Employee: Perhaps we should take some measurements so you won't waste time looking at suits that won't fit. Is that OK? (1)

Customer: [brusquely] *No.* Thank you, but no. I'd rather look.

Employee: That's fine. That may be a good idea, since if you find something you really love, but we don't have it in your size right now, we can probably order it for you. (2)

Customer: Yeah, that's right. I want to see what I like first.

Employee: If you'd like, I can show you some of our newest items. Or you can look around on your own and give me a shout if you would like some help. (1)

Customer: OK, I'll just let you know, then.

Employee: OK. [walks off to straighten the tie rack]

EXPLANATIONS

It may seem odd that this customer might not want the employee to know his size, particularly since someone is going to have to ring up his purchase (if he makes one) and will obviously see the information anyway. But it really doesn't matter, because good customer service dictates that we try to make the customer as comfortable as possible. That means accommodating individual quirks and eccentricities when possible.

This example is fairly straightforward. You can see that the employee offers choices to the customer (1) and gives him control of the interaction. Notice how the employee uses the "face-saving out" (2). When the customer says he wants to browse and he seems upset at the prospect of the employee taking measurements, the employee provides a plausible explanation for why browsing could be a good plan, in essence agreeing with the customer, rather than arguing that they should determine the customer's size right away. This technique is intended to avoid embarrassing the customer by any mention of his size.

HINTS

Whenever possible, try to accommodate the customer's desire for privacy. If you cannot do so, then make sure you explain why you need the information to assist the customer.

Stay alert to customer quirks and potential areas that may be embarrassing for the customer. Remember that a customer may be embarrassed by things that would not embarrass you and that it's your job to try your best to be sensitive to that fact and to make the customer comfortable.

See Also: 30. When a Customer Makes an Embarrassing Mistake, 59. When a Customer Asks Inappropriate Questions

32. When a Customer Threatens Bodily Harm or Property Damage

THE SITUATION

One of the most stressful situations in customer service occurs when a customer threatens bodily harm or property damage. Apart from the obvious sense of concern that an employee feels about his or her welfare, stress is magnified because of the uncertainty of the situation. When threats occur, questions flood in. Will the person actually carry through on the threat? What should you do? How can you stay safe?

There are many kinds and degrees of threat, which compounds the difficulty. Some threats are made from a distance, where the employee isn't in immediate danger. Some are general, some specific. Some are direct, some indirect. Since dealing with threats is complex and the consequences of making a wrong decision can be severe, in most situations, an employee should rely on the organization's policies and procedures for dealing with emergencies or threats and let law enforcement or security professionals make the tough decisions. They are trained for it. You are not.

When a customer utters a threat of any kind, the issue is no longer customer service, but safety, protection, security, and law enforcement. For this reason, detailed discussion and advice on dealing with most threats are beyond the scope of this section. However, we will look at a situation where the employee is not in immediate danger and a general threat has been made over the phone. We'll add some extra explanation and hints to this particular example that apply to other kinds of threat situations.

TECHNIQUES USED
- Use Customer's Name (1)
- Empathy Statements (2)
- Setting Limits (3)
- Contact Security/Authorities/Management (4)

DIALOGUE

A clearly upset customer calls and, during the phone call, makes a generalized threat.

Customer: I'm absolutely fed up with you people. I have a mind to come down there and show you can't mess with me. You know I can get you if I want.

Employee: Mr. Jones, (1) I understand that you're concerned and worried about [summarize issue]. (2) I will do the best I can to help you with this, but I can't do so if you talk in an aggressive way.

Customer: Maybe you'll be more helpful if I come down there with a crowbar.

Employee: Mr. Jones (1), if you continue to talk in a threatening way, I'll have to end this conversation. It's up to you whether you want to continue to talk right now. (3)

After the conversation ends, the employee then informs security, the authorities, and/or management, according to the organization's policies and procedures, in order to maximize safety and security. (4)

EXPLANATIONS

This situation involves an indirect threat, but in any threat situation it's important to remain calm, sound calm, and not overreact. That's why the employee's initial response involves using the customer's name (1) and an empathy statement (2). The interaction may not be doomed: the employee is still trying to work to resolve the problem or at least to get the customer to tone down the discussion. This is more appropriate when the threat is indirect and there is no obvious immediate danger.

The customer steps up the threat, making it more specific by mentioning the crowbar, at which point the employee decides that if the threats continue in any shape or form, the conversation must end. He sets a limit, which he will enforce if necessary. If the customer does not calm down or rescind the threat, it's absolutely essential that the employee report the threat to his manager, the authorities, and/or security. The most compelling reason to do so is to alert them to a possible problem so they can prepare to deal with it if it occurs.

If the employee succeeds in calming down the customer and the phone call or interaction is resolved calmly and constructively, whether the employee reports the incident or not is a judgment call. However, since uttering threats is illegal in most places and since a customer may make a habit of threatening employees, it's probably best to report threats even if the situation seems to have been resolved.

HINTS

Err on the side of safety and security. While many verbal threats are just words born of anger and frustration, you won't know which of the threats is serious and sincere.

Let the professionals decide. The police and security should have more experience in these situations and better training. That's why it's best that all threats be reported, at minimum to management.

If you feel you are in serious danger, contact the police, even if your company prefers you don't. Better to deal with an angry boss than become a violence statistic.

It is important that you remain calm in threat situations. When you react emotionally, you may be providing the threatening person with reinforcement (or reward) for making the threat. In a situation where you may feel endangered, the more emotional you get, the more unpredictable your behavior may be, and that behavior may startle or upset the person threatening you.

After any threat incident, you will want to make some notes about the situation, the context, the person making the threat, and so on to provide to management, security, or the police. For example, if the threat is made in person, you might want to note any information you might have about the person—physical description, characteristics, voice, etc. If on the phone, you might want to note the caller's number, the tone and kind of voice, and any background noises.

Your company or organization should have guidelines and procedures for these kinds of situations. Follow them unless you feel that doing so will result in immediate harm to you, your colleagues, or other bystanders. If your company does not have such guidelines, it should. Suggest that management develop them. In the absence of guidelines, talk to your manager so he or she and you are on the same wavelength about how these situations should be handled.

See Also: 36. When a Customer Refuses to Leave, 39. When a Customer Might Be Stealing

33. When a Customer Is Confused About What He or She Wants or Needs

THE SITUATION

In many customer service situations, the employee's role is to help the customer buy or obtain something, in a situation where the customer is fairly clear about what he or she wants. In other situations, the customer may not be clear about which product or service to buy, which person to speak with, or other matters. When a customer is confused, the employee needs to help the customer clarify his or her wants or needs.

TECHNIQUES USED

- Probing Questions (1)
- Empathy Statements (2)
- Active Listening (3)
- Expert Recommendations (4)
- Above and Beyond the Call of Duty (5)

DIALOGUE

In this example, which occurs in a government office, a customer is very unclear about the person to see or talk with or even what she wants. The customer has a problem, but has no idea how to use government services to solve that problem.

Customer: I'm a single mother and I need financial help to pay for my children's school.

Employee: OK. I'm not sure this is the office you need, so I'm going to ask you some questions so I can suggest who you need to speak with in order to get some help. OK?

Customer: Sure. I'm a little lost with all this.

Employee: Understandable. You're probably pretty worried about your kids and navigating the various government offices can be confusing. (2) First, let's start with who you've talked to so far. Is this your first government visit about this? (1)

Customer: Yes.

Employee: [asks questions about the age of the children, the income level of the customer, whether the father is paying support, etc., which the customer answers] (1)

Employee: All right. I think I understand. Let's see if I have this right. You have two children and your husband has left you and is refusing to pay support to help pay for school supplies. You're wondering what your options are. Is that right? (3)

Customer: Yes. I just need to get by this rough spot.

Employee: OK. We don't handle requests for temporary assistance in this office, but I can help. Here's what you need to do. You can apply for short-term assistance at the Department of Family Affairs on Green Street, which is right around the corner. (4) They can help you with that end. I'd also suggest that you contact the Child Support Enforcement Agency as soon as possible for advice. (4) It may turn out that there are ways to encourage your husband to pay for the school supplies, but you need to talk to the experts. They are also on Green Street. (4)

Customer: OK. Can you give me directions?

Employee: Yes, I'll do that. I'm also going to give you my card, so you'll have a specific person to talk to if you need more help on this. (5)

EXPLANATIONS

Most of this conversation consists of the employee using probing questions (1) to get enough information to provide expert advice to the customer. Clearly, to give proper advice, the employee must take the time to understand the customer's situation. Once the employee believes he has enough information to provide that advice, he checks out his understanding of what the customer has said, using active listening to summarize the customer's situation. (3) This is an essential step, because if the employee misunderstands, the customer may end up going to the wrong places, because the advice will not fit. Active listening provides an opportunity for the customer to correct the employee's understanding.

Then the employee offers expert recommendations. (4)

Pay special attention to the last sentence, where the employee offers his card so the customer will have a known point of contact. (5) This is something the employee is not required to do; it's above and beyond the regular call of duty. It's offered as a means of reassuring the customer that she can call a specific person if she gets lost in the bowels of the government system.

HINTS

Make sure you understand the customer's situation before handing out advice. It's easy to jump to conclusions and not listen effectively—and end up not helping at all.

If you do not have enough knowledge to provide expert advice, then don't. Either refer the person to somebody who is more expert or be honest and simply admit you don't know.

34. When a Customer Makes a Racist Remark

THE SITUATION

One of the most offensive things one person can say to another is to make a racist remark—a negative comment about the person's ancestry, culture, heritage, or skin color. It's unacceptable in any civil social situation and it's no less unacceptable during an employee-customer interaction. And let's not make the mistake of assuming that racist remarks are uttered only by those in the "dominant culture." No particular group has a monopoly. Racism is racism.

But how can you handle such a situation in a professional way that does not open you up to a long, drawn out argument?

TECHNIQUES USED

- Setting Limits (1)

DIALOGUE

In this example, the customer makes a remark about the employee's skin color. In this example, we'll use the color green to refer to the employee's skin color.

Customer: Well, I guess I shouldn't expect you green people to have any brains at all. All of you are brought up in barns or something.

Employee: I'm willing to help you conduct your business with us, provided you don't make any further comments about my background. If you do make any further remarks like that, I'm going to end this conversation and ask you to leave. (1) It's up to you, but I need your agreement before we can continue. (1)

Customer: I have a right to my opinions. It's a free country.

Employee: It seems like you've made your choice, so I'm ending this conversation. If and when you are willing to talk without negative remarks, I'm willing to help. But right now, this conversation is over.

EXPLANATIONS

This is a volatile situation and there is no perfect solution. What you want to do is make it clear that the customer must meet a certain requirement—to stop making racist/negative comments—if the conversation is to continue. That's why the major technique involves setting and enforcing limits (1). In setting the limits, it's important to do so in as neutral and matter-of-fact tone as you can muster. The less you show emotional reactions, the less likely the situation will escalate.

Setting limits is a first step. The much harder part is enforcing the limits you set. If this conversation occurred on the phone, you could terminate the conversation, since that's something you have control over. If it occurs in person, let's say in your company's office, that's much tougher, since you do not have direct control over whether the unpleasant customer leaves or not. You can refuse to interact further, but that raises a question: What do I do if the person doesn't leave the area? The answer: it depends on your company policy and whether you have security personnel available to enforce the limits and the consequences you set. What's clear is that you should never take it upon yourself to try to remove such a person from the office. Situations like this can escalate to violence if not handled properly.

If the person refuses to leave, probably your best bet is to remove yourself from the vicinity. For example, if the person is in your office, you can get up and leave. If you can't do that and the person is interfering with business, then this may become a security or law enforcement issue.

If this occurred outside of the office, let's say on the premises of the customer, then you would leave, applying the consequences you mentioned in setting the limit.

HINTS

While you may be completely outraged by the remarks, keep in mind that your job is not to make the customer into a better human being. You will always lose if you engage in a long lecture about making racist remarks. Keep things short and simple. Don't argue.

When applying a consequence, like ending an interaction or asking the person to leave, you should always consider your own physical safety and the safety of those around you. There are times when the best path is to do nothing to get the person to leave. Try not to escalate and try not to back yourself into a corner, literally and figuratively. Safety first.

See Also: 35. When a Customer Makes a Sexist Remark, 37. When a Customer Accuses You of Racism

35. When a Customer Makes a Sexist Remark

THE SITUATION

While customers probably use sexist language less these days, employees still encounter sexist remarks much more frequently than many of us would think. Both men and women can be the victims of sexist comments, but women are more likely to be the targets. In this example we'll look at one way to deal with a somewhat indirect, demeaning, sexist remark.

TECHNIQUES USED

- Not Taking the Bait (1)
- Refocus (2)
- Pros and Cons (3)

DIALOGUE

The employee is a car mechanic who is highly qualified and expert at her job. The customer, unfamiliar with having a woman work on his car, expresses a lack of confidence in an obnoxious, sexist, and insulting way.

Customer: Look, I want someone to look at my car who knows what he's doing. Isn't there a man around?

Employee: If you are concerned about my experience, I've been a mechanic for over 10 years and I've had my license at least that long. Now, you mentioned a funny noise coming from the engine. Can you describe it for me? (1, 2)

Customer: I don't see how a woman can know anything about cars.

Employee: Well, the thing is that if you want your car fixed today, I'm the only person available. So it's up to you what you want to do. Do you want to discuss the problem with your car so we can get it done for you? (3)

Customer: OK, let's do it.

EXPLANATIONS

While the sexist remarks are exceedingly demeaning and insulting, notice that the employee refuses to be drawn into an argument about the ability of women to fix cars. She realizes that if the customer is sexist, it's not likely that arguing with him is going to change his mind. So, first she avoids the bait (1). She very briefly assures the customer that she is experienced and skilled, *but* almost in the same breath she refocuses (2) back to the customer's reason for being there—the problem with the car.

Unfortunately, the customer responds to the refocus with another sexist comment. The employee responds by providing incentive for the customer to put aside his prejudice (really a Pros and Cons technique) (3), by explaining that if he wants the car problem repaired today, she's the mechanic he will have to deal with.

Faced with this reality, the customer gives in.

HINTS

There is a difference between sexist remarks and behaviors and a legitimate desire to work with a man or a woman. For example, a man arranging a psychotherapy session may have a legitimate desire to work with another man (or a woman) because he feels more comfortable and his comfort may be essential to the success of psychotherapy, at least for him. His request to work with a man (or woman) isn't based on any prejudice about male or female competencies. However, when a request is phrased in terms that imply one gender or the other is inferior, then the request is sexist.

While sexist remarks may cause considerable anger, remember two things: you aren't going to change the other person and the person is a stranger whose opinions shouldn't be allowed to control your emotions. There's no point in arguing.

However, when a customer makes sexist remarks over and over and it's clear that his or her attitude is going to prevent you from doing your job to help, you can consider terminating the conversation or giving in and arranging for the customer to be served by someone else—of the preferred gender. It's a judgment call. You can also refer the individual to a supervisor.

See Also: 13. When the Customer Insults Your Competence, 34. When a Customer Makes a Racist Remark

36. When a Customer Refuses to Leave

THE SITUATION

While it is rare, you may find yourself in a situation where you have exhausted all constructive mechanisms of conversation and have decided to terminate the conversation with a customer. You politely ask the customer to leave, but he or she refuses. What do you do?

TECHNIQUES USED

- Setting Limits (1)
- Disengaging (2)
- Contact Security/Authorities/Management (3)

DIALOGUE

This situation occurs in the office of the employee. The customer is angry at not getting what he wants and has become abusive. The employee sets some limits, indicating that unless the customer ceases his abusive behavior, the employee will ask him to leave. The customer responds abusively.

Employee: I don't think we can continue this conversation, so I'm going to ask you to leave.

Customer: I told you I'm not leaving until I get what I want. I'd like to see you try to make me leave.

Employee: I'm not going to force you to leave, but I'm not going to continue with you. I'm going to leave.

Customer: Well, I'm not going anywhere.

Employee: Fine. If you are still here when we close our office in 20 minutes, we'll have to contact the authorities to escort you out of the building. I don't think anyone wants that.

Customer: I'm not moving.

Employee: [leaves the office and informs manager and/or security of the problem] (3)

EXPLANATIONS

The employee recognizes it isn't his job to remove the customer and chooses the path of least resistance. Since there is no immediate safety threat and the customer is not actively interfering with the business of others, the employee decides to let the customer sit in the office. Faced with refusal to leave, the employee sets forth the limits and consequences if the customer stays (1) and then disengages by leaving the office (2).

When the customer realizes he is sitting in an office by himself, without anyone to talk to, he may choose to leave on his own, understanding the whole process has become pointless. If he tries to stay beyond closing, then there is no choice but to contact security or the authorities to have him removed.

This situation is a potentially serious one that may impact safety and security, so it's important that the employee, upon exiting from the office, inform his supervisor or security immediately, so he or she can decide on the best course of action.

HINTS

In this example, the employee could have checked back with the customer after allowing him to sit by himself for five or 10 minutes. For example, "Mr. Smith, if you are willing to discuss your situation in a quiet manner, I'm willing to do that." Sometimes an angry customer will reconsider after having had a few minutes by himself or herself and either act more civilly or choose to leave.

There is no magic solution to this kind of situation that guarantees everyone wins. Keep safety and security firmly in mind and do not escalate or raise the stakes. Above all, don't take on the responsibilities of the police or security.

See Also: 32. When a Customer Threatens Bodily Harm or Property Damage, 39. When a Customer Might Be Stealing

37. When a Customer Accuses You of Racism

THE SITUATION

One of the most offensive verbal attacks a person can make on another is to accuse him or her of being racist. While these kinds of attacks don't happen that often, when they occur, self-control is essential for keeping the situation from becoming even uglier and more destructive. In this example, we assume that the employee has not done anything at all to justify the accusation.

TECHNIQUES USED
- Empathy Statements (1)
- Refocus (2)
- Referral to Supervisor (3)
- Not Taking the Bait (4)
- Offering Choices/Empowering (5)

DIALOGUE

In a government office, a person from a minority group (we'll call it the "green" group) is frustrated and angry because he is not being given what he asks for. He strikes out verbally at the employee.

Customer: If I wasn't green, you'd give me what I'm asking for. I think you are just prejudiced against green people.

Employee: It sounds like you are pretty frustrated. (1) I can explain how to appeal the decision, if that's what you want. (2, 4, 5)

Customer: What's the point? All of you people are the same. You don't like green people.

Employee: If you would like to talk to my supervisor about the decision, I can help you arrange that. Is that what you'd like to do? (3, 5)

Customer: Yeah, I guess so.

EXPLANATIONS

The most important thing to notice here is that the employee, while indirectly acknowledging the "racist accusation," doesn't focus on it, but continues to turn the conversation to the issue (whatever the customer came in to discuss). He responds calmly and refuses to get into or encourage an argument about the accusation of racism, in essence refusing to rise to the bait (4).

Notice that the employee uses an empathy statement (1) that acknowledges the customer's feelings of frustration, without directly acknowledging the racist accusation. The employee offers a suggestion or choice about explaining the appeal process (2, 3), which the customer refuses or ignores.

Sometimes a customer will accuse an employee of racism as a way to get attention or intimidate the employee into doing what he or she wants, even though the customer does not really believe the accusation. Responding positively and not getting pulled in can encourage such people to back off the accusation.

However, in this case, that doesn't happen. The customer repeats the accusation, this time suggesting that everyone discriminates against green people. Since this kind of accusation is something that the employee cannot ignore if the customer continues to bring it up, the employee decides this situation would best be handled by the supervisor. He offers the possibility of speaking with the supervisor (3) and leaves the decision up to the employee (5).

HINTS

Accusations of racism need to be taken more seriously than other kinds of accusations or insinuations, because the customer may decide his concerns (legitimate or not) should be aired in the media or to senior company staff. Generally, you should try to acknowledge any anger but without addressing the accusation directly, until such time as you believe the customer is serious. Then you need to address it more directly.

Self-control here is crucial. Your natural reaction may be to defend yourself, but that reaction usually fuels an argument. The accusation may be unfair and unjustified. However, you aren't going to change the accuser's mind when he or she is persistent. Arguing isn't likely to result in the accuser stopping the accusations. Arguing *will* cost time, and result in even more frustration.

See Also: 34. When a Customer Makes a Racist Remark, 35. When a Customer Makes a Sexist Remark

38. When a Customer Plays One Employee Off Another ("So-and-So Said")

THE SITUATION

On occasion you may come across a customer who plays one employee off another. There are two situations where a customer may do this. In one situation, a customer contacts one employee (a coworker of yours) and then contacts another employee (you) and receives information that is inconsistent. In that situation, a customer might say, "But I spoke to John (coworker), and he said that I could …." In this situation, the customer is acting in good faith and is confused about the conflicting information he received.

In the second situation, the customer is not acting in good faith: he or she lies about getting different information from another employee and is hoping that you will bend the rules and buckle to the pressure of "what so-and-so said" to do what he or she wants. Customers will sometimes contact a number of employees, hoping to find someone who gives the answer the customer wants. You may recognize this as similar to what children sometimes do with their mothers and fathers.

The challenge is that it's hard to tell if a customer is playing off one employee against another as a way of manipulating or whether it's a good-faith effort to resolve conflicting information. How do you handle a situation where you don't know whether the customer is being honest about what another employee said, or whether the customer might be honestly mistaken?

TECHNIQUES USED

- Not Taking the Bait (1)
- Offering Choices/Empowering (2)
- Summarize the Conversation (3)

DIALOGUE

In this situation, the customer calls to try to get an employee to make an exception to a particular procedure. The employee cannot tell whether the caller is legitimately asking for clarification or trying to manipulate when he uses the "so-and-so said" phrasing. The employee informs the caller that he is unable to do what the customer asks.

Customer: Well, I don't see the problem. I spoke to John McGee yesterday and he said there wouldn't be a problem in getting this done.

Employee: I can't address what John McGee might have said to you, since I wasn't part of the conversation. Which leaves us a few options. You can get back in touch with John and continue the discussion with him or we can talk about your situation a bit more to see whether we can find some way to accommodate you that works for both of us. Which would you prefer? (2)

Customer: Well, John's hard to get in touch with, so maybe we can continue to talk about this, since I have you on the phone.

Employee: OK. Let's see if I understand your situation properly. You want to [fill in relevant information] and you would like us to make an exception because [fill in relevant information]. Is that right? (3)

EXPLANATIONS

When a customer starts the employee-versus-employee tactic, it creates a problem. If the employee deals directly with what the customer says as if it is true and accurate, the employee may end up manipulated. On the other hand, if the employee completely ignores what another employee might have said, that can result in inconsistencies or even conflict between employees. So, the employee's first response is to avoid taking the bait (1). The employee acknowledges that he heard what the customer said, but does so in a way that doesn't commit to further discussion about what the other employee might have said. At this point, there is little reason to go into any detail about what John said, unless John is involved in the discussion.

However, since the employee doesn't know what's happened, what's true, and what John really said, he provides the opportunity for the customer to go back to John to finish conducting his business. This sends the message that the employee is being flexible and helpful and leaves the decision with the customer (2).

If the caller is not quite telling the truth about what John said, then it's likely the caller will not want to go back to John. In effect, offering this choice is a way of calling the customer's bluff, if it is a bluff, without being obvious or offensive about it.

When the customer decides not to contact John, the employee returns the conversation to the issue at hand by summarizing the situation as he sees it (3). Apart from showing he is listening, summarizing addresses the possibility that the employee has missed something important about the situation that might have caused John to give conflicting information. It's a form of clarification, just in case.

HINTS

In a "so-and-so said" situation, you really can't comment on a conversation you were not a party to, no matter how much the customer wants to push you into it.

Remember that you simply don't know what John said or what information John used to draw his conclusions. Either avoid the bait or, involve John in the discussion.

Keep in mind that even if a customer is providing an honest recollection of what your colleague said, that recollection may be inaccurate, incomplete, or garbled.

See Also: 40. When a Customer is Playing to an Audience of Other Customers, 41. When a Customer Exhibits Passive-Aggressive Behavior

39. When a Customer Might Be Stealing

THE SITUATION

Strictly speaking, theft and shoplifting shouldn't be customer service issues, but it's not uncommon for an employee to have suspicions or be confronted by situations where a "customer" is stealing. What to do?

TECHNIQUES USED

■ Contact Security/Authorities/Management (1)

DIALOGUE

This situation is different from most, because what counts is not what you say to a suspected shoplifter, but what you do. In this situation, an employee observes someone stuffing an item into his pocket, apparently with the intent of stealing.

There should be no dialogue with the suspect. (See Hints.) When the employee observes someone he believes is stealing, he does not approach the suspect, but contacts security or appropriately trained staff. (Normally, a company would tell employees who to contact in theft situations.)

EXPLANATIONS

When you observe someone stealing, your first reaction might be to confront the person. That's wrong and that's dangerous. You probably aren't being paid to police the environment; certainly your job isn't to put your health on the line. No shoplifting situation is serious enough to place yourself in danger. The bottom line is that you need to let the professionals handle these situations, since they will be better trained in theft management and suspect apprehension techniques. Follow whatever procedures your company has mapped out for you, but you are far better off not intervening directly unless you are a trained security professional. (1)

HINTS

Keep in mind that, regardless of size or age, any person may carry a weapon or something that can be used as a weapon. That's a major reason why you should not approach a suspected criminal, regardless of size, age, or gender.

You may take personal offense to someone who may be stealing in your department or jurisdiction and that's understandable. You might feel obligated to take direct action and confront. Don't. Put aside your outrage or anger and let the professionals handle it.

See Also: 32. When a Customer Threatens Bodily Harm or Property Damage, 36. When a Customer Refuses to Leave

40. When a Customer Is Playing to an Audience of Other Customers

THE SITUATION

In offices open to the public, you may come across a situation where an angry or upset customer "plays to the audience" of other customers. The presence of an audience can increase the severity of the customer's angry behavior, and can also increase the length of the angry outburst. One way you can determine whether the angry person is playing to the audience is to observe whether he is glancing at the onlookers, or speaking to them. Here's a way of dealing with this situation.

TECHNIQUES USED

- Empathy Statements (1)
- Privacy and Confidentiality (2)
- Disengaging (3)

DIALOGUE

This discussion occurs in a government office, more specifically in a public waiting area that has several customer service windows. There are about 10 customers waiting and one customer is angry and interacting with the employee and playing to the audience.

Customer: You have no right to disallow my permit. Look at all these people.... I bet you're screwing over all of them. [turning to the waiting room] Isn't that right? [turns back to employee] I bet if we took a vote of all these good people, they would agree with me.

Employee: I can see that you disagree with the decision and that you are upset and want to talk about this. (1)

It's not very private here and I'm sure you don't want your personal information heard by others, so why don't I arrange to talk about this so your confidentiality is protected? If you want to step this way, we can continue the discussion. [guides customer to a room or other area away from other customers] (2)

When the customer is seated in the private area, the employee continues.

Employee: I'm going to get your file, so we can look at whether we missed something in deciding about your permit. It will just take a minute. Can I get you a cup of coffee or water?

Customer: Coffee, black, please.

Employee: [goes to get file and coffee and returns in less than two minutes] (3)

EXPLANATIONS

The employee recognizes that so long as there is an audience, the customer is going to continue to complain angrily, hoping to get moral support from the audience. First, the employee uses the front-line response, empathy statements, as a preliminary way to begin the defusing process. (1) She then takes action to remove the "audience effect," by suggesting the conversation continue in a venue that "protects the confidentiality of the customer." (2) Make special note of the way she presents this option, suggesting it ostensibly for the protection of the customer.

Once they have moved into the more private area, she uses the disengagement technique. (3) Angry people will often calm down if they have a few moments to themselves, particularly if they realize they have acted inappropriately or uncharacteristically. The employee leaves the customer alone for a few minutes, after offering two reasonable explanations for leaving the area (files and coffee), while demonstrating consideration for a "guest."

HINTS

A disengagement allows both parties (employee and customer) the opportunity to calm down and pull things together. You can use disengagement when you find you are getting overly frustrated and need time to recover.

When arranging for more privacy, keep in mind that safety is an important concern, particularly with a customer who seems unstable, is exceedingly abusive, or has a record of verbal or physical violence. For this reason, it's often best to use a location that is not completely isolated. For example, if you take the customer to an office, it may be best to keep the door open.

See Also: 41. When a Customer Exhibits Passive-Aggressive Behavior, 42. When a Customer Uses Nonverbal Attempts to Intimidate

41. When a Customer Exhibits Passive-Aggressive Behavior

THE SITUATION

The passive-aggressive customer can be exceedingly frustrating to deal with, and in some cases, a passive-aggressive person can be more intimidating than someone who is overtly and obviously hostile. Luckily, most passive-aggressives are…well passive, and are unlikely to do anything that is truly dangerous.

Before we discuss what you can do with passive-aggressive customers, we need to be clear about what the term means. Passive-aggressives are uncomfortable with expressing their anger in clear and obvious ways, and choose to get their angry message across more subtly, through the use of voice tone, nonverbals like staring and glaring, rolling of eyes, and sarcasm.

TECHNIQUES USED

- Not Taking the Bait (1)
- Acknowledge Customer's Needs (2)
- Assurances of Results (3)

DIALOGUE

In this situation, the customer wants to return some merchandize. There is really no problem with the return process, but this customer is exceedingly passive-aggressive, and makes his displeasure known through "passive" behavior.

Customer: [stands in front of employee with arms crossed, glaring at employee while he makes his return request]

Employee: I bet you want to get this done quickly. (1,2) If you can just fill in the top part of this form, we'll get your refund.

Customer: Yeah. Right. More paperwork. [begins to fill out the form, and when completed waves it in front of employee and says] There, here's your form.

Employee: Good. I'll just get the manager to approve this. It will be just a minute. (1,3)

Customer: Uh huh. That will be the day.

EXPLANATIONS

In this scenario the employee knows that the customer is upset, or at least in a bad mood, and the customer insists on showing it in a rather covert way. The problem with the passive-aggressive is that if you ask about or comment upon the customer's negative feelings, the customer will deny them. So, it's best to ignore these childish, passive-aggressive behaviors. The employee simply refused to take the bait throughout the interaction. (1)

The employee also acknowledged the customer's apparent need to get the refund quickly (2), and assures the customer the refund will be processed almost on the spot.

HINTS

Passive-aggressive behavior on the part of a customer is different than passive-aggressive behavior coming from someone closer to you—let's say a spouse, child, co-worker or boss. In the latter cases, it's important, for the purposes of building and maintaining relationships, to deal with the person's discomfort. With a customer, it's usually not worth exploring why the customer is upset. The passive-aggressive customer won't tell you.

Deal with the passive-aggressive in a calm, businesslike and task-oriented way. Don't take the bait, and don't indicate the behavior is putting you off balance.

Passive-aggressive behavior tends to be fairly ingrained in people who use it. You won't be able to change that in casual encounters with customers. Get the business done, and move on. The customer may still be angry or upset, but unless he or she takes some responsibility to work with you to become less upset, there's nothing you can do.

See Also: 42. When a Customer Uses Nonverbal Attempts to Intimidate

42. When a Customer Uses Nonverbal Attempts to Intimidate

THE SITUATION

When some people get angry, they will use some specific nonverbal techniques to make the other person feel uncomfortable, threatened, or cornered. These techniques include staring and glaring, invading personal space (getting too close), and using height differences to force the other person to look upwards (a subservient position). There are some ways to counter these behaviors. Here's an example.

TECHNIQUES USED

■ Managing Height Differentials/Nonverbals (1)
■ Distraction (2)

DIALOGUE

This situation occurs in a garage, where the customer is having his car examined to get an estimate of damage for an insurance claim after an accident. The insurance adjuster is a female, about five foot two inches tall; the man who owns the car is about six foot three. The two are standing face to face as the adjuster is outlining the damage she has identified. The customer moves closer and closer, into her personal space, which also forces the adjuster to angle her head upwards more and more.

Employee: I'm seeing some rear bumper and headlight damage on the right, but I need to get the car on a hoist to take a look at the suspension.

Customer: [glaring and moving closer] What the hell are you talking about? Any idiot can see that the suspension is shot.

Employee: [shifts a quarter turn away from the customer, breaking eye contact for a moment] (1) Mr. Smith, we'll look at the suspension in a moment, but right now, take a look at the right side panel. [points to a spot below eye level] Do you see a dent there? We don't want to miss anything. (2)

Customer: [bends down, breaking eye contact and moving out of the employee's personal space] Yes, I think I do.

EXPLANATIONS

When the customer moves into her space, the adjuster faces a dilemma. If she moves backwards, she sends a message that the customer is intimidating her and controlling the interaction. If she moves forwards, into a confrontational position, she increases the risk of more anger and even physical violence, particularly if any contact is made, however accidental. So, she turns her body to one side, so she is at a 90-degree angle to the customer (1). This position is much less confrontational than a face-to-face situation and she can also break eye contact without appearing subservient. When a person breaks eye contact at the same time as he or she moves, it appears less "weak."

At about the same time, she uses the distraction technique (2), directing the attention of the customer away from her, away from his anger, and toward a specific and concrete point. That causes the customer to look at that point (the car panel). When he bends to look, he is now lower and has lost his dominating physical position. In that stance, he can no longer stare (extend eye contact).

HINTS

When you face a person invading your space, it's never good to move closer, because of the possibility of violence. This applies whether you are bigger, smaller, or the same size.

If someone tries to intimidate by moving closer and towering over you while you are seated, then you need to get out of your chair. Do so slowly and without placing the palms of your hands on your knees or the arms of the chair, since those actions can be construed as aggressive.

The distraction technique is exceedingly valuable whenever you deal with an angry customer. You can direct his or her attention to any physical object—a computer screen, pamphlet, other piece of paper, clipboard, etc. However, you *must* direct his or her attention verbally—"Take a look at this because ... "—and nonverbally—point to the specific spot you want the customer to look at. The distraction technique will not work if you simply provide something and say, "Please look at this."

See Also: 41. When a Customer Exhibits Passive-Aggressive Behavior, 43. When a Customer Makes Persistent and Frequent Phone Calls

43. When a Customer Makes Persistent and Frequent Phone Calls

THE SITUATION

A customer who calls over and over again when there is no clear constructive point in doing so is enough to drive any employee to frustration. Customers do this kind of thing for various reasons—perhaps in the hope of being so annoying the employee will give them the answer they want or simply because they are exceedingly anxious. Apart from being annoying, the bigger problem is that persistent and pointless phone calls interfere with getting real work done and serving other customers. While you can't really control who calls and how often, there are some things you can try.

TECHNIQUES USED
- Broken Record (1)
- Acknowledge Customer's Needs (2)
- Finding Agreement Points (3)
- Setting Limits (4)

DIALOGUE

In this situation, the caller wants to speak to the manager, who is away from his desk for most of the day. During the first call, the employee who answers explains that the manager will be unable to return the call today, but will likely do so tomorrow. Unfortunately, about 30 minutes later the customer calls again, asking if the manager is in yet.

Customer: This is John Smith. I called earlier, but I need to know if the manager is back yet.

Employee: As I said, he won't be available until at least tomorrow. I will make sure he knows you urgently want to talk to him. (1)

Customer: OK. Bye.

About an hour later, the customer calls again and repeats the question.

Employee: Mr. Smith, I realize you are anxious to speak to the manager and I've promised you I'll convey a sense of urgency to him. (1, 2) You can save yourself a lot of time by waiting until you hear from us tomorrow, and I'd really like to ask you to refrain from calling until tomorrow.

Customer: Yeah, well, I'll do what I want.

Employee: I'm sure you will. (3) If you do call back today, though, your call is simply going to get routed to voice mail. Best to wait until tomorrow. (4)

EXPLANATIONS

This is a difficult situation because the customer controls whether he calls back or not; the employee can only encourage restraint. The basic approach is to avoid getting into an argument by doing a "broken record" of the same message—that the manager is not available and will call tomorrow. (1)

Despite this, the customer calls back again, asking the same question. Once again the employee uses the broken record (1), but couples this with an acknowledgment that the caller feels the situation is urgent. (2) The customer does not respond favorably and indicates he will do what he wants. Rather than arguing, the employee agrees that he can do as he pleases. (3)

The employee also sets a limit. (4) He indicates that further calls will not be answered and will simply go to voice mail. In other words, he is trying to get across the point that additional calls will simply waste the caller's time. Of course, if the employee lacks the facility to do this (caller ID), then this particular consequence won't work.

A second option for setting limits goes like this. "I appreciate that you want to speak to the manager, but if you call again today, I'm not going to be able to speak to you, except to repeat what I've already told you." And then enforce that consequence/limit.

HINTS

The worst thing you can do is get angry or let your frustration show, since this will almost always precipitate an argument, which will eat up more of your time.

You can explain why you can't continue to respond to the same questions, but the challenge is to do so in a way that does not send the message that you have "more important things to do." If the customer gets that message from you, whether implicit or explicit, an argument is likely.

See Also: 14. When a Customer Won't Stop Talking on the Phone, 23. When You Need to Route a Customer Phone Call

44. When Someone Else Is Not Responding (No Callback)

THE SITUATION

In the workplace, we all work with and depend upon other employees. Unfortunately, colleagues may not return calls in a prompt manner, or fulfill their commitments to customers. On occasion you may run into a situation where you receive a call from a customer complaining that one of your colleagues has not responded to phone messages from the customer. Since the customer has managed to contact you, it's likely he's going to vent his frustration on you. How do you deal with this situation, particularly without casting aspersions on your colleague?

TECHNIQUES USED

- Empathy Statements (1)
- You're Right! (2)
- Providing Explanations (3)
- Offering Choices/Empowerment (4)
- Arranging Follow-Up (5)
- Apologize (6)

DIALOGUE

In this situation, the caller has been trying to get in touch with Bob, and has left several urgent messages requesting that Bob return his call. He manages to call you.

Customer: I've left at least three messages for Bob, in the last two days, and I haven't heard from him. What kind of outfit are you running here? Doesn't anyone return calls?

Employee: That's got to be frustrating for you. (1) We try to ensure that all calls are returned within one working day, but obviously something has gone awry. Let me check to see whether Bob has been in, or perhaps he's been sick. (3)

Customer: Even if he's sick, shouldn't someone be covering his calls? Or don't you follow proper business practice.

Employee: You're right! (2) Whatever the circumstances, you should have received a return phone call. I'm checking right now to see if Bob is in. Yes, he just returned from a meeting. I'll tell you what. (3) If you give me your name, and what you are calling about, I'll walk down the hall, and explain the situation to Bob. If Bob can't call you within an hour, I'll see if someone else can. One way or another, someone will call you within the hour, let's say by 5:30. Is that Ok? (4)

Customer: No, it's not OK. I want to know what's happening now, before I hang up.

Employee: I can do that. If I can place you on hold, I'll talk to Bob right away, or I can call you back in five minutes. (4)

Customer: Ok. Call me back then.

The employee ends the conversation by apologizing, then speaks to Bob. Whatever the outcome, the employee personally calls the customer back (5,6) (following up), and tries to solve his problem.

EXPLANATIONS

These situations can be frustrating because both you and the customer may be quite annoyed because of someone else's behavior over which neither of you have control. As with most irate customer situations, the employee begins the response with an empathy statement (1), and then explains that the company strives to call customers back within one business day. (3) Notice the explanation about callbacks is kept short, because the truth is that the company policy is of little relevance to the customer at this point in time.

When the customer points out that someone ought to be covering the phone for an absent employee or one taken ill, the employee takes the opportunity to use the "You're Right!" technique. (2)

The next part of the conversation is directed at trying to solve the customer's immediate problem—getting in touch with Bob, or someone else who can help him as soon as possible. The employee offers alternatives so the customer gets to choose what would be best for him from a range of possible options. (4)

Finally, the conversation ends after an agreement has been struck about follow-up (5), and with the employee offering an apology. Needless to say the employee (or someone) *must* follow up in the agreed upon fashion, or risk the customer going from irate and frustrated to full bore angry.

HINTS

It is very important that you do not make any disparaging remarks about the coworker who has not returned the call, even if that coworker has a history of this kind of behavior. For example: "Oh, Bob is always late returning calls" is completely inappropriate and puts Bob, your company, *and* you in a negative light. It can also cause problems with your coworker.

The more you can go above and beyond the call of duty in resolving this difficulty, the better. You can't necessarily deflect the customer's anger resulting from a sloppy colleague, but you can act in ways so that you won't get painted with the same brush.

See Also: 56. When a Reservation/Appointment Is Lost and You Cannot Meet the Commitment, 58. When a Customer Complains About a Known Problem

45. When You Need to Clarify Commitments

THE SITUATION

Customer service isn't always a one-way street where the employee is the only one with commitments to keep. There are situations where both you and the customer have to do certain things to meet the customer's needs. While this situation exists in normal interactions with customers, it's far more frequent when you are working with internal clients.

TECHNIQUES USED

- Summarize the Conversation (1)
- Probing Questions (2)

DIALOGUE

Over the course of this conversation, the employee has committed to developing a formal proposal to be forwarded to the client. Since the proposal is based on information that must first be sent from the client to the employee, the client also has to make and keep a commitment to get the material sent to the employee. The conversation below is an example of clarifying and summarizing commitments.

Customer: So, you're going to get the proposal to me by the end of the week, right?

Employee: Yes, but I can do that only if you send me the portfolio information by fax sometime today. Can you do that?

Customer: Yes, I'll do that.

Employee: OK, let's make sure we are on absolutely the same wavelength. You're going to send me the portfolio by fax. That document includes [details]. I should receive that today. Then I'll use that to draft a proposal that includes [details] and get it to you by the end of the week. Is that what we are saying? (1)

Customer: Yes.

Employee: Good. One more thing. I don't see anything that might cause me to be unable to get the proposal done on time. Is there anything that might come up that might interfere with your getting the portfolio here? (2)

EXPLANATIONS

This is a relatively straightforward discussion that includes a bit of negotiating and the use of a basic communication technique to avoid the consequences of misunderstanding. The initial part of the conversation involves both parties agreeing to meet some specific commitments by specific deadlines. In this scenario, both parties must keep their commitments in order for the customer to receive the proposal he wants. Once the initial agreement is made, the employee summarizes the conversation. (1) This might seem like overkill to you, but it's always better to err on the cautious side. Making sure communication is working is better than running the risk of a project going askew due to a misunderstanding.

At the end of the conversation, you'll notice the employee doing something interesting. He uses a probing question (2), asking whether the customer can foresee any possible barriers to keeping his commitment to fax the material. Why? Because sometimes people will make commitments to do something without actually thinking enough about the commitment. By using this probing question, the employee encourages the customer to think a little more carefully. Since the employee's ability to keep his end of the bargain is dependent on the customer keeping his commitments, it makes sense to do that.

HINTS

Whenever commitments are made, the conversation should end with a summary of those commitments.

See Also: 12. When the Customer Needs to Follow a Sequence of Actions, 51. When an Internal Customer Isn't Following Procedures to Request Service

46. When a Customer Wants Information You Are Not Allowed to Give

THE SITUATION

Customers will sometimes ask for information that you are not permitted to give out, because it might compromise the privacy of others, pose a security threat, or result in the sharing of proprietary information the company does not allow to be circulated. The trick here is to refuse in a professional and polite way that is less likely to create a long, drawn-out argument.

TECHNIQUES USED
- Acknowledge Customer's Needs (1)
- Explain Reasoning or Actions (2)
- Providing Alternatives (3)

DIALOGUE

In this short interaction, the customer asks for the home phone number of the manager of the department.

Customer: Since he's not in, I'd like to contact him at home. What's his number?

Employee: I understand you want to resolve this quickly, (1) but I'm not allowed to give out that information. Everyone deserves some time off from work and our staff isn't available for home phone calls. (2) What I can do is arrange for you to talk to someone else who is available right now who can help solve your problem. (3)

EXPLANATIONS

In this example, the employee handles the situation by acknowledging the customer's desire to deal with his problem quickly (1) and then provides a brief explanation of why she can't give out the number. (2) The reason it's good to provide an explanation is that it makes the response sound less bureaucratic or arbitrary. Finally, the employee offers an alternative (3). This tends to soften the refusal.

HINTS

When refusing, offer an explanation of why you are refusing. That sends the message that you aren't being arbitrary, but are interested in helping the customer understand the reasoning behind the refusal.

Explanations should be short, followed by offering some sort of alternative that might address the customer's needs.

See Also: 20. When You Don't Have the Answer. 59. When a Customer Asks Inappropriate Questions

47. When a Customer Makes a Suggestion to Improve Service

THE SITUATION

One of the best ways to find out how to improve customer service is to get information from customers. In this situation, a customer volunteers a suggestion about how to improve the service at a bank.

TECHNIQUES USED

- Thank-Yous (1)
- Arranging Follow-Up (2)
- Closing Interactions Positively (3)

DIALOGUE

Sometimes employees will encounter customers who make suggestions for how to improve service. Because employees are often not trained to do anything with these suggestions, they will listen politely hoping the person will finish what he or she has to say so they can get on with finishing a transaction. It doesn't have to be that way as this dialogue shows. Listening to such suggestions and then in fact acting on them can affect both your relationship with customers and improve your ability to serve them.

Customer: You know, when I come to this branch at lunch, I'm always surprised that you have less staff during the period most people come to the bank. I'd bet you'd do much better by making sure there are more tellers on at lunchtime.

Employee: Thanks for the suggestion. I happen to agree and I know this issue has come up before. What I'd like to do is pass your suggestion on to the manager of the branch, since she's the one who would have to arrange more staff. And, if you like, I can also have the manager follow up with you on your suggestion, if only to explain why it might not be practical. Is that something you'd like?

Customer: Well, yes, I'd appreciate that. My name and phone number are ….

Employee: OK. It might be a few days before you hear from Marsha Smith, who is our manager. I also appreciate that you thought enough about us to offer a suggestion about how we can provide better service to you. Have a good day. (3)

EXPLANATIONS

This is a relatively straightforward situation, because the customer is making a suggestion in a constructive and neutral way. The employee thanks the customer for the suggestion (1). What's more critical here is the employee's offer and commitment to pass the suggestion on to the branch manager and arrange for follow-up if the customer desires it (2). Why is this so important? Because it tells the customer that the employee is taking her seriously and that she is important to the employee and the branch.

Finally, at the end of the interaction, you see an effective "close," where the employee reiterates an appreciation of the customer's time and effort in offering up the suggestion.

HINTS

When you make a commitment on behalf of someone else (in this case the bank manager), be absolutely sure that the other person will keep the commitment you made.

When you make a commitment for someone else, it's always a good idea for *you* to follow up with the person who is supposed to fulfill the commitment. In this case the employee would talk with or remind the bank manager to contact the customer in a day or two.

It's good customer service to treat *every* suggestion as important, even those that seem impractical or "poor." Above all, don't argue.

See Also: 49. When You Are Following Up on a Customer Complaint, 53. When You Want Feedback from the Customer

48. When You Can't Find a Customer's Reservation/Appointment

THE SITUATION

In any business where the customer needs to make a reservation or appointment to be served, there's always a risk or possibility that the reservation or appointment information may be lost. How you recover from this situation means the difference between a satisfied customer and one who might complain, argue, vent, and otherwise take up a lot of your time.

Situations like this can occur with airlines, hotels, restaurants, doctors' or dentists' offices, or similar environments.

TECHNIQUES USED

- Apologize (1)
- Assurances of Results (2)
- Bonus Buyoff (3)
- You're Right! (4)
- Contact Security/Authorities/Management (5)

DIALOGUE

This situation takes place in a hotel lobby. The customer arrives with a reservation number, but the hotel clerk has no record of the reservation. In this example, the employee can accommodate the customer's needs, but perhaps not without some degree of inconvenience for the customer.

Customer: What the heck do you mean, you can't find my reservation? I made it at least two weeks ago.

Employee: I'm sorry for the inconvenience, (1) but it shouldn't be a problem to get you into a room even without the reservation. (2) It should only take a minute or two....I just need to get some information from you and, once we're done, I'll find out what we can do to compensate you for the inconvenience. (3)

Customer: Well, this is stupid. It just shouldn't happen.

Employee: You're right, (4) it shouldn't, and once we get you settled I'll let my manager know about the problem so we can do our best to make sure it doesn't happen again. (5)

EXPLANATIONS

Since the company has probably made an error, the first step is to apologize (1). It's possible the customer has made the error, but even in the case where the customer has arrived at the wrong time or place, it's best to assume the company has made the mistake, since arguing will alienate the customer and waste more time.

In this situation, there is a vacancy, so the problem is relatively minor. The employee wants to communicate as quickly as possible that the customer *will* be accommodated and the inconvenience will be minor (2).

The employee suggests that the hotel will offer some sort of compensation, or bonus buyoff (3), as a concrete indication that the hotel is truly sorry for any inconvenience. The employee may need to follow through on this, perhaps talking with the manager on duty to determine the exact nature of the compensation.

The employee uses the "You're Right!" technique (4), emphasizing that she agrees with the customer that this should never have happened. By following this up with a promise to contact/notify management that the reservation was lost (5), she solidifies the customer's perception that the employee and the hotel take these problems seriously. Because the employee does this, it's more likely the customer will return to the hotel.

HINTS

Customers sometimes get confused about their reservations or blame their own error on the company. While it may seem unfair to take responsibility for a problem that is not your fault, that was really caused by the customer, nothing is gained by arguing with the customer or focusing on who is to blame.

Even if you are not personally responsible for a mistake, apologize on behalf of the company.

See Also: 56. When a Reservation/Appointment Is Lost and You Cannot Meet the Commitment, 58. When a Customer Complains About a Known Problem

49. When You Are Following Up on a Customer Complaint

THE SITUATION

Believe it or not, one of the biggest opportunities to show a customer how much you value him or her involves how you recover when the customer has a complaint. Of course, if you can address the customer's complaint immediately, that is a major and critical step. What most companies and people don't realize is that following up on customer complaints can complete the recovery cycle, and transform a complaining customer into a customer for life.

TECHNIQUES USED

- Use Customer's Name (1)
- Offering Choices/Empowering (2)
- Probing Questions (3)
- Thank-Yous (4)
- Above and Beyond the Call of Duty (5)

DIALOGUE

In this case, the manager of a retail outlet has employees notify him of any significant complaints on the part of customers, along with any contact information the customer is willing to offer. Here's how the manager follows up on complaints via phone calls.

Manager: Mr. Jones (1), this is John Roberts from the Loveme Emporium. You may remember about a month ago you had some concerns about [describe situation] , and I'm phoning to see how everything worked out, and if you are satisfied with the result. Have you got a minute? (2)

Customer: Sure. What did you want to know?

Manager: Well, let's start with whether you were satisfied with the outcome? (3)

Customer: Yes and no. I'm satisfied that we got things solved, but I have to tell you that the whole process took far too much time—time I didn't have to waste.

Manager: I can understand what you are saying. Is there anything specific we could have done to shorten the time? (3)

Customer: [offers some suggestions]

Manager: Thank you for the ideas. (4) I'm going to pass those on to the District Manager. Here's something I can suggest to you right now though. If you ever come across a similar situation, please feel free to contact me directly at 555-1212 or in person. I hope this doesn't happen again, but if it does, I can make sure it's settled much more quickly in the future. (5)

Customer: Well, thank you. You know, it's pretty rare to get this kind of personal contact from anyone these days. I'm impressed.

EXPLANATIONS

The techniques used here are fairly straightforward. First, we have the basic courtesy ones; using the customer's name (1), and Thank-Yous (4). In addition, you can see that the manager asks permission (choices/empowerment) to give the customer the option of answering a few questions or not. (2)

However, the critical component here is (5) where the manager goes above and beyond the call of duty by offering the customer "special" access in the event that a similar problem occurs. It reassures the customer that the phone call is sincere, and that the manager is offering something significant to help him.

What really makes this kind of follow-up succeed is that the customer perceives that he is getting very personalized service. To this end, the manager used his name, and demonstrated that he took the time to familiarize himself with, and remember the customer and his situation. Personalized service is so rare these days that customers who receive it can become very loyal indeed.

HINTS

When following up on a complaint, it's absolutely essential that the person following up take the time to familiarize himself with the customer's situation, *and* prove to the customer that he has put in the time to do so. That's where the power of the follow-up lies.

While this example focuses on a manager following up, non-management employees should be encouraged to do this. It's a low-cost way of demonstrating to customers that they are important.

See Also: 47. When a Customer Makes a Suggestion to Improve Service, 55. When You Need to Respond to a Customer Complaint Made in Writing

50. Properly Identifying the Internal Customer

THE SITUATION

When working with internal customers it's important that you identify who has the power and authority to make decisions, and that you interact directly with that person. Sometimes you may be approached by someone who lacks the decision-making power that will permit you to help the customer. Here's a process you can use to identify the real customer, and request direct contact.

TECHNIQUES USED

- Probing Questions (1)
- Active Listening (2)
- Questioning Instead of Stating (3)
- Explain Reasoning or Actions (4)

DIALOGUE

In this situation the employee works in the Information Technology Division (IT). He is approached by someone from the Insurance Division about a software development project the Insurance Division needs. The IT employee is not clear about who the real customer/decision maker will be and seeks to identify and contact that person.

Employee: Fred, I know that projects of this size usually have a lot of people who need to be involved and considered. Before we move forward we need to involve those other people. (4) Can you suggest who needs to be involved in our discussions? (1)

Customer: Sure, I'm the lead person on this. Then, there's the Supervisor of Underwriting. Also, my manager needs to sign off on the project.

Employee: OK, so what you are saying is that, ultimately, your manager is the one who is the final decision maker. Is that right? (2)

Customer: Yes, ultimately, but I make the recommendations to my manager, so pretty much what I suggest is accepted.

Employee: OK. That makes sense. I want to make sure that we get this project on the right path and don't have to redo things, so I'd like to arrange a meeting with your manager. (4) Can we do that? (3)

EXPLANATIONS

This example is a bit trickier than it looks. The employee wants to be careful not to alienate the customer she is interacting with, by insinuating that he is incompetent or the wrong person. That's why she uses a gentle approach, rather than a more direct approach.

The employee uses some gentle probing questions (1) to get the customer to identify the key players. Even though the employee knows the answer, it's a good tactic to encourage the customer to identify the other players, if only to confirm the employee's understanding is accurate. To put the question in context, the employee explains the reasoning behind the question (4).

After the customer provides information regarding other people that need to be involved, the employee uses an active listening response (2) to show she is paying attention and to confirm that she understands the customer's response.

Once again, the employee explains why the manager

should be involved (4) and follows up by asking a question, "Can we do that?," rather than making a direct request or demand. The employee does this to avoid the possibility the customer will feel demeaned or marginalized.

HINTS

People don't always feel comfortable admitting they don't have the power or authority to complete an arrangement. You need to be aware of that and use gentle probing questions to identify who really has the authority.

Since you may work with the same internal customers over long periods of time, remember that you have two concerns. One is to get the project going and meet the needs of the customer. The other, which is as important, is to build relationships with those internal customers and avoid poisoning those relationships by being too aggressive or task-oriented.

See Also: 45. When You Need to Clarify Commitments, 51. When an Internal Customer Isn't Following Procedures to Request Service

51. When an Internal Customer Isn't Following Procedures to Request Service

THE SITUATION

Internal customers, due to their familiarity with staff, sometimes go directly to an employee to ask for help, when they should be making a formal request for service. This can complicate life for the unit providing the service, since it makes it difficult to coordinate requests. What do you do if you are approached directly to provide service, but your work unit requires that the internal customer make a formal request?

TECHNIQUES USED

- Providing Explanations (1)
- Empathy Statements (2)
- Expediting (3)

DIALOGUE

In this situation, a member of the Accounting Department (internal customer) contacts a computer technician in the Information Technology (IT) Department. IT has a set of procedures it wants internal clients to use so it can coordinate and prioritize requests.

Customer: Our computers have been down for about 20 minutes and we can't process our month-end invoices. It's a real mess. Can you come up and see what the problem is?

Employee: That's a pretty serious problem. (2) We need to get on this right away, but I'll need you to complete a request for service form and get it to our job coordinator.

Customer: We don't have time for that stuff. I need this fixed yesterday. Can't you just come up and take a look?

Employee: I'll tell you what. We can get something moving on this within the hour if you get the request for service done. How about if I come up right now and get the request for service form, and I'll hand-walk it to the coordinator for approval? (3) The whole thing should take about 10 minutes.

Customer: Well, I don't see why that's necessary, since we're talking right now and you're the one who has to fix the problem.

Employee: I understand it's frustrating. (2) Let me explain why we want to have a formal request. [explains] (1)

Customer: OK. I guess that makes sense. Can you come up right now?

EXPLANATIONS

It's easy to understand why the Accounting Department employee is upset and concerned, because it appears that he is being tied up in red tape. It's also easy to understand why the IT department needs to coordinate and prioritize service. In this situation, the IT employee knows that this *will* be a high-priority job, provided the formal request is made.

Notice the use of empathy statements (2) by the employee to show concern and understanding. What's really important in this example is the promise of immediate help (expediting) (3). By offering to get things going immediately, the employee is sending the message that the customer's needs will be met and the employee will help the customer navigate the process of making a formal request. Finally, you can see that the customer isn't understanding why the request is necessary. The employee explains the reasons for the procedure (1).

HINTS

When explaining the purpose of a policy or procedure, it's important to highlight any benefits of the procedure from the point of view of the customer or customers.

Explain policies or procedures in plain language without using jargon. The exception is when the customer is conversant with the jargon.

See Also: 12. When a Customer Needs to Follow a Sequence of Actions, 50. Properly Identifying the Internal Customer

52. When the Customer Wants Something That Won't Fill His Need

THE SITUATION

You may find yourself in a situation where the customer thinks he wants something that you know will not make him happy or fill an important need he has expressed. While you might think that giving the customer what he wants is generally a good thing, it may not be so in this situation. Your role should be to make sure the customer remains happy over time. Here's how to help the customer make a better choice.

TECHNIQUES USED

- Active Listening (1)
- Probing Questions (2)

DIALOGUE

In this situation, which takes place in an automobile dealership, the customer has expressed a strong concern about the importance of fuel efficiency, but has also indicated he wants a sports utility vehicle (which has particularly poor fuel efficiency). The employee uses questions to help the customer clarify his priorities.

Employee: OK. If I understand what you are saying, you would like a fuel-efficient SUV, maybe a Blazer. Is that correct? (1)

Customer: Yes. I really like the Blazer.

Employee: I want to be sure you won't be disappointed in whatever choice you make, so let me ask you a few questions. First, given the mileage you've said you drive, the Blazer will cost you about $250 per month in fuel.

On the other hand, going to a smaller hatchback like the Sentra would cost you about $80 a month in fuel. Are you comfortable paying that extra money every month for the Blazer? (2)

Customer: Wow. It's that much difference?

Employee: Yes. So which is most important to you, having something that's more fuel-efficient or having the extra space of the Blazer? (2)

Customer: Well, I like the Blazer, but I'm not sure I really need one. On the other hand, I don't want to be spending over $3,000 in gas each year. Maybe we should look at those other vehicles. You're suggesting that a Sentra might be a good way to go, right?

EXPLANATIONS

Notice that the first step in this example involves the use of active listening, reflecting back what the customer has said to ensure that the employee understands (1). An additional benefit of this is that the customer knows the employee is paying attention.

The probing questions used here are an alternative to the employee offering expert advice and pros and cons directly. While the latter techniques can be useful or combined with the use of probing questions, the advantage of the probing questions lies in gently leading the customer to consider issues he may not be thinking about. The employee is helping the customer to "connect the dots."

HINTS

Probing questions can be used in conjunction with expert recommendations and a more direct discussion of pros and cons. When combined, usually the probing questions would be used first.

Active listening is almost always a good technique to use in all kinds of situations. What's important is that the active listening responses sound natural and comfortable. Active listening responses should never sound artificial, or too "touchy-feely."

See Also: 33. When a Customer is Confused About What He or She Wants or Needs

THE SITUATION

We usually think of customer service as the process of providing something—services, information, or products *to* the customer. There's another component of customer service, and that involves the process of getting feedback *from* the customer so you can improve how you provide for the customer. Most people involved in serving customers don't think of this as part of their jobs, but it can be useful. How do you elicit feedback that might help you and your company improve service?

TECHNIQUES USED

- Offering Choices/Empowering (1)
- Probing Questions (2)
- Active Listening (3)
- Arranging Follow-Up (4)
- Use Customer's Name (5)
- Thank-Yous (6)

DIALOGUE

The setting is a bank. The employee wants to find out (with the support of the manager), how customers see the service they are receiving, and whether they have any suggestions or comments for improvement. Here's how she does it.

Employee: Mrs. Jones (5), we're interested in hearing what you think about our service at this branch. If you have just a minute or two, I'd appreciate it if you could answer some quick questions. Is that OK? (1)

Customer: Sure. If it's short.

Employee: Yes, it's short. On a scale of one to ten how would you rate the service you receive at this branch? (2)

Customer: Well, I guess a six.

Employee: Is there anything specific that we could do to raise that rating?

Customer: Well, yes. The thing that gets me is that I always come in at lunch time, and it seems that's when you have the most people waiting, and the least number of tellers working.

Employee: So, if we could reduce the waiting at lunch time, that would help? (3)

Customer: Yes, it would.

Employee: [asks one or two other short questions] Well, thank you Mrs. Jones (5). I'm passing these suggestions on to our bank manager, and if you like, I can follow up with you to let you know the result. Would you like that? (4,1)

Customer: Well, no, that's not necessary. I'm in every week, so I can talk to you then.

Employee: OK, well thanks again.

EXPLANATIONS

This is a fairly straight-forward process. Make special note that the employee offers the customer the choice of answering the questions or not (1), and uses the same technique at the end of the interaction to determine if the customer wants to be contacted. It's about offering choices.

When asking for information from customers, it's best to provide some form of follow-up option. (4) This tells the customer that you (and your organization) are sincere about the information the customer provides, and that you are willing to try to do something to accommodate the needs of the customer. It moves the feedback process beyond "just talking."

You can also see the use of two techniques that should be part of almost all customer interactions—common courtesy. They are using the customer's name (5), and using thank-yous. (6)

HINTS

The same basic techniques can be used if your company has some form of feedback form customers can fill out, and drop off.

Collecting feedback from customers, and then doing nothing—no feedback and no fixing of problems, is worse than collecting no feedback at all. That's because it will seem phony to customers. If you collect feedback on your own initiative, make sure you pass the information on to those in your organization that should have the information.

See Also: 47. When a Customer Makes a Suggestion to Improve Service, 55. When You Need to Respond to a Customer Complaint Made in Writing

THE SITUATION

All organizations have policies, procedures, and paperwork. Some organizations, particularly those associated with government, seem to have inordinate amounts of red tape involved in getting things done. Customers often get frustrated at the paperwork and red tape needed to accomplish something and may vent their frustration on you. How do you deal with this situation?

TECHNIQUES USED

- Active Listening (1)
- Providing Explanations (2)
- Empathy Statements (3)
- Some People Think That (Neutral Mode) (4)
- Offering Choices/Empowering (5)
- Broken Record (6)

DIALOGUE

This situation occurs in a government office, but could occur in any organization that has fairly complex procedures and requires filling out lots of forms (e.g., banks and medical facilities). Here, the customer wants to apply for a driver's license. We join the conversation in progress.

Employee: OK. Let me explain the process. I need a copy of your birth certificate and one other piece of ID, and then we need to schedule your written test and your driving test.

Customer: What? This is going to take forever. I went through all that three years ago. Why the hell do I have to do it all over again?

Employee: I understand that you don't want to go through that again, (1) but the problem is that you haven't had a valid license in two years, so it's like starting over again. (2)

Customer: What a pile of crap! You government folks will do anything to make things hard for us taxpayers. I pay your salary, you know.

Employee: I know it's frustrating. (3) Some people do think that the laws are strict, (4) but you know, they are there to protect everyone and to make sure the streets are as safe as we can make them. (2)

Customer: Well, it's just plain stupid.

Employee: It's up to you what you want to do. If you would like to speak to my supervisor, I can arrange that, or we can go ahead and set up the appointments. Which would you prefer? (5)

Customer: Neither. I don't like either.

Employee: Well, those are pretty much the options. Which would you prefer? (6)

EXPLANATIONS

The first technique used is active listening (1), where the employee tries to put herself on the same side as the customer by showing she is paying attention and understands where the customer is coming from. She follows this up by offering an explanation for the requirements (2).

When the customer expresses his frustration, the employee uses an empathy technique (3) and "neutral mode" (4) to try to soften the news.

The customer continues to make angry comments, so

the employee shifts gears to get things moving by offering two alternatives—speaking to the supervisor or making the appointments, leaving the choice to the customer (5). She does this because no amount of arguing or discussion is going to result in changes to the policies and laws, over which neither of them has control. When the customer indicates his displeasure with the options, she uses the broken record technique (6), presenting the options to him once again. She does this to push the customer into making a decision and not wasting more time arguing.

HINTS

When explaining a policy or set of procedures, it's important to do so in plain language without quoting specific laws or policy numbers. Unless asked for detailed explanations, it's best to keep explanations short and to the point.

There are situations where the red tape cannot be explained rationally. You may not know why it's necessary or it may be one of those things that really is unnecessarily complex. In that situation, it's best to admit you don't know why and offer access to someone who might be better able to explain it. In these situations, focus on placing yourself on the same side as the customer, emphasizing empathy statements and active listening.

Avoid arguing with the customer about procedural necessities. No amount of talking is going to change them, since they are beyond your control. If the customer insists on arguing, it's better to direct him or her to someone who has the authority to change the procedures.

See Also: 6. When a Customer Has a Negative Attitude About Your Company Due to Past Experiences, 7. When You Need to Explain a Company Policy or Procedure

55. When You Need to Respond to a Customer Complaint Made in Writing

THE SITUATION

A customer who complains in writing is a customer who is angry enough to take the time to write a letter. That means the person is pretty angry. The usual response is to reply in writing, but that's only part of the process of offering superior customer service.

TECHNIQUES USED

- Use Customer's Name (1)
- Explain Reasoning or Actions (2)
- Offering Choices/Empowerment (3)
- Probing Questions (4)

DIALOGUE

The employee has been asked by his manager to draft a written response to a customer complaint letter. He drafts the response, but realizes that a written response, while necessary, is not going to be sufficient to convince the customer that she is receiving top-notch service. Here are two options.

In option 1, the employee drafts a response and follows up via phone before sending the letter.

Employee: Mr. Smith, (1) this is John Jones from Acme. I'm following up on a letter you wrote outlining a concern you had about [explains what the customer wrote about]. I'm sending out a written response you should have within two days, but I wanted to talk to you personally, to clarify the situation. (2) Can I ask you a few questions? Then I can go over what's in the letter. (3)

In option 2, the employee composes the reply, sends it, and then follows up with the customer after the customer has received the reply. It goes like this.

Employee: Mr. Smith, (1) this is John Jones from Acme. I wanted to follow up on our response to your letter, to see if you had any questions about our position and where things are right now. (2) First, have you received our response? (4)

Customer: Yes, I got it today. Thanks for taking the time to call.

Employee: Was there anything in our letter that we didn't make clear? (4)

EXPLANATIONS

In both examples, the employee uses the customer's name (1) and also identifies himself. He does this to personalize the call and to show that he has made the effort to remember the name.

Also, in both examples, the employee quickly explains the purpose of the call (2). Once that's done, he basically asks permission to continue, giving the customer the choice (3). This comes across as considerate and respectful, while trying to maintain control over the interaction.

In the second example, you can see the use of probing questions (4). Again this shows that the employee and, by extension, the company, are interested in the customer's problem. The questions, particularly when he asks, "First, have you received our letter?" provide information the employee needs to guide how he handles the phone call. Clearly, if the customer has not received the letter, he needs to handle the call differently.

What's important here is that the employee, through actions and words, demonstrates that the complaint is being taken seriously and that the company wants to do all it can to address the customer's concerns.

HINTS

Responses to written complaints should be accompanied by some form of more personal follow-up. At the best of times, written words tend to come across as cold and distant.

When writing a response to a complaint, it's important to draft something that is informal and uses plain language. A common mistake is to sound stiff or bureaucratic in written responses, which guarantees the customer will be even angrier.

See Also: 7. When You Need to Explain a Company Policy or Procedure, 47. When a Customer Makes a Suggestion to Improve Service

56. When a Reservation/Appointment Is Lost and You Cannot Meet the Commitment

THE SITUATION

In dialogue 48, we dealt with a situation where the customer's reservation was lost, but the employee could accommodate the customer with only minimal inconvenience for the customer. What happens when the customer cannot be accommodated and it appears the fault lies with the company?

TECHNIQUES USED
- Preemptive Strike (1)
- Assurances of Results (2)
- Providing Alternatives (3)
- Empathy Statements (4)
- Bonus Buyoff (5)
- Contact Security/Authorities/Management (6)

DIALOGUE

As with the example in situation 48, this occurs in a hotel. The employee discovers there is no record of the reservation and, unfortunately, the hotel is booked solid and cannot offer the customer the room that was promised.

Employee: Mr. Jones, I can't find any record of your reservation, but I can promise you that we will find a place for you to stay. (1, 2) Unfortunately, we're completely booked, but I will find you alternate accommodations that won't cost you any more than you'd spend here. (3) It may take a few minutes, but I *will* find something for you. (3)

Customer: What kind of outfit do you run here? I shouldn't have to run all over the city when I made a reservation for here.

Employee: I'd be upset too if it was me. (4) Am I correct that you want to stay in this general area? If that's the case, I'll phone around to other hotels and arrange a room close by. I can probably arrange a significant discount. (5)

Customer: Well, I guess that's better than nothing, but this should never happen.

Employee: I'm going to inform the manager about this so the next time you come to our hotel, it won't happen again. (6) Sound fair?

EXPLANATIONS

One of the key elements in this example involves assuring the customer that he will not end up with no place to stay the night. The employee addresses this issue as early as possible in the conversation, using a preemptive strike (1) and assurances of results (2). In this case, the preemptive strike involves addressing the customer's concern about having a place to stay *before* the customer expresses that concern.

The employee suggests an alternative to solve the problem (3), to "make it right." In this situation, all the words in the world aren't going to bring the customer back if the situation isn't "made right."

You might notice that while the employee is doing his best, the customer is still irate. That's typical and understandable. That's why the employee uses an empathy statement (4).

Before making calls to other local hotels to arrange for

a room, the employee "sweetens" the situation by mentioning the possibility of a bonus buyoff (5) and reassures the customer that the hotel will investigate and take every effort to prevent a recurrence. The employee promises to bring this situation to the attention of the manager (6).

HINTS

There are two prongs to this approach. One is to do everything possible to "make it right," which means finding a room and arranging things for the customer. The other is to show that the employee and the hotel take these situations seriously and that the customer and his needs are important. *Both* prongs are essential: solve the problem and, at the same time, send the "you are important" message.

While we've used a hotel example, the procedures are the same whenever the company might be at fault for a lost reservation or appointment. Minimize inconvenience. Express concern. Compensate for inconvenience. Solve the immediate problem.

See Also: 48. When You Can't Find a Customer's Reservation/ Appointment, 58. When a Customer Complains About a Known Problem

57. When Customers Are Waiting in a Waiting Room

THE SITUATION

This is a situation you will relate to from the customers' perspective. It's not uncommon in this era of under-staffing and unexpected delays for customers to have to wait in a waiting room, even if they have appointments that are long past. What do you do when there are delays and you have a room full of people who have been waiting for some time?

TECHNIQUES USED

- Empathy Statements (1)
- Explain Reasoning or Actions (2)
- Apologize (3)
- Providing Alternatives (4)

DIALOGUE

This situation takes place in a doctor's office. There are about 10 people waiting to be called for their appointment. Unfortunately, the doctor is running between 30 and 50 minutes behind schedule, so some people have been waiting quite some time. Here's what the receptionist does.

Employee: [Loud voice to waiting customers] If I can have your attention for a moment, I'll explain the delay and what you can do.

Customers: [Look up]

Employee: The doctor had an emergency earlier today that caused a delay of about 45 minutes, so everyone has been pushed back. (2) I know that's really frustrating for everyone, including us (1), and I apologize. (3) I want to offer you some alternatives, particularly for those of you who have appointments between three and four o'clock.

First, if you would rather not wait the extra 45 minutes, please come up to the desk and we will reschedule at no charge. If you want to wait because you feel you have to see the doctor today, you don't have to remain in the waiting room. If you want to do something else, just make sure you let me know, and get back here about 35 minutes after your scheduled appointment. That way you won't lose your place. (4)

EXPLANATIONS

Despite what you may think, the most annoying part of having to wait in a waiting room is not the delay or even the lost time, but the uncertainty. The customers are asking themselves, "Should I wait?" "Do I need to call home to arrange child care?" "Can I go and come back?" and similar questions that come from not knowing the situation.

That's the reason why it's absolutely critical to inform waiting customers of the situation. In this example, the receptionist explains the reason for the delay (1). She does this so that the customers know the delay isn't a result of sloppy scheduling or lack of consideration, but due to an unavoidable situation.

She follows this explanation with an empathy statement (2) and an apology. (3) That's basic common courtesy.

Finally she wraps up by providing some alternatives and answering some of the unspoken questions customers probably have. The alternatives, while not perfect, are intended to help the customers make decisions about what they can do to make the delay more tolerable.

HINTS

When making an announcement to a group of people, first ask for their attention. Once you have their attention, then deliver the announcement.

Don't assume that every customer will have heard the group announcement. Some people may not be listening, and it may be necessary to approach each customer individually to explain, just in case he or she didn't hear.

See Also: 2. When a Customer Is in a Hurry, 3. When a Customer Jumps Ahead in a Line of Waiting Customers

58. When a Customer Complains About a Known Problem

THE SITUATION

Sometimes with a product there are problems that employees are aware of, but have not yet been able to correct. The ideal situation is for the employee to inform customers of the problem before the customers have committed to or purchased the problematic item, but that's not always possible. What do you do when a customer complains about a problem that has been identified by employees and/or the company?

TECHNIQUES USED

- Explain Reasoning or Actions (1)
- Apologize (2)
- Bonus Buyoff (3)

DIALOGUE

In this situation, the customer goes to the service desk of a hardware store with a complaint about the bargain gas barbecue he purchased yesterday. His concern is that the product is dented and seems to be missing some parts. This is the third such instance today. The hardware store has determined that the entire shipment is faulty—which it discovered only after selling a number of them.

Customer: I bought this yesterday. There are at least two pieces missing and the top is dented. Why are you selling this junk?

Employee: We only discovered a problem with the shipment this morning, so I apologize for the problem. (1, 2) I'll tell you what I can do to compensate you for the inconvenience. We can exchange this item for the more expensive model, so you'll get more features and quality for the same price. If you have a few minutes, we'll check the more expensive model for you to make sure it's complete. (3) How does that sound?

Customer: Well, OK. That sounds like a good deal.

EXPLANATIONS

Notice that the employee offers a brief explanation of the source of the problem and offers a reason why the customer ended up with a faulty unit (1). The explanation should be brief, because the customer is less interested in the *why* than having a working unit. The employee apologizes for the inconvenience (2), even though he wasn't personally responsible for the problem. He makes his apology on behalf of the company. However, an apology without compensation would be perceived as rather empty.

The employee offers a means of solving the customer's problem by offering two bonus buyoffs (3)—an upgrade to the more expensive model and an offer to inspect the replacement to ensure it is in working order. Pay special attention to the employee's explanation of why the upgrade will be beneficial for the customer.

HINTS

If you do not have the authority to offer a bonus and you are aware of a problem that may affect more than one customer, ask your manager for the authority to deal with this specific problem by offering a bonus. That way, you don't have to involve the manager for each and every instance.

See Also: 55. When You Need to Respond to a Customer Complaint Made in Writing, 56. When a Reservation/Appointment is Lost and You Cannot Meet the Commitment

59. When a Customer Asks Inappropriate Questions

THE SITUATION

You may come across situations where a customer asks questions you deem to be personal and/or not related to the customer service process. These kinds of questions may be quite benign or quite personal and even offensive. How do you handle these situations in a diplomatic and tactful way?

TECHNIQUES USED

- Refocus (1)
- Broken Record (2)

DIALOGUE

During a normal conversation with a customer, the customer starts to ask questions that don't seem to be related to the discussion. Here's how that situation can be addressed.

Customer: So, what's it like to work here?

Employee: I don't want to take up your time talking about my experience here, so perhaps we can get back to discussing the features of the services you are interested in. (1)

Customer: Well, I really want to know what it's like to work here. So what's the scoop?

Employee: It's like any place, really. So, you're interested in our computer repair services? Is there something specific you'd like to know about that? (1, 2)

Customer: Well, I was hoping to apply for a job here and was hoping for a bit more information. But yes, I have a problem with my computer that I need to have fixed.

Employee: I understand. I can't help you with the job, but I can help you with your computer problem. Let's see what we can do. (1, 2)

EXPLANATIONS

While the customer's questions are not that intrusive, the employee does not want to be put in an awkward position by answering them. In this example, the employee layers two techniques, refocus and broken record. Refocusing (1) is intended to encourage the customer to return to the issue that the employee is able and willing to help with. Broken recording (repeating the same theme) is used to reinforce the idea that the employee won't be responding to off-topic questions (2).

HINTS

The broken record technique helps the employee avoid any direct argument and sends a firm but not aggressive message.

The broken record technique works best when you send the same message but in different words. You don't want to repeat the same sentence verbatim. Vary the dialogue.

See Also: 46. When a Customer Wants Information You Are Not Allowed to Give

60. When a Customer Tries an Unacceptable Merchandise Return

THE SITUATION

Most companies have some limits on merchandise returns. Some of those restrictions have to do with safety and/or hygiene reasons (e.g., the return of over-the-counter drugs or undergarments). There is little flexibility possible for accepting returns of such items. Companies may also establish time limits or other conditions regarding returns. For example, they may limit returns to two weeks or allow only exchanges (no refunds) on some items, such as videos and CDs.

Understandably, when you refuse to allow a customer to return an item, it's likely that he or she is going to be upset. Here's a way to handle it.

TECHNIQUES USED
- Probing Questions (1)
- Acknowledging Without Encouraging (2)
- Preemptive Strike (3)
- Providing Alternatives (4)

DIALOGUE

In this situation, the customer is requesting a refund for a boxed set of DVD movies. As is standard, due to the possibility of copying, the store does not accept returns for refunds but only allows an exchange, identical title for title. We join the conversation after the customer has requested his money back.

Employee: I need to ask you one or two questions before we can process this for you. First, were any of the DVDs defective?

Customer: No, they play fine. I just changed my mind.

Employee: Sure, that happens sometimes. (2) When you bought the DVDs from us, did anyone point out our policies on returns and refunds for DVDs? (1)

Customer: I don't remember.

Employee: OK. What I have to tell you isn't going to make you all that happy. (3) Our store and, for that matter, almost all other stores that sell DVDs have an exchange-for-identical-item policy and don't offer refunds. I'd be glad to explain why it's done this way if you'd like, but the bottom line is that we can't refund or exchange it for a different item since the DVD has been opened.

Customer: So you're saying I'm stuck with this?

Employee: Yes, I'm afraid so. As far as I know, we've never made an exception to this rule, but you could talk to the store manager if you'd like. (4)

Customer: No, I can't be bothered. But I'm curious, how was I supposed to know about this "policy," since nobody told me?

Employee: It's so common in the industry that it's possible the cashier forgot to mention it. We also have the policy posted on each rack of DVDs, just in case.

Customer: Well, OK, then.

EXPLANATIONS

In this example, the customer's reactions are relatively mild, and he can best be described as disappointed rather than angry, but that reaction is partly a result of how the employee handled the situation. As soon as the employee learns that none of the DVDs is damaged, he knows the customer isn't going to get what he wants. Rather than simply blurting out "the rule," the employee uses the probing process (1) to build a little bit of rapport with the customer before giving the bad news. He also acknowledges the validity of changing one's mind by acknowledging without encouraging (2). Notice the phrasing, "that happens sometimes," which doesn't agree or disagree with the possibility of a change of mind. The employee does *not* want to make the customer feel stupid and is trying to allow some face-saving here.

In saying, "What I have to tell you isn't going to make you all that happy," the employee uses a preemptive strike (3). Anticipating that the customer may be disappointed, he is the first to identify that the customer is likely to be unhappy with the result. When you acknowledge a customer's emotions in advance, he or she is less likely to harp on those emotions.

In offering the customer an alternative (4), speaking to the manager, the employee is mostly making a gesture of goodwill to placate the customer and show that he is taking the issue seriously, even though he cannot offer the customer what he wants.

Finally, take a close look at how the employee answers the customer's final question about how the store lets people know about the policy. It would be normal to wonder how this customer could not know about this policy that is common in almost every retail store on the planet, could have missed the signs prominently displayed, and could claim he wasn't informed. A less professional employee might have commented in a way that the customer might find offensive or, worse, in a way that might encourage the customer to argue. But this one didn't. He answered the question asked of him and tried to do so without blaming the customer. Why? Because the surest way to generate an argument and waste large amounts of time is to point a blaming finger at a customer, even if it's deserved.

HINTS

When refusing a customer request, it's always good to make some sort of goodwill gesture to the customer along with the refusal. That's not always possible, but if you can, it smoothes the waters. A goodwill gesture would be something that gives the customer "a little something," although not what he wants.

Blaming a customer is plain stupid, even if the customer is to blame. Blame is about embarrassment and humiliation, and people fight back. However, it is appropriate to identify what might have caused a problem, for the purposes of fixing it, which is an unemotional process of gathering information.

See Also: 7. When You Need to Explain a Company Policy or Procedure, 12. When a Customer Needs to Follow a Sequence of Actions

About the Authors

William T. Brooks was considered America's foremost sales strategist. The author or coauthor of 14 previous books, he was CEO and Founder of The Brooks Group, a sales and sales management screening, development, and retention firm based in Greensboro, NC.

An honors graduate of Gettysburg College, he also held a master's degree from Syracuse University. One of the country's most in-demand sales and business speakers, he was a Certified Speaking Professional, Certified Management Consultant, and member of the Speaking Hall of Fame.

Mr. Brooks numbered among his clients some of the world's best-known and prestigious organizations in more than 400 industries. Once a college football coach and military officer with 23 months' duty in Southeast Asia, he delivered more than 3500 keynotes, speeches, seminars, and workshops. A sales award winner, he was president of a national sales organization with over 3500 salespeople.

Since the early 1990s **Robert Bacal** has trained thousands of people in how to deal with difficult customers through his "Defusing Hostile Customers" seminar. His clients have included people from a wide range of specializations, ranging from health care, law enforcement and security, social work, education, and manufacturing.

He draws from a range of disciplines, including psychology and psycholinguistics, and has incorporated a number of customer service techniques that have come from some of the attendees at his seminars. He holds a masters degree in psychology from the University of Toronto, and a B.A. from Concordia University in Montreal.

He is the author of the *Defusing Hostile Customers Workbook For Public Sector* and a similar book written for school board officials, teachers, and educators. He is also author of two titles in McGraw-Hill's Briefcase Books series, *Performance Management* and *Manager's Guide to Performance Reviews* as well as *The Complete Idiot's Guide to Consulting* and *The Complete Idiot's Guide to Dealing with Difficult Employees.*

He makes his home near Ottawa, Canada, where he continues to write, and offer customer service related seminars. He also hosts The Customer Service Zone on the Internet, at **www.customerservicezone.com**, where you can find free help and suggestions on customer service improvement.

The Right Phrase for Every Situation...Every Time.